LAVARACK: RIVAL GENERAL

LAVARACK
Rival General

Brett Lodge

ROBINSON·REYNOLDS
London

BY THE SAME AUTHOR

The Fall of General Gordon Bennett

To NX206228, Lodge, N. W. B.

First published by Allen & Unwin in 1998.
This revised edition published in 2021 by
Robinson Reynolds,
London
www.robinsonreynolds.com

Every effort has been made to ensure that no rights have been infringed in the production of this book. All photographs are in the public domain and sources are credited. In the event of any omission the publication will be updated at the earliest opportunity.
Email: legal@robinsonreynolds.com
Cover photograph: AWM
Author Photograph: Staton Winter

ISBN: 978-1-914973-50-5

Contents

Maps & illustrations

Abbreviations

AA	Australian Archives
ATk	Anti-tank
AA&QMG	Assistant Adjutant and Quartermaster-General
ABDA	American, British, Dutch, Australian
ADC	Aide-de-Camp
ADMS	Assistant Director Medical Services
Adv	Advance
AFV	Armoured Fighting Vehicle
AGPS	Australian Government Publishing Service
AHQ	Army Headquarters
AIF	Australian Imperial Force
AMF	Australian Military Forces
ANU	Australian National University
AOC-in-C	Air Officer Commanding-in-Chief
AWM	Australian War Memorial
BCOF	British Commonwealth Occupation Force
Bde	Brigade
BGS	Brigadier General Staff
BMRA	Brigade-Major, Royal Artillery
Bn	Battalion
C-in-C	Commander-in-Chief
Cav	Cavalry
CGS	Chief of the General Staff

CIGS	Chief of the Imperial General Staff
CMF	Citizen Military Forces
CNS	Chief of the Naval Staff
CO	Commanding Officer
Comdr	Commander
Coy	Company
CRA	Commander, Royal Artillery
CRE	Commander, Royal Engineers
CRS	Commonwealth Record Series
DAAG	Deputy Assistant Adjutant-General
DADMS	Deputy Assistant Director Medical Services
DAQMG	Deputy Assistant Quartermaster-General
DC-in-C	Deputy Commander-in-Chief
DCGS	Deputy Chief of the General Staff
Div	Division
DSO	Distinguished Service Order
Fd	Field
GDL	Gallica Digital Library
GHQ	General Headquarters
GOC	General Officer Commanding
GSO1	General Staff Officer, Grade 1
HMSO	Her Majesty's Stationery Office
HQ	Headquarters
inf	infantry
instn	instruction
LHQ	Land Headquarters
LMG	Light Machine Gun
LoC	Library of Congress
lt	light
MG	Machine Gun
MGGS	Major-General, General Staff
MHR	Member of the House of Representatives
MUP	Melbourne University Press
NAA	National Archives of Australia
NCO	Non-Commissioned Officer
NEI	Netherlands East Indies
NLA	National Library of Australia
NMM	National Maritime Museum (London)

offr	officer
ops	operations
pdr	pounder
Pnr	Pioneer
posn	position
PRO	Public Record Office (London)
RAAF	Royal Australian Air Force
RAF	Royal Air Force
RAN	Royal Australian Navy
rd	road
Regt	Regiment
RHA	Royal Horse Artillery
RN	Royal Navy
SAA	Small Arms Ammunition
SEAC	South-East Asia Command
SLQ	State Library of Queensland
SLV	State Library of Victoria
SWPA	South-West Pacific Area
SWPC	South-West Pacific Command
tps	troops
WDF	Western Desert Force
WO	War Office

Preface

to the 2021 Edition

PHILIP L. GRAHAM, the former president and publisher of the *Washington Post*, is often credited with coining in 1963 the phrase that journalism is 'the first rough draft of history'.[1] His words imply that eventually there will be a final, irrefutable version of some important historical event or the biography of a prominent person. It is an enticing prospect.

Unfortunately, although at any time there may appear before us the latest draft, a final, definitive history remains a chimera. Historical events reveal themselves by stages. In war, for example, initially there are the censored accounts of war correspondents and the carefully crafted official communiques. Soon after the fighting is finished (if not before) begins the flood of memoirs, private histories, biographies and official despatches of the commanders. Not long afterwards the official histories start to appear.

Then, as the years pass, records are released to the public from government archives (perhaps two, three or more decades after events have occurred); private papers and diaries are bequeathed to libraries for interested parties to read and interpret; and all the while more first-hand accounts and autobiographies are published before memories fade and time runs out. At each stage historians delve ever deeper into the past to weigh the significance of new facts and opinions, and so produce articles and books which illuminate a subject from hitherto unseen perspectives.

Over time, diligent research and constant re-evaluation can bring us closer to a definitive history of an event or biography of a person, but—like one of Zeno's paradoxes—arrival at historical certainty, although growing tantalisingly nearer all the time, will remain ultimately unreachable. Nevertheless, although we may not be able to know every detail about a momentous event of the past, or every facet of an exceptional person's life, each new revelation adds to our knowledge and understanding of the history which has shaped our present and may guide our future.

And so it is with this biography. Sufficient new material has emerged in the two decades since *Lavarack: Rival General* was first published to justify a revised edition. More archival records have been released; the accessibility of private papers has provided additional personal details, permitting a fuller idea of the man's background and character; and books by other scholars, both in Australia and abroad, have provided extra detail of some of the events in which Lavarack was involved and throw light on the lives of the people with whom he dealt.

The impetus to take advantage of this new material originated, appropriately, in Beirut where I happened to be stationed on the 70th anniversary of the Australian army's campaign in Lebanon. The Australian ambassador there, Lex Bartlem, graciously invited me to speak at the opening of the embassy's exhibition commemorating the 1941 campaign, which had strengthened the long-standing bond between Australia and Lebanon. Thus the idea of a new edition of Lavarack's life was planted, though work on it could not begin until I had finally left Lebanon some years later.

The result is this edition, published on the 80th anniversary of that gruelling, but successful, campaign conducted by Lavarack. The book now has an expanded text, redrawn maps and more photographs illustrating Lavarack's life. While not repudiating the broad conclusions of its predecessor, I hope it offers a deeper and more nuanced account of Lavarack's tumultuous and varied career, and in the process inches us a little closer to that elusive goal of a 'definitive history'.

Even so, there will remain questions to be answered and gaps to fill. There always are. Facts emerge slowly and inchoately, which perhaps explains why it took more than forty years before the phrase 'the first rough draft of history' was more accurately attributed in 2010—not to Philip Graham, but to another American reporter writing during the Second World War, Alan Barth. Yet there is speculation that even he may not have been the originator. History is never quite finished.

Brett Lodge
July, 2021

Introduction

ERUDITE, TENACIOUS AND VOLATILE, Lieutenant-General Sir John Lavarack was head of the Australian army during one of the most critical periods in the country's history. His career see-sawed between success and failure as he battled rivals in the government, the civil service and the army itself, both on and off the battlefield. At times his fights may have been ill-chosen, but he brought to each a keen intelligence and a dogged determination.

As Lavarack rose to prominence after 1918, so did the major challenges facing the Australian army: the widespread acceptance of a crippling inter-war defence policy; the minefield of political-military relations; the bitter rivalry between regular and citizen officers; the difficulty of commanding an Australian force in action overseas after 1939; and the powerful influence of personality in war. All these factors influenced Lavarack's professional fate, but none was so effective in thwarting his military career as personal animus.

Lavarack's eclipse would come eventually, but after successful service during the First World War his star was in the ascendant and he was given a number of increasingly important posts in the Australian army in the 1920s and 1930s. Almost without exception, those who served with Lavarack recall that he was impressive in appearance: well-built and tall, with a dark complexion which earned him the nickname of 'Black Jack' when he was commandant of the Royal Military College (his more

1

common nickname was 'Joe'). His distinguished and soldierly bearing could be daunting; in the words of one senior officer: 'as a general, he certainly always looked the part'.[1]

Lavarack possessed an equally formidable temperament, most notably an unpredictable and 'wicked temper which rose like a flash and often subsided quickly'.[2] His personality did not always win him supporters. Brigadier Sir Charles Spry has described Lavarack as an 'irascible gentleman of the old school'[3] and Lieutenant-General Sir Sydney Rowell, who served with Lavarack at Army Headquarters and later as his chief operational staff officer in the Syrian campaign, encapsulated his character when he wrote:

> Lavarack had a fine brain; he wrote brilliantly and spoke convincingly. He did not possess the most equable of temperaments and could be a difficult master. But at other times he was a delightful character with a wide range of interests.[4]

Yet, those who came to know Lavarack warmed to him. Despite the fiery side of his character, Lavarack was respected and often characterised as charming. Brigadier Sir Frederick Chilton has recalled that although Lavarack had the reputation of being 'somewhat temperamental' he was also 'a man of considerable presence and charm'[5]. Likewise, Sir Kingsley Norris, a citizen soldier who was Lavarack's senior medical officer in the 7th Division in the Middle East, wrote in similar terms that 'J.D.L., as we called him, was a man of singular charm', a view shared even by a hostess who had endured Lavarack overturning a table in her home after losing at cards.[6] Lavarack's circle of friends extended beyond the army. Major-General R.N.L. Hopkins, who served on Lavarack's staff before the Second World War, recalled Lavarack's participation in the annual Bench and Bar versus Army golfing competitions in Melbourne:

> Joe was on excellent terms with the justices and seniors of the bar and was always greeted by them with both enthusiasm and respect. Obviously they looked forward to his presence. He was a good and interesting conversationalist, with plenty of ideas.[7]

Clearly the lawyers and judges were willing to overlook Lavarack's intensity when it came to sport, as Hopkins also related:

Playing golf with him, in a tight match, I have sunk a long and curly putt to win the hole to find JDL glaring at me, his face literally black with rage. It might be two or three holes before he would speak to me but then it was as if nothing had happened. You can imagine the effect on people who didn't know him well.[8]

Of all Lavarack's traits, though, the pre-eminent was intelligence. General Hopkins recalled of his time on Lavarack's staff that 'one's abiding impression was his acute brain. Quickness of thought—excellent in discussion—careful, even precise, in his language'.[9] His intelligence, reinforced by an excellent memory and a detailed knowledge of history, led him to hold strong opinions on many subjects, not just military matters. (He was convinced, for example, that Shakespeare's plays had been written by someone other than the Bard himself.)[10]

Intelligence can, however, beget less admirable attributes. Writing in *The Bulletin* in 1957 the journalist and historian M.H. Ellis recalled that although Lavarack was 'throughout his career, active, vigorous in thought and action, determined, self-sufficient, clear-thinking' he was also 'dogmatic—some thought too dogmatic'. There is no doubt that his determination sometimes overcame prudence, as again Hopkins remembered: 'I've seen JDL flush to the roots of his hair with sudden anger and start out of his chair to confront some senior officer whom he thought was misguided'.[11] These elements of his character—determination, intelligence and volatility—were to dominate his career throughout the 1930s and 1940s.

However, in the decade after the First World War Lavarack's undoubted abilities had marked him early as a potential Chief of the General Staff (CGS). He was the most prominent of a number of young army officers who criticised inter-war defence policy based on promises of a British fleet being sent to Singapore in the event of war in the Pacific. (Collectively they were labelled 'the radical "Young Turk" group' by the influential Secretary of the Department of Defence, Sir Frederick Shedden, who disagreed deeply with Lavarack's views and would become one of his most dogged opponents.)[12] Lavarack was the first Australian army officer to attend the prestigious Imperial Defence College course in London and, after postings as Director of Military Operations and Intelligence and later as Commandant of the Royal Military College, he would supersede a number of officers to become CGS in 1935.

As Chief of the General Staff Lavarack continued to champion a more realistic defence policy for Australia based on self-sufficiency, not on unrealisable British assurances of naval help in an emergency. Later events were to prove him all too prescient. But for the time being his most conspicuous achievement was to alienate his political masters and antagonise powerful civil servants, who began to turn against him because he had dared to confront their long-cherished, but ill-founded, policies on defence. They took their revenge soon after the outbreak of war. In October 1939 Lavarack was replaced as CGS with a British officer and consigned to a military backwater.

Another man may have been tempted to resign himself to fate, but Lavarack fought on to ensure that, even if he could no longer be Chief of the General Staff, on relinquishing his desk at Army Headquarters he would pack his kit for active service and take Australians into battle. So it was that in 1940 Lavarack salvaged what appeared to be a stagnant career by dropping a rank to major-general in order to join the Second Australian Imperial Force (AIF) and see active service overseas. The move was vehemently resisted by the talented, but vindictive, General Sir Thomas Blamey who commanded the AIF. Blamey had served with Lavarack in the previous war and feared him as a rival.[13] Undeterred, Lavarack soldiered on and did so with conspicuous success, to Blamey's chagrin.

For almost the first half of the Second World War Lavarack was the only regular army, or Staff Corps, officer to exercise senior command. All the other division commanders were part-time citizen officers of the militia, and Blamey (who became a citizen officer when he resigned from the Staff Corps in 1925) the only other to command an Australian corps. Lavarack successfully fought Germans and Italians at Tobruk and soon afterwards, as the Australian corps commander, the Vichy French in Syria (a tough campaign in which two Victoria Crosses were awarded to Australians and the AIF lost almost as many men killed and wounded as in the fighting in Greece and Crete combined).[14] Not only was Lavarack the sole regular officer to command a division or a corps in the Middle East campaigns, he was the only regular general to command both a division and a corps in battle during the whole war. Not until the campaign against the Japanese in Papua in 1942 did an officer of the regular army other than Lavarack take a formation larger than a brigade into action.[15]

However, although more senior Staff Corps officers rose to command divisions and corps against the Japanese, this was an opportunity denied Lavarack who, after his victories in the Middle East, was kept firmly on the sidelines of the Pacific War by Blamey who had been made Commander-in-Chief of the Australian Military Forces in early 1942. Indeed, without Blamey's obstruction, Lavarack could have been the first regular army officer to command a division, a corps and an army on the battlefield. But in Blamey's mind, Lavarack was a threat to his own position and therefore deserved as much obscurity as could be heaped upon him.

It is hardly by chance that Lavarack's name is not as well known in the annals of the Australian army as some of his contemporaries, like Blamey, Morshead and Mackay. The powerful Blamey rarely missed an opportunity to belittle Lavarack's achievements, such as his victory at Tobruk in April 1941, and keep him from the limelight. A major Australian army base might bear his name, but in many ways Lavarack remains Australia's forgotten general, and undeservedly so. His position in the history of the army is unique. He was at the centre of the country's momentous debate over defence policy before the Second World War and became one of the most senior and successful Australian commanders during the war. But it was in the midst of war that he would confront his greatest rival, Blamey, and his professional fate would be sealed. Through bitter experience Lavarack would learn that winning the argument in a government committee or standing victorious on a foreign battlefield could constitute sins never to be forgotten or forgiven.

1

The Foundations of Controversy

1885-1929

AFTER THEIR ARRIVAL in Australia from Britain, Lavarack's parents settled in Queensland where his father, Walter, took a job as a draughtsman with the State Lands Department and later bought a property at Julia Creek. The young John Lavarack applied to join the army as soon as he left Brisbane Grammar School, where he had been prominent in the cadet corps. He had harboured an ambition to be a doctor, but an older sister (Lavarack had eight siblings) was already studying medicine and the family could not afford the extra fees. The army provided a good alternative, and one with which the family was familiar. His father was a major in the Queensland Defence Force and his mother, Jesse, was the daughter of a British army officer, Colonel Robert Mackenzie. And so, less than twenty years after his birth in Brisbane on 19 December 1885, John Dudley Lavarack was commissioned in the Australian army as an artillery officer. Lavarack's average of more than 92 per cent in the officer entrance examinations was an indication of the intellectual capacity for which he would become renowned in the army.[1]

During the five years after he received his commission in June 1905, Lavarack filled junior regimental posts in New South Wales, Victoria, Queensland and on Thursday Island. In January 1911, while still a lieutenant, he applied to sit the examinations for entry to staff college. At the time Colonel J.S. Lyster, the district commandant in Queensland, reported that Lavarack was 'a zealous and industrious officer' possessing a 'vigorous brain and a very good memory' and likely to be a good staff officer. Nevertheless, despite this report and the support of his commanding officer, Lavarack's application was refused because there were already too many artillery officers absent from the regiment. Coincidentally, a Captain T.A. Blamey was also given approval to apply that year.[2]

The next year Lavarack, who was by then a captain also, was successful in his application to sit the entrance examination for the staff college at Camberley. Although he only just passed the papers on military engineering and military geography, he showed himself to be well-versed in other subjects, particularly mathematics, in which he had excelled at school, and his overall performance earned him a place in the two-year course beginning on 1 February 1913. Although support for his application was not as great as it had been the year before (in the interim he had been accused of 'gross neglect of duty', but details of the charge are now lost), his was the only application received and it was approved. Before leaving for Camberley, Lavarack married Sybil Nevett Ochiltree (the daughter of Dr E.C. Ochiltree of Ballarat) at St George's Anglican Church, Queenscliff on 10 October 1912.[3] Not long afterwards the newlyweds set sail for England.

The Lavaracks seemed to have settled easily into the social life of the staff college. There were dinners, balls, riding and boating, and renewing contacts with English relatives. Perhaps Lavarack was enjoying his time at Staff College a little too enthusiastically, for he found himself in trouble during the first year. In late 1913 he incurred the displeasure of both the Australian CGS and Director of Military Training because he failed to produce the customary quarterly report on his work at Camberley.

Nevertheless, it appears to have been the only blemish on his time there (which saw the birth of the first of the Lavaracks' three children, John, who would serve briefly in his father's division during the Second World War). By mid-1914 Lavarack's overall progress at Staff College had been good enough for the Australian government to request that, on completion of his course in December, he remain in England for a further year to gain experience in a series of attachments with the British army.[4]

The First World War

World events were to intervene to prevent Lavarack and his fellow students at Camberley completing the full course. On the outbreak of war in

August 1914 the college was closed and its students were scattered, Lavarack being posted to the War Office in London as a junior staff officer. It would be almost two years before he saw service with the Australian Imperial Force (AIF), but he was not to be the only Australian walking the corridors at the centre of the Empire's war effort: the man who was to become his nemesis in another world war, Thomas Blamey, had also been attached to the War Office at about the same time.[5]

In February 1915 Lavarack was enlisted in the AIF, but was immediately detached for service with the British army. Although he still only held the rank of captain, Lavarack left London for a posting as brigade-major of the British 22nd Division Artillery during its formation and training. In September this appointment was confirmed and Lavarack crossed to France where the divisional artillery was concentrating on a comparatively quiet part of the front north of Amiens.

Lavarack's time in France on this occasion was short. On 1 November orders were received that the 22nd Division was to move to Marseilles and embark for Salonika, in Greece, en route to Macedonia. The campaign in Macedonia was intended to relieve German, Austrian and Bulgarian pressure on Serbia. Lavarack was one of a number of Australians serving there, including Captain (later Brigadier Sir) K.A. Wills who would serve on his staff in the next war, and who considered the campaign one of the most interesting of his service. While in Macedonia Lavarack was promoted to major and later transferred to HQ 16th Corps as Staff Officer Royal Artillery. After some months in that post he applied for a transfer to the AIF and on 15 July 1916 he left again for France where he would serve for the first time with the AIF.[6]

Once back in France, Lavarack was posted to the 2nd Division Artillery in time for the attack on O.G.1, O.G.2 and the Windmill near Pozières at the end of July. His two months with the 2nd Division were divided between commanding the 17th and 104th Batteries and working on the headquarters staff. Then, as one of the few Australian officers who had attended staff college, he was appointed brigade-major of the 5th Division Artillery, AIF. During Lavarack's time with the 5th Division it saw action on the Somme and at Bullecourt.

Then, in mid-May 1917 Lavarack was transferred to the headquarters of the 1st Division as a GSO2 where his immediate superior was Colonel Blamey. A few months after his arrival, the division took part in the Battles of Menin Road, Broodseinde and Passchendaele, during the latter part of which, and for some weeks thereafter, Lavarack (who had been promoted to lieutenant-colonel on 23 July) was acting GSO1 owing to Blamey's absence because of illness. Lavarack and Blamey worked together in the 1st Division for seven months, and it is all but certain that this period saw the beginnings of the 'feud', as one staff officer put it, between the two men. At the least, their time serving together would have provided opportunity enough to establish that, although both were able and professional, they were essentially different in character and so the chance of any deep rapport developing between them was remote.[7]

Early in December the two men were separated when Lavarack was posted temporarily to HQ 3rd Division as Monash's GSO1 until, on 19 December (his 32nd birthday), he assumed duty as GSO1 of the 4th Division, commanded by a British officer, Major-General E.G. Sinclair-MacLagan. It was in this post that Lavarack was to spend the last year of the war, seeing action at Dernancourt, Villers-Bretonneux, Hamel, Amiens, and the Hindenburg Outpost-Line, building for himself a reputation as a gifted staff officer. The official historian, C.E.W. Bean, recorded an incident during the German offensive on the Somme in late March 1918 which illustrates Lavarack's calm determination and initiative. The 4th Division was pushed forward to hold the line in front of Amiens and Lavarack was moving ahead of his divisional commander:

> On the road he had passed a brigade of British siege artillery, which had been withdrawing before the German thrust. 'You Australians think you can do anything,' said its commander to Lavarack, 'but you haven't a chance of holding them.' 'Will you stay and support us if we do?' asked Lavarack. 'Right you are,' said the brigadier—and he did.[8]

Undoubtedly Lavarack proved his worth as a staff officer during the war. For his work he was made a Companion of the Order of St Michael and St George, awarded the Distinguished Service Order and mentioned in despatches on three occasions, as well as receiving the French Croix de Guerre. In four years of war Lavarack had served with the British army and in all five of the Australian divisions involved in the fighting (the 6th was short-lived and was disbanded before seeing action). He had risen from the rank of captain to lieutenant-colonel to occupy the most important staff position in a division. However, not unusually for a regular officer, the war had offered him scant opportunity to command.

At the end of the First World War Lavarack did not return immediately to Australia. Sybil Lavarack took their two children home (a second son, Peter, had been born in August 1915), while Lavarack remained in England to fill a post at AIF HQ in London. There he worked for a time under Brigadier-General C.H. Jess, one of several officers he would later supersede to become Chief of the General Staff. Eventually, after conducting an instructional tour of the recent battlefields for young officers, Lavarack returned to Australia in September 1919—he had been away almost seven years. Shortly thereafter his appointment in the AIF was terminated.

The next fifteen years would see Lavarack occupy posts in the Australian army of increasing importance, beginning in 1920 when he was appointed Director of Military Art (effectively the second-in-command) at the Royal Military College, Duntroon, in Canberra. It was perhaps the perfect posting after the years of war. In a serene environment the Lavarack family was able to be together again and welcome a new addition, James, born in 1922. Professionally, Lavarack enjoyed the time at Duntroon, taking great interest in the training of a new generation of army officers. He was able to mix easily with the academic staff of the college and found time for his favourite sports, golf and tennis.

After four years at Duntroon, Lavarack was posted for a year as a staff officer on the headquarters of the 2nd Division, a militia formation based in Sydney. Then came another staff posting to Army Headquarters (AHQ) in Melbourne which lasted only two months before he was given the key post of Director of Military Training and assumed responsibility for the training policy of the entire army.[9]

The Imperial Defence College

That Lavarack was being groomed for a senior post in the army became even more apparent when he was selected to attend the second course at the prestigious Imperial Defence College (IDC) in London, which was due to commence in 1928. In fact, it had been suggested by the Minister for Defence that Lavarack attend the inaugural course the year before, but he could not be spared from Army Headquarters, and so Commander C.J. Pope, RAN and Wing Commander S.J.Goble, RAAF became the first Australian students at the IDC. Curiously, although originally Lavarack had been nominated for 1927, the Minister suggested another army officer, Colonel W.J. Foster, for 1928. The reason for the minister's change of heart is not clear. It may have been an early manifestation of the distrust some politicians would come to feel for Lavarack as his views on defence became better known, but more likely, given the nature of his job, it was Lavarack's indispensability in his current post. However, Foster fell ill and Lavarack took his place to become the first of six Australian army officers who were to attend the IDC before the outbreak of war in 1939.[10]

The year 1928 was to be pivotal for Lavarack. Not only would he befriend a British officer on the course, Ernest Squires, who would eventually succeed him as Chief of the General Staff, but there was another Australian on Lavarack's course, Mr F.G. (later Sir Frederick) Shedden, who would become Secretary of the Department of Defence in 1937 during Lavarack's time as CGS. Lavarack and Shedden would become relentless opponents the next decade as Lavarack battled to expose the dangers of relying on a defence policy based on promises of a British fleet coming to Australia's aid in the event of war.[11] The seeds of their opposing views were sewn at the Imperial Defence College. The commandant of the college in 1928 was Admiral Sir Herbert Richmond, who held firmly to the ideal of imperial defence based on seapower. It was a proposition which Shedden, but not Lavarack, came to embrace fully, paving the way for future heated battles within the Department of Defence.

The range of subjects dealt with at the IDC was broad and pitched at a higher level than those covered at staff college. The nature of the course was more concerned with national strategy than military operations and tactics: there were lectures on the political and economic situations in various countries, the functions of government in war, international law, civil defence, manpower and industrial mobilisation, diplomatic duties during hostilities, the higher direction of war, control of the sea, and imperial defence, as well as exercises and papers to be completed on similar topics. At the end of the course Richmond reported on Lavarack:

> An officer whose military knowledge, personality, sound sense and
> sense of humour have been of the greatest value to the College. His
> knowledge of Australian problems has made him take a leading part in
> the studies of Imperial Defence. He can argue a case with tact, tonefulness and good humour, while showing determination in keeping to his
> point. He is an excellent colleague. He has taken every opportunity to
> profit from the course and to enable the other students to profit from his
> presence here.[12]

The combination of Lavarack's education, experience and personality now set the stage for the most important years of his career. During the next decade he would grasp every opportunity to question the soundness of Australian defence policy founded upon the British navy and its base at Singapore, hoping to better prepare the army and the country for the war which he, and many others, felt certain would come too soon. Lavarack's arguments against the navy's Singapore strategy would be eloquent, forceful and too cogent to ignore, much to the frustration of its supporters, especially his Australian classmate at the IDC, Shedden, who by the end of the course was in thrall to British seapower. The effects of their disagreement on Lavarack's career would persist into the Second World War as Shedden's power and influence grew, and his support for Blamey increased.

2

'A brilliant thinker'

Director of Military Operations and Intelligence, 1929-1932

AFTER HIS RETURN from the Imperial Defence College course in February 1929, Lavarack took up the key post of Director of Military Operations and Intelligence (DMO&I) at Army Headquarters in Melbourne. Initially the appointment was to be for a short time only, perhaps no more than six months, during the absence from the post of Lieutenant-Colonel E.F. Harrison, who had temporarily assumed the duties of commandant of the Royal Military College. But unexpectedly Lavarack was to remain DMO&I for almost four years, until December 1932.

General Rowell, who as a major served under Lavarack during the latter part of his time as DMO&I, has recalled that the General Staff Branch at Army Headquarters at that time was not large by modern standards. There was, for example, no Director of Staff Duties, a key officer who would have had the task of co-ordinating the staff work at the headquarters. Consequently, the position of DMO&I was that much more influential and Lavarack found himself to be the principal adviser to the CGS, who in 1929 was General Sir Harry Chauvel, the esteemed leader of the Desert Mounted Corps during the war. (Coincidentally Blamey had been Second Chief of the General Staff under Chauvel until a few years before, when he resigned from the regular army.) The scope of Lavarack's responsibilities as described by Rowell indicate the demanding nature of the appointment:

We covered the whole range of Army policy, since our conclusions were the basis of the recommendations which the Chief of the General Staff had to lay before the Military Board...[which] was the main source of advice to the Minister of Defence on Army matters.[1]

By definition, Lavarack was responsible for planning the employment of the Australian Military Forces in peace and war, and for the gathering of military intelligence. It was the planning, however, which occupied most of his time since Australia relied almost exclusively on the United Kingdom to provide it with military information. Working under the CGS, Lavarack threw himself into the task of preparing the army for war, devoting most of his energies to three main considerations: coast defences and the protection of defended ports; completing the plans for the despatch of an expeditionary force; and, most important, the strategic defence of Australia in which the army had been given a secondary role because of reliance on British promises of protection by the Royal Navy.[2]

The seeds of the argument concerning the army's role—whether it had to be prepared primarily to repel sporadic raids or be ready to meet an enemy invasion—were to be found in the policy of relying on British naval forces, to be based at Singapore in time of war, to protect Australia. The Singapore strategy did not allow for the possibility that the Royal Navy might fail to prevent an invasion force reaching Australian beaches. So, in the absence of official recognition that the Royal Navy might be unable to provide protection in some circumstances, the primary roles of the army and the air force were reduced to repelling raids.

The army, though, had been in no doubt about its task since the Senior Officers Conference of 1920: they had warned that Japan would most likely attack while Britain was engaged elsewhere, a warning that Admiral Lord Jellicoe had uttered the year before when he visited Australia to advise on defence in the Far East. The Chief of the Naval Staff (CNS) at the time, Rear-Admiral Sir Percy Grant, had also warned of the pitfalls of relying on a fleet being sent to Singapore. These expressions of doubt by senior British naval officers were to become rarer in the coming years as the orthodoxy of the Singapore strategy became entrenched in naval and government circles. Within the army, though, the peril already had been identified clearly: invasion was possible and planning against it was essential.

Lavarack thus found himself working at the heart of the growing divergence of views on defence within, and between, the Australian political and military establishments: the dispute over the likelihood of Australia being invaded was for the army, and for Lavarack in particular as DMO&I, the crux of Australian defence policy. Lavarack's views on national defence coincided with Chauvel's, and were probably shared by every senior army officer: the fundamental flaw in defence policy was that the promise to despatch a British fleet to the Far East was no guarantee to Australia of protection against a Japanese attack. If the army were to be prepared to meet an invasion by its most likely adversary, Japan, it would need more men and modern equipment.

However, by 1929 the Australian army had endured successive reductions in funding. The amount allocated for the financial year 1928–1929 was the smallest in five years and shortly after Lavarack became DMO&I the services had been told to make further economies. Chauvel's biographer, Alec Hill, has observed that the members of the Military Board 'were at their wits' end' after already having stripped the fat (and even some bone) from the army. Chauvel had been fighting to maintain the framework of the army since his appointment as CGS in 1923, and even before as Inspector-General, but with limited success. Although he had made some progress, he reported that overall the army had

> reached the bitter end of the process of robbing Peter to pay Paul, and cannot in future be expected to maintain the ground it has gained even if the funds provided are not again reduced.[3]

The army could be built up again only if the government decided that it would have an anti-invasion role.

As the main adviser to the Chief of the General Staff, Lavarack was closely involved with the issue and began concentrating his efforts on exposing what he saw as the weakness of Australian defence policy. He hoped to strengthen the country's preparedness by having a larger role for the army officially sanctioned.

His first significant opportunity came in July 1929 when the Prime Minister's Department asked the Defence Committee (which usually consisted of the heads of the three services and a civil servant from the Department of Defence as secretary) for an opinion on whether Australia's interests would be adequately safeguarded by British troops quartered only in the Suez Canal zone. The protection of the canal had a direct bearing on the time it would take a Royal Navy fleet to reach

Australia—if the canal were blocked, the fleet would have to take the longer Cape of Good Hope route around Africa to reach the naval base at Singapore.

Lavarack drafted the report, concluding that an interruption of traffic through the Suez Canal might well be disastrous for Australian defence. Therefore any agreement by Australia to proposals for the contraction of British forces in the wider region around the canal would be tantamount to accepting a much greater risk in case of war with a Pacific power. The effect of such a blockade would be a potentially disastrous delay to the arrival of the British fleet in the Pacific until three months after the outbreak of hostilities. And even that bleak assessment was based on the assumption that the situation in Europe would be stable enough to allow the fleet to be despatched immediately. (The Army's position would soon be fortified by an exercise conducted at the Imperial Defence College the next year when the ease with which Japan could block the Suez Canal became worryingly apparent.)[4]

Lavarack, though, already well aware of these potential problems, went beyond his remit in the report to question the likelihood of a British fleet being despatched to Australia at all. He argued plausibly that a delay in the arrival of the fleet in Singapore was not the most serious possible consequence of the blocking of the canal. Denial of access to the Indian Ocean via Suez might encourage Britain to retain the fleet in the Mediterranean and the Atlantic:

> It must be constantly borne in mind that the Royal Navy is primarily the main defence of the British Isles, and that any expedition that threatens to remove that defence for an indefinite period is likely to be vetoed by political and public opinion.

The answer was obvious: bolster the dangerously weak Australian army and air force for local defence.[5]

Lavarack had clearly strayed from the purely technical into the realm of politics to challenge the wisdom of current defence policy. The political dimension of his report was overlooked, however, and the Defence Committee forwarded it to the minister without amendment. That did not necessarily mean, though, that Lavarack's scepticism of British promises had gone unnoticed. His implication that stronger local forces were needed would become more explicit in later arguments, when he would indeed be taken to task for his political remarks.

Scullin and The Great Depression

In the meantime, any attempt by the army to achieve recognition of the unbalanced nature of Australian defence policy, and the precarious premises on which it was based, was to be swamped in October 1929. The Scullin Labor government's victory in the election that month coincided with the collapse of the New York stock market, precipitating the onset of the Great Depression. These events were to expose the Australian armed services to a blizzard of austerity, the chill of which would be felt for years.

From 1 November the Labor government suspended all compulsory service obligations under Part XII of the Defence Act. The army bore the brunt of the effects of the suspension of compulsory training, which might have been expected considering its size relative to the other services. Almost 90 per cent of the money saved would come from cutbacks in the army (£292,700 compared to £43,000 for the navy): 755 officers of the Staff Corps, quartermasters and warrant-officers would be retrenched, whereas the RAN would lose 106 officers and ratings, and the RAAF, in which no-one was compelled to serve, would maintain its establishment.[6]

The Australian army's overall strength would be reduced from 48,000 in the citizen forces to 35,000, and senior cadets from 16,000 to 7,000. Not only were the establishments of units to be reduced to achieve this aim, but five infantry battalions and two light horse regiments would no longer be maintained. Although on paper the army's divisional strength remained largely unchanged—the equivalent of five infantry divisions and two cavalry divisions, with the role of defending against a possible attack by three enemy divisions—in reality the army lacked the capability to oppose a serious attack successfully (for example, it had ammunition sufficient for only two major engagements).[7]

Prepared as the Scullin government was to make such radical changes, it might also have been expected that perhaps it would be willing to resolve the raid versus invasion dispute and so settle an issue on which the army and navy had been long divided. Scullin, though, would refuse to take the bull by the horns and would pass the problem to the heads of the services, with the comment that it was not a political decision but one to be made by them. It is not clear by what circuitous reasoning Scullin could arrive at the conclusion that the determination of government policy was not a political decision. However, it is obvious that the Prime Minister was not much interested in the problem, in spite of the efforts of his Minister for Defence, A.E. Green, who encapsulated the difficulty of trying to base a defence policy on a shifting premise:

> Conflict of opinion and indefiniteness are therefore the characteristics of the technical opinion on which the Government at present relies for an important phase of its policy entailing an annual expenditure of many millions of pounds.

The disagreement between the services first became apparent to the new government during discussions with the chiefs of staff in November 1929. So, early in February 1930, Green suggested to Scullin that a parliamentary committee be appointed to examine the existing defence policy and explore future possibilities. When that was done, advantage could be taken of the Imperial Conference to be held that year to obtain advice upon the principles which had been decided on. Scullin, however, 'was not favourably disposed towards either of these suggestions' and so, in the absence of a civil umpire, the service teams were left alone on the field.[8] By his inaction Scullin permitted the debate on raids or invasion to continue in the Council of Defence and the Defence Committee, as well as in service papers, with little hope that the issue would ever be resolved by the services themselves.

Not surprisingly, the next few months were to see great diversity of opinion in defence circles over policy, a debate to which Lavarack contributed generously. Lavarack relished the intellectual challenge of arguing the broad defence issues which passed across his desk. Always interested in finding the right terms in which to express his views, one member of his staff recalled that

> JDL would come into our office and sit on the corner of someone's desk. His practice was to throw some problem which was on his mind into the ring so to speak. On occasions he might read out a bit of some draft he had written or ask for a quotation to be completed or again, with some pride, expound his latest apt expression. I remember great joy one day when he worked 'mutatis mutandis' into some strategic paper he was concerned with. He was in high good humour and rolled the phrase over his tongue as if it was a sip of claret he was tasting.[9]

However, it seems that Lavarack's intelligence and fervour were not always matched by prudence and that he was to a degree oblivious, or perhaps even careless, of the enemies he was beginning to make. Most notable amongst these was Frederick Shedden whose influence in the Department of Defence had increased with his recent appointment as the secretary of the Defence Committee upon his return from the Imperial Defence College course in London.

Lavarack attacks Shedden

In December 1929, not long after returning to Australia from the United Kingdom, Shedden had submitted for consideration a lengthy paper he had prepared at the Imperial Defence College the year before. It was strongly in favour of Imperial defence based on the Royal Navy. Shedden's excellent relations with the college commandant, Admiral Richmond, and with Sir Maurice Hankey, the secretary of the Committee of Imperial Defence in London, would develop his belief in 'blue water strategy'. The depth of Shedden's regard for these two men, and the corresponding influence it generated, can be gauged by his assessment of them some years later: Richmond 'is the greatest living writer on naval history and strategy', while Hankey, 'as Secretary of the Committee of Imperial Defence, demonstrated the possession of a great strategical mind'. That Shedden had found his sea legs in Britain is evident from Richmond's comments on his paper:

> I return herewith your paper which I have read with the greatest care and pleasure. I have made some minor suggestions...but I wish to say that in its broad lines I think it quite the best analysis of the problem that I have yet seen. I agree entirely with all your major principles. You have expressed the ideas which I believe to be right, which I advanced in my teachings at the Imperial Defence College...[10]

Richmond even went so far as to write that when he completed his book (subsequently published as *Statesmen and Sea Power*) he felt that he would be regarded as a plagiarist by those who had also read Shedden's paper. Shedden told the Secretary of the Department of Defence, M.L. Shepherd, when presenting his paper, that

> As the opinion of the Australian General Staff on invasion is well known, particular attention has been paid to the Admiralty view of the

employment of the British Fleet in a war with Japan, and the security it furnishes to Australia against invasion.[11]

The army view, of course, did not coincide with Shedden's. In March 1930 the Australian CGS, Sir Harry Chauvel, presented a report prepared by Lavarack rebutting Shedden's paper with the comment that:

> Mr. Shedden has taken an immense deal of trouble and is to be congratulated on his work which is ably compiled. I am afraid, however, that nothing new is disclosed. The facts arrayed and the conclusions arrived at, which are all based upon undisputed command of all the seas, have been put forward time and again but have never yet been accepted by Australia and it is hoped never will be until the Singapore Base is completed and there is reasonable certainty that the British Fleet will always be available for employment in the East.[12]

Lavarack's accompanying paper was a seminal analysis of Australia's strategic position which, broadly, would be just as relevant decades after the end of the Second World War. Not only was it prescient and well-argued, it was also biting. Shedden would be stung by Lavarack's straightforward criticism, and it is difficult to imagine that it had no influence on Shedden's later actions affecting Lavarack's career.

Lavarack began his analysis with some general comments, reiterating that there was 'nothing new' in the facts presented by Shedden, that he had not considered the practical obstacles which would work to prevent his ideal concept of imperial defence from operating, and that in any case his argument was incomplete. In the detailed comments which followed, Lavarack concentrated on two contentions put forward by Shedden which, although not constituting the whole of the latter's thesis, were to Lavarack's mind 'the fundamental basis of its main argument'.[13]

The first of these was that complete control of sea communications could be established by British naval forces at will and thus Australian interests were protected. Consequently, it was superfluous to make preparations for an independent land- or air-based defence against an invasion which could not happen. Lavarack made it clear that he did not oppose the defence of Australia by naval forces per se 'were it certain that the sea forces of the Empire could obtain command in every theatre of war the question of invasion would not arise'. However, while Britain had in the past generally been able to succeed in achieving this goal, the existing situation had never been faced before to the same degree. Certainly, Britain had never had to reckon with a powerful Asian navy, as she now had to with Japan's. In light of that development, and returning to the argument he had put forward before when assessing the danger of the Suez Canal being blocked, Lavarack again warned that

> the despatch of the British battle fleet to the Far East for the protection of Imperial (including Australian) interests cannot be counted upon with sufficient certainty, and the risk that it will be withheld, added to the risk of the non-completion, capture, or neutralisation of Singapore, results in a total risk that no isolated white community such as Australia would be justified in taking.[14]

Lavarack's arguments were obvious and, as events would show in little more than a decade, well-founded. The Royal Navy of the 1920s was not strong enough to meet the demands of imperial defence—naval parity and international disarmament conventions prevented the increase of the navy to a size able to meet those demands. Even without the restraints upon the size of British seapower imposed by international agreements, the financial burden of increasing the navy to an adequate size would be too great for Britain to bear in its depleted state after the Great War.[15]

Lavarack also addressed another major contention in Shedden's paper: that a Japanese invasion of Australia would not be necessary. Shedden believed that if the enemy could gain sufficient control of sea communications to allow an invasion, then it could more easily defeat Australia through economic strangulation than by a major military confrontation on land. Consequently, according to Shedden's view, building up Australian land and air forces to guard against invasion was pointless.

Lavarack felt that Shedden's analysis was simplistic. Instead of either Britain or Japan gaining complete control of the approaches to Australia, to Lavarack's mind it was more likely that command of the seas would be divided. Shedden had ignored the possibility that Japan might control the western Pacific but that Britain would retain command of the Suez and Cape routes through the Indian Ocean. Thus, while trade might be severely curtailed, it could not be stopped completely. However, the situation could be dramatically different if the army and air force were not strong enough to resist the Japanese:

> Such a situation, however, in the absence of provision for land defence

against invasion, would leave Australia quite helpless and would give Japan time to establish herself on land in a position that would soon become practically impregnable.

In Lavarack's opinion Shedden had exaggerated an enemy's power to stop Australia's maritime trade, while underestimating the country's capacity to endure any disruption to trade that might occur. Critically, Shedden

> ... has not taken into consideration the third and most probable case of divided command at sea, in which the existence of land forces in Australia would be a vital necessity. The land forces are in fact not a 're-insurance', as stated... but an essential part of the insurance, of which sea power is the main ingredient.[16]

Lavarack, determined to hit on the head every nail he could find, went on to attack Shedden's confident assertion that the

> provision of the requirements for defence of trade therefore simultaneously furnishes in the most economical manner security against invasion by seaborne land or air forces. If...enemy forces cannot cross the ocean to reach the shores of a territory, the provision of troops and aircraft for defence against them is not necessary.

Here Lavarack could even call upon an eminent sailor to support his case, referring to the views of Admiral Lord Jellicoe who had visited Australia and advised on defence in 1919:

> Lord Jellicoe's statement that 70 cruisers would be sufficient to-day must be accepted, though it is difficult to reconcile it with his other statement that 140 were insufficient in 1914, since the number of trade routes to be guarded is no less and the potential enemy relatively stronger. But the Empire is to be allowed 50, not 70, cruisers, and her strength in large cruisers of great endurance, the only kind that is of value for trade attack from the Japanese point of view, is to be 15, while Japan, for example, is to have 13.

Obviously, if there were insufficient ships to protect trade, it could not be assumed that the same forces could furnish protection against the greater threat of invasion as well. Indeed, Shedden had referred to the Admiralty's view, of the same year in which he had written the paper, that the 'naval strength at present provided is not sufficient for the protection of trade'.[17]

The paradox of Shedden propounding the advantages of seapower in providing protection against invasion as well as defending trade when he was aware that there were insufficient forces even for the latter role could hardly be lost on Lavarack, who added that the British position vis-à-vis other powers was weakening, not improving. It is difficult when faced with such inconsistencies to disagree with Lavarack that Shedden was extolling the ideal without allowing practicalities to mar the formula for defence concocted by the wizards in Whitehall, under whose spell he had clearly fallen.[18]

Having disposed of the major issues, in the remainder of his paper Lavarack dealt with other aspects of Shedden's argument which touched more particularly upon army interests. For example, Shedden postulated that effective guerrilla warfare could be waged against an invader (though this was surely a purely hypothetical case from Shedden's point of view when he was so confident of Royal Navy protection) to increase beyond practicality the size of a Japanese attacking force. To bolster this argument Shedden drew an analogy with the Boer War in which 'it took 240,000 well-equipped troops to subdue 40,000 Dutch farmers'. Lavarack made it clear, however, that in his opinion ad hoc civilian resistance was no substitute for a trained army:

> Australia's population is largely concentrated into centres of vital indus-
> trial importance, in which talk of unorganised resistance of any kind is
> idle...The country population of Australia is unarmed and unorganised,
> whereas the Boers were a genuine pastoral and agricultural people, were
> practically all armed, were trained in the use of the rifle, and were or-
> ganised in commandos in a very suitable manner for the type of warfare
> that took place. Passive resistance and sabotage would receive short
> shrift at the hands of the Japanese. The Australian people, in fact, is very
> ill-adapted for unorganised resistance.[19]

Having shot that idea down, Lavarack then challenged Shedden's assessment of Japanese military psychology. Shedden wrote that a 'study of Japanese psychology in relation to their campaigns indicates that they are prudent and prefer over-insurance to risk', and gave the Russo-Japanese War of 1904-05 as an example. Lavarack retorted pointedly:

> Every student of the Russo-Japanese war knows that the Japanese ac-
> cepted very real risks in the despatch of the earlier parts of their Expedi-

tionary Force to Korea and even the neighbourhood of Port Arthur itself before they had put the Russian fleet in the Far East out of action.

(One can only wonder if Shedden had altered his view of Japanese military timidity by the time of the audacious Japanese attack on Pearl Harbor and Malaya just over a decade later.)[20]

Overall, Lavarack had been hard on Shedden's paper, writing that it was scattered with untenable assumptions and unsound conclusions. He admitted that building a navy of an adequate size was the ideal solution, but 'finance, parity, and disarmament combine to render the ideal unthinkable'. The ramifications for the army were that the possibility of invasion had to be faced: '[Shedden's] conclusion that provision against possible invasion is unnecessary in Australia's case has been shown to be based on an incomplete analysis of the probable situation'. Thus, Lavarack concluded that he could not accept Shedden's thesis as a 'practical guide' to Australian defence policy, 'although it certainly is a brilliant and thoughtful contribution to the general question of Empire Defence'.[21]

As soon as his paper had been released by Chauvel, Lavarack sent a copy to Shedden with the observation that 'You will I know accept my criticisms in good part, and will realise that I don't regard what I have written as the last word, by any means'. Lavarack also despatched with his critique another paper of his own dealing with war in the Pacific 'because it gives my idea of how the economic pressure situation might work out at greater length than in the earlier paper'. The impression that he was trying to educate Shedden was not dispelled by the last sentence of his letter: 'My motto is "We live and learn".'[22]

Shedden attacks Lavarack

Naturally Lavarack's views did not go unchallenged. The Naval Staff produced a short critique of his paper which did little to advance the argument and at one point seemed to sail precariously close to inter-service churlishness:

Invasion of Australia...is an operation of the utmost complexity and magnitude and can easily be upset by the obtrusion of comparatively minor forces. This fact is completely disregarded in the paper under review. It is, moreover, an entirely Naval matter in which Naval views will necessarily prevail. If Japan[ese] Naval advisers are incompetent, Japan will be riding for a fall.[23]

However, it was Shedden who, not surprisingly, led the counter-attack against Lavarack. His reaction showed that he had been shaken by Lavarack's criticism. He began by questioning Lavarack's knowledge, asking 'What does the writer know of the probable method of employment of the British Navy?' But it was on the raid-invasion issue that Shedden really attacked him. Lavarack's appreciation that 'the provision for trade defence cannot be assumed to provide assurance against attacks on territory as well as on trade, which the [Shedden] thesis claims that it should' provoked Shedden to reply that

> No one said that Australia was immune from attacks on territory. The whole question is "Invasion". The writer [Lavarack] does not appear to understand the difference between Raids and Invasion.

Shedden was grasping at straws. It is quite clear that Lavarack, in using the phrase 'attacks on territory' was referring to an invasion, for the sections of Shedden's paper to which he referred dealt exclusively with the relationship between defence of trade and defence against invasion.[24]

Shedden, who had invested heavily in the naval school of thought, obviously felt his reputation to be under threat:

> I am concerned [about Lavarack's critique] in so far as [his] criticism of illogical thought is concerned. The facts are to be judged by others. Col. L. acts as his own judge.

In reply to Lavarack's assertion that 'the conclusions drawn by Mr. Shedden [are] fallacious', Shedden wrote—with what seems to be a mixture of anger and desperation —that 'Col. L's jumping to conclusions shows [his] opinion is valueless'. Shedden even drew on his mentor from the IDC, Admiral Richmond, for support, asking him to comment on statements made by 'military critics of my papers'. As might be expected, Richmond castigated those who attacked Shedden. Of the possibility that the British government might refuse to permit the fleet to sail for the Far East, Richmond wrote:

> I have never heard a more stupid statement...No representative on the General Staff can have the smallest knowledge whatever of what the ac-

tion of the Government would be as regards sending ships to the Far East. If strategy required ships there[,] there is not the smallest doubt in the world that they would be sent. Of that I am absolutely confident. I suppose the representative of whom you speak is harping on that old old string of the Far Eastern war coinciding with a European one. It is one of those almost incredibly foolish things against which Lord Salisbury found it necessary to take a stand. A hypothetical situation of a highly improbable nature is first taken, and then the action which would result is given, or asserted, in terms to suit some preconceived idea or policy. I can imagine no worse way of stampeding a Government into waste of money.[25]

Richmond did a great deal to bolster Shedden's morale, but in reality produced little to undermine Lavarack's argument. In Lavarack's opinion the observations of Richmond, to which Shedden had referred as support for his own paper, were 'his personal views, which are not necessarily those of the British Admiralty'. Within weeks Lavarack's assessment was amply borne out by events: Richmond was informed by the Admiralty that because of the views he had recently expressed in the London *Times* he could consider his career at a standstill. Richmond told Shedden: 'The Admiralty were angry about them and have informed me that I shall not be offered any further employment'. Nevertheless, Richmond advised about the army critics: 'Don't let these Humbugs get away with it, my dear Shedden'. But obviously both were worried about Lavarack and others in the ranks of the army like him, such as Colonel H.D. Wynter. Shedden warned Richmond that Wynter was attending the IDC that year. Richmond expressed his misgivings about this:

I knew that Colonel Wynter was at the I.D.C. Of course he will have put forward his views. My anxiety, Shedden, is that our officer—naval—at the College will not have the knowledge to confute his assertions.[26]

Richmond had cause to be concerned. While both Shedden and Lavarack firmly believed in the merits of their respective cases (and both had as a result overstated their arguments at times), Lavarack possessed the more realistic appraisal of defence policy given the weakened state of the Royal Navy at the time. He had also shown himself to be an articulate critic of government policy and a champion of the army cause. But in so doing had made a professional enemy who would come to wield great power in the Department of Defence.

More strategy than money

Lavarack's next foray into defence policy came soon after he had finished his critique of Shedden's paper. At a meeting of the Defence Committee on 6 March 1930 the heads of the services had to decide in what proportions the reduced defence vote would be allocated.

The CNS submitted at length his views on Australian defence, which naturally stressed the efficacy of sea power, the danger of economic strangulation and the unlikelihood that Japan would attempt an invasion of Australia, in part because it would be a great risk and, echoing Shedden, 'on the whole the mentality of the Japanese is opposed to risk'. He argued against a *pro rata* reduction by all the services. Instead the money available should be 'apportioned amongst the three services to the best advantage' and there was no doubt in his mind that the navy should be the service to endure the least cut in expenditure:

> It will be seen that an adequate Navy insures against both forms of major attack [economic strangulation and invasion], while the Army is a deterrent against one form only and that the less likely of the two.

Naturally, Chauvel did not agree, arguing that the army had not accepted that the navy could protect Australia from invasion: since 1918 the Royal Navy's strength had declined as the Japanese navy's had grown.

With no agreement in sight between the service chiefs it was decided that a full review of the Defence Committee's 1928 appreciation covering the eventuality of war in the Pacific was necessary and a sub-committee was appointed to carry out the task.[27] Lavarack was appointed chairman of the sub-committee, with the naval and air members being Pope and Goble, both of whom had attended the IDC the year before Lavarack. But, as Lavarack's difference of opinion with Shedden had shown, attendance at the IDC did not guarantee unanimity of opinion when it came to defence policy.

The army and air force representatives, Lavarack and Goble, could not agree with the naval representative, Pope, who argued that invasion of Australia was practically impossible and that consequently the maintenance of mobile land and air forces was unnecessary. As a means of resolving the issue of how the reduced defence vote should be distributed amongst the services, the sub-committee was a failure—it simply reflected the disagreement in the Defence Committee itself. At the end of discussions Lavarack reported:

> The Committee has not been in agreement on certain essential points, and as a result the Naval representative has submitted an independent review; the Army and Air Members are in agreement and have collaborated in the production of a joint review.[28]

It was not hard to see who had taken the lead in producing the joint review: the points made were reminiscent of those in Lavarack's appreciation of the defence of the Suez Canal and in his critique of Shedden's paper on imperial defence. In conclusion, Lavarack and Goble decided that Australian defence 'depends upon the effective co-operation of the three fighting services and cannot with safety be entrusted to one of them.' However, they felt that money spent on the army and the air force would be a better investment because those two services were concerned solely with local defence, whereas the navy was designed to become part of the Empire's defence, and not just protect Australia. In the light of this they made a controversial suggestion in an effort to pass a substantial portion of the navy bill to Britain:

> In the interests of efficiency and economy, therefore, it is considered that the position of the Australian Naval Forces should be examined with a view to their re-organisation and administration as an Australian unit within the British Navy, and not as a separate Navy at great additional overhead cost for staffs and shore establishments.[29]

This unexpected proposal served to spice the debate considerably and immediately put the navy on the defensive.

As might be expected, the report quickly came under attack from the CNS, Vice-Admiral Munro Kerr, when it was tabled at the Defence Committee. A lively discussion on defence followed, but the argument proceeded, in the words of one member of the committee, 'in circles without progress' and so the meeting was adjourned. When the Defence Committee met again six days later, the CNS resumed his comments on the review furnished by Lavarack and Goble. Having had more time to consider the report, the heads of the services were better prepared for debate, but neither that day, nor during the next, could any agreement be reached on the services' primary responsibilities and hence on the proportions in which the defence vote should be divided. Eventually it was decided that a *pro rata* distribution of the new vote was the only solution in the circumstances.[30]

The review furnished by Lavarack and Goble had done little but fuel an already heated debate in the Defence Committee. Realistically, however, it could be expected to do little else. The chiefs of staff had referred the problem to a sub-committee which, if anything, had even less chance of resolving the issue of apportioning the meagre defence vote than they had themselves—junior officers would be bound to follow the policy of their respective services.

The essence of the problem, however, was broader in that the government had given no clear direction to the services on policy, and was unlikely to do so while Scullin's incomprehensible opinion that it was a matter for the services held sway. For as long as the government refused to resolve the issue of raid or invasion (and hence all the corollaries which attended it) there was hardly the smallest likelihood that agreement amongst the services would ever be reached and the Defence Committee had little recourse but to reiterate the importance of receiving some guidance from the government.[31]

However, as well as producing the joint report with Goble, Lavarack also wrote another, more polemical, appreciation of his own dealing with Australia's position should war come to the Pacific. In it he pounded over the familiar ground upon which army policy was built, but in colourful language:

> In the Pacific...the possibility of war with the yellow races is just as
> frankly recognised as in the case of the U.S.A. it is denied. Obviously
> this must be so. To us the East is inscrutable. Its motives and political
> morality lead its peoples in directions diametrically opposite to those we
> must take. Providence has left, in Australia, an obvious field of
> expansion for the yellow and brown races, but 6 millions of white
> people cling (in Japanese and Chinese opinion, selfishly) to this empty
> land.

For the defence of Australia by sea to be certain, Lavarack argued that absolute reliance would have to be placed on 'the presence of the British main fleet, or a considerable proportion of it, based on a completed Singapore Base'. Not only that, he added prophetically, but the fleet would have to arrive quickly enough 'to prevent the Japanese from establishing prior command' in Singapore.

Unfortunately, with the Royal Navy reduced to a one-power standard (i.e., equal in size to only one potentially belligerent foreign navy), there appeared to be little hope that the British government and people would ever sanction the despatch of the fleet to the other side of the world:

> The issue is simple. Command in the Atlantic is of vital importance to the British people, command in the Far East is not. The Imperial Navy, (with the insignificant exception of the R.A.N.), belongs to the British people. Whatever therefore the Admiralty may design to do, the Government and people are unlikely to accede to the transference of a considerable portion of the main fleet to the Far East if there is danger or the possibility of danger nearer home. Japan, on the other hand, will not make war unless she is certain that the British main fleet can be safely eliminated from the equation she has to solve.[32]

Lavarack sent a copy of this markedly logical appreciation to Shedden, which would have done little to ease the ill-feeling growing between the two men over the issue.

The 1930 Imperial Conference

Lavarack's arguments were becoming well-known at senior levels within the government by this time and his next paper certainly reached the Prime Minister. Scullin had decided to attend the Imperial Conference in London in late 1930 and before his departure he asked the Military Board for a memorandum on army policy and organisation. Since it was intended for public consumption Scullin asked that 'it should be as informal and as picturesque as the nature of the subject permits'. The Prime Minister had wanted a paper of about 3,000 words by 16 June, but Lavarack provided him with a memorandum of almost twice that length by 5 June and one which, although picturesque, hardly seems to have been what Scullin had in mind when he made the request.[33]

Lavarack began by outlining the threat posed to Australian security by the growing awareness in nearby Asian countries that the 'ubiquitous white man' had usurped their place in Australia. Australia, he went on, must be prepared to back the provocative White Australia Policy by force if necessary. However, providing for local defence (which Lavarack termed the 'Primary Responsibility') from Australian resources depended upon the strength of the British navy. When Britain had enjoyed unchallengeable naval supremacy

> the sea-power of the British Empire was, to all intents and purposes, an absolute guarantee of security for all Australian interests, possible attack being limited to raids on the coast and sporadic attacks on trade.

Lavarack attempted to place words in Scullin's mouth when he wrote that, as a result of the effects of naval parity and disarmament agreements which were still reducing the margin of security,

> Australia feels, therefore, that she cannot rely, as completely as in the past, upon the British Navy, and that she is becoming more and more dependent upon her own resources for her security against possible aggression.

The best way of achieving the self-reliance necessary under the circumstances was to make the army the mainstay of the defence forces.[34]

In an effort to undermine the naval argument, Lavarack appealed to the Scullin government's primary concern about defence—its cost: '[I]t should be here stated that the main argument in favour of military, as compared with Naval and Air defence, is its extraordinary cheapness.' He criticised decisions by several governments to curtail expenditure which had arrested the development of the army, except for that which might be achieved in some small way by 'personal effort and personal efficiency, and [by] making the best of the equipment available'. He went further, observing that although there was much talk of an imperial defence policy, no such policy had ever, in reality, existed:

> [N]o genuine Imperial Defence policy exists and consequently there is no basis for a properly co-ordinated Australian Defence policy. The Army, in common with the other Services, thus finds itself distinctly at a loss when questions arise which demand the guidance afforded by a common policy.

As an example he cited the difficulty of distributing the defence budget among the services when no clearly defined priorities existed.[35]

The lack of a straightforward policy meant that the army could have a role no more defined than to co-operate with the other services in preparing to defend the country. 'This is admittedly a nebulous policy, but nothing more definite is possible under present conditions.' The remedy, Lavarack suggested, was 'the formulation of a clearly defined defence policy for the Empire as a whole', but unfortunately the machinery through which this might be achieved did not exist. Therefore, he proposed that the matter be raised at the Imperial Conference with a view to forming a body which would consider the question of overall policy for the empire and report to the next conference (which was the same point he had made in his critique of Shedden's paper on imperial defence). He admitted that this would be a slow process, but

> it would, at any rate, hold out some hope of eventual agreement, the lack of which is at present a very considerable handicap on the proper co-ordination of defence activities, and prevents the attainment of the ideal of efficiency with economy.[36]

As notes for a speech by Scullin, Lavarack's paper was of course far too controversial. Unlike a similar paper prepared by the navy, Lavarack had roamed freely across political ground. It was liberally sprinkled with statements which, if used by Scullin in a public speech, could have caused considerable embarrassment to the government.[37] Nevertheless, it had provided a vehicle for the army view to reach the highest political level, although it was unlikely to have much effect on a government which had shown itself to be largely uninterested in defence. Later, after he became CGS, Lavarack was to attempt something similar when he tried to have the Minister for Defence commit himself to the possibility of invasion. As events were to show, it was not the kind of ploy politicians appreciated.

Naturally, however, Lavarack was viewed favourably within the army for his efforts. The post of DMO&I had given him limited entrée to the arena of policy considerations and even attendance at a meeting of the Council of Defence (composed of the prime minister and selected members of the government) to which senior military officers and civil servants would usually be summoned. Lavarack had been quick to take advantage of his position to question the soundness of current policy. By 1930 his well-known, percipient views, as well as his professional abilities, had marked him early for high rank.

In April of that year, shortly before his retirement as CGS, Chauvel had placed Lavarack's name before the Minister as a future Chief of the General Staff. Chauvel had identified Jess and Lavarack as the two officers most deserving of succeeding him as CGS, but felt that Jess would be much better suited to the command of troops and suggested that he be given a senior command when one became available. Of Lavarack he wrote:

> Colonel Lavarack possesses all the qualifications except that of a command in the field. He also recently attended a Course at the Imperial Defence College. Colonel Lavarack, however, is also comparatively junior and has fifteen, or, if promoted to Major-General, seventeen years still to serve. It would not appear to be in his own interest or that of the Service that he should be placed now in a position from which there is at best only one more step. Colonel Lavarack's claims should not, however, be lost sight of when another change is made.[38]

Chauvel's recommendation was a tribute to the quality of Lavarack's work as DMO&I and a significant acknowledgement of his ability to grasp political and diplomatic issues as well as military problems. Lavarack had shown himself, in the words of General Hopkins, to be

> a brilliant thinker, astute and often ahead of service opinion. As DMO he never seemed over-awed by his superiors, not even by the conclusions of the prestigious (in the 1930s) Committee of Imperial Defence.

Even so, the extent to which his arguments had influenced policy was minimal, which is not surprising considering his relatively junior appointment. It is interesting, however, that in February 1931 the Minister agreed to place before Cabinet the proposal, amongst others, that the RAN be handed over to Britain, which Lavarack had earlier suggested.[39]

Whatever the effect of Lavarack's arguments during his years as DMO&I, the government, the Defence Department and the other services had been put on notice that there was a rising star in the ranks of the army. Little wonder that the successive Chiefs of the General Staff under whom he worked were disinclined to hobble such an articulate critic of what they saw as a dangerously flawed defence policy which imperilled the nation. Lavarack had shown himself to be as intelligent and capable as many had thought him to be, and it seemed only a question of time before he became the head of the army in Australia when the entrenched views of the Singapore strategy would come under more prominent attack.

3

'A bit of an "invasionist"'

Commandant, Royal Military College
1933-1934

LAVARACK'S CAREER TOOK a turn away from the recurring wrangles about defence policy with his appointment in December 1932 as Commandant of the Royal Military College, Duntroon and Army Schools of Instruction. It was an important posting which carried increased pay and an advancement in rank from brevet colonel to temporary colonel (as a brevet colonel, Lavarack had been entitled to wear the rank but not receive the pay of a colonel). It also removed Lavarack from Melbourne, the focus of the strategic debate, to Sydney where the college had been temporarily relocated at Victoria Barracks to save money. But Lavarack's official absence from the dispute over defence policy was only planned to be temporary. In reality the new appointment was simply a posting in which Lavarack could mark time until he could be brought back into the strategic debate to fight the army's corner inside the Department of Defence at a more senior level.[1]

Lavarack's role as commandant was hardly stretching for someone of his ability and interests, and in some ways the posting was not as congenial as his earlier time at the college a decade before when it had been located in Canberra. The Depression had taken its toll and cuts in defence spending had not only restricted training but also had reduced the number of cadets recruited. Nevertheless, Lavarack threw himself into the new task with characteristic verve, if not always good humour.

One cadet recalled a tennis match in which Lavarack hardly set an example to his young charges of the good-sportsmanship perhaps to be expected of a senior officer in such a position:

> [Lavarack] displayed a most violent temper. J.D.L. was partnering Professor Morrison against me and my partner, who either 'aced' him or passed him down the sideline. The general threw his tennis racquet at my partner with no ill-effects except making an indelible mark on my memory which has lasted nearly fifty years.[2]

Lavarack's intense competitive spirit was not limited to his own performance. As commandant he identified with the college sporting teams, taking to heart any setback they suffered, as another ex-staff cadet remembers:

> He followed the Duntroon teams around in all weathers and I well remember him standing on the sideline in the rain at rugby matches, smiling broadly when we scored a try and looking as black as his moustache if we were losing or if he thought the referee had ruled incorrectly against us.[3]

Although the new post precluded Lavarack's official participation in the strategic debate, his views were still being aired. In the same month that he became commandant, the British *Army Quarterly* published an article Lavarack had written entitled 'The Defence of the British Empire, with Special Reference to the Far East and Australia'. It was a response to another by Admiral Richmond in the same journal six months before. Lavarack's penchant for the apt quote led him to begin his article with: 'I think there be six Richmonds in the field'. But there the levity ended. Lavarack challenged Richmond's arguments, called his article 'highly provocative' and charged that he dealt with policy and strategy 'on the broadest lines', apparently content 'to limit himself to the consideration of an ideal defence, unconditioned by world agreements, Dominion policies, finance, disarmament and pacifism'. To Lavarack's mind, Richmond was propounding the impracticable: British ships in the Mediterranean and Atlantic 'could hardly be accepted as sufficient protection' for Australia and New Zealand in the event of war in the Far East.[4]

Lavarack's piece was timely, for although Labor had been defeated at the polls by the centre-right United Australia Party led by Joseph Lyons, the new government had decided upon an anti-raid policy for the army, so ensuring that the raid-invasion debate between the services would continue. And the opinions Lavarack expressed in the article epitomised the army view and publicly encapsulated the ideas he had been putting forward to that time in his career, ideas which would soon guide his actions as Chief of the General Staff in dealing with the army's *bête noire*, the Singapore strategy.[5]

In the article Lavarack expounded familiar arguments: the Royal Navy no longer had ships in sufficient numbers to protect both the Atlantic and the Far East, and, as a war in the Far East would most likely coincide with hostilities in Europe, 'the possibility of the detachment of adequate forces [to the Far East] would be remote'. He was adamant that the 'conditions of the problem have fundamentally changed with the disappearance of unchallengeable British supremacy at sea' and thus 'security based on the control of sea communications alone is a counsel of perfection...'. To offset these changed circumstances Lavarack proposed that, as well as co-operating in naval defence, Australia should build up its land-based forces to prevent an enemy obtaining a base on mainland Australia. Such a base would be needed, he argued, to maintain an effective naval blockade of the entire Australian coastline.[6] But to counter that threat would be difficult if the army and air force remained under-funded.

After quoting the galling defence expenditure figures of the previous ten years (the Royal Australian Navy had enjoyed 63 per cent of the defence budget, the army and air force 28 per cent and 9 per cent respectively), he made it clear that such a trend could not continue without serious ramifications: 'Naval defence already gets the lion's share; any more and the harmless, necessary cat and dog must perish'. Lavarack was adamant, however, that he was not fighting merely to increase the size of the army for its own sake, that he did indeed take a broader, imperial view of defence which encompassed all services. But for the time being:

Australian faith in the omnipotence of naval defence is not so great as it would be were the main Fleet stationed in the Far East, instead of the North Atlantic, and this is largely the reason why a mobile garrison in a nucleus form is kept in being. By no stretch of imagination, however, could this be described as an army maintained in a state of instant readiness to resist attack. Destroy this nucleus and the Dominion will be helpless, both to assist in the land defence of the Empire, and to provide for its own defence in the contingency, remote or otherwise, of attack on its own territory. The nucleus in some form, therefore, is necessary, and no more has ever been suggested.

The concluding sentence was a counter to charges that there was an attempt to confine Australia's military forces to a purely local and defensive role. But such a movement, according to Lavarack, was no more widespread than the belief that the earth was flat.

Lavarack's article expressed views held by other senior officers in the army who wanted the government to commit itself no further to the Singapore strategy until work on the base was completed and until there were guarantees of a fleet being based there or sent in time of need. Such advice was sound: Britain's naval strength in the Pacific was then so weak that the British chiefs of staff were of the opinion that if Japan attacked in the Far East, the Royal Navy would be fortunate to be able 'to disappear into the blue'. Not only that, but the base at Singapore was, according to the First Lord of the Admiralty, 'little more than a hole in the earth'.[7]

Nevertheless, Lavarack was subsequently criticised by Admiral Richmond for 'labouring under a particularist influence very common today—that of the doctrine of national self-sufficiency'. Whether Richmond at this time believed in his arguments in favour of the Singapore strategy, or was merely espousing Royal Navy dogma without the hindrance of critical thought, is difficult to determine. But it is notable that in a work published just after the Second World War, Richmond would finally admit that there had been little hope of a fleet being despatched to the Far East.[8] The pity is that he, and his British naval colleagues, did not admit as much in 1933.

The next Chief of the General Staff

Throughout Lavarack's time at RMC discussion continued about who would replace Major-General Sir Julius Bruche as Chief of the General Staff. Bruche was due to retire from the army in April 1934 and so it was that Lavarack's name came to the fore again in late 1933. It might be thought that a government concerned about criticism of its defence policy would be keen to remove the sting from the army's opposition by having a more malleable, less outspoken officer than Lavarack.[9] However, unless the government had been prepared to throw away efficiency with criticism, there was little choice but to appoint an opponent of defence based upon the navy—even had it been possible to find an army officer who agreed with the policy, which was unlikely.

A Department of Defence paper made it clear that, since the new CGS was to be the principal military adviser to the Minister on topics such as defence plans, preparations for war and expeditionary forces,

> It is essential that the officer selected for this appointment should be so fully equipped to tender this advice that it can be accepted with confidence. He must be a highly educated officer and graduation at Staff College is therefore essential. But he should also be in close touch with post war thought and development.
>
> It must be admitted that there has been a considerable degree of stagnation in this direction in Australia. Only one or two somewhat junior officers have had an opportunity since the war of rubbing shoulders with the leaders of the Empire Forces who make a continuous study of developments.[10]

Clearly, such criteria narrowed the field considerably. Of officers holding the rank of colonel and above, only Brigadier-General Sir Carl Jess could claim a sufficiently high standard of education, having attended staff college soon after the end of the war. In addition, he had been the senior staff officer of a division during the war and commanded a battalion and a brigade. However, appointments in Australia had prevented him from establishing and maintaining contact with post-war developments.

Considering substantive lieutenant-colonels, E.M.Williams and P.M. McFarlane had both been to staff college, but their war experience had been considerably less than Jess's. The next staff college graduate was Lavarack. He had had varied war experience in staff appointments up to GSO1 of a division, although no significant experience of command since he had been a subaltern. But his post-war training was considered the most recent and valuable in the army, especially after his time at the Imperial Defence College in 1928. It was not thought necessary to look further for a candidate, especially since originally it had not been intended to draw candidates from so far down the seniority list:

> It would appear that the two officers who can be considered most nearly eligible are Brig. Gen. Jess and Lt. Col. Lavarack. But it is suggested that neither can be confidently recommended immediately. Brig. Gen. Jess

because of his lack of personal experience of post war developments and Lt. Col. Lavarack because of his lack of experience in command.

Before either could be considered ready to take over as CGS their relative shortcomings would have to be rectified, but both were comparatively young and so there was much to be gained by investing time and money in both.[11]

Despite being junior to Jess, clearly Lavarack was favoured for the post, as a letter from the Minister for Defence, Sir George Pearce, to Australia's High Commissioner in London, S.M. Bruce, made clear. After outlining the difficulty in finding a suitably qualified successor to General Bruche in Australia and suggesting that one might be found in the British army, Pearce continued:

> Complementary to this, my idea is that one of the most promising of our younger officers, say Colonel J.D. Lavarack, C.M.G., D.S.O., should proceed to England for training in Staff and Command duties which would ultimately fit him for appointment as Chief of the General Staff, and he might perhaps be considered as an exchange with the officer selected by the War Office. Colonel Lavarack at present holds temporary substantive rank whilst Commandant of the Royal Military College, but it is possible that he will shortly be promoted permanently.[12]

Means of alleviating the difficulties created by Bruche's imminent retirement were still being explored less than three months before he was due to leave the post. At the end of January 1934 Shepherd wrote to Pearce that although it was possible to extend Bruche's appointment for one, or even two, years,

> The other alternative is to appoint Laverack [sic] as C.G.S. as soon as Bruche's time is up in April this year.
>
> This would simplify all problems and make the proposed exchange with a British officer easier as it w[oul]d then be an exchange with our C.G.S. and secure a much more senior officer than w[oul]d be otherwise available.
>
> Laverack's [sic] qualifications are of the highest character—possibly highest in the C[ommon]wealth Military Forces.[13]

Two days later Pearce received a reply from Bruce to the effect that a suitable British officer could be made available, but at a pay rate substantially higher than would normally be granted to an Australian CGS. In addition, Australia would be liable for the travelling expenses of the officer and would have to contribute to his pension. These financial considerations, coupled with the opinion of the Chief of the Imperial General Staff (CIGS) that training Lavarack in the United Kingdom would be difficult to do without depriving a British officer of some opportunity, put paid to the idea. Consequently, Shepherd's suggestion that Bruche's appointment be extended for one year was accepted. Nevertheless, it is obvious that by early 1934 Lavarack was not just one of two candidates for the post of CGS, but appears already to have been accepted in the minds of Pearce and Shepherd as Bruche's successor.[14]

However, there were many outside the army, both in Australia and the United Kingdom, who were nervous about the prospect. One of those was Sir Maurice Hankey, the Secretary of the Committee of Imperial Defence (CID) in London and one of Shedden's mentors, who arrived in Australia in late 1934 to advise on defence matters. Lavarack would meet Hankey and later, in concert with Bruche, savagely attack his report.

The Hankey Visit

At the time of Hankey's visit in late 1934 the government of Prime Minister Joseph Lyons had been trying to restrict defence spending further, especially on the army. These financial constraints had again fuelled the bitter dispute between the navy and the army on the degree of trust to be placed in British promises of despatching a fleet in the event of war in the Pacific. The one-power standard of the Royal Navy was appearing increasingly feeble in the light of the deteriorating situation in Europe and the decline in Anglo-Japanese relations after the recent crisis in Manchuria caused by Japanese aggression. In the words of the British official historian:

> The despatch of the main fleet to the Far East could no longer be
> regarded with equanimity in face of the increasing danger of finding an
> enemy in Europe at the same time.[15]

This was precisely the argument that Chauvel, Lavarack and other army officers had been making for some time. The ability to maintain a naval two-power standard, which would allow full-strength Royal Navy fleets to be in Europe and the Pacific at the same time, was beyond Britain's means. So, why continue to pour the major part of Australia's defence budget into the Royal Australian Navy whose contribution, even beside a large British fleet in the Far East—should it arrive—would be negligible? Instead, why should funds not be channelled into the army and air force in Australia? It was hoped that Hankey's tour in 1934 would resolve the question.

Hankey knew that he was stepping into a political minefield. Once in Australia he would have to extol the efficacy of the Singapore strategy, while aware that in Britain there was opposition by some members of the British government (such as Neville Chamberlain, the Chancellor of the Exchequer) to pouring money into defence measures in the distant Far East. Concerned, Hankey sought an assurance before leaving Britain that the first stage of the Singapore base would be completed by 1938 'with the object of enabling the Fleet to proceed to Singapore in any major emergency in the Far East'. This he received from Stanley Baldwin, the influential Lord President in Ramsay MacDonald's National Government.

Having had his position reinforced, Hankey set out for Australia. En route he wrote to Baldwin on 23 August that the Australian Minister for Defence, Pearce, had sent him two large files dealing with the country's defence. Hankey was surprised at the 'highly secret and confidential' nature of the material, which included correspondence between the Minister for Defence and the chiefs of staff. He went on:

> The controversy is between the Naval Staff, who contend that Australian defence must be based on sea power, that is to say on the assumption that the British fleet will, in a war in the Pacific, proceed to Singapore, and the Army and Air Staffs, who say in effect that we are not to be trusted, and that Australia, instead of cooperating in the maintenance of the Empire's sea power, would do better to build up an Army and an Air Force to deter and resist an invasion.
>
> The trump card of the latter school is that the British Labour Party, each time that it has come into power, has suspended work on the Singapore defences.

Referring to a speech made by Pearce on 25 September 1933, Hankey continued that 'the Commonwealth Government...has so far taken the big view'. However:

If there was any weakening on the part of the [UK] National
Government as to their intention to assert our sea-power in the Pacific
in a war emergency, I am convinced, after reading these papers, that the
effect would be absolutely shattering. No greater blow could be dealt to
the unity of the Empire... [16]

In Hankey's final sentence lay the crux of the problem of defending
Australia by relying on promises of British naval superiority. The two
sides were playing the same game, but for each the goal was different:
Australia wanted to ensure its national security, but Britain wanted to
ensure the integrity of a flagging empire, even if it meant putting
Australia at risk by making far-fetched promises based on wishful
thinking. And Hankey was well-placed to try to achieve Britain's aim. Not
only did he occupy a key position in the scheme of imperial defence, but
the staunchly patriotic Hankey also embraced, according to his
biographer, the 'certainties of a late Victorian imperialist, whose policies
sought to maintain British domination abroad' and whose 'sensitivity to
processes of historical change proved limited'.[17] Given the uncertainty
about the Singapore strategy which existed in London, let alone amongst
the Australian services, Hankey approached his task in Australia with
some trepidation, as he told Baldwin:

I am glad I obtained from you and the Chancellor of the Exchequer
[Chamberlain] that little bit of paper about the Far East (Singapore etc).
Without it I should feel I was walking on a bog and even with it I shall
have to tread warily![18]

Immediately he arrived in Perth, Hankey's foreboding about the task
ahead of him was borne out. He was met by Pearce who told him that the
dispute between the services about defence had become 'acute': the army
wanted approval to prepare for full-scale invasion, the air force
expounded the efficacy of air power in defeating an invasion and the navy
saw no need to prepare for an eventuality as unlikely as an invasion.

In Hankey's opinion the prospects for inter-service co-operation were
not much improved when, a short time later, Pearce was replaced as
defence minister by Sir Archdale Parkhill who 'did not greatly impress me
when I met him London last year'. Hankey, mindful that the Department
of Defence was at that time located in Melbourne, elaborated:

Parkhill hates Melbourne and has a house at Sydney. He told me that he used to run the Post Office by long-distance telephone! How, I ask you, is he to co-ordinate the three services unless he is in constant contact with them?[19]

During the few weeks he was in Australia Hankey travelled widely, accompanied by Shedden, the secretary of the Defence Committee. Previously Shedden had been attached to the Committee of Imperial Defence in London, which had allowed him to strike up a friendship with Hankey whom he saw as a role-model—so much so that the stubby Shedden (he was 5 feet 7 inches, or 170cm, in height) soon acquired the nickname of 'the pocket Hankey'.

As well as attending six meetings of the Defence Committee between 19 October and 13 November, Hankey visited major cities and defence installations around the country. On 24 October, during his visit to Sydney, he met one of the Singapore strategy's greatest critics when Lavarack conducted him on a tour of the city's coastal defences.

Three days later they met again at the Royal Military College. Hankey thought Lavarack to possess 'by far the brightest intelligence I met among the senior men', even though he was 'a bit of an "invasionist"'. He hoped that by speaking frankly to Lavarack and taking him into his confidence army criticism might be forestalled. He noted in his diary that he had a 'Long talk with Brigadier Lavarack...[and] Gave him a full account of proposed military policy for Australia as Mr. Parkhill had indicated that he would be the next C.G.S.'[20]

Hankey was aware, of course, of the stands Lavarack had taken in the past on defence policy and would not have been comforted by the knowledge that he was to be the next head of the army. In fact, during his visit Hankey had again suggested, almost certainly with Shedden's ready concurrence, if not connivance, a year's training in the United Kingdom for the new CGS, no doubt in the hope of watering down army opposition to the Singapore strategy.

Finally, on 14 November, Hankey handed Parkhill a carefully worded report intended to bolster Australian confidence in the navy and the Singapore strategy.[21] Hankey could not admit to shortcomings in the Singapore strategy without undermining his own position and discrediting pledges made in London. Consequently, in his report to the Australian government he stated:

[E]ven in the very extreme case of simultaneous trouble in Europe and the Far East without our having allies in either theatre the ratio of naval strength in capital ships (15:9) is sufficient to enable a numerically superior battle fleet to be sent to the Far East and yet to leave a small margin of strength in both theatres... [22]

Hankey would be more frank in a letter to the War Office written afterwards:

I was careful to make clear that we had undertaken no commitment to send the Fleet to Singapore in an emergency but I pointed out, as an earnest of intention, that we had decided to spend a lot of money on Singapore and other ports east of Suez, and that we had tremendous interests in the East... [23]

So, regardless of the strategic uncertainties and their attendant risks, Hankey proposed that as a consequence of the 'protection' afforded by Singapore the Australian army could be reduced.

By the time he left Australia Hankey also felt that the heads of the services had largely buried their differences during his visit, which he summed up in a letter to Baldwin on 17 November, two days before his departure:

[T]hey all seem pleased with my reports... I have felt rather lonely in this work of advising on defence. I do hope we shall not let down the Navy. Everything depends on it here, and the vacillation of past Governments over Singapore etc. have [sic] created a most deplorable impression. I have made clear that our Government has taken no commitment to send the fleet to Singapore,—any more than Australian Governments will take commitments to help us (they can't, though they will come all right on the day so far as their resources permit). But I have emphasised... the large sums we are spending on Singapore and the Far East, and the immense interests we have at stake there, which are covered by the assumption of the fleet going to Singapore. I hope I shall be backed at home. No-one has criticised my line here.[24]

Hankey was puzzled by the absence of criticism. He told Baldwin that although just before he had arrived in Australia there had been a bitter debate raging over the size of the military forces, which of course was connected with the raid versus invasion controversy, by the time he reached Melbourne some two weeks later 'something had happened—I never discovered quite what...I found the Defence Committee in complete agreement to recommend a reduction from the five Infantry and two Cavalry Division basis' to the equivalent of three divisions, plus several independent formations.[25]

When Hankey departed for New Zealand on 19 November Lavarack was on the dock to see him off, the two men no doubt having bade farewell with few regrets but any number of misgivings. In mid-December Hankey wrote to Shedden: 'I wonder often whether anything will come of my Reports. I fear the circumstances are not too favourable'.

He was right. His optimistic opinion that the Australian chiefs of staff 'have got together better lately' was soon shown to be very wide of the mark. As the imperial historian, John McCarthy, has pointed out,

> as soon as Hankey left, their important differences were again revealed. The navy accepted the wisdom and authority of Hankey's report with little question; the army rejected Hankey as an adviser on Australian defence planning almost entirely.[26]

The army would do all in its power to resist any action being taken on Hankey's advice, but it had made no attempt to challenge Hankey's conclusions while he was in the country—an open confrontation with such an eminent figure was bound to end with the army as the loser. In particular, Bruche and Lavarack may have calculated that an attack on Hankey's views during his visit might have jeopardised Lavarack's chances of being announced publicly as the next CGS in favour of a less articulate and more biddable army officer.

Despite Hankey's assurances, it was obvious to Lavarack and others that British warships did not exist in numbers large enough to permit the splitting of the fleet between Europe and the Far East without compromising one or both theatres of operations. In any case, it was increasingly unlikely that a naval force of any effective size would be sent to the Far East at all.

Lavarack was to be intimately involved in the official evaluation of the Hankey report and any hopes that Hankey may have harboured that his meeting with Lavarack would dilute army criticism were soon shown to be forlorn. Lavarack would question the whole basis of existing defence policy, and in so doing openly challenge the views and abilities of serving officers, civil servants and politicians in both Australia and Britain.

4

'The fullest co-operation is expected'

Chief of the General Staff Designate, 1935

IN EARLY 1935 it was time to finalise Bruche's replacement as Chief of the General Staff. The new Minister for Defence, Sir Archdale Parkhill, whose egotistical nature would make him as unpopular with senior army officers as he was with his political colleagues, was having difficulty in deciding whether to recommend Jess or Lavarack to Cabinet, although he had already told Sir Maurice Hankey during his visit only two months previously that Lavarack would be the next Chief of the General Staff.[1]

It was a knotty problem for Parkhill, as his Defence Secretary, Shepherd, reminded him on 22 January:

> There are difficulties from whatever angle the selection of an officer for the appointment of Chief of the General Staff is approached. The choices are X [Jess] and Y [Lavarack], and in both cases it is a matter of weighing advantages and disadvantages in order to reach a conclusion.

Shepherd observed of Jess (51 years old) that he was the senior of the two, the second senior colonel in the Staff Corps and also held the ranks of brigadier and honorary brigadier-general. If appointed he would supersede only one officer, who could not be considered as a candidate. Lavarack (then 49 years of age) was junior not only to Jess, but to a number of other officers as well—if he were appointed he would supersede five lieutenant-colonels and five colonels. Shepherd compared the two men:

X [Jess] is reported to be headstrong by nature, and hard to work with. The absence of these failings in Y [Lavarack] would appear to make him a safer selection, but his credit balance under the heading of personality is somewhat reduced by a tendency to an egotistic and patronising manner. The effects of this are, however, mainly reflected in his personal popularity, and not in his work.

Jess's war record was the better, but Lavarack had better academic qualifications, having attended both staff college and the Imperial Defence College. In concluding his comparison, Shepherd wrote:

To sum up, X [Jess] compares less favourably in personality but more favourably in war service, while Y's [Lavarack's] academic qualifications are better. Though it is an open question whether the balance on these points is in favour of Y [Lavarack], a further consideration has to be borne in mind. Should Y [Lavarack] be promoted, he would supersede many officers including X [Jess] and cause considerable discontent. Full co-operation has been lacking in the Military Board, and the promotion of X [Jess] would be the more likely to effect a change, as he would have the fuller and more cordial support of the senior officers.

Perhaps Shepherd also favoured Jess because he could not match Lavarack's incisive and outspoken criticism of current policy. His reluctance to have Lavarack as CGS had also led him to suggest that Sir Brudenell White come out of retirement to take the post, or failing that it could be offered to Blamey, who could leave the part-time militia and rejoin the permanent army. At the time Blamey was the controversial Chief Commissioner of Police in Victoria and so had been able to sidestep the dispute between the army and the navy over defence policy.[2]

Parkhill had to make the decision quickly. The Cabinet meeting at which the new CGS would be named was to be held on 2 February. Already the names of Jess and Lavarack had been published in connection with the appointment of Bruche's successor, and the claim in one newspaper that the government was considering the appointment of a British officer forced Parkhill to issue a less than accurate denial, saying that the suggestion was 'a sheer fabrication' with 'no foundation whatever'. At the Cabinet meeting Parkhill not only recommended that Lavarack be appointed CGS but also made several other proposals which would affect the careers of all senior army officers. The military members of the Military Board—the CGS, Adjutant-General, and Quartermaster-General—were all to receive the same salary, although the allowance provided for the CGS significantly increased his income. The same amount was to be paid also to the divisional commanders and commandants of the 2nd and 3rd Military Districts. All of these appointments were to be of four years' duration, except that of CGS which would be five, and all officers filling them were to be eligible for appointments on the Military Board, including that of CGS. In addition, the CGS might fill one of the other posts after his five years had expired.[3] The aim of rotating senior officers between posts on the Military Board and commands in the districts was to avoid any officer feeling that he had a claim on a particular post and to foster a 'corporate outlook in the senior group, promote co-operation, and improve the standard of administration and training'. On 2 February Cabinet approved Lavarack's appointment as CGS, to take effect in April with the temporary rank of major-general.[4]

Naturally there were some who harboured misgivings about what Lavarack's appointment might bring. On the day Lavarack's appointment was announced Shepherd wrote to the Military Board hinting that any ill-feeling about the new CGS had to be subsumed in the interests of the army and defence in general:

> It is important that Colonel Lavarack should report for duty at Army Headquarters as early as possible in order to become conversant with current questions, and to ensure a quick and satisfactory take-over from Major-General Bruche who retires on 20th April.

> Several questions of Policy are at present before the Defence Committee and will later be submitted to the Council of Defence. It is essential that the Minister should be aware of the views of the new Chief of the General Staff before decisions are taken, as the success of future Policy will largely hinge on the loyal co-operation of this officer and the support that he can command from the Staff Corps and senior Militia Officers.[5]

Shepherd also seems to have been worried by the prospect of so articulate a critic of the Singapore strategy as Lavarack becoming CGS. Earlier he had spelt out in more detail his ideas on the loyalty of the new CGS and told Parkhill:

It has been the practice in Britain for the Prime Minister before offering appointments to officers selected as Chiefs of Staff to make clear to them the Policy of the Government in respect of their services, and to indicate that the appointment is offered to them only on an unequivocal assurance that they will loyally seek to carry out the Policy of the Government. It is suggested that ... the Minister, on selection of the Officers for the posts of Chief of the General Staff, and Commanders of the two Divisions, should make it clear that ... the fullest co-operation is expected to render effective any decision that may be taken by the Government ... regarding Army Organisation.[6]

Obviously the navy was not overjoyed at Lavarack's appointment. Although, as CGS Designate, he was granted access to the meetings of the Military Board as a matter of course, in March the chairman of the Defence Committee, Vice-Admiral Sir Francis Hyde, following the letter of the regulations, would not let him attend the Committee meetings, which effectively halted consideration of Sir Maurice Hankey's report on Australian defence.[7] Accordingly, Parkhill wrote to the secretary of the committee, Shedden, reminding him that a direction had been given on 6 February that Lavarack was to proceed to Army Headquarters as soon as possible and that it was essential that he be consulted about the issues raised by the Hankey report currently before the Defence Committee. As it was essential that he should have Lavarack's views on the Hankey report before taking a decision, Lavarack was to be granted access to all meetings.[8]

Thus, Lavarack found himself propelled once more into the arena of defence policy, but this time as one of the leading participants. Although the level at which he was participating had been raised considerably, his views on defence remained substantially the same, as his assessment of the Hankey report would show.

The Hankey Report and the Services

The first shot in the battle of words precipitated by the Hankey report was fired by the navy. As a precursor to discussions in the Council of Defence on the strength of the army arising from the suggestions made by Hankey, Admiral Hyde produced a paper in early February entitled 'The Invasion Bogey'. The paper complemented an earlier suggestion by him that the

United Kingdom give a pledge that the British fleet would move to the Far East in the event of war and that, in return, the Australian government agree to place the Royal Australian Navy under the command of the Admiralty. Shepherd told Parkhill that:

> Both [Hyde's suggestion and his paper] represent an early Naval move in the forthcoming discussion by the Council of Defence on the strength of the Army. The latter hinges on the question of invasion and the security of the first line represented by British Naval strength, the Singapore Base, and the movement of the British Fleet to the Far East.[9]

Hyde pointed to a number of factors which, he said, ruled out the possibility of an invasion of Australia. These included the nearness to completion of the Singapore base; Britain's interests in the Far East; the technical and logistical difficulties the Japanese would have to overcome to mount the invasion; the probability of a lengthy warning of enemy intentions; and the absence of a worthwhile reason to invade the country. Hyde argued that invasion of Australia was impracticable as long as Singapore was held; the British fleet remained capable of moving to the Far East; the air force was maintained in accordance with the recommendations of the Salmond Report; and a new army organisation based on three divisions was maintained.[10]

The army presented its views on Hankey's report at a meeting of the Defence Committee on 21 March 1935. They were markedly different from the navy's. Both Bruche and Lavarack were unequivocal in their criticism of Hankey's paper. Bruche began by questioning the appropriateness of Hankey advising on Australian defence:

> Sir Maurice Hankey's opinion by reason of his great experience in Imperial affairs must be viewed with respect. Nevertheless the direct responsibility for military advice upon the problem of the defence of Australia rests upon the naval, military and air advisers of the Australian Government.

Bruche argued that organising the country's defence on the expectation of only minor attacks or sporadic raids was 'definitely unsound and insupportable'. The army should be organised, trained and equipped to meet the largest force an enemy could transport to Australia and the air force developed to provide reconnaissance and attack capabilities commensurate with the threat. Local production of munitions should be increased with the aim of achieving self-reliance. He condemned strongly the current defence policy:

> The most unsatisfactory feature of the operation of defence policy at present is that the bulk of the funds available go to [the] R.A.N. Since the role of the latter is not local defence and since naval defence as a whole is now and for a long time must remain inadequate, the result is that we go on from year to year getting nothing right. The time has clearly arrived when in the allotment of funds available for defence a definite concentration of effort should be made to put the Army and Air Force and M.S.B. [Munitions Supply Board] on a sound footing. The time may conceivably arise when we should again concentrate upon our Navy but in view of the existing conditions regarding naval agreements and the general unlikelihood of gaining any appreciable preponderance over other nations (e.g. the re-attainment of the [naval] two power standard) that time is assuredly not now.[11]

Hankey had recommended that the army organisation be reduced to two infantry divisions, three cavalry brigades, four mixed brigades and garrison troops (giving a total strength of 35,000), but Bruche, although he had not challenged the proposal during Hankey's visit, declared:

> I most strongly urge that Sir Maurice Hankey's recommendations be not accepted as the basis of the organisation of the Army. I recommend on the contrary, that the general sense of the recommendations of the Senior Officers' Conference of 1920 be adhered to as the basis of our military organisation and of the development of our land forces.
>
> If the Government, despite my advice, are inclined to accept the views of Sir Maurice Hankey, I must strongly urge that before doing so they approach the British Government for a tangible guarantee concerning the completion of the Singapore Base and the despatch of the British Fleet to Singapore without delay on the outbreak of war with Japan.[12]

As Chief of the General Staff Designate, Lavarack also stressed the value of land and air forces which, in his opinion, had been greatly underestimated. For that reason he recommended that the defence budget, which he felt unduly favoured the navy, be distributed more evenly. He, too, recommended that no further commitment to the Singapore strategy be made until the British government had guaranteed the date of completion of the base at Singapore, the strength of the naval forces to be despatched there in an emergency, and the time which would elapse before the arrival of the fleet.

Admittedly these views were very similar to those of Bruche, and indeed Lavarack had read Bruche's paper before preparing his own and stated his complete agreement with the views expressed by the CGS. Lavarack's words, however, were not empty carriages running on the official line. His own memorandum, he explained, was designed to 'amplify certain points dealt with by the C.G.S. and to express personal views which have been formed during a fairly long and intimate experience of the question at issue', an assertion supported by his article of 1933 and by the papers he had written as DMO&I, especially his earlier critique of Shedden's paper.

Turning specifically to Hankey's recent report, Lavarack contended that Hankey had simply re-presented the established views of the Committee of Imperial Defence and the naval lobby:

> Perusal of Sir Maurice Hankey's report leaves me with the very definite impression that it contains nothing new. Fundamentally its basis is precisely the same as that of the various papers on the subject of Imperial Defence in general, and Australian Defence in particular, which have been written since the Committee of Imperial Defence came into existence before the Great War. That basis is the doctrine that British sea-power is, and will remain, sufficient to protect the territories and external interests of the Empire as a whole, and that arrangements for local security are a matter of minor concern.[13]

The problem was, as Lavarack correctly pointed out, although such a doctrine may have been valid before 1914, the Royal Navy was no longer at a two-power standard, and as naval power declined relative to other nations so too did the security derived from Britain's unchallengeable supremacy at sea. Therefore, he stated flatly that

> Sir Maurice Hankey's views are out of date, since they do not take sufficiently into account the decline of British sea power which has taken place since the Great War.

Moreover, not only were Hankey's views out of date, but they were unlikely ever again to be practicable. The economic lead which Britain had enjoyed over other countries and which had permitted great naval preponderance had been irretrievably reduced. To complicate matters, Britain (reduced to a one-power naval standard and lacking the economic means to reconstruct a two-power Royal Navy) had now to face not only the prospect of war with European nations, but also with Japan in the Far East. Given these factors Lavarack thought it obvious that less reliance should be placed on naval defence than had been the case in the heady days before 1914.[14]

In these changed circumstances, Lavarack identified the problem facing those responsible for Australian defence as being 'how to adapt our Australian defence system to post-war, or modern conditions, the chief of which is the definite and permanent decline of British sea-power'. Naturally, he warned, each service's opinion would be coloured to a degree by its own interests, but none so much as the navy, which enjoyed the support of a British Admiralty attempting to spread its costs among the Dominions. Lavarack stressed that the search for a solution to this problem was one for Australians to undertake and that no panacea, such as 'all-pervading sea supremacy', would provide a lasting answer.

Using this as a springboard for a direct attack on Hankey, Lavarack made what must have appeared to be an extraordinary statement considering the close relationship which then existed between Australia and the United Kingdom:

> [I]n such a matter as the detail of Australia's defence system, Sir Maurice Hankey is not qualified to give an opinion...His report shows clearly that his mind is obsessed with the idea of obtaining from all parts of the Empire forces which can be employed in the solution of the general defence problem. In this from his own point of view he is right, for the solution of this problem is his proper task. The local defence problem, however, remains, and is the first and personal responsibility of each part of the Empire. Incidentally the provision of adequate and proper forces for local defence solves the problem presented to Sir Maurice Hankey, but he must use what is provided, and cannot, and should not, dictate to Dominions what they are to provide.

More than one political alarm bell must have been ringing at this drift into imperial heresy. But, although Lavarack emphasised the importance of local defence being an Australian problem, he was not arguing in principle against co-ordination with the United Kingdom. Consultation, however, should be concerned mainly with preparing joint plans and guarantees, and any advice from British authorities originating during these consultations should be carefully weighed. He made the reasonable and valid point that 'there is very little better reason for following British advice on local defence than there would be for following Australian advice on the defence of London against air attack'. So, on the question of local defence preparations dovetailing with imperial plans, Lavarack was unequivocal:

> Australian plans for local defence should not be made contingent on the presence of the British Main Fleet at Singapore unless there is a very firm guarantee from the Government in the United Kingdom as regards the strength of the naval force to be sent and time of its arrival at Singapore.

Examining more closely the relationship between sea power and local defence, he outlined three factors which reinforced the need for stronger local defence to help protect Australia against invasion: Australia may have to stand alone for some time while waiting for the fleet, especially if it is delayed; in any case, its arrival is no guarantee of victory and if the fleet were defeated, Australia would have to fall back on its own resources; and, the likelihood that the fleet may not be sent at all owing to complications west of Suez.[15]

Consequently there was a need for increased expenditure on forces which could be used for local defence, namely the army and the air force. This would entail decreased expenditure on the small Australian navy, which was so insignificant as to be practically useless if the main fleet did not arrive in the Far East or if it were defeated after its arrival. In any case, the RAN would be a negligible contribution to the bulk of the British fleet even if it were to arrive. As far as Lavarack was concerned,

> it is contrary to common-sense to spend, as is now done, more than 50% of the total defence appropriation on a naval force which will either be merely supplementary to the British main naval forces, or will, in their absence, be totally useless.

Even in the event of an attempted economic blockade of Australia by an enemy, the land-based forces would provide a deterrent effect by denying to the enemy the necessary bases on Australian territory from which such an operation could be sustained. As the size of these forces increased, a blockade tended to become impossible:

In fact the value of Naval Defence is generally over-estimated, and may, in the event, be nil, while the value of Land and Air Defence is generally under-estimated, although such defences may, in the event, be the only form possible. At present, unfortunately, the Land and Air Forces are practically powerless and it can therefore happen in an emergency that Australia may be left without any defence at all.

Lavarack ended his memorandum with a list of succinct conclusions he had reached from his examination of Australian defence and Hankey's report. They expressed the essence of his views on Australian defence and promised to be the basis of army policy for the next four years:

(A) That the whole matter is one for the Australian Government to decide on the representations of its own advisers, and that the advice of Sir Maurice Hankey, whilst receiving the respect and attention due to his high authority, should not be allowed to obscure consideration of the detail of what is a purely Australian problem.

(B) That owing to the decline of British Sea-Power since the Great War, the relative importance of Local Defence measures, (as compared with contribution to General Defence measures, i.e., the British Navy), has greatly increased.

(C) That Australia's contribution to the British Naval forces is merely supplementary to the Royal Navy and does not increase the general naval strength of the Empire.

(D) That efficient Land and Air forces are of much greater value as regards both trade and territorial defence than is realised. Their importance to Australia in any system of defence would, in fact, be greater than is that of her contribution to general naval defence, and they would be more valuable in Imperial Defence than would increased Naval construction.

(E) That expenditure on the three services is not properly balanced, to such an extent that over-expenditure on the Naval forces is gradually throttling the Land forces, and is preventing the proper development of the Air forces.

(F) That no further increase in Naval expenditure should take place; and that the present Naval proportion of the total appropriation for defence purposes should actually be reduced to below 50% of the total, while the effect on recurrent annual expenditure of new construction should be very closely scrutinised.

(G)   That the re-conditioning of the Land forces and the expansion of the Air forces are both overdue and should be undertaken at once by the allocation to them of an increased proportion of the total defence appropriation.

(H)   That even if this and other memoranda are disregarded no action should be taken on Sir Maurice Hankey's recommendations until full guarantees have been obtained by H.M. Government in Australia from H.M. Government in the United Kingdom on the following points:

(a) The date of completion of the Naval Base at Singapore.
(b) The strength and composition of the Naval forces to be despatched to the Far East in certain emergencies.
(c) The time that will elapse before the arrival of such Naval Forces in the area of operation.[16]

The papers by Lavarack and Bruche have been described as 'the only rigorous examination of Hankey's report', but naturally they were not appreciated in all quarters, especially at Navy Office. The Chief of the Naval Staff, Hyde, leapt to the defence of the Singapore strategy. He would have limited even further the roles of the army and air force in defending Australia and roundly attacked the memoranda by Bruche and Lavarack. To judge by his comments, it was Lavarack's memorandum which Hyde found the more offensive. He began by defending Hankey against Lavarack's charge that there was nothing new in his report:

There is, indeed, nothing new in Sir M. Hankey's report, for it is based on the time honoured and well tried doctrine that sea-power is, and will remain, the principal factor in the defence of Empire territories and external interests.

Hyde went on to argue that if this doctrine does not work it is not proof that the doctrine itself was faulty, but that those responsible for defence throughout the empire did not recognise its importance and act accordingly. Hyde challenged Lavarack's assertion that Hankey was not qualified to give an opinion on Australian defence:

Sir Maurice Hankey made no attempt to give an opinion on details. What he did was to advise on principles of defence, upon which he is eminently qualified to give an opinion, and to suggest the outlines of the Naval, Military, and Air Forces required.[17]

However, even Hyde was forced to agree with some of Lavarack's observations, but not always without qualification. He admitted, for example, that British sea power had declined (it would have been difficult to argue otherwise):

> It is agreed that the present power standards do not provide a reasonable margin of safety. They were accepted by the Imperial Government as a post war measure of economy, and the risk taken, in view of existing political conditions, was not appreciable until very recently. All previous naval agreements are now in the melting pot and there are signs that the naval holiday is at an end. Leaving the U.S.A. out of account, it will be well within the capacity of the Empire to attain once more a 2-power standard of naval forces, and the Dominions must be prepared to do their share.

How a two-power standard was to be regained Hyde didn't say. Instead he clung doggedly to naval defence simply because he could envisage no alternative:

> It is agreed that modern developments have increased the difficulties of defence. Unfortunately we are just as dependent upon sea supremacy for victory in war as we were in 1914. There is no other solution of the problem.

Hyde took this line despite his opinion that '[i]t would obviously be impossible for any Government' to guarantee that the fleet would be despatched to the Far East. The discrepancy between what was promised and what was possible had presented Hyde with a circle he couldn't square, but to reinforce his tenuous thesis, Hyde attacked Lavarack's theory that a strong army supported by a well-equipped air force would able to prevent invasion and blockade if the navy was defeated:

> The size and efficiency of Australian Land Forces cannot possibly affect the establishment of enemy blockades, once our command of the seas is

lost. A million trained men armed to the teeth, won't stop the Japanese fuelling their ships in a hundred inaccessible anchorages round our coasts.[18]

He did admit, though, that strong land forces would prevent an enemy capturing bases in Australia, but argued that such forces could not further the defence of the Empire. Implicitly Hyde was arguing, like Hankey, that the Empire must come first, which perhaps was the inevitable corollary of having a British-born, ex-Royal Navy officer in command of the Australian navy.

Essentially, Hyde's argument amounted to a mixture of nostalgia and faux pragmatism: the navy had to be Australia's first line of defence because the Empire had always depended on the navy, and in any event there was no alternative, even though British sea power had declined dramatically. However, as weak as the navy's case may have been, the army had little hope of achieving a major change in defence policy, despite the logic of its case. This was not just because of the costs involved, but also because of a sense of tradition and a reflexive deference to Britain permeating Australian decision-making which at times could obscure the diverging interests of the two countries.

Ironically, to a degree Hyde and Lavarack were arguing at cross-purposes since both were in favour of imperial defence *per se*. The CNS was presenting the case for imperial defence based on British seapower, with the secondary benefits it could have for Australia; Lavarack was arguing that by strengthening local defence Australia was not only being secured, but a contribution was being made to imperial defence as well. The fundamental difference was that Lavarack was giving priority to Australia, not the empire.

In Shepherd's summation of the differing opinions contained in the navy and army papers he perched on the fence as far as the substance of the argument was concerned, though he spared a few acerbic words for the protagonists:

> The papers from the Services unfortunately illustrate the conflict of opinion that has existed for long among the technical advisers on whom the Government and the Minister rely for advice on the basis of Defence Policy. Though the Services have the common aim of national security in view, the preference for controversy rather than agreement reminds

one of combatants that 'shriek and sweat in pigmy wars' where ink is shed and not blood.

(Shepherd's opinion of the country's military leaders was readily reciprocated. Soon after his Australian visit Hankey had reported to London that at least the services had reached agreement on Shepherd 'whom all the Chiefs of Staff unite in detesting'.)[19]

Thus, in the end, neither Hankey's report, nor the various memoranda it generated, resolved the dispute about Australia's defence. As Parkhill noted in May 1935, a month after Lavarack had taken over as CGS:

> It had been hoped that unanimity of doctrine among the Chiefs of Staff would be established by Sir Maurice Hankey ... [T]he Defence Committee, after consultation with Sir Maurice, agreed on a recommendation to reduce the Army Organisation from seven Divisions to three Divisions, but ... the then Chief of the General Staff [Bruche] later withdrew his adherence. He was supported in this attitude by the present Chief of the General Staff [Lavarack].[20]

The army's approach, as expounded by Bruche and Lavarack, although perhaps exaggerating the likelihood of invasion, was the more realistic, and would have been seen to be so had the Australian government been privy to a cabinet paper then being circulated in Britain. At the time when Hankey was reassuring all but the army in Australia that the Royal Navy would sail to the Pacific in a crisis, the British Chancellor of the Exchequer, Neville Chamberlain, and the Foreign Secretary, Sir John Simon, had concluded that sufficient naval forces would not be available in the event of a two-front war to protect the Indian and Pacific Oceans. Consequently, they agreed, in those circumstances Australia and India would find themselves in 'dire peril'.[21] And, with Japanese aggression in Asia growing and Hitler's power increasing in Europe, the prospect of a two-front war did not seem as remote as it had several years earlier.

In Australia though, the Hankey report had reinforced the idea of security through naval defence, at least for the government and the navy. The report had also focused attention on the new CGS, who had shown himself to be a vigorous and articulate critic of the Singapore strategy. No doubt Parkhill, Shepherd, Shedden and the navy could see squalls ahead with Lavarack at the army's helm.

5

'Treat our part of the business as strictly confidential'

Chief of the General Staff,

1935-1936

WHEN LAVARACK SUCCEEDED Bruche as Chief of the General Staff on 21 April 1935 his aim was straightforward: to prepare the Australian army for the war which he was convinced would come within the next few years. In pursuing that objective Lavarack would come dangerously close to exceeding his mandate as CGS and would imperil his career. His was a battle waged for the most part against politicians and bureaucrats, and there is no denying that during the years of deprivation imposed upon it by the Singapore strategy, the army had become deeply distrustful of civilians, whether they decided policy, advised on policy or carried it out.

This potentially volatile situation could hardly benefit from the differences between Lavarack and the new Minister for Defence as individuals. The ambitious and diminutive Parkhill (he stood 5 feet 4 inches, or 163 centimetres, in height) dressed in a dandyish fashion, favouring cravats and grey shoe spats, which he would wear even to sporting events. After being knighted he adopted a British accent until ridiculed by parliamentary colleagues, with whom he was generally unpopular. The former Prime Minister, W.M. Hughes, compared Parkhill (who had acquired nicknames such as 'Sir Spats', the 'Archduke' and 'Sir Kewpie') to a 'caricature of a Botticelli cupid'.[1]

With the image-conscious Parkhill as minister, and the autocratic

Shepherd and pro-navy Shedden occupying key positions behind the scenes in the Department of Defence, Lavarack had much to worry about as the latest in a succession of army leaders trying to compensate for the years of neglect the service had endured since the end of the Great War.[2] In 1935 the field army was in a parlous state: a nucleus of slightly more than half the fighting units was being maintained, but considerably less than half the maintenance and support units existed. Although equipment and ammunition for training was available, it represented only a fraction of war requirements and generally dated from about 1916. The list of deficiencies covered almost every item in the army's inventory, as Lavarack told Shepherd:

> The Field Army has only a negligible number of out of date armoured fighting vehicles, no anti-aircraft artillery, no anti-tank weapons, no modern mortars for close support, no army field artillery (which is essential to supplement Divisional Artillery in order to give the field army a reasonable fighting chance in operations against a modern enemy), an inadequate quantity of medium artillery and no heavy artillery. The quantity of medium artillery... is so low as to cause grave concern. The development of plans for the manufacture in a crisis of complementary stocks, particularly of gun ammunition, will require some considerable period and consequently, for the present, the provision of considerable stocks is the only sound course to follow.

The army would need at least six months training to reach a rudimentary readiness for general operations and although a division could be despatched overseas in half that time, it would be suitable only for garrison duties. Overall, the army was incapable of 'sustained resistance to organised landings by trained regular troops' and the Military Board could foresee no improvement in the situation in the next two years 'since funds allotted are being devoted mainly to Coast Defences'.[3]

Under such circumstances there were two main avenues by which Lavarack might achieve the goal of preparing the army for war. First, take every opportunity to argue forcefully against the current defence policy of unrealistic dependence on the Royal Navy in the hope that it would be scrapped in favour of greater self-reliance. Second, in the meantime take advantage of whatever latitude he could find, or contrive, within the confines of the current policy to strengthen the army.

The Campaign Begins, 1935-1936

The government's defence policy, under which the army's priority was fixed coast defences, was re-affirmed less than two months after Lavarack became CGS, at a Council of Defence meeting on 19 June 1935. The Council was also in favour of the existing army organisation of seven divisions being maintained. But this was an army on an anti-invasion scale, so any additional funds could only be spent on a smaller anti-raid organisation which Hankey had recommended—two divisions, four mixed brigades and three cavalry brigades. The confusion caused by having apparently competing organisational commitments was compounded when the Principal Supply Officers Committee (PSOC) was given the task by the Defence Committee of investigating the capacity of Australian secondary industry to supply an anti-invasion force of more than twice the size of the anti-raids force approved by the government.[4]

From Lavarack's point of view this confusing, if not contradictory, state of affairs seemed to favour attempts to achieve greater recognition of the need for a stronger army. So, in July 1935 he challenged the root of defence policy when the question of coast defences was considered in the Defence Committee. The Council of Defence had already endorsed in principle the priority of the coast defence scheme and had passed it to the Defence Committee so that technical aspects, such as the priority of ports to be defended, could be considered. But Lavarack went further to question the basis of Australia's defence policy, namely the likelihood of a fleet being despatched to Singapore:

> I consider that the whole tenor of the resolutions passed at this meeting of the Council indicated that reliance could not be placed implicitly on "the arrival of the Main British Fleet at Singapore with a minimum of delay after the outbreak of war in the Far East".[5]

He requested that his views accompany the report on the scheme when it was placed before the Committee of Imperial Defence in London and stressed (perhaps somewhat naively) that, since the foundation of the Australian system of defence had been questioned, the opportunity of giving the matter full consideration should not be allowed to pass.[6]

When Lavarack's suggestions were referred to the next meeting of the Council of Defence he was officially rebuked by Parkhill, who had been influenced by the views of Hankey and Shedden:

The special observations of the Chief of the General Staff involve implications of a highly political nature and the subject is one solely for the United Kingdom and Commonwealth Governments. The Services have a definite basis on which to proceed with their plans, and in transmitting the revision of C.I.D. Paper 249C [dealing with the coast defence scheme] to the Committee of Imperial Defence, its remarks are to be requested on the purely technical aspect of the scheme.

Lavarack replied that he had based his observations only on strategic considerations and, perhaps disingenuously, that he had not intended to trespass upon political ground. Nevertheless, he had been officially censured by the Minister. More than a year had passed between these meetings of the Council (as Hankey wrote in 1934, it 'is an absolutely dud show and never meets') and there is little doubt that events during that time contributed to the Minister's decision to chastise Lavarack, in particular his efforts to have Australian defence policy move away from almost total reliance on the Singapore strategy and to strengthen the army.[7]

In August 1935, for example, Parkhill complained that Lavarack was flying in the face of policy by suggesting, in concert with the Chief of the Air Staff, Air Vice-Marshal Richard Williams, that no more additions to the navy be made until several other conditions were met: the coast defences completed, the RAAF increased to a size sufficient to repel raids, first-line army units modernised, and the ability to despatch an expeditionary force realised. Lavarack also wanted to increase the number of troops (both permanent and militia), to improve service conditions and to provide better training, especially for regular soldiers, militia leaders and specialists. However, given the priorities laid down by the government and only a voluntary system of enlistment operating, it was difficult to maintain even the bare nucleus of the army because of the high turnover of personnel. Consequently, Lavarack favoured the reintroduction of compulsory training, under the new name of national service. Although the idea did not have political support, Lavarack would fight hard to have it introduced, at no small cost to himself.[8]

In April 1936 the Military Board produced a paper outlining ways in which the voluntary system could be improved so as to reach the peacetime ceiling of 35,000 personnel, but Parkhill was not impressed. The strength of the army was about 27,000 at that time and Parkhill blamed the Board for the shortfall:

The real facts of this matter are that the Military Board apparently made no provision to provide 35,000 men when the funds for the 3 years' programme were being distributed. An additional amount of £110,000 is now necessary to bring the Militia up to that strength.

Parkhill told Cabinet on 21 April 1936 (the first anniversary of Lavarack's appointment) that in the first year of the three year programme, 1933-34, the army had been given all the additional funds it had sought in order to maintain the organisation. But the Military Board held a different view:

The improvement of the general standard of defence preparations, and of the Militia Force, is essentially dependent on the provision of additional funds. The ordinary votes are inadequate to maintain the existing Army organisation apart from undertaking any improvement.

Parkhill was also critical of the suggestion made by Lavarack and the other members of the Board that the peace-time nucleus of the army be raised to 130,000, a figure which could only be attained by the introduction of compulsory training:

It is not considered that a stage of crisis in national security has been reached at which Universal Training should be re-introduced ... The Military Board, in basing its views on its own interpretation of the international situation, has really exceeded the limits of its functions. The Government alone can be the sole judge of the international position in view of the political considerations involved, and it is for the Service Advisers to recommend a scheme of defence in the light of the Policy laid down by the Government and the Vote made available. The Minister does not recommend any variation in the present basis of Policy. To deviate from the objective of completion of the defence against raids, would be an unwise dispersion of our limited financial resources and provide security against neither raids nor invasion.

An irritated Parkhill concluded firmly:

Whilst the loyalty of the Army Staff to carry out the Policy of the Government is not doubted, it is proposed to place on the Army Staff in very definite terms, the responsibility for exerting every effort to make a success of the Voluntary System.[9]

Shedden, at that stage still secretary of the Defence Committee, used the disagreement to strike at Lavarack by suggesting (in what appears to be a blatant appeal to Parkhill's *amour propre*) that an inspector-general be appointed 'in view of the importance of making the Voluntary System a success from the political aspect of Policy and the prestige of the Minister'.[10]

Old enmities were dying hard in the Department of Defence and Shedden himself was doing a reasonable job as 'inspector-general' of the army. At around this time Lavarack, eager for a direct source of information about imperial defence policy, attempted to have Lieutenant-Colonel John Northcott, who was already in the UK, attached to the secretariat of the Committee of Imperial Defence without reference to Parkhill. Although the attachment was initially only to be for three months, it would afford Lavarack access to discussions of policy affecting Australian defence. Shedden, who had maintained contact with Hankey, warned against it:

> There is no apparent reason why an Army Officer should be attached to the C.I.D. for discussion of the higher aspects of Australian Policy, and from the aspect of inter-Service controversy in Australia, it is undesirable that the Army should have access to information relating to the other Services which may prove an embarrassment to the Minister and the Government.

When asked to explain its reasons for the proposed attachment, the Military Board replied that Northcott was to be attached to study air-raid precautions and 'for general purposes'. Parkhill gave his approval for Northcott to be attached to that sub-committee of the CID dealing with air-raid precautions, but did not approve the attachment so that Northcott could gain a general knowledge of the working of the CID. He also directed, despite Lavarack's efforts, that in future all extension of officers' attachments overseas were to be approved by him and not the Military Board.[11]

Lavarack may not have been making much headway after a year as CGS, but he would not give up. In June 1936, thwarted thus far in having compulsory training resurrected, he proposed that more of the army's allocation be spent on the field army than on fixed coast defences—artillery embedded in a concrete blockhouse could not be hitched to a truck and towed to the battlefield. Parkhill told him to adhere to the guidelines laid down by government policy. Not to be deterred, Lavarack challenged the Minister through the Military Board and argued that the emphasis given to fixed and anti-aircraft defences 'is completely unbalanced and will perpetuate a very dangerous condition of affairs'. He characterised the present army priorities as 'most unsound' and suggested to Parkhill that emphasis be placed on the field army. Parkhill directed that the Board resubmit its proposals. He also told Lavarack several days later that, in principle and within the constraints of policy and the limits of finances, the Military Board was responsible for the most effective allocation of funds.

As a result of this discussion the Board re-presented its proposals on the army programme, again favouring the field army. Parkhill was annoyed and clearly had not intended Lavarack to interpret his remarks as authority to alter the priorities he had laid down as Minister. He replied that the 'basis of Policy as at present laid down does not...authorise the bulk of new expenditure being allotted to the Field Army' and left Lavarack in no doubt the powers of the Military Board:

> On the question of powers, it cannot be agreed that the Board is responsible for determining the use of its allotment and that the Minister's powers (inferentially) are confined to fixing the amount of the allotment. It is the Board's duty and responsibility to make recommendations, but, in the last resort, the Minister must reserve the right of approval, variation or selection, as was done in this case.

Parkhill again stressed that any proposals 'must be within the four walls of Policy as laid down by the Government' and warned Lavarack that the question of fixed defences was set to divide service opinion (the navy, unlike the army, gave fixed defences the highest priority among army responsibilities).[12]

Nevertheless, Lavarack would not back down and the Military Board presented Parkhill with a paper arguing the necessity not for fixed defences alone, but also for a well-equipped mobile army. Although couched in deferential terms, Lavarack made it clear that he considered the Minister to be making a mistake in attempting to force the army to spend the bulk of its allocation on fixed defences:

> The Board now feels that since questions of such fundamental

importance as the basis of army policy and the powers of the Military Board have been raised, it is desirable that a fairly complete review should be made, but at the same time it desires to deny absolutely any attempt to depart from the basis of policy laid down by the Government, or to claim (even by inference) powers of decision which must necessarily belong to the Minister.

... The Minister is the interpreter of Government policy, and his interpretation governs the general distribution of funds. Nevertheless, it must be abundantly clear that in the transmutation of policy into action, a stage must be reached at which the Minister will require advice as to the detailed distribution of funds, and it is here that the main responsibility of his expert advisers begins. If this stage occurs too late, the responsibility of the expert adviser, and his influence on the purely military solution of the specific problems presented, may be too greatly restricted.[13]

Lavarack then presented a submission on the priority of army spending for the next Council of Defence meeting. In his opinion the re-armament of the fixed defences and the strengthening of the mobile forces to defend them (which had been identified by the Council of Defence in June 1935 as the army's two most important objectives) should have equal priority. He therefore requested that at the next meeting of the Council, this resolution be confirmed unambiguously so as to allow the mobile forces to be developed concurrently with fixed defences. This was a deft attempt to use the Council's views to provide political cover for increased spending on men and equipment which would benefit a field army in wartime.

Parkhill referred the matter to the Defence Committee instead of the Council of Defence, which decided to defer any decision on Lavarack's proposals until after the 1937 Imperial Conference. As Shedden later told Shepherd:

This matter goes to the very roots of the basis of Policy, and the discussion at the Defence Committee meeting threatened to re-open the divergences of opinion between the Chiefs of Staff... After tracing the history of the matter since 1932, I suggested that the Chiefs of Staff should be more helpful to the Minister than repeatedly asking him to referee on the merits of their conflicting views.[14]

The Press Campaign

While Parkhill, aided by Shepherd and Shedden, had been trying to keep a tight rein on Lavarack's criticisms of policy and his attempts to build up the field army, a series of politically embarrassing articles on defence policy had been appearing in the press in 1936. These placed great pressure on Parkhill and caused suspicious glances to be cast in Lavarack's direction. Parkhill did not trust Lavarack and soon became convinced of army involvement in the appearance of publications critical of government policy.

To a degree Parkhill's suspicions were warranted, though perhaps not in the way he imagined. In late 1935 Lavarack and Colonel H.D. Wynter, the Director of Military Training at AHQ, commented on proofs of E.L. Piesse's book *Japan and the Defence of Australia*, which was published that year under the nom de plume of 'Albatross'. Lavarack told the author that in making the comments on the book: 'We have not undertaken a campaign of counter-propaganda, and have not even stated our own case, because we pride ourselves on our traditions of loyalty to the Government'. Nevertheless, Lavarack was aware of the risk of misinterpretation by Parkhill and told Piesse that although 'there is nothing in any of our comments that should not be published... of course we must request you to treat our part of the business as strictly confidential'.

Even so, both Shepherd and Parkhill suspected that there had been some army collusion in the production of the book. Their suspicions were to grow as the series of newspaper articles critical of the government appeared at the same time that Lavarack was pressing for the re-introduction of compulsory training.[15]

In February 1936 a member of parliament, A.G. Cameron, was quoted as saying that the voluntary system of training had been a failure and the compulsory training would have to be reintroduced. He said that 'Mr Parkhill cannot produce any competent military authority to show that the full establishment of 35,000 is sufficient for the defence of Sydney or Melbourne alone'. According to Cameron, total enlistments comprised only 75 per cent of that 35,000, and called on Parkhill to declare just how large was the effective fighting force of the army and how many of those who enlisted under the voluntary system completed their training. Naturally Parkhill was not pleased and called on the Military Board to comment on Cameron's remarks.[16]

Lavarack told Parkhill that the army had a strength of 21,000 and that since 1931 only slightly more than 8,000 men had satisfactorily completed their three years of service under the voluntary system. However, he was not content to supply Parkhill with just simple facts. In a six page memorandum the whole basis of defence policy was questioned once again:

> The remarks of Mr. A.G. Cameron M.P. raise the question of the effectiveness of the existing military preparations for defence, and particularly the effectiveness of the present peace establishment of the A.M.F. (35,000), for the protection of Sydney and Melbourne. On this question, the Board is of the opinion that the Voluntary system of military service has served the valuable purpose of maintaining a bare nucleus of the Army organisation. The Board has also stated... that it is desirable that the Voluntary system of service should be given a fair trial, before another system is substituted, but that if the Voluntary system then fails to produce the required results, the Board would welcome a return to compulsory training, from which an improvement and strengthening of the organisation would result.[17]

The deteriorating international situation, and Britain's response to it, added force to Lavarack's argument. Germany was re-arming in violation of the Versailles Treaty and had introduced conscription. In East Africa Italy had launched an invasion of Ethiopia, which adjoined the British colony of Kenya and British-controlled Sudan. As a result, not long before Lavarack produced his memo, the First Lord of the Admiralty had disclosed in January 1936 what Lavarack and others had long suspected would happen: the British Main Fleet would be restricted to the North Atlantic and Mediterranean for several years. This had serious ramifications for Australian defence, especially since war was expected in 1939.[18]

The sabre-rattling by Germany and aggression by Italy, as well as growing militarism in Japan—taken with the reduced effectiveness of the Royal Navy, which was now even less reliable than before—left Australia's weakened army with much to do if it were to be ready for war. Lavarack told Parkhill that there were three essential steps to take. First, the provision of modern arms, equipment and ammunition. Second, the maintenance of a nucleus of commanders, staffs, non-commissioned officers and specialists in numbers sufficient to permit the necessary expansion of the army within a few weeks (which Lavarack considered might be the only time available). Third, the completion of all plans as soon as possible so that the army could become effective in the shortest time after the outbreak of hostilities.

Lavarack's priorities showed that, like Bruche before him, his primary aim was to put the army's slice of defence money into more tangible assets which could benefit the field army and which could not be taken away by the government as easily as manpower. Manpower, though, was far from ignored: the Board once more estimated that a peace nucleus of 130,000 was required (which was in accordance with the recommendations of the 1920 Senior Officer's Conference). Moreover, with war probably only three years away, it could see no alternative to the re-introduction of compulsory training, or national service, and recommended to Parkhill that a decision be taken soon.[19]

While Lavarack had been preparing this report, another parliamentarian, Harold Holt, had publicly criticised the voluntary system of enlistment in the *Herald* newspaper on 3 March, offering the opinion that 'for nearly seven years the voluntary system had been on trial, and by no stretch of the imagination could it be said to be satisfactory'. He said he was 'reliably informed' that at best most units could achieve only 50 per cent attendance at parades and that the official strength of 27,000 men 'was entirely fictitious'. Naturally Parkhill was not pleased with this development, nor with Lavarack's report on the earlier article by Cameron, which the Board suggested also covered Holt's criticism. Parkhill wrote:

> The report referred to above does not answer either Mr Cameron's or
> Mr Holt's statements and I desire the Military Board to give further and
> immediate consideration to the matter and submit specific replies to the
> points raised.[20]

However, no matter how many times Parkhill ordered Lavarack and the Military Board to resubmit reports, the message would be the same: government defence policy was wrong. In both the latest reports the Board had made it clear that it agreed with Cameron and Holt on almost every major point raised. There were serious weaknesses in the voluntary militia system (such as unrealistic training owing to a shortage of troops) and compulsory recruitment appeared to be the only alternative. Lavarack told Parkhill that 'the Voluntary System has so far failed to produce the numbers required'. He conceded, though, that 'the Military Board has at present no option but to continue the trial until the Government decides to adopt National Service'.[21]

Parkhill's displeasure with the way that Lavarack's reports had taken the opportunity to criticise government policy and had left him floundering in parliament was clear in his reply:

> When asking for this reply to the statement made by Mr. Cameron, M.P.,—and the same thing applies to statements by Mr. Holt and others— I desired a reply that is based on the present policy of the Government. What I received is a statement which refers to an entirely different policy, which has yet to be considered by Cabinet.
>
> It is obvious that I cannot use the views contained in the statement in any reply that I make to Mr. Cameron.[22]

Not surprisingly, Parkhill's suspicions grew that senior army officers had been leaking confidential information. On the same day he wrote to the Board about the Cameron and Holt articles, another article appeared in the *Age* of Melbourne which began: 'Drastic reorganisation of the Australian military system has been strongly recommended by the army experts to the political head of the Defence department, Mr Parkhill.' It conjectured that compulsory training would be introduced under the title of 'national service' a name suggested by Lavarack in January. The article concluded:

> It was stated at the Defence department that the Minister had been provided with overwhelming proof that Australia's present defence system had been based on the presumption of immediate and adequate assistance from Great Britain in the event of war: the contention of Australia's experts being that the sooner the local defence organisation became more self-contained and self-reliant the better.
>
> That no official statement concerning this most important plan, which so vitally affects the nation, was made by the Minister affords yet another deplorable example of the Government's unwillingness to face the facts and take the people into its confidence.

As a result of the article Parkhill was besieged by journalists in Canberra. Shepherd sent a copy of the article to Lavarack with the following note:

[The] Minister has asked by phone whether [the] Military Board or
military officials have supplied the press with information to enable this
article to appear...He desires to be furnished with a report on [the]
matter and that inquiry be made to ascertain how this leakage
occurred.[23]

Lavarack replied that he had already seen the article and begun an
investigation. All officers with any knowledge of the matter were
questioned and all denied involvement with the press. However, he
pointed out that since an announcement had already appeared in the
press that Parkhill had called on the Military Board to submit a report on
the voluntary training scheme:

It was therefore only reasonable to assume that the Board would be
submitting recommendations and that they would be in front of the
Minister at this particular time, i.e. the beginning of a new session.

Lavarack also observed that the figures quoted (such as a reference to a
nucleus strength of 45,000) had never been mentioned in any paper by the
Board. He gave his assurance that all reasonable care had been taken to
prevent the leakage of information.[24]

Parkhill was far from satisfied with Lavarack's explanation, especially
as another article appeared in the *Age* the next day. He wrote to Shepherd
on 11 March 1936:

The attached report is unsatisfactory, and it would appear that any
enquiry that has been made by the Military Board seems to have been of
a perfunctory character. The fact is outstanding and must be well known
to members of the Military Board, that no sooner is a report made to me
on any subject, than reference to it, and portions of it, appear in the
Press, and which are ascribed to 'army experts', 'officers of the
Department' and 'others connected with the Defence Forces'...I desire
that a more thorough enquiry should be made into these expressions,
and more definite steps taken to prevent publication of information
which is extremely embarrassing in many ways.

At the same time Parkhill released a statement in which he declared that
articles in the press referring to 'a sharp difference of opinion between the

Minister and the Military Authorities on the question of military training... [were] entirely wrong'.[25]

Lavarack's anger at Parkhill not accepting his initial assurance that there had been no leak was evident in the reply of the Military Board:

> [T]he Military Board regrets that the Minister has seen fit to convey the rebuke of perfunctoriness, as everything possible has been done to trace the source of information. As stated in the Board's report, contact with papers under consideration has been limited to a very small number of persons. All of those under control of the Military Board were personally interrogated before the despatch of the Board Memorandum on the subject, dated 10th March 1936, to which the Minister has taken exception. All have denied absolutely having supplied the Press with information. This includes everyone, from members of the Board down to the typists who prepared the documents and who are regarded as perfectly reliable. The drafts from which the final copies were made were burnt. File copies are carefully locked up in the Military Board and General Staff safes, and do not pass to Records.

In addition, Lavarack told Shepherd that the Military Board had raised the issue of compulsory training in the context of Cameron's statements, not as a recommendation to alter policy, so charges in the press that the Board and the Minister had disagreed on policy were untrue. The inaccuracy of such reporting, he argued, indicated that the articles were conjecture. The report concluded that while all care had been taken to avoid leakages,

> the Board realises the embarrassment which such incidents must cause the Minister, and wishes to assure him of their complete loyalty, both as a Board and as individuals, to himself and to the Government.[26]

It seems improbable that Lavarack had anything to do with providing information to the press—he was more likely to confront Parkhill personally. But, despite Lavarack's protestations, clearly the Military Board disagreed with the government's policy of voluntary training. Somewhat provocatively, Lavarack had used the opportunity of commenting on the papers by Cameron and Holt to put the army view that the navy could not be relied upon and therefore the army had to be built up, which could not be done if the present government policy continued.

Parkhill's suspicion of Lavarack and the Military Board deepened a week later with the publication of another article on defence, again in the *Age*. The article criticised him for 'dallying with the report on military training which the Military Board presented to him two weeks ago' and referred to the approval given previous articles by 'leaders at the Defence Department'. Parkhill demanded 'an immediate statement' regarding the reference to senior officers of the department.

In reply he was told that 'all members of the Military Board deny absolutely having supplied "The Age"...with any information'. To drive home the point, the Board had ordered that all officers at Army Headquarters certify in writing that they had not communicated with the press and attached their statements. The Board told Parkhill that confidential inquiries amongst journalists had revealed that the *Age* 'has an animus against the Minister for Defence and seizes every opportunity for such harassing tactics...' In an accompanying statement the Adjutant-General, Jess, referred to the embarrassment which was being caused both to the Minister and the Board, and suggested prosecution of the newspaper.[27]

Parkhill was mollified for the time being at least, and replied: 'I accept, without reservation, the views regarding the nuisance which the continued publication of these statements causes to everybody concerned'. Four days later, in response to a question in parliament, Parkhill defended the Military Board and other officers at the AHQ, describing them as 'an honourable body of men'.

However, despite his assurances to parliament, Parkhill's confidence in the Military Board, and Lavarack in particular, had been shaken and the press farrago was to set in train events which would undermine the post of CGS. Shedden, of course, was suspicious of the Board and now used the issue of the newspaper articles to suggest to Shepherd that the post of inspector-general of the army be resurrected: 'My own opinion is that the Minister would be wise to establish this check', which of course would act most upon Lavarack.[28]

There was a lull in the press campaign until late July when the *Bulletin* published an article which declared:

If the Government is sincere in its efforts to provide for the defence of the country, and not content merely to shelter behind Britain's skirts, it must consider restoring compulsory service, and it should not let Opposition outbursts, pacifist aggressiveness or fear of election consequences deter it.

As usual Parkhill wanted the Military Board's views on the article and, as usual, Lavarack's reply a week later did not satisfy him:

> The Board considers that if a really effective military force is to be provided, something more than the requirements as set out in Part XII of the Defence Act is necessary. The form of training advocated in the article would be a very suitable basis for consideration, if and when the Government decided to re-introduce a system of National Service. This would, of course, necessitate amendments to the existing Defence Act.

Lavarack referred to the Senior Officers' Conference of 1920 which had recommended a form of training similar to that advocated in the article, and told Parkhill that eventually it would have to be introduced. However, as lip-service to ministerial authority, he added that 'the Board also fully realises that it is for the Government to decide when such action should be taken'.[29] A draft statement for Parkhill to use in reply to *The Bulletin* article was also provided. In it there were several references to the necessity for expanding the army considerably. After reading the statement Shepherd told Parkhill:

> By these remarks you are committed sooner or later to introduce compulsory training, yet the Policy of the Government is voluntary enlistment. It is rather a wet blanket at a time of endeavour to make the voluntary system a success.[30]

The divergence of opinion between Lavarack and Parkhill which had been simmering was now brought to the boil. Parkhill told the Board that he had no intention of using the draft statement which had been provided 'as it might be taken to appear that the Military Authorities are not in favour of the present efforts to increase the Militia' through voluntary enlistment. He made it clear that he viewed this particular instance as part of a wider problem:

> I have observed that on this and other occasions when the policy of the Government is being criticised, the Military Board has, more than once, expressed itself in agreement with the criticism and has provided little, if any, argument in support of the policy laid down and at present being carried out by Parliament, the Military Board and all parties concerned.[31]

He emphasised that the government laid down the policy and, until the government decided to alter it, 'it is the duty of the Military Board to carry it out and support it in every way possible.' In conclusion, he accused the Board of inconsistency:

> Finally, I would add that the advice which the Military Board proffers on this subject loses, I regret to say, some of its value by its inconsistencies. An increase in the number of men is urgently advocated in several of the minutes I have read, whilst statements that other matters are of more importance and should be dealt with first, are made with equal, if not greater, strength. My view is that when a policy is decided upon and laid down, it should be wholeheartedly supported, and the expression of and agreement with opinions that pertain to other policies are disturbing and unsettling.[32]

In reply, Lavarack turned the Minister's own words against him, referring to Parkhill's public references to invasion:

> The draft statement was intended to cover the Government's policy, with reservations to enable any change made necessary by future developments to be covered also. The Minister's remarks on 'Invasion', in his speech on 'Australian Defence' on 11th May, 1936, and in other speeches, have been taken as implying the need for such reservations, and the Board's references to the manpower question were intended only as an expansion of these remarks. Certainly there was no intention of causing the Minister to commit himself. The Board notes that future statements are to be drafted so as to cover present policy, without reservations.[33]

Furthermore, Lavarack rejected Parkhill's charge of inconsistency and told him that the Board always commented within the framework of the hypothesis under consideration. If an article assumed that large-scale attack was imminent, then the Board agreed under such circumstances a rapid increase in manpower would be essential. On the other hand, when told by the Minister that only limited funds are available and that attack was not likely, the advice was to concentrate on commanders, staffs and equipment rather than raw manpower. He told Parkhill that

> the Board had therefore consistently advised that available funds should be devoted to the development of commands, staffs, and material, and

that expenditure on Militia units should be limited to the necessities of upkeep and training.[34]

Lavarack might have left the matter there, but he decided to go beyond mere explanation and criticised Parkhill obliquely for not keeping the Board informed:

[T]he lack of official information regarding the world situation is the cause of the Board's occasionally expressed uneasiness with regard to the international situation. The Minister has now given his assurance (to the Chief of the General Staff on Tuesday, 25th August, 1936) that the Government does not regard the situation with any anxiety, but the Board desires to explain that previously it had interpreted various passages in his recent public speeches as indicating a change in the outlook, and a change for the worse.

Lavarack therefore requested that from time to time the Board be advised of the government's latest appraisal of the international situation. He told Parkhill that the Board commented freely on the subject of defence only with him and operated on the assumption that frankness was the only attitude to adopt. He concluded that

the Board wishes once more to assure the Minister of its entire loyalty. At no time has it had the intention, when commenting on articles, etc. referred to it by the Minister, of supporting any adverse criticism of the policy laid down by the Government.[35]

Shepherd found this hard to accept and in a note to Parkhill attacked the Military Board's statements as revealing explicitly

what has been more or less apparent by inference on occasions, that though the Government's Policy is to give priority of defence to raids, the Military Board really hold in their minds certain reservations regarding its wisdom.

Shepherd said that this assessment was borne out by Bruche's refusal to stand by the agreement made during Hankey's visit to reduce the army to three divisions; and by Lavarack's frequent favourable references to compulsory training and his proposal to halt development of the fixed coastal defences in favour of developing the field army. Shepherd concluded:

The remainder of the Military Board minute seems to be hedging in an endeavour to cover themselves both ways. If war comes and there is an outcry against the lack of trained man-power, it will have been due to the Government, notwithstanding that, on the advice of its technical advisers, the training of man-power is placed last in priority.[36]

Parkhill suspected that the Military Board was trying to force him into committing himself on the invasion issue. He told the Board that, while he did not doubt its loyalty, it was 'unnecessary for the Board to provide for reservation in regard to Government policy in their statements, as this is a Ministerial matter'. The tone of the correspondence between Parkhill and the Military Board made it clear that an air of mutual confidence was hardly all-pervasive, and soon the affair of Colonel H.D. Wynter was to create a permanent rift between Lavarack and Parkhill.[37]

6

'Your luck is out'

Chief of the General Staff,
1937-1939

BY THE BEGINNING of 1937 Lavarack's well-known views on defence policy and his obdurate attempts to change its direction had done his reputation in political circles considerable damage. Nevertheless, he would continue the fight against the Singapore strategy and for greater military self-reliance, further alienating himself from politicians and civil servants. There were several events to come which stand out as sealing Lavarack's fate as CGS: the Wynter affair which came to a head in 1937; pivotal meetings of the Council of Defence in late 1937 and early 1938; and the impression he made on politicians at the time of the Munich crisis. The year 1937 would be a difficult year, but 1938 would prove to be decisive in determining the future course of Lavarack's career.

The Wynter Affair

The Wynter affair had begun in November 1936 when Parkhill drew the attention of the Military Board to a speech delivered in parliament by the Leader of the Opposition, John Curtin. Parkhill argued that parts of Curtin's speech bore a similarity to information contained in General Bruche's paper of the previous year criticising Hankey's report and also to a paper by Lavarack in August 1935 regarding the readiness of the army for war.

In fact, Curtin had drawn on arguments put forward by the Director of Military Training, Colonel H.D. Wynter (who had prepared the draft of Bruche's paper), in a talk he had given at a meeting of the United Services Institution (USI) in August 1935 with Lavarack's permission.[1] Wynter echoed arguments he had put forward almost a decade before in another lecture he had given at the USI, warning against placing too much faith in British sea-power and advocating self-reliance in Australian defence. Although the press had been excluded from the talk, Wynter provided copies to interested army officers and members of parliament, one of whom was Senator H.C. Brand, a former regular major-general. Brand in turn circulated a summary of the paper to other parliamentarians and so it came into the hands of Curtin, who used it against the government.[2]

Parkhill was embarrassed in parliament as a result of Curtin's speech. He said that he had hoped to raise the issue of defence above party politics so that continuous development of the services could be achieved and to that end had made speeches in parliament on 11 September and 5 November. However,

> the whole fabric was destroyed by the Leader of the Opposition rising immediately after me and making a speech the essence of which was in the C.G.S. secret memorandum of 5th March, 1935, and the bulk of which was in Colonel Wynter's notes.

Parkhill claimed that in addition to Curtin's speech, an article in Sydney's *Daily Telegraph* of 3 April 1936 was similar to a secret defence document. Wynter admitted that it was 'not improbable' that his elder son, a journalist who had attended the meeting of the USI in August 1935 in an unofficial capacity, had written the article from knowledge he had gained informally from his father. The Military Board had admitted at the time that the views in the article 'almost entirely coincide with those of the Board'.[3]

Parkhill wanted an explanation from the Military Board. In the first instance Lavarack alone prepared a report for him down-playing the issue and had the secretary to the Military Board sign it. Clearly annoyed, Parkhill wrote that

> though the subject was before the Military Board three times, it was not considered by the Board in session until the third occasion. This is the responsibility of the CGS as chairman of the Board.

Parkhill was in no doubt where Lavarack stood on the issue: 'the criticisms of Government Policy are shared by the present CGS' and declared that

> The Government will not tolerate propaganda by Service Officers on the political aspect of Defence Policy, and the Military Board being responsible for discipline should consider Colonel Wynter's position in the matter. On receipt of its recommendation I shall consider the assessment of the degree of responsibility resting on the CGS.

Parkhill concluded that he expected an immediate reply as he considered the previous one had taken far too long to produce.[4]

Lavarack's hand was forced: clearly, if he did not agree to punish Wynter, Parkhill intended to take the issue much further, possibly using it as an opportunity to muzzle Lavarack and the Military Board. Shedden appears to have had a hand in the production of this threat, for he later told Shepherd that the object was 'to make the Military Board face up to its responsibilities and abandon its "whitewashing" attitude'. He also raised the possibility of officially censuring Lavarack, who seems to have brought some of this upon his own head to judge from a ministerial minute by Parkhill:

> I would also place on record the substance of a verbal statement made to me by the C.G.S... Major-General Lavarack explained that his purpose in originally dealing with the matter personally in the name of the Military Board and without the full Board considering the case was inspired by a personal desire 'to white-wash Lt.-Col. Wynter'. (This was his own expression.)[5]

In a memorandum to the Prime Minister, Joseph Lyons, Parkhill complained that Lavarack

> has sought to excuse the action of Colonel Wynter, and, though responsibility for discipline in the Army is a matter in the first instance for the Military Board, it has been reluctant to deal with this officer, and left the judgement to me.

> ... this is not the first occasion in recent times on which there have been leakages of information or apparently inspired criticisms of Government Policy, but the Military Board on enquiry has been unable to locate the source in other cases.[6]

In January 1937 Parkhill insisted that Wynter be moved from his post at Army Headquarters. He was sent to Brisbane, reverting to his substantive rank of lieutenant-colonel with a reduced salary. Wynter told Lavarack that the Military Board, in carrying out Parkhill's wishes without allowing him personally to state his case, had done him a 'most grievous wrong'. He did concede, however, that the Military Board had been the 'medium through which a punishment has been inflicted' by the 'political authority'. His request to be judged by a court-martial was denied by Parkhill. Wynter felt that he had been unfairly singled out for attention:

> If I was wrong in discussing matters of so called high military 'policy' with my son—which was not policy at all—then surely Lord Milne must have been wrong in discussing such matters with the whole world in the press and Admiral Richmond, General Lavarack and many other writers are wrong in publishing articles discussing the general merits of the problem...[7]

Wynter had a point, of course, but the atmosphere was too politically charged for anyone to concede it publicly. He was also naive if he thought he could disclaim all responsibility for information imparted to his son, a journalist, who then published the material. (Wynter, though, would not have to wait long for redress—Parkhill would soon be ousted as minister, after which Lavarack would oversee Wynter's promotion to colonel, backdated to July 1937, and soon thereafter his appointment to command the newly-established Command and Staff School.)[8]

Wynter was not the only army officer in Parkhill's sights. He called Lavarack's permission for Wynter to deliver the lecture 'an imprudent decision'. In retrospect it was unwise, especially given the problems with press articles criticising government policy and the deteriorating relationship between minister and CGS. However, Lavarack assured Parkhill that he had no intention of being a party to criticism of the government's policy:

> I had no suspicion, when I read the lecture, of its identity or similarity with the previous C.G.S. Memorandum...I suggest that it would have required a most unusual feat of memory to have recalled the fact that the same wording had previously been used in the earlier memorandum.[9]

Lavarack may have been innocent of any ill-intent, but his prevarication over Wynter's future at successive meetings of the Military Board had done nothing to allay Parkhill's suspicions.

The Wynter affair had brought to a head the difference of opinion between Lavarack and his political masters. Although Lavarack was criticised by some within the army for not doing more to shield Wynter from Parkhill's excessive vindictiveness, he had done what he could to protect him. Beyond that there was no option for Lavarack but to take a stand on the issue and resign, which of course would have been welcome to both government politicians and civil servants in the Department of Defence, such as Shedden and Shepherd. Had he resigned there was not a soldier of the same calibre who could replace him and the army would have been the poorer for his absence.

Lavarack had the worst of both worlds because of the affair, being criticised by some officers within the army and punished by the government. Parkhill, again encouraged by Shedden, withdrew his recommendation for Lavarack to be created a Companion of the Bath. It was a telling manifestation of the resentment felt for Lavarack within the government and civil service.[10] More broadly, it was decided as a result of the Wynter affair that a proposal to have Curtin, as Leader of the Opposition, attend meetings of the Council of Defence would be taken no further, and so the opportunity for bi-partisan consultation on defence was squandered by Parkhill.[11]

Given the distrust and ill-feeling the Wynter affair had engendered, it is not surprising that the Australian government refused to allow Lavarack to attend the 1937 Imperial Conference as an adviser. Nevertheless, his presence would be felt: the British official historian, Roskill, has noted that the 'penetrating questionnaires' presented by the Australian delegation were probably influenced by the local defence advocates. Even so, the probing questions asked by the Australian and New Zealand delegates were fobbed off with more assurances from the British chiefs of staff who were eager to disguise the extent to which the Singapore strategy had become impracticable. Naturally Lavarack was criticised after the conference for suggesting, against the prevailing wisdom, that development of the navy be maintained at the present level to allow for improvements in the army and the air force, although he had been putting his views to the CIGS in his periodical liaison letters.[12]

Lavarack's position was hardly eased in November 1937 by the appointment of Frederick Shedden as the new Secretary of the

Department of Defence, replacing Shepherd. Intelligent, status-conscious and fixated on his work, Shedden would rule the department by fear, as Sir Frederick Chilton recalled: 'He was ruthless with those who crossed him, and devastating with those in his Department who could not rise to his exceptional standards of performance'.[13]

The new Secretary was keen for the Council of Defence, which included Blamey as a co-opted member, to meet more frequently. The December 1937 meeting of the council concentrated on the results of the Imperial Conference, and in particular the cornerstone of Australia's defence policy, the country's reliance of British promises to send a Royal Navy fleet to Singapore in case of war. Not surprisingly, the Chief of the Naval Staff, Sir Ragnar Colvin (a British officer) supported the plan. Lavarack and the Chief of the Air Staff, Williams, preferred boosting defences in Australia in readiness to meet any threats. Blamey, however, steered a more political course saying that he was 'gratified with the very clear and definite statement which had been presented', congratulated those responsible for the defence scheme and stated the orthodox view, which was that if Singapore could hold out all would be well.

That view was not accepted by the External Affairs Minister, W.M. Hughes, who, like Lavarack, had doubts about such a policy. Hughes likened relying on Singapore to hold out against the Japanese to 'living in a fool's paradise'. It was no surprise that Hughes' view was challenged immediately by Colvin who, rendering himself a hostage to fortune, assured the council that Singapore was impregnable and could therefore hold out for the 70 days it would take the British fleet to reach the Far East[14]. One can only imagine Colvin's feelings when, less than five years later, the Japanese stormed the Malay peninsula to capture Singapore in precisely 70 days after sinking the only two British capital ships sent to bolster the defence. But that calamity was yet to come and for the time being the country's policy of relying on the Royal Navy and the Singapore base remained intact, thus impeding greatly the development of the army and air force.

The meeting had also been the first for the new Minister for Defence. In November H.V.C. Thorby replaced Parkhill, who had lost his parliamentary seat in recent elections, taking the defeat so hard that he refused to shake hands with his victorious opponent. Lavarack tried to capitalise on the change in political masters to help the army. Frustrated at delays in obtaining approval for alterations to the army works programme (in particular for coast defences), at Lavarack's instigation it was suggested that the Minister delegate to the Military Board some of his authority in order to speed up the process.

This proposal was not well-received by Thorby, a 'rugged' and 'pugnacious' farmer, who viewed the services with suspicion. Lavarack was unwilling to accept no for an answer and told the other members of the Board that

> I think we must take up as a major question of policy the whole procedure in future in obtaining Ministerial approval and the question also of the degree of delegation which the Board should be empowered to exercise.

Thorby, however, was not likely to be moved on the issue, for as he later wrote of the chiefs of staff, 'any Minister who accepts all they have to tell him uncritically may well imperil the nation'.[15]

The Council of Defence

The next Council of Defence meeting, held on 24 February 1938, was to be significant. Thorby went on the attack, criticising the army's use of the money allocated to it in the defence vote, claiming that too much money had been spent on buildings and not enough on armaments. Lavarack replied that the buildings were necessary to house troops who were to man the fixed coastal defences, to which the government had given priority.

The Minister for External Affairs, W.M. Hughes, again weighed in, saying that he was 'very dissatisfied' with the state of the army and telling the council that he had been assured during Parkhill's ministry that the field army had not wanted for recruits. However, he had since learnt that in some units there were more NCOs and officers than men. Moreover, it now appeared to him that the army was short of essential weapons and that little was being done to obtain more.

Lavarack offered that although the army had only thirteen tanks, they were sufficient to fulfil the government's policy of preparing solely for defence against raids. Hughes became even more alarmed and said that such a small number of tanks in an age of increasing mechanisation not only was insufficient, but left the government open to criticism. He asked

Lavarack how well-prepared the army was as far as field artillery was concerned. Again Lavarack replied that sufficient guns were held to meet the requirements laid down under the current policy of defending against raids, but that reserves of ammunition would be expended in meeting only a minor raid. Hughes then placed on record his opinion that he was not convinced that a policy of defence against raids alone was sound: 'The initiative under our present policy would lie with the enemy, and we should be prepared to meet an attack from an invading force.'[16]

Lavarack had once again set the stage for a declaration of doubt from a government minister about the fiscally convenient policy of relying on the Singapore base and the Royal Navy to defend Australia against a major attack. While Hughes' statement would have been music to the ears of most of the soldiers in the room, the navy and its supporters were alarmed. In a re-run of the previous meeting, the Chief of the Naval Staff, Sir Ragnar Colvin, responded that Hughes' remarks had strayed from government policy: if defence against invasion were to be adopted as a policy many more ships would have to built or purchased, and as it was the navy was not even equipped to meet raids. The Chief of the Air Staff, Williams, then admitted that the RAAF was in a similar position.

This revelation so disturbed the Treasurer, R.G. Casey, that he disclaimed any responsibility for the situation, saying that he had given the Department of Defence everything that had been requested. He demanded from Lavarack and Williams explanations of why their services were so unprepared for war in terms of munitions and other equipment. Lavarack retorted that he had not in any year since becoming CGS received the amount he had requested and referred Casey to a submission for money he had made at the previous council meeting which had been greatly reduced. (In September 1935 Lavarack had advocated the provision of considerable stocks of ammunition and again in March 1936 had told Parkhill that the army's first priority was the provision of modern arms, equipment and ammunition.) He also reminded Casey that the government had given priority to the fixed coast defences and he had been directed to spend most of the army's funds in that area.[17] Defence policy came under closer scrutiny and on cue the CNS leapt to the defence of the Singapore strategy as the best means of defending Australia, a view which, naturally, was challenged by Lavarack.

Blamey, however, disagreed with Lavarack and supported the navy view that the Japanese would do nothing which laid open their lines of communication to attack, such as launch an invasion of Australia. Bearing in mind the assurances of the chiefs of staff in the United Kingdom, 'he felt that it was reasonable for the Council to assume that invasion was unlikely' and that efforts should be concentrated on defence against raids. No doubt Blamey's words reinforced the impression in the minds of the politicians that he was far more sound and reliable than Lavarack. And, as for the reaction of the Secretary of the Defence Department, Blamey's biographer, Horner, has observed that 'Whatever Shedden thought of Blamey's views he would certainly have found them more acceptable than Lavarack's'.[18] Lavarack's reaction to Blamey's remarks is unknown, but having been acquainted with Blamey for decades he may not have been overly surprised at a response from him which smacked more of coming from a politician than a soldier.

Although there was no obvious change in defence policy afterwards, the meeting did have the beneficial effect of stirring the government to take more strenuous action towards becoming self-sufficient. The council had suggested that the Prime Minister, Lyons, do whatever he could to speed up delivery of equipment from the United Kingdom and that local production be accelerated. In March Lyons announced that the government proposed to spend £43,000,000 on the armed services and munitions production—more then twice the amount spent in the previous three years. It was encouraging, but the army received the smallest proportion of the funds.[19]

It was a small victory for Lavarack, but it came at some personal cost. Shortly after the Council of Defence meeting which had been the catalyst for the increased defence spending, Lyons also made an announcement which must have gratified some politicians and civil servants, especially Shedden: an inspector-general to the Australian army was to be appointed. Lavarack's forensic criticism of defence policy, and a feeling within the government that he was not to be trusted to support his political masters, had contributed to the decision to appointment Lieutenant-General E.K. Squires, a British army officer, as Inspector-General. Also criticism of defence policy in the press had continued sporadically after Parkhill's departure as minister. So the question of army officers making statements or supplying information to newspapers continued to dog Parkhill's successor and the government in general, doing little to dispel suspicions about Lavarack's loyalty. (Lyons, for example, was extremely perturbed to see in the press the agenda of the

February Council of Defence meeting he was about to attend.) Lieutenant-General Sir Edmund Herring told Blamey's biographer:

> I knew Dick Casey [who was then Treasurer]. He told me the Government thought Joe wasn't telling them what they should know but what he thought they ought to know. That was why they brought out Squires.[20]

It may be just as accurate to say that Lavarack was telling the government too much of what it did not want to hear: that its defence policy was bankrupt.

Lavarack received the news of Squires' appointment with equanimity (they had been friends since meeting at the IDC in 1928) and telegraphed Squires that 'your appointment [is] very welcome to me. Looking forward to seeing you here'. Lavarack said that he considered Squires to be a fine soldier and that his posting would be beneficial to the Australian army. He added that because Squires was junior to himself there would probably be criticism, but not from him. (Jess, however, resented Squires and the next year would attempt to challenge his appointment as acting CGS during Lavaracks's absence abroad.)[21] Squires was indeed a distinguished soldier who had held a number of important posts throughout his career, his last before coming to Australia having been Director of Staff Duties at the War Office. Intelligent and personable, he brought with him, in Rowell's words, 'a wide knowledge of all aspects of army life'.[22]

In the meantime, despite the fact that his position was being undermined and his influence being whittled away, Lavarack kept up the pressure on the government. In May 1938 he suggested that the instability of the international situation warranted the government giving early consideration to 'preparations for defence against a higher scale of attack, including the introduction of a form of National Service'. At the same time W.M. Hughes told Lyons that there were some important questions about defence policy which needed clarification, such as the strength of the naval force Britain would send to the Far East and, indeed, if there was any guarantee that a force would be sent at all. Thorby demurred, feeling that the nebulous British replies given to similar queries at the 1937 Imperial Conference answered Hughes' questions.[23]

Three months later Lavarack reiterated the call for urgency in the Defence Committee on 16 August. The international situation was hardly comforting to a CGS at the head of an army almost devoid of resources: the Italians and Germans were involved in the Spanish Civil War and full-scale fighting had broken out between China and Japan, which, like Germany, had increased the pace of rearmament. Although Lavarack said he did not advocate any 'drastic change in Government policy', he nevertheless asked for radical action in the form of compulsory training and a decision to prepare for defence against attacks larger than raids, though he refrained from using the word invasion. However, both the CNS, Colvin, and the CAS, Williams, disagreed with Lavarack and, as they formed a majority, reports tabled by Lavarack were not considered.[24] Lavarack had been defeated, but the international crisis which occurred the next month was to impart to Australian defence preparations some of the impetus he was fighting to achieve.

The Munich Crisis

The Munich crisis of September 1938 underscored the alarm which had been experienced at the Council of Defence meeting earlier in the year and showed that Australia was still lamentably unprepared. Lavarack thought his misgivings about the unpreparedness of the army were soon to be realised, and expressed his anxiety in the Defence Committee. According to Menzies: 'He made a bad impression on Ministers at the time of Munich when he seemed to be excited and jittery'.

Lavarack's concern and frustration, however expressed, can be understood when it is recalled that in 1938 the diminutive and threadbare Australian army had no anti-tank guns; had only begun the laborious and expensive process of mechanisation; was seriously deficient in many vital items, such as ammunition, clothing, bridging equipment, wireless sets and steel helmets; and existing equipment was ludicrously out of date—in an age of growing military mechanisation the Australian army's field artillery was not even on rubber-tyred wheels. In any case, if Lavarack were indeed 'jittery' he was certainly not the only one. According to the British High Commissioner in Canberra, the Prime Minister, Lyons, 'worked himself into a kind of desperate anxiety' at the time. As a result of the crisis the defence budget was again increased, this time the army finally receiving the largest share.[25]

The crisis also showed how well Lavarack and Squires could work to-gether. They proposed that, in the event of mobilisation, either of them

should be appointed commander-in-chief and suggested to Shedden that
he support the idea when he communicated with the Minister (coincidentally, they also recommended that Blamey be given command of the vital New South Wales District). Shedden obviously had reservations about
their suggestion regarding the appointment of a C-in-C, for on the 29th
he sent a telegram to Thorby which read in part:

> As there are important aspects I would like to discuss personally with
> you, I replied that... it was inopportune to put forward any suggestion at
> this stage.
>   In case [the] matter should be raised with you by Squires or by
> Squires with [the] Prime Minister, I suggest that neither you nor [the]
> Prime Minister commit yourself to any opinion. Events of [the] last few
> days have confirmed certain views held by me.

Unfortunately Shedden did not elaborate, but perhaps he suspected that
Lavarack and Squires were working too well together, or at least better
than he had expected.[26]

Indeed, they enjoyed a surprisingly harmonious relationship
considering the circumstances. The only temporary disagreement
between the two arose over part of Squires' report on the army submitted
in December 1938, which was critical of some aspects of the army's
administration and organisation. Initially, Lavarack and the other
members of the Board disagreed with some of Squires' criticisms, but soon
withdrew their opposition—most of the problems had been caused by
political neglect rather than any failing on the part of the CGS or the
Military Board. For his part, Squires supported Lavarack's policy of
spending money on equipment and also recommended the formation of a
permanent force of two brigades.[27]

The Munich crisis may have caused the defence wheels to turn faster,
but by January 1939 Lavarack was still concerned that a sense of urgency
in war preparations had not developed and so told Shedden that 'we do
not appear to have benefited from the crisis in September last'. In February he again urged that defence policy be altered to allow for the army to
prepare against invasion and not just raids. He referred to statements by
ministers which mentioned defence against invasion, arguing that 'it is
well understood that this is the eventual objective of the Government's
policy, although at present the Military Board is still... limited to the Raid

Policy.' He suggested that the matter be clarified (as indeed Squires had also recommended earlier that month) and submitted a statement of requirements which would be necessary to complete army preparations to repel an invasion. These included an army organisation of seven divisions: one mobile (or armoured), two motorised and four infantry divisions, plus army and corps troops. He suggested that at least half the establishment of the mobile division should consist of regular troops.[28]

The Chief of the Naval Staff, Colvin, was worried and told the Admiralty in London on 14 March that there was a danger of 'Australia turning to military self-dependence', which he considered to be 'illusory and impossible' but attractive to an uninformed public. Of course the Naval Board in Australia was still expressing the expectation that the British Main Fleet would steam to the Far East in an emergency. Ironically, Colvin himself was being kept in the dark by the Royal Navy's First Sea Lord, Sir Roger Backhouse, so permitting Colvin to advocate naval policy in Australia without reservation.

It had been decided in London in early March to avoid, as far as possible, communicating with Australia and New Zealand on the size of the fleet to be sent to the Far East. At this time Hankey's preferred successor to his position as the secretary of the Committee of Imperial Defence, H.L.Ismay, was trying to undo the damage caused by the inadvertent passing, through 'gross stupidity', of a British Defence Committee document to the acting Australian High Commissioner in London, J.S. Duncan. The document cast grave doubts upon the likelihood of a fleet being sent to the Far East, but Ismay extracted a promise from Duncan (who surprisingly seems to have decided that his loyalty lay more with Britain than his own country on this occasion) that he would not tell the Australian government.[29] Thus, as war approached, so London's obfuscation—if not duplicity—mounted.

However, the truth could not be concealed for long. On 20 March the British Prime Minister, Neville Chamberlain, delivered a 'bombshell' to Australia: he told Lyons that the size of the force to be sent to Singapore in an emergency could not be specified in advance, but would depend on whether Britain was occupied in Europe with Germany and Italy at the same time. Then in April the Naval Staff in the United Kingdom could not say when a fleet would be sent to the Far East in an emergency, let alone how large it might be—indeed it was cautiously acknowledged that interests in the Mediterranean might preclude a force being sent at all.

The spectre of the two-front war which the Australian army had been warning successive governments about for years had materialised. The next month Thorby's successor as Minister, G.A. Street (a former army officer who had served in the First World War and later reached the rank of brigadier in the militia), directed that the chiefs of staff review the basis of Australian defence policy.[30]

Lavarack's fight for a realistic defence policy was all but over: the policy was to be reviewed and he was due to leave on a tour of the United Kingdom. Being proved right may have been a professional vindication for Lavarack, but it was not a personal victory. By mid-1939 Lavarack's stocks could hardly have been lower in political circles and the army had come to be viewed with suspicion by both the government and the opposition, which had experienced similar difficulties with its leaders when in government a decade earlier. Not many people outside the army would be sorry to see Lavarack leave for Britain. The visit was in itself not a good omen (the Chief of the Air Staff, Williams, had been sacked in January and sent to England for two years) and Lavarack would not be kept well-informed of changes to the army during his time abroad.[31]

Before Lavarack's departure for the United Kingdom he and Squires drew up a list of appointments to come into effect in July. They recommended that either Squires or, in a significant gesture, Wynter act as CGS during Lavarack's absence, and that on his return (by which time his five-year term as CGS would almost be over) Lavarack be promoted to lieutenant-general and become General Officer Commanding (GOC) Eastern Command. Sturdee would then be appointed CGS, also with the rank of lieutenant-general and the appointments of CGS and GOC Eastern and Southern Commands would become interchangeable.[32] As it turned out, Lavarack would instead be appointed GOC Southern Command soon after his return from England, but in circumstances very different to those he and Squires had envisaged.

War, 1939

Lavarack planned to spend the first few weeks in the United Kingdom at the War Office and then attend field exercises. However, in August he was recalled to Australia because of the imminence of war. On 3 September, while he was still at sea, the Australian Prime Minister, Menzies (who had assumed the premiership in April after the death of Lyons), declared that 'in consequence of a persistence by Germany, in her invasion of Poland, Great Britain has declared war upon her and that, as a result, Australia is also at war'. There could be little doubt that an expeditionary force would be raised for service abroad. The question of who would command such a force was of great concern to many, especially senior army officers. It seemed likely that the appointment would be offered to one of seven substantive major-generals on the active list of the Australian army. The most senior of these was H.G. Bennett, followed by Blamey, Lavarack, Jess, Phillips, E.A. Drake-Brockman and I.G. Mackay.[33]

At first glance Lavarack, at 53 years of age and the current Chief of the General Staff, appeared to stand a good chance of being appointed to command an expeditionary force, but he faced stiff competition from the other contenders. Although it had been seven years since Bennett had commanded a division, at 52 he was the youngest and possessed a reputation as an outstanding fighting commander during the First World War. However, his strong criticisms of regular officers and defence policy had done little to enhance his chances. Blamey, too, had considerable war experience, notably as Monash's chief of staff, and had the advantage of being well-known to Cabinet through Menzies and Casey. Largely at Shedden's instigation Blamey had recently been given the position of Controller-General of Recruiting and then Chairman of the Manpower Committee to bring him out of semi-retirement after the debacle of his time as Chief Police Commissioner in Victoria (a post from which he had been dismissed in 1936). The appointment enhanced Blamey's chances of command if war broke out, but on the other hand he had been on the army's unattached list for two years and was two years older than Lavarack.

Next in line were Jess, 55, and Phillips, 57, both of whom had been members of the Military Board during Lavarack's time as CGS, although neither had made his task easier (as far as Lavarack was concerned Jess was obstructive, unscrupulous and assuredly resentful of being superseded, while Phillips was pleasant but ineffectual). Both had been identified by Squires as men who should be 'axed' in what he called a 'much-needed "purge"' of senior Staff Corps officers in an attempt to increase the efficiency of the army. Drake-Brockman, 55, and Mackay, 57, were both militia officers, commanding the 3rd and 2nd Divisions respectively and both, like Bennett, had commanded brigades in France, but Drake-Brockman was probably not physically fit enough to be considered.[34]

There were indications, though, that the decision to place Blamey in command had been already taken by the time Menzies announced on 15 September that a division, soon to be known as the 6th Division, would be raised. Menzies said that the 'Divisional Commander, the Brigade Commanders and Battalion Commanders—in fact, all commanding officers—will be provided by our Militia Forces'. Thus, Lavarack or any other regular officer was not a candidate. Menzies' view was that Blamey was the only man for the job:

> I well remember how my Government, on the outbreak of war in 1939, had to choose a commander for the new Australian Imperial Force. Australia had two or three other senior soldiers at the time who, as military technicians, were probably Blamey's equals, perhaps his superiors, but none nearly matched him in the power of command—a faculty hard to define but impossible to mistake when you meet it.[35]

In reality, though, the decision had been made long before the outbreak of war. During the Munich crisis in September 1938, when Menzies thought Lavarack had over-reacted, he and Casey had decided that Blamey should be placed in command of an expeditionary force if war broke out, as Menzies later admitted:

> The matter of the appointment of Blamey really began in 1938 just after Munich. Casey and I particularly were convinced that war was coming...We decided that Blamey was the man to appoint C-in-C...There was no need for us to seek outside advice. Casey had served with Blamey on the same staff throughout the last war. I knew Blamey quite well and I had been Attorney-General in Victoria when he was Commissioner of Police there. Both of us were convinced that he was the only man who had the necessary ability and experience.[36]

After Menzies' public announcement favouring citizen officers over regulars for the new overseas force, Squires wrote to Lavarack, then still en route back to Australia, that Blamey was the preferred candidate as its commander and that the government had decided that commands down to battalion level in the Second AIF would be given only to citizen officers: 'The Prime Minister announced *(without any reference to anybody)* that the commands in that division would go to Militiamen'. Although Menzies claimed that all these proposals had originated with the Military Board, Squires told Lavarack by telephone, after the ship returning him to

Australia had docked in Perth on 27 September, that the Military Board had recommended Lavarack to command the new division, but Menzies' announcement had trumped that recommendation. Thus, Squires told Lavarack: 'Your luck is out'. And indeed it was, for apart from Blamey's appointment, Squires had another blow for Lavarack: he was soon to be replaced as CGS by Squires himself.[37]

Lavarack flew at once to Melbourne where was met by Squires, who expanded on what he had already told Lavarack during their telephone conversation and noted that Lavarack accepted this drastic change in his fortunes 'very nicely'. Lavarack later told the official historian that on this occasion Squires

> informed me that he and I, (he as Inspector-General and I still C.G.S.), were to sit as a committee of two to select and recommend to the Government a non-regular officer as G.O.C. 2/A.I.F. and the 6th Australian Division. We considered the various possibilities very carefully and decided to recommend Sir Thomas Blamey to the Government as our selection. I do not remember whether this was done verbally or whether the recommendation was written. In any case the recommendation was accepted and the appointment made at once. I may say that, in accordance with my invariable practice, I made no personal protest.

However, it is doubtful that any recommendation by Lavarack could have been influential at this stage, the decision having been made long ago by Blamey's supporters, Menzies and Casey. Thus on 28 September the War Cabinet decided that Blamey would command the 6th Division, Squires would soon take over as the Chief of the General Staff and Lavarack would take up the less prestigious post of GOC Southern Command, encompassing Victoria, South Australia and Tasmania. The effect of Lavarack being replaced as CGS and Menzies' statement preferring militia officers was a natural resentment amongst Staff Corps officers.[38]

Later, when Lavarack told Menzies that many of the difficulties in the army were the result of attempting to exclude regular officers from commands in the 6th Division, Menzies replied that his announcement was not a ruling but simply a statement of fact. He said that he had told Cabinet that 'we did not want any funny business about regular soldiers in this war…'. Lavarack's remarks prompted Menzies to observe that Lavarack 'cannot forget his grievances'. If Lavarack harboured grievances, then perhaps in this case it was not without reason: as Horner has remarked in his biography of Blamey, it is conceivable that 'Menzies had deliberately made the comment to exclude Lavarack from the appointment' to command the AIF.[39]

Typically Squires tried to soften for Lavarack the effect of being sidelined peremptorily:

> I imagine, from what you've said to me at various times, that this would
> suit you...and someone like yourself, who will really take charge, is
> badly needed in Southern Command...I shall envy you—at a time like
> this one wants to be near the troops, not sitting on a stool.

Still, despite Squires' solicitous remarks, it was bitter news for Lavarack, but he could do nothing to alter the decision. As from 13 October Squires was officially the head of the army in Australia, Blamey the commander of the expeditionary forces, and Lavarack, running a poor third, GOC of Southern Command which, as some consolation, carried the rank of lieutenant-general.

Even at this early stage, though, the seeds of wartime rivalry were already being rekindled: Blamey later told Lavarack that he believed Lavarack had deliberately arranged the promotion to lieutenant-general for himself which accompanied the position in order to be the senior of the two men. Lavarack wrote:

> This was certainly not so, as I emphatically told him. In any case there
> could be no question, in my opinion, of his right to the rank [of
> lieutenant-general] as G.O.C. 2/A.I.F. even if the extra divisions had
> never been approved.[40]

Nevertheless, Blamey later took steps to ensure his seniority over Lavarack and another grudge between two men was born, to Lavarack's bemusement.

So, the senior commanders chosen, the Australian army prepared to go to war once again. In 1936 Lavarack had written that to get the defences on their feet 'a war scare is our chief hope'. Two years later the Munich crisis had the desired effect, but by that time Lavarack had done serious damage to his career in attempting to get modern weapons and equipment, trained commanders and staffs, and more troops for the field army.[41] His spirited attempts to rectify military deficiencies and his often-expressed fears that the army would not be ready for a major conflict alienated politicians. As CGS Lavarack had turned a blind eye to government policy when possible and had tried to free the Military Board from ministerial constraints in an effort to prepare the army for war. His motives were above question, but it was inevitable that his methods would bring retribution. Far from being lauded as a far-sighted patriot, he had been removed as head of the army, denied command of the expeditionary force and relegated to a military backwater.

Lavarack's efforts to rebuild the army in the late 1930s had been hobbled by an ultimately useless defence policy which had forced him to expend a disproportionate amount of the army's inadequate vote on the coast defence installations. In that sense, Lavarack's tenure as CGS had been similar to his predecessors. Even so, he had managed to wrest some victories from the army's point of view: a Directorate of Staff Duties had been established at AHQ, a permanent School of Signals had been set up and the Australian Command and Staff College opened.

Although throughout his time as CGS he had been a trenchant critic of the reliance by Australia on British seapower which had hobbled the army, Lavarack was not opposed to the principle of Imperial defence, as he had explained in a letter to Admiral Richmond in 1936:

> All that I do is to query the freedom of action, in all circumstances, of the Royal Navy. I consider that those who believe that the 'period before relief' in the Far East will be only a few weeks are dangerous optimists, and that Australia may have to be prepared to hold her own territories and protect her own local interests for many months, or even a few years...I am a firm believer in Naval defence for the Empire, but I believe that the standard of Naval power is too low for safety...
> ...I have never opposed Australia's Naval contribution, though I have opposed its extension towards the point at which it would entail the annihilation of the other Services.[42]

Lavarack's motto, as he told his friend Sir John Dill, was 'Trust in the Navy, but keep your powder dry'. He added ruefully, however, that 'the RAN doesn't think it necessary to have any powder but their own, much less to keep it dry'.[43]

Lavarack's broader goal had been a more balanced policy relying on the three services, but he had been unable to realise it in the face of over-whelming, and sometimes duplicitous, British advice to the contrary and political expediency in Australia. Lavarack might have resigned, but clearly he saw that to do so would do nothing to advance defence preparedness and would have served only to satisfy his opponents in the Department of Defence. Although at times he overstated his case, Lavarack had shown that he possessed a far keener appreciation of strategic and political problems than his protagonists, notably the Secretary of the Department of Defence, Shedden, who had all too readily swallowed the British line.

But logic and facts had been defeated by uncritical acceptance of British views, championed by Shedden. Shedden's trump card was the influence he had with the politicians, as the Chief of the Naval Staff at the time, Admiral Colvin, recorded:

> [Shedden] always had the ear of the Prime Minister and could generally get the Chiefs of Staffs view and wishes overridden. Still... he was an able and knowledgeable man and though one couldn't trust him personally his views were generally sound.

Considering that Colvin would almost certainly regard Shedden's views 'generally sound' because they were the same as his own, the CNS's opinion was hardly a ringing endorsement of the Secretary of Defence's character (indeed one of Colvin's successors as head of the navy would refer to 'that little bastard, Shedden' because of Shedden's tendency to undermine the heads of services behind the scenes).[44]

Lavarack, unlike Shedden, had demonstrated that he could maintain a distinctly Australian outlook within the general context of Imperial defence. Despite almost two years spent in the United Kingdom at staff college, two years attached to the British army during the First World War, a year at the Imperial Defence College in London, and the close military ties between Australia and the United Kingdom, Lavarack had retained independence of thought and possessed a broader vision well-adapted to the gradual decline of British power. Lavarack's Imperial defence was one which benefited from a well-protected and self-reliant Australia, not a near-defenceless sycophantic Dominion which gratefully accepted unrealistic British promises of protection.

However, the time for discussion was over—Australia was at war and the fleet was not coming.

7

'The crown of any officer's career'

Raising the 7th Division, 1940

AFTER THE OUTBREAK of war competition for men and equipment between the existing formations in the Australian Military Forces and the new 6th Division of the Australian Imperial Force became keen. Although Army Headquarters had laid down that the AIF was to have priority, which in some commands necessitated withdrawing equipment from militia formations, there was a degree of natural resistance to the policy. General Rowell recalled that while Blamey was determined to do the best he could for the AIF, there were

> senior officers, both Regular and CMF, who were just as determined that their formations were not going to be unduly weakened in favour of a division that might never go overseas.

According to Rowell, this was especially notable in Lavarack's Southern Command where 'the situation became almost a scandal' until Squires stepped in to resolve the difficulties. The problems were probably exacerbated in Southern Command because the headquarters of Blamey's 6th Division had been established within its area at Puckapunyal in Victoria. According to the renowned war correspondent Chester Wilmot, Blamey's scandal-dogged years as the Victorian Chief Commissioner of Police—beginning in 1925 when his personal police badge was found in a Melbourne brothel and ending in 1936 when he was forced to resign after he lied to a Royal Commission—had left him with a less-than-lustrous reputation which followed him into the army and undermined 'the loyalty of so many of the Victorians who joined the AIF. Knowing that Blamey had the reputation of being a crook they did not serve happily under him'. Nor would Blamey's questionable past have encouraged commanders serving in Southern Command to give up their resources for him, especially at a time when rumour had it that Blamey was taking a cut of the laundry contractor's profits at the Puckapunyal camp.[1]

For Lavarack, though, the issue would have been more straightforward: he would have argued that it was his duty as a commander to do the best he could to maintain the effectiveness of his own command, as it was Blamey's to do the best he could for his new AIF formation. Soon, however, Lavarack himself was to join the AIF, with the task of raising and training a second division for service abroad.

The suggestion that a second AIF division be formed had been considered at a meeting of Cabinet as early as November 1939. There were several arguments advanced in favour of forming the division: there had been an easing of tension in the Pacific; home defences had been strengthened by calling up drafts of the militia; the formation of another AIF division would not endanger Australia's safety while the present home defence policy was maintained and the equipment necessary to implement it remained in Australia; and, finally, the survival of the Empire and Commonwealth, and so Australia, depended upon the defeat of Germany. Although the proposal had the support of both the Australian and British chiefs of staff, no action was taken immediately. However, General Squires and the Minister for the Army, G.A. Street, continued to press for the new division and on 28 February 1940 the War Cabinet approved the raising of the 7th Division and necessary corps troops.

Tragically, four days after War Cabinet approved the formation of the 7th Division, Squires died and was replaced by General Sir Brudenell White (who had been CGS from 1920 to 1923 and came out of retirement to resume the post). White recommended that Blamey be given command of the new AIF corps, with the result that a commander had to be found for the 6th as well as the 7th Division.[2] Street, probably mindful of Menzies' statement in September 1939 that commands in the 6th Division would be given to militia officers, felt that one of the commands should go to a Staff Corps officer, the other to a militia officer. Of the former he considered Lavarack, Sturdee and Wynter, and after consulting White recommended that Lavarack command the 6th Division and that the citizen soldier to command the 7th be Mackay.[3]

The recommendations came before the War Cabinet on 21 March, when it was decided to reverse the order of the divisional commanders, so giving Mackay the 6th and Lavarack the 7th. There is little doubt that this change was made because of, as Rowell put it, 'Blamey's violent opposition to Lavarack's appointment as a Divisional Commander and the arguments about it in War Cabinet just before Easter' in 1940. Menzies informed Blamey personally of the proposal to appoint Lavarack before the meeting of the War Cabinet:

> Blamey told me that he would not work with him. I said to Blamey:
> 'Well that is a very important matter. You had better talk to Cabinet
> about it'. At the Cabinet meeting Blamey was strongly critical of
> Lavarack, not on the grounds that he lacked technical accomplishments
> but on the grounds that he had defects of character[4].

There was a certain irony in a man of Blamey's dubious personal reputation arguing against Lavarack on grounds of character, especially since Lavarack had risen to the top of the army as CGS at the very time Blamey's career outside the army was faltering under a cloud of impropriety. One of the government ministers who attended the meeting was the Treasurer, Percy Spender, who said that Blamey didn't want Lavarack because of his 'quick and uncontrollable temper'. Such a trait, as unsettling it may have been on occasion, was hardly a reason to ignore Lavarack's claim, and perhaps to the members of the Cabinet it smacked of something other than genuine professional concern. In the event, Blamey's objections had no effect, as Menzies related: 'Cabinet overruled him and later on Lavarack did very well in the Middle East.[5]'

Blamey had not remained at the meeting and was travelling by car to New South Wales when the decision was taken to appoint Lavarack despite his opposition. Rowell recalled that:

> White spoke to me on the telephone but refused to tell me the decision
> as he felt he had to give it to Blamey personally in view of the latter's
> feelings on the matter. So Blamey had to be brought back to Melbourne
> and I had to contact all the police stations up the Hume Highway. We
> finally caught him at Benalla. He wasn't a bit pleased to be brought back
> to receive this news.[6]

On the other hand, of course, Lavarack was pleased with the appointment and perhaps not greatly disturbed that he had been given the 7th Division instead of the 6th, although it probably meant that Mackay, not he, would be the first to take Australian troops into action. For the time being the paramount consideration for Lavarack was that he had a command in the AIF. He told a journalist shortly after his appointment was announced that he was 'very delighted and proud to be going abroad on active service, which, after all, is the crown of any officer's career'.[7]

Still, Blamey's animosity for Lavarack had resurfaced vehemently and publicly. General Herring observed that Lavarack 'was the very antithesis of the kind of man Blamey wanted to command his troops', but the strength of Blamey's opposition suggested more than the objective misgivings of a military commander about a subordinate. The ill-will between the two men, dating from their contact during the First World War, had been fuelled in the 1930s by Lavarack's criticism of Blamey's personal conduct while police commissioner in Victoria, when Blamey was also a senior officer in the militia whose behaviour also reflected on the army. Yet, although Blamey was not the kind of man Lavarack could respect, he would not allow subjectivity to play a role in official decisions affecting Blamey. As the newly-appointed CGS in 1935 Lavarack had recommended that Blamey's tenure in command of a militia division be extended, noting Blamey's 'conspicuous success' in the post. Three years later during the Munich crisis Lavarack (with Squires) had recommended Blamey for the command of the New South Wales District. At the outbreak of war he, again in conjunction with Squires, had recommended Blamey as the commander of the Second AIF. In the years to come, as the Second World War unfolded, Lavarack would give loyalty to Blamey as his commander, despite the personal rift between them, and could not comprehend why Blamey did not return it.[8]

Blamey, however, seemed conscious only of the threat he saw in Lavarack and jealously guarded his position from the beginning of his time as GOC of the AIF. It rankled Blamey that Lavarack retained the rank of lieutenant-general for some time after his appointment to command the 7th Division, which would usually be commanded by a major-general. On 19 April Blamey met Sir Owen Dixon, a judge on the High Court of Australia (and later Chief Justice of the court), to discuss the powers of the War Cabinet to reduce the rank of a general officer appointed to a command holding a lower rank. Dixon gave the opinion that the 'Crown could reduce or take away rank or commission at will'. Later that day Blamey attended a conference at Army Headquarters at which the rank of divisional commanders was discussed, and soon thereafter Lavarack reverted to major-general on the AIF list. It was Blamey's right as a corps commander to raise the issue, and indeed it could be argued that it was his duty to ensure that no disparity of rank existed between his divisional commanders. Nevertheless, probably he was more motivated by what Rowell described as a fear of being 'stabbed in the back':

> He was very suspicious of some people; Lavarack and Bennett, even White. He believed the AIF would be built up to two-corps size and [that] White would get command of the Army.

Perhaps he envisaged Lavarack as the second corps commander. In any case, he was determined to retain the lead over his potential rivals.[9]

Like most senior military men, Lavarack was ambitious as well and that ambition no doubt played a part in his decision to accept a drop in rank to command an AIF division. But the decision, which was applauded by the commander of the First AIF, Field-Marshal Lord Birdwood, was also a measure of Lavarack's enthusiasm and professionalism. Even so, John Hetherington, in his biography of Blamey, speculated that Lavarack

> hid his resentment [of Blamey's opposition to him]. And at least he was now a member of the AIF hierarchy of commanders. That was the important thing. To become GOC 7th Division he had to drop back to major-general from his Staff Corps rank of lieut-general but that was a minor price to pay. The war would last a long time and who was to say how the wheel might not turn within a year or two, or even less?

There is nothing to suggest that Lavarack was plotting to unseat Blamey or to undermine him. In any case, in April 1940 any ambitions Lavarack may have had to be promoted or to command a corps had to be put aside as he faced the demanding task of forming a division for overseas service.[10]

GOC 7th Division

Lavarack's first priority in building his new command was his divisional headquarters. He selected the officers for his staff and telegrams were sent to the area commands in which they were serving, asking if they were medically fit and prepared to accept the appointments offered. Unfortunately, those who accepted were not released from their previous appointments until replacements could be found, which meant that, in the early stages, some positions in the headquarters of the 7th Division were vacant or operating on a part-time basis, although officially the officers concerned were posted to the division from 4 April, the day of Lavarack's appointment. By early May the situation had improved greatly, but even as late as June officers were being withdrawn from divisional headquarters to return to their previous duties, or to take appointments in Blamey's corps headquarters which was also being formed.[11]

Lavarack's first choice as his chief staff officer (or GSO1) had been a regular officer, Colonel F.H. Berryman (a fellow artillery officer and Duntroon graduate with whom he had served briefly during the First World War), but he was appointed instead to the 6th Division as Mackay's GSO1. Lavarack then chose Colonel John A. Chapman, another regular, who had served as a staff officer during the First World War and had attended Staff College at Camberley. Lavarack's senior administrative officer (the AA&QMG) was Colonel A.J. Boase, also a regular officer with First World War experience as a staff officer and was a staff college graduate. (Boase and Chapman were later promoted to the rank of major-general in the AIF in March and August 1942 respectively.) After Lavarack had chosen the senior officers of his staff they in turn suggested the names of more junior officers who, if considered suitable, were interviewed by Lavarack, after which he chose the men to be appointed. One of Lavarack's brigade commanders later testified to the quality of the officers Lavarack had chosen and recalled that '7th Divisional Staff, at that stage, was certainly a hand-picked group'. All the headquarters staff except his senior medical officer (the ADMS) Colonel F.K. Norris, were members of the Staff Corps.[12]

Concurrent with the selection of staff officers and the establishment of divisional headquarters was the selection of formation and unit commanders. Lavarack chose another regular officer, Brigadier E.J. Milford, as his artillery commander (CRA). Milford had ended the First World War as brigade-major of the 2nd Division artillery and later attended the Staff College at Camberley. His last appointment before joining the 7th Division was Director of Artillery at AHQ. In January 1941 Milford would also be promoted to major-general and from April 1942 would command the 5th Division. Of the three infantry brigadiers, two

were militia officers (J.J. Murray and J.E.S. Stevens) and one Staff Corps
(H.C.H. Robertson). Murray had been a major in the First AIF and a
battalion and brigade commander in the militia between the wars. He was
given command of the 20th Brigade. Stevens was a signals officer who had
risen from the ranks of the First AIF to be commissioned as a second-
lieutenant in January 1917. By 1926, enjoying the rapid promotion shared
by many of his militia colleagues between the wars, he was a lieutenant-
colonel. In October 1939 he had been given command of the 6th Division
Signals, and then joined the 7th Division on promotion to command the
21st Brigade. The third brigade commander, Robertson, had served in the
light horse at Gallipoli and in Palestine, and between the wars had
occupied a number of staff appointments, as well as attending staff college
in the United Kingdom. He was a flamboyant and ambitious officer who
was not well-liked by Blamey.[13] By April 1942 all three of Lavarack's
infantry brigadiers would be major-generals.

After Lavarack had chosen his brigade commanders, they in turn
selected their brigade-majors and battalion commanders, and so on down
to sub-unit commanders. There were some restrictions, which meant that
commanders did not always get the officers they wanted (for example, the
commanding officer of a unit and his second-in-command were to be a
mixture of Staff Corps and militia officers), but by 26 April battalion and
equivalent commanders had been appointed. The official historian, Gavin
Long, commented:

> An interesting aspect of the appointments to the new division was that
> two brigadiers (including Brigadier Milford, the artillery commander),
> one battalion commander, and the commanders of several of the corps
> units were officers of the Staff Corps, whose members had been
> grievously disappointed when none were allotted commands in the 6th
> Division.[14]

Even so, the 7th Division did not meet the recommendations made by
the Military Board on 17 January when it suggested that not only should
as many regulars as possible be allotted, but also that they should get all
the important staff appointments and at least one in three command positions. Certainly most of the staff appointments went to Staff Corps
officers, and one of the infantry brigadiers was a regular, but only one of
the nine battalion commanders (R.F. Marlan, commanding the 2/15th Battalion) was a regular officer. The reasons for the scarcity of regulars in the

AIF at this stage were several: a desire to retain permanent officers in Australia for home defence (although this policy was more prevalent at the time the 6th Division was being formed); the idea held by some that regular officers were best suited to staff work and not command; and the uncooperative attitude of some area commanders unwilling to lose their staff to the AIF. The conflict of interests between the home forces and the AIF had been a problem in the First World War and had surfaced again in the Second. In Long's words,

> no effective link was established between the AIF and the home army, with unhappy results that became apparent within a few weeks and were to persist until the end of the war.[15]

At Lavarack's first conference for commanders and staff on 11 April the problems which would hamper the preparation of the 7th Division for operations were discussed. Already some were becoming obvious in establishing the headquarters, such as obtaining staff and finding a suitable location. The problem of which city in Australia Lavarack's headquarters would be located was not resolved until 20 April, and even then there remained the question of where in Melbourne it could be situated. At one stage Lavarack's headquarters was scattered between 466 St Kilda Road, K block at Victoria Barracks and a basement at Headquarters Southern Command. At one time it was suggested that it move into Sleight's Funeral Parlours in Flinders Street. It had found three other locations by the end of the next month. In July, the Headquarters had to give up its rooms at Victoria Barracks. The final move was made on 17 August, just two months before leaving Australia, when HQ 7th Division moved into 441 St Kilda Road.

Other problems appeared as units were raised, including acute shortages of weapons, equipment and recruits, but the most obvious at this early stage was that the division would not be concentrated before going overseas. Soon after the decision was taken to form the 7th Division it had also been decided to adopt the British organisation of nine infantry battalions per division instead of twelve. Since the 6th Division had been formed with twelve battalions, the three surplus would form a brigade of the 7th. Thus the 2/4th, 2/8th and 2/12th (later replaced by the 2/11th) Battalions of the 6th Division were allotted to form the 19th Brigade, and, since they were already in the Middle East, Robertson left to take command of them there in June.[16]

Once commanders and staff had begun arriving for duty, the most important task was to recruit the men needed to bring units up to strength. A cadre of instructors had to be established before recruits could be received and by 8 May a nucleus of officers and NCOs had been collected at Ingleburn west of Sydney, where the 20th Brigade and other units were to begin their training. A week later the training cadre at Puckapunyal (for the 21st Brigade and some units) had begun to function. Recruits had begun arriving in the camps at almost the same time as the training cadres, but in small numbers. On 15 May the two battalions of the 20th Brigade in Ingleburn camp numbered only 85 men each, and five days later only 158 and 124 respectively. The 21st Brigade was faring only a little better, having in its three separated battalion camps on 13 May a total of only 364 officers and men.

Difficulty was still being experienced in having junior Staff Corps officers and NCOs from the Australian Instructional Corps released for duty with the AIF and by 22 May, when the formation of the 8th Division was authorised, only 6,000 men had enlisted in the AIF since the announcement of the formation of the 7th Division on 6 March, and some of these had been allocated to corps troops. A further 24,000 men would be required to complete the 7th Division and corps troops. The prospects were not good, but world events were to resolve the problem. On 10 May Germany had ended the 'phoney war' by invading Holland, Belgium and Luxembourg, and little more than two weeks later was forcing the evacuation of the British Expeditionary Force at Dunkirk.[17]

The fall of France had a galvanising effect. On 16 June 1940 the Australian government decided to raise the strength of the home defence force to 250,000, of which 30-40,000 would be AIF troops in training in Australia. By the end of July there were sufficient men to fill the 7th and 8th Divisions with 50,000 to spare. The government had helped by relaxing the enlistment conditions relating to height and age, and recruits and recruiting officers assisted by unauthorised relaxations of manpower restrictions (for example, those who wished to enlist but were in reserved occupations could be listed as labourers to permit their recruitment). Although there was still a shortage of some officers, Lavarack's recruiting problem, short-lived but nonetheless serious, had been solved and he could devote his attention to turning raw recruits into trained soldiers.[18]

Like the 6th Division (which had followed the example of the 1st Division in 1914), troops for the 7th were to be drawn from all over the country and most units would complete their training in the state in which they were raised, regardless of the location of their formation headquarters. These policies resulted in the division being spread literally over the length and breadth of the country, necessitating a great deal of travel for the divisional commander and his staff and preventing the concentration of even brigades, much less the whole division.

The dispersal of the 7th Division is well illustrated by the locations of its infantry, armour and artillery units. HQ 20th Brigade and two of its battalions were in New South Wales, but the third was in Darwin. HQ 21st Brigade and one battalion were in Victoria, but the other two were in South Australia and Western Australia. HQ 26th Brigade (which had by then replaced the 19th Brigade) was in New South Wales with one its battalions, but the other two battalions were in Victoria and South Australia. The artillery headquarters was in Melbourne, one regiment was at Puckapunyal in Victoria and the other two were in New South Wales. The divisional cavalry regiment had two squadrons in Queensland and the remainder in New South Wales. Tasmania did not have any of the fighting units at this stage, but did have the divisional ammunition company and the salvage unit.[19]

The arrangements for raising and training the AIF were, to say the least, cumbersome. In addition to being responsible for the training of his own troops in camps all over Australia, Lavarack was allotted units from corps troops to train, and all units of the 7th and 8th Divisions and corps troops located in Southern Command were under his administrative command. The commander of the 8th Division was in a similar position in Eastern Command.[20] A shortage of accommodation and equipment, a desire to have AIF units in every area to bolster home defence, and an inclination towards tradition had led the Australian government (so keen to ensure that its forces were not broken up overseas) to adopt a policy at home which resulted in formations being scattered around the nation.

Consequently Lavarack travelled often and far. For example, in the period 2–13 September he visited Adelaide, Alice Springs, Darwin, Townsville and Sydney to monitor the progress of his units before returning to Melbourne. However, apart from the difficulties in administering such scattered forces at the division and brigade levels, the dispersal did not greatly hamper Lavarack's training schedule. Training up to unit level could be carried out no matter where the battalion or regiment was located. However, if the bulk of the division could not be not concentrated after unit training finished, then serious problems were possible as training progressed to formation level.[21]

As the size of the 7th Division grew with the influx of recruits, so did Lavarack's difficulties in accommodating and equipping such a large body of men from meagre resources. Compounding the problems, the 7th Division recruits marched into army camps around Australia at the beginning of winter. There was a widespread shortage of accommodation, equipment and uniforms—even sufficient underwear could not be issued. The available barracks could not provide adequate protection against the weather during June, July and August. The huts at Puckapunyal, which one unit historian described as 'bitterly cold and bleak', were unlined until Lavarack intervened, and the first six stoves to heat the division's units there did not arrive until June.[22]

The combination of inadequate winter accommodation and lack of warm clothing resulted in an epidemic in nearly every 7th Division camp of upper respiratory tract infection, known to the troops in general as 'Dog's Disease' and locally by names such as 'Pucka Throat'. When Lavarack visited the camps to see what could be done he found that not only had the lack of winter amenities contributed to the epidemic, but also that the division was ill-equipped to deal with it—at one camp in Tasmania there were no beds for the sick. He immediately took the matter up with the Director-General of Medical Services, Major-General R.M. Downes, but with little result. Brigadier Stevens wrote that 7th Division requests for assistance were 'treated with disdain. Downes seemed to be too far removed from troops to have any great sympathy with them'. To be fair, medical units were just as short of equipment as fighting units and Downes was just as limited by lack of resources as the commanders of fighting formations. Mostly through self-help units again became fully effective.[23]

Lavarack's equipment problems were more serious. When the division was formed it was decided that it would be equipped with small arms and Bren carriers in Australia, but that the remainder of its weapons and transport would come from British sources when it arrived in the Middle East. Throughout the training period in Australia arms and transport were in short supply and slow in arriving at units when they were available. There seemed to be a shortage of everything, from drill cartridges, copies of AIF Standing Orders and colour patches to every kind of weapon and vehicle. The 2/2nd Pioneer Battalion, under the command of the 21st Brigade at Puckapunyal for training, had by the middle of June 1,000 men but only 100 rifles. As late as July the 2/16th Battalion was short of rifles and had not been equipped with 2-inch and 3-inch mortars, Bren guns, carriers and even the outdated Lewis gun (it was entitled to 48 and had none).[24] The 2/27th Battalion had no Bren guns and 2-inch mortars and anti-tank rifles were represented by wooden dummies. Signallers were trained with flags because there were no telephones or signal lamps. Prismatic compasses were scarce and the battalion was equipped with binoculars by donation from the civilian population. An officer of the 2/13th Battalion recalled that his unit 'was in the same plight and was little better off when it met the Germans at Er Regima' on 4 April 1941.

As far as the artillery was concerned, the 2/4th Field Regiment in July even lacked sufficient of the outdated, wooden-wheeled 18-pounder field guns and the 2/5th Field Regiment, owing to the shortage of equipment, practised 'mechanised silly b____s':

> Members of the battery would fall in, in the same places that they would have occupied if the guns, vehicles and motor-cycles actually had been present. On the command, "Inspect Maintenance', for example, drivers would crawl about their imaginary trucks, kick non-existent tyres for air pressure, lift mythical bonnets and gaze wisely at non-present engines. Phantom radiator caps would be unscrewed and visionary water added. At the command, "Mount', the gunners who had meanwhile been playing similarly with their share of nothingness, would leap to their places on these supposititious vehicles, officers and N.C.Os jumping on to unreal front seats and slamming hypothetical doors with loud bangs.[25]

Lavarack visited units in an attempt to alleviate problems, but eventually he had no option but to tell commanding officers that there was no possibility of being equipped with items such as Bren guns, carriers or mortars for some time. The widespread shortage of vehicles was also a major problem which, despite Lavarack's efforts, was never solved in Australia and so the division made the best of a bad situation until it arrived in the Middle East.[26]

It was ironic that Lavarack had to deal with precisely the problems he had forecast as CGS and fought to prevent. The results of the economic depression, misguided disarmament policies and faulty strategic appreciations of the inter-war years had reached the zenith of their pernicious effects on Australia's military preparedness. Until the German invasion of the Low Countries in May 1940 the Australian government was content to maintain a part-time army for home defence and to allow Britain to produce most of the arms the Australian forces would require. After the fall of France, however, Britain faced the enormous task of almost completely re-equipping its army, which had left most of its materiel on the Continent. Subsequently Australia could no longer expect to rely on Britain for equipment, and in fact would have to divert its resources to help the British forces.[27] How empty the inter-war promises of British protection for Australia must have begun to seem.

The shortage of modern equipment was one of the two crucial strategic shortcomings of the Australian army on the outbreak of war. The other was that the Australian Military Forces (AMF) consisted of troops who were liable for service only in Australia, hence the necessity to raise a separate force—the AIF—for service abroad. On 12 July the Military Board discussed with Lavarack and the General Officers Commanding Eastern and Southern Commands the arrangements for raising the strength of the AMF to 250,000 and the use of AIF units in Australia in the event of an emergency. The General Staff conclusion was that AIF units would have to make up the numbers needed because of the shortage of equipment which would exist until local production increased:

> If we have to mobilise in Australia before the Militia Forces can be brought up to war strength, it must be clearly understood that the A.I.F. will have to be used to provide the necessary officers, N.C.O.s and specialists to complete the A.M.F. units. We cannot mobilise the A.M.F. and maintain [the] existing A.I.F.

In detail it was proposed that

> all A.I.F. units in each Command should be organised to form a complete Division for home defence, Corps Troops units being used as appropriate, i.e., a Pioneer Battalion to complete an Infantry Brigade or other suitable Corps Troops in lieu of non-maintained units.[28]

Again the army and government leaders were advocating at home what they would never have countenanced overseas: the splitting of brigades and divisions.

The system for mobilisation recommended by the General Staff was unwieldy and had all the appearances of having been devised in haste. In an emergency the AIF would be broken up to fight alongside the only partly-formed militia in ad hoc formations, when instead it should have been concentrated. Lavarack considered the scheme 'impossible' and 'negative' and produced a counter-proposal for consideration by the Military Board. In it he stated that it was fallacious to assume that any difference existed between home and imperial defence. Consequently all new Australian forces should be raised on a general service basis (in effect giving them AIF status) and that existing AMF divisions should be converted to general service formations. Men who did not wish to remain on a general service basis could be transferred to garrison formations and be replaced by volunteers.

Lavarack also criticised the dispersal of battalions and brigades around Australia, arguing that AIF formations should be concentrated to reach a high standard of training as soon as possible instead of squandering their potential effectiveness by scattering them piecemeal about the country. He concluded:

> If this brings up the vexed question of non-voluntary service abroad I believe that this problem could and should be faced now. If, for political reasons, it cannot be faced, I believe still that the divisions provided could be raised on a general service basis, provided that the public is warned that men will be called up in any case for full-time home service. It is not the idea of service abroad that deters men from service so much as the fear of losing their jobs. I should therefore make it known that any call-up would be for full-time duty, [and then] men would enlist for G.S. rather than be called up.[29]

There was logic in Lavarack's proposal. The AIF had been given priority in training and equipment and so should have been concentrated to reach as high a standard as possible so that it could provide a well-trained and cohesive home defence force, a nucleus about which the other divisions (which had to be raised to reach the target of 250,000) could be formed. This would have happened if Lavarack's proposals had been accepted, with the added advantage that the new divisions would in effect, if not in name, also be AIF formations. Not only would this have streamlined the system in 1940, it would have pre-empted the controversy about conscription for service overseas which would arise after Japan's entry into the war. However, nothing came of Lavarack's suggestion, as he later noted:

This proposal was not given much consideration [at the meeting], largely, I think, because the Minister, the C.G.S., and the M.B. had already decided what they intended to do before the conference met.[30]

In any case, Lavarack had no time to dwell on it. Apart from the problems of men and equipment there were other obstacles which he had to overcome, in particular the changing order of battle of his division. In June the 7th Division had two brigades in Australia (the 20th and 21st) and one in the Middle East (the 19th), and the 6th Division had two brigades in the Middle East (the 16th and 17th) and one in the United Kingdom (the 18th). So that the 6th Division would be complete it was decided to incorporate into it the 19th Brigade and transfer the 18th Brigade to the 7th Division. This arrangement persisted until the next month, when it was decided that the 18th Brigade would no longer be part of the 7th Division and that a new brigade, the 26th, would be formed in Australia to bring the division up to strength. So after July Lavarack had the task of raising a new brigade with all its teething problems, and as a result the division would not be at a uniform standard of training for another three months, at about the time it was due to leave Australia.[31]

The destination of the 7th Division, and at one stage whether Lavarack would go with it, had not been foregone conclusions. When the 7th Division was raised it had been decided that it would go to the Middle East after training in Australia, but in late June it seemed possible that, as the formation most advanced in training, it could go to Singapore in response to a British request. After the fall of France and the entry of Italy into the war Britain was in a difficult position. Without the aid of the French fleet the Royal Navy could not contend with the German and Italian navies in the Atlantic and the Mediterranean and still send a fleet to Singapore, as it had been promising to do for two decades. However, the British view was that Singapore was just as likely to be attacked from the landward side, through Thailand, as it was by sea. Therefore the land defences at least should be reinforced. And so on 28 June Australia was asked to provide a division for the defence of Malaya and Singapore.[32]

After the Australian chiefs of staff and the War Cabinet had considered the issue for two months, it was finally decided to inform the British government that it would be preferable to have the 7th Division sent to India to relieve an Indian formation for duty in Singapore, but should this not be possible it was agreeable that the division go to Malaya.

The War Cabinet had ratified a conclusion reached by the chiefs of staff which was difficult to distinguish from those made ten and more years before: that the dominant factor in the defence of Australia was the security of the naval base at Singapore. The foundation for this conclusion was the assurance given by Churchill on 12 August:

> If, however, contrary to prudence and self-interest, Japan set about invading Australia or New Zealand on a large scale, I have explicit authority of Cabinet to assure you that we should then cut our losses in the Mediterranean and proceed to your aid, sacrificing every interest except only the defence position of this island on which all depends.[33]

Churchill's words were meaningless. As Lavarack and others had pointed out years before, Japan was likely to invade only when Britain could not come to Australia's aid.

Fortunately for Lavarack he was to be spared the irony of being the commander of the force sent to Malaya to bolster the crumbling Singapore strategy which he had fought to expose as CGS. On 18 September, in reply to the Australian offer of the 7th Division, the British government requested that the division now go to the Middle East as originally planned: the division's training could be completed more quickly in the Middle East, its presence there would help internal security, it would release other troops who had completed their training, and to have the division in India would benefit neither the Middle East nor Malaya. The Australian War Cabinet agreed on 23 September.[34]

Then, a few days later, it seemed that Lavarack's division might not go overseas at all. On the 27th Japan signed a pact with Germany and Italy, which prompted the Minister for the Army to raise the question whether this development would require the retention in Australia of the 7th Division. The official historian has written that

> The War Cabinet's estimation of the effect of the Axis pact is indicated by the fact that when the question was raised... it was decided that the original decision should stand and the army should proceed with the embarkation of the division for the Middle East.

The Australian government 'still fervently hoped for peace with Japan and believed in the possibility', and besides, as far as Australian expeditionary forces were concerned, its hearts and minds were in the Middle East.[35]

So the 7th Division was bound for the Middle East, but perhaps if Lavarack had had his way the division would have embarked without him. On 13 August an aircraft carrying the CGS, the Minister for the Army and several other key government figures crashed near Canberra killing all aboard. Immediately the news reached Blamey in the Middle East he cabled the Prime Minister that he was at the disposal of the government should it wish to recall him to Australia. Rowell believed that Blamey would have been happy to replace White and a letter Blamey wrote to Menzies four days later made it clear that he wanted to be CGS:

> In sending you a cable, I was influenced by the fact that if consideration
> of my recall came up you might think that I might feel it would be a
> little hard on me to be recalled from the Field Command. This would, of
> course, be the case normally ... The whole lot is somewhat less than a
> Major-General's command, and Mackay is quite capable of handling it, if
> I am wanted elsewhere.[36]

Apparently Lavarack was of the same mind, for the day after the accident he was in Canberra to discuss White's replacement with Menzies, but after speaking to the Prime Minister he felt that it was most likely that Blamey would be recalled. In the end, neither Blamey nor Lavarack was appointed CGS, White's place being taken by Sturdee who vacated the command of the 8th Division to take up the post in early September. Perhaps the government did not wish to change the commander of the 7th Division so close to embarkation, but it is more likely that Lavarack's previous unpopularity as CGS ensured that he did not fill the post again. Menzies especially was unlikely to allow him back into Army HQ again as CGS. The die was cast: Lavarack would embark for the Middle East the next month as a division commander in the AIF under Blamey.[37]

Clockwise, from top left: **Beginnings.** Lavarack in 1887 aged two years; newly-commissioned Lieutenant J.D. Lavarack, 1905; John and Sybil Lavarack on their wedding day in 1912 shortly before leaving for England where Captain Lavarack would attend the prestigious two-year staff college course at Camberley. (SLQ)

Above: **United Kingdom, 1913.** John and Sybil Lavarack epitomise Edwardian England while boating on the lake at the Staff College, Camberley. (SLQ)

Below: **Staff College, Camberley.** Lavarack (centre) surrounded by other soldiers of the empire in a detail from a photograph of his staff college class. Their course was truncated because of the outbreak of hostilities in 1914. The war in which they were about to fight would weaken their empire irretrievably and eventually put Australia at risk. (SLQ)

Above: **The First World War.** Lavarack, Blamey and staff of the 4th Division, AIF, with the French Prime Minister, M. Georges Clemenceau, during his only visit to the Australian front. Lieutenant-Colonel J.D. Lavarack is second from the right (between an unidentified French officer and Major-General E.G. Sinclair MacLagan). Brigadier-General T.A. Blamey is second from the left. The careers of Lavarack and Blamey were to be intertwined for years in rancorous rivalry which began around this time. (AWM)

Left: **Lieutenant-Colonel Lavarack in 1918.** The war offered Lavarack scant chance to command troops, but he had shown himself to be a gifted staff officer during service with both the British and Australian armies in Macedonia and France. For his valuable, and progressively more responsible, work he was made a Companion of the Order of St Michael and George, awarded the Distinguished Service Order, the French Croix de Guerre, and was mentioned in dispatches three times. (SLQ)

Above: **The Governor-General of Australia.** Viscount Stonehaven, who served from from 1925 to 1930, is pictured with his aides-de-camp. Lavarack is fifth from the right. Two steps below him, Brigadier-General Blamey converses with Stonehaven. (SLQ)

Left: **Commandant of the Royal Military College.** In 1935 Lavarack relinquished this post to become Chief of the General Staff. Although still relatively junior, his intelligence and undoubted ability had ensured that he would supersede a number of officers to lead the army through one of its most difficult periods. The post-Depression years saw the army starved of funds because of the misplaced faith of successive Australian governments in British promises of Royal Navy assistance in the event of war in the Pacific. As expectations grew of another world war, Lavarack argued that Britain was too weak to come to Australia's aid. (SLQ)

Right: **Sir Maurice Hankey, Secretary of the Committee of Imperial Defence, London.** Lavarack was critical of Hankey's advice to the Australian government on defence policy which championed the role of the Royal Navy, to the detriment of the Australian army and air force. Hankey's influence over Australian policy makers, especially the Secretary of the Department of Defence, Sir Frederick Shedden (who acquired the nickname of 'Pocket Hankey'), and the Minister of Defence, Sir Archdale Parkhill, would generate conflict with the Military Board and greatly inhibit the country's preparedness for war. (LoC)

Below: **The Military Board, c.1935.** The CGS, Major-General Lavarack (far left), and the Minister of Defence, Sir Archdale Parkhill, with the Military Board. Lavarack clashed with the bumptious Parkhill over defence policy. Neither Major-General Sir Carl Jess, the Adjutant-General (on Parkhill's left), nor the other military member of the Board, Major-General O.F. Phillips, the Quartermaster-General (far right), eased Lavarack's task as CGS: Jess was obstructive and Phillips amiable, but ineffectual. (SLQ)

Right: **The CGS with with government ministers.** Discussing the effects of the Depression are (from left to right): former Prime Minister and Minister for External Affairs, Billy Hughes; the Treasurer, Richard (later Baron) Casey; and the Chief of the General Staff, Major-General Lavarack. (SLQ)

Below: **The Australian Council of Defence, 1938.** Standing, left to right: Major-General J.D. Lavarack, CGS; Air Vice Marshal Richard Williams, CAS; General Sir Harry Chauvel; Arthur Leighton, Controller-General of Munitions Supply; Noel Brodribb, Inspector-General of Works and Supplies; Major-General Sir Thomas Blamey, Controller-General of Recruiting; and Lieut-Gen Sir Brudenell White. Seated, left to right: Admiral Sir Ragnar Colvin, CNS; Frederick Shedden, Secretary of the Department of Defence; Geoffrey Street, Minister for Defence; Joseph Lyons, Prime Minister; Stanley Bruce, High Commissioner to the United Kingdom; and Richard Casey, Treasurer. (SLV)

Above: **Powerful Triumvirate.** The Prime Minister, R.G. Menzies (centre), shares a drink with the commander of the Second Australian Imperial Force, Lieutenant-General Blamey, and the Secretary of the Department of Defence, Frederick Shedden, during a visit to the Middle East in early 1941. After the outbreak of war Lavarack's career was largely in their hands. Blamey had not wanted Lavarack in the AIF and had tried to deny him a command, but was overruled by the government. Menzies was a Blamey supporter who would later refuse to promote Lavarack to full general. Shedden had clashed with Lavarack over defence policy in the years before the war and worked against him behind the scenes. (AWM)

Above: **Division Commander.** Lieutenant-General Lavarack, then GOC Southern Command, is congratulated by his staff in March 1940 on his being given command of the 7th Division in the Second AIF. When Blamey failed to prevent Lavarack being appointed to the AIF, he reversed the proposed order of division commanders so that a militia officer, Major-General Iven Mackay, not Lavarack, would command the better prepared 6th Division and so be the first to depart for the Middle East to take Australian troops into action. (SLQ)

Right: **Once more a major-general.** Lavarack, wearing the diamond-shaped shoulder patch of the 7th Division, in late 1940. After his appointment to the Second AIF Lavarack did not hesitate to accept a drop in rank to major-general to raise the 7th Division and take it abroad on active service. (AWM)

Right: **Preparing for war.** Lavarack with Sister M. Brown of the Australian Army Nursing Service and Brigadier J.E.S. Stevens. All wear the 7th Division's diamond-shaped shoulder patch. Stevens, a citizen officer, would command the 21st Brigade of Lavarack's 7th Division during the campaign in Syria. His skill and determination in advancing on Beirut along the narrow coast road, against stiff opposition, would earn the admiration of Lavarack who called the brigade the 'perfect team, and Stevens the master'. (AWM)

Below: **Embarking for war.** Major-General Lavarack, GOC 7th Division (centre, rear), and some of his 'hand-picked' staff aboard HMT *Mauretania*, before sailing for the Middle East in October 1940. Lavarack's GSO1, Colonel John Chapman (who as a major-general would be deputy chief of the general staff in 1944), stands to his left. Next to Chapman is Major Henry Wells, a future chief of the general staff. Second on Lavarack's right is Colonel Allan Boase, who would rise to the rank of lieutenant-general. Lavarack's ADC, Captain Curtis Wilson, is seated centre front. (AWM)

Left: **The 'Desert Fox'.** Generalleutnant Erwin Rommel, the commander of German and Italian forces in North Africa, monitors operations at Tobruk. Rommel's *Afrika Korps* halted the westward advance of the Allies in early 1941 and began pushing them back towards Tobruk and Egypt. In April 1941 Lavarack was given the task of stopping him. (AWM)

Below: **Tobruk Defenders.** Men of the 2/48th Battalion man a forward post on the Tobruk perimeter on 14 April 1941. Although the battalion was transferred to the 9th Division in early 1941, it had originally been raised and trained as part of Lavarack's 7th Division. Lavarack's plan for the defence of Tobruk in the 'Easter Battle' of 1941 was bold and depended upon the Australian defenders separating the German infantry from their tanks, which they did with devastating success. Beginning with Lavarack's victory, the garrison at Tobruk resisted all Rommel's attempts to take the town and its strategically important port until June 1942. (AWM)

Above: **Tobruk Victim.** A German Panzer Mark IV, which was destroyed during Rommel's unsuccessful attack on 14 April 1941, is examined by members of the defending garrison. (AWM)

Below: **Tobruk Prisoners.** An Australian intelligence officer talks to German POWs. In the 'Easter Battle' Lavarack inflicted the first defeat on Rommel in North Africa. Some German troops were so shocked at the failure and their heavy losses that they wept. Yet Blamey made sure that Lavarack was replaced in Tobruk only days after his victory. (AWM)

8

'What sort of person does he think I am?'

Palestine, 1940-1941

EARLY IN THE MORNING of 20 October 1940 Lavarack and the headquarters of the 7th Australian Division departed St Kilda Road to board HMT *Mauretania* at Port Melbourne. The next afternoon outside Port Phillip Bay the *Mauretania* joined the *Queen Mary* and the *Aquitania*, which had sailed from Sydney with units of the 20th and 21st Brigades, and the convoy sailed for Fremantle in Western Australia escorted by HMAS *Perth*. After pausing in Fremantle to embark the 2/16th Battalion the convoy made its way into the Indian Ocean. Almost two-thirds of the division was now en route for the Middle East and the 26th Brigade would follow in November, with the last few units travelling in the December convoy. On board the same ship as Lavarack was his eldest son, John, who had fulfilled his father's early ambition of becoming a doctor and had been assigned as a medical officer to a field ambulance unit which sailed with the 7th Division.[1]

On 4 November the division arrived at Bombay. There it transferred to smaller ships for the final leg of the journey to the Middle East because it was considered unwise to risk the loss of the larger ships in which it left Australia. At Bombay Lavarack temporarily parted company with his command. He left by aircraft for the Middle East with four of his staff on 7 November and two days later, after one engine failure and almost colliding with a hillside while landing, arrived in Palestine. He was met by Brigadier Rowell and Major K.A. Wills of 1st Australian Corps Headquarters, and then driven to Jerusalem, where he spent the night before travelling to Gaza to meet Blamey on 10 November.[2]

One of the first tasks Blamey gave Lavarack was the temporary command of the 6th Australian Division because Major-General Mackay, and his 17th Brigade, had been ordered to Crete to bolster the defence there by the Commander-in-Chief, Middle East, General Sir Archibald Wavell. Although Wavell reversed his decision a short time later, Lavarack's preparations for the job would consume valuable time and require additional travelling in the fortnight after his arrival. During those two weeks Lavarack met senior British officers, inspected the camp sites for his own troops and ensured that all was in readiness for their arrival.

On 23 November he drove from Cairo to Ismailia on the Suez Canal where the first groups of the 7th Division had arrived. He visited Brigadiers Murray and Stevens aboard their ships and the next day drove to Kantara to watch the disembarkation of his troops. Unfortunately he could not remain long because he had fallen ill the previous night. Two days later he was admitted to hospital with dysentery, but continued to administer the division from his bed until his discharge at the end of the first week in December. The division's chief medical officer, Colonel F.K. Norris, thought that Lavarack's illness, although unfortunate from a personal point of view, was

> a blessing for the Division, as henceforth I had only to suggest to him
> any measures to prevent the prevalent bowel disorders (the "Gippy"
> tummy) when he would immediately issue blistering orders and enforce
> them; it was too easy.[3]

By the end of November the 7th Division (less four battalions, the divisional cavalry regiment, a field regiment, a field company and a field ambulance) was settled in Palestine, occupying a series of camps extending some twenty-five miles northwards from Gaza to Qastina along a sandy, sparsely-vegetated coastal plain. Norris recorded that Lavarack's headquarters was established

> on a gently sloping hill overlooking what had once been the fertile fields
> of Philista [sic], but which over the centuries had been sterilised and
> buried under dunes of drifting sands. Nearby was the typical Arab
> village of Deir Suneid, a collection of mud huts separated by unpaved
> muddy lanes down which ran all the village drainage. Along the

alleyways at all hours of the day moved black-robed women with faces hidden by their yashmaks, except for their dark eyes.[4]

In mid-December the next convoy arrived, carrying with it the 26th Brigade and by the end of the month the division was complete except for one battalion, the divisional cavalry regiment and a field ambulance, all of which would come under Lavarack's command during the first two weeks of January 1941.[5]

However, although the 7th Division had left Australia behind, many of the difficulties which had beset it there persisted in Palestine. Contrary to expectations, arrival in the Middle East was not the panacea for equipment problems, which were to continue to dog Lavarack for several months to come, as one unit historian illustrated:

> From the day that the first man had reported into Ingleburn, the Regiment had been encouraged by the prospect of its fighting equipment's being "just around the corner". During the last few weeks before sailing, each man had consoled himself with the certainty that it would be waiting on disembarkation. During the voyage all had imagined that one day very soon the Regiment would march through the "IN" gate of some huge depot, and roll through the "OUT" gate, complete in every detail. On arrival at Deir Suneid, they said "This is IT!" Probably no one then realised the effects and the extent of the disaster in France. The depots were practically empty, even of their emergency reserves.

Not only was there a shortage of equipment, but even of the forms needed to indent for equipment. One of Lavarack's greatest problems was that materiel, especially transport, was being taken from the 7th Division for use by the 6th in preparation for the planned attack on Bardia in early January. The entry in the 7th Division war diary for 31 December reads:

> The month closes with training equipment in a most unsatisfactory position. Essential MT Lorries 3-ton and 30-cwt are so scarce that training in movement is impossible. The supply of SAA is so limited that even reinforcements could not complete a recognised course and LMG practices are quite out of the question. The Div Arty have not yet been issued with either Fd gun, How, or A-Tk gun [sic]. The scale of issue of A-Tk rifles—3 per bn—is totally inadequate for anything more than cadre training.[6]

Infantry battalions began to receive anti-tank rifles and Bren guns for the first time in January, but not in sufficient numbers to permit effective training. On a visit to the 2/16th Battalion on 7 January Lavarack observed that during weapon training there were too many men around each light machine gun for one instructor to manage. Artillery units fared no better, as one unit historian recorded:

> There was a little consolation, only as a sign that the worst might be over, when four very antiquated howitzers, together with an 18-pounder gun of equally archaic vintage, arrived on 8 January. There were no sights, gun stores or anything much else. Someone made crude sights out of cardboard…It was all of such little help in keeping nearly 700 men 'on their toes'.

When the 2/4th Field Regiment supported the 21st Brigade in an exercise all the field guns and transport of the division had to be pooled for the purpose. In mid-February the 2nd Anti-Tank Regiment was supplied with captured Italian guns, but even by mid-March the division's senior artillery commander (or CRA) could complain that his units remained so short of equipment that it was impossible to conduct one troop drill per troop even once a week. At about that time the 21st Brigade was still trying to secure blade foresights for all its Bren guns and enough ammunition to zero them. One battalion did not fire the Boys anti-tank rifle in training because ammunition for it was never issued and in another unit each man was able to fire only one round. In March transport was still being withdrawn from Lavarack for the benefit of other formations and ammunition for training remained in short supply throughout the division.[7]

Personnel problems also persisted and there were so many changes in staff appointments after arrival in the Middle East that Lavarack's headquarters was rarely at full strength. On 26 November he lost his senior administrative and logistics officer, the AA&QMG, Colonel Boase, who was promoted by Blamey and placed in command of the AIF Administrative Base and Line of Communication Units. The move was especially annoying since Boase's replacement was, according to General Vasey, 'a most useless fool'. Another blow to Lavarack had been the loss of his CRA, Milford, who left on promotion in early December. However, his replacement, Brigadier Berryman (an exceptional officer who, it will be recalled, had been Lavarack's first choice as GSO1), was a most welcome addition to the division, but did not take up duty until 25 January, which meant that Lavarack was without his artillery commander for six weeks.[8]

By the end of January the disruption of staff throughout the division had become one of Lavarack's most pressing problems. Brigade training in particular was being hampered seriously by the lack of trained brigade-majors. It was not until the end of February that brigade-majors for the 21st and 26th Brigades arrived, but that was offset by Lavarack losing his deputy administrative officer (DAAG). Divisional headquarters and the brigades continued to lose officers, some to Blamey's headquarters, as late as March.

To ameliorate the personnel problem Lavarack had been trying to have those of his staff officers who had been detached, rather than trans-ferred, returned to the division, but without much success. Visits by senior staff officers to units and formations were perforce curtailed. Lav-arack, however, was the exception—he made frequent visits to units and was often seen during exercises, as a battalion historian noted: 'General Lavarack took a close interest in the exercises, and was apt to be present at unlikely times and places'.[9]

These visits to units occasionally allowed Lavarack to indulge his taste for history. He took great interest in areas which had been the scene of past campaigns or still showed evidence of Roman occupation. Perhaps he wondered if the legates in command of the long-gone Roman legions suffered similar interference from senior commanders while they were in Palestine almost two millennia before, for as well as individual members of staff, Lavarack also lost units and sub-units for varying periods. In December the 2/17th Battalion took over garrison duties at the Suez Canal from a British regiment. At the same time GHQ Middle East ordered him to detach a field company to construct a prisoner of war cage. The next month Lavarack lost his CRE, the senior engineer in the division, and most of his field companies when they were placed at Wavell's disposal and moved to Egypt. A week later the sole remaining field company was taken away for work on the Suez Canal. The next day a signals company was ordered to Egypt. In March the divisional cavalry regiment was taken from the division and later sent to Cyprus. Like the problems with personnel, there was little that Lavarack could do to prevent such frustrating unit detachments.[10]

However, despite all these unforeseen difficulties and distractions, it was paramount that training continue. By the time the bulk of the 7th Division had embarked in Australia it had reached a reasonable standard considering the difficult circumstances under which it was raised. (The exceptions were mainly in the 26th Brigade which had been formed later than the other two, and as a consequence individual training in that formation had begun only in the second half of August.) But after the long sea voyage the efficiency of the division had declined. Training on board ship had been restricted to rifle and respirator drill, map reading and physical training, and after leaving India in the smaller transports even this programme had been curtailed. Only hard training in Palestine could first restore, and then surpass, the standard reached in Australia. At least Palestine's rocky, undulating hills, almost devoid of trees, were perfect for the kind of training which was now needed. To the disgust of the troops, however, they first had to endure elementary drill, weapon-handling and field-craft refresher courses to regain the standards of individual proficiency and physical fitness achieved in Australia before progressing to unit and formation training.[11]

Although some unit training had begun in Australia, little had been achieved before embarkation. In mid-January Lavarack called a conference of his brigade commanders and other senior officers to review progress since the division's arrival in the Middle East. From the outset Lavarack had insisted on high standards and stressed particularly the need for troops to be able to operate effectively at night and to develop an aggressive spirit against tanks and aircraft. He now emphasised that the division must be ready in the shortest possible time to go into action and that desert warfare, while uppermost in most minds at that time, should be considered as only one type of operation—the division had to have sound training in all types. It would not be long before the wisdom of that approach would become readily apparent to the men of the 7th Division.

Lavarack hoped that by the end of the month he could begin sending each of his brigades into the line for a short time so that they might have some experience of battle conditions. It would be a little longer, however, before they would be ready for action. Although Stevens was confident in mid-January that the 21st Brigade was ready for a brigade exercise, Murray (20th Brigade) told Lavarack that it would be a week before he could begin battalion exercises. Tovell (26th Brigade) said that it would be another month before platoon training was completed, an unsurprising delay since the 26th had been formed three months after the other two brigades. As the official historian wrote: 'In short, the soldiers had been trained to fight but the officers and staffs had not yet been trained in battle management'.[12]

Nevertheless, progress was steady, especially by Steven's 21st Brigade, and by the end of February the divisional war diarist could record:

Training was advanced at a greater speed during the month and all battalions carried out exercises which involved considerable powers of endurance on the part of all ranks. 21 Aust Inf Bde increased its pace and successfully carried out a brigade group exercise extending over five days.

Three weeks later Lavarack arranged that an advanced divisional headquarters and the divisional signals would operate in another 21st Brigade exercise.

It would only be several more weeks before the division reached a uniform standard of training, after which Lavarack's command would be ready to join the fighting. When the Prime Minister, Menzies, visited the 7th Division early in February he referred to it as a 'crack division'. It was the first feather in Lavarack's cap as the commander, but his ADC noted during the Prime Minister's visit that 'Blamey watches over him to see that the other AIF generals do not get too much of his ear'. Blamey, of course, had Menzies' ear and it was at this time that Menzies (who was accompanied by Lavarack's erstwhile opponent during the Singapore strategy debates, Frederick Shedden) arranged for Blamey to be promoted to lieutenant-general in the Australian Military Forces as well as the Australian Imperial Force. The impetus behind the promotion was Lavarack. Although Blamey had engineered Lavarack's reduction in rank to major-general in the AIF, Lavarack still held the rank of lieutenant-general in the AMF and was thus senior to Blamey in the Australian army at home.[13]

Regardless of Blamey's machinations, Lavarack was pleased that the 7th Division was progressing so well. But his efforts to weld his command into an effective fighting formation were dealt a severe blow in late February. Earlier that month Wavell had been ordered by the British War Cabinet to make the provision of aid to Greece his primary aim, and initially he intended that the Australian 7th and 9th Divisions would be used for that purpose. Blamey, however, insisted that the 6th Division go to Greece and that it be replaced in the western desert by the 9th. He then ordered an extensive reorganisation of the Australian divisions in preparation for the expedition to Greece. This had profound ramifications for the 7th Division. On 24 February Lavarack was told that two of his brigades (the 20th and 26th) would be transferred to the 9th Division. The next day he learnt that they would be replaced by the 18th and 25th Brigades which had originally formed the nucleus of the 9th Division.[14]

The divisional war diarist wrote that the reorganisation was a blow, especially as far as the 20th Brigade was concerned since it had been with the division since its formation. For those leaving it was also a wrench and some regarded it as a type of collective demotion. Naturally Lavarack was not happy either, as he recorded in his diary:

> 20 and 26 Bdes to join 9 Div and be replaced by 18 and 25 Bdes...Reason given [is that the] latter [are] better equipped and more ready for immediate service work. Don't like losing our Bdes and fear that quality of new ones, especially 25th, will be inferior.

After seeing the 25th Brigade (which had been formed in England in June 1940 from technical troops and personnel from the 18th Brigade) he felt that most of its senior officers and adjutants were weak. Lavarack was keen on promoting from the ranks and therefore also felt that with the changes he had lost two good reservoirs of potential officers.

It was not all bad news, though. Lavarack had little to fear as far as the quality of the 18th Brigade was concerned—it had been formed as part of the 6th Division in 1939 and was one of the best trained brigades in the AIF. Moreover, both brigades were relatively well-equipped and, all things considered, the 7th Division probably benefited from the re-organisation more than it suffered. Lavarack's nephew, Brigadier J.G. Ochiltree, then a staff officer at 26th Brigade headquarters, has recalled of Lavarack that 'although disappointed at this move he was philosophical about it and re-garded the transfers as being in the best interests of the AIF'.

Even so, it was difficult for Lavarack to see his command dismembered at Blamey's behest. When the 20th Brigade left for Egypt on 26–27 Febru-ary he wrote that it was the 'beginning of [the] break-up of Bob Menzies' "crack division"'. He expressed the same sentiment about the 26th Bri-gade's departure on 11 March, adding: 'Begins to look as though 7 Div will miss the bus again'.[15]

Blamey's senior staff officer, Brigadier Rowell, suspected personal motives had played a part in Blamey's decision to reorganise the AIF divisions and to send the 6th Division to Greece. Rowell agreed with Wavell's decision to send Lavarack's division first because it was 'concentrated in Palestine, had a reasonable standard of efficiency and could be brought up to G.1098 [war] scale in equipment and M[otor] T[ransport]', whereas the 6th Division, 'on the other hand, was in Libya after the 1940-41 campaign. It was down in personnel, MT and equipment, and it was getting a bit battle worn', but:

> Mainly for the reason that Blamey did not like Lavarack...and did not want his Div first into Greece, he demurred at [the] C-in-C's decision and there was a first class row. As a result, it was decided to relieve 6 Aust Div in Libya by 9 Aust Div. In view of the existing state of communications and general lack of transport, this was a most difficult move. Personally, I never agreed with Blamey's attitude, which gave everyone a severe headache and resulted in us getting in Greece a formation (6 Aust Div) which was no better than 7 Aust Div, although untried in battle, would have been.[16]

Officially Blamey denied that the issue had caused any trouble between himself and Wavell, and told the Minister for the Army that he had decided to send the 6th, and not the 7th Division, first because it was the most highly-trained of his formations. But Rowell saw the incident as being similar to Blamey's insistence the previous year that Lavarack be given the 7th Division and not the 6th and therefore as another example of the way in which Blamey was prepared to allow personal motives to overcome professional considerations. However, Blamey's ADC, Carlyon, dismissed such allegations:

> Some critics have alleged that Blamey was influenced in this by his dislike of Lavarack...and that he wanted to deny Lavarack the chance to be the first Australian commander to oppose Hitler's Army in Greece. That is nonsense. Blamey made the realistic decision that the formation which had just been toughened and tested in the Western Desert fighting was the one better prepared to take the first impact of German blitzkrieg tactics.[17]

That there were sound reasons for reorganising the AIF divisions in the Middle East and for changing the order in which they went to Greece cannot be denied. But equally there is little doubt that Blamey did not want Lavarack to be the first on the ground in Greece despite Carlyon's protestations (which are entirely understandable from a young aide-de-camp who is almost bound to see events through the eyes of his military master). More than that, though, Blamey soon made it clear that he didn't want Lavarack in Greece at all.

On 27 February Lavarack received a signal from Blamey urgently summoning him to Cairo, preferably the next day. To Lavarack's surprise, when he met Blamey at Shepheard's Hotel in the evening of the 28th, he was offered command of AIF Rear Headquarters in Egypt during Blamey's absence in Greece. To make it more palatable, Blamey also offered Lavarack succession to the command of the AIF in the Middle East if he did not return. Lavarack, after noting that Blamey had no authority to guarantee his successor, wrote in his diary later that night:

> Fortunately [Blamey] gave me [the] option of accepting or refusing, so refused at once. What sort of person does he think I am? Refused without hesitation. T.A.B. then, without regard to my refusal, asked me to take till next morning "to think it over".

The next morning Lavarack, as he recorded, met Blamey again:

> Repaired to T.A.B.'s office and there positively refused to accept offer of job at rear H.Q. during his absence in Greece. T.A.B. then said [he] would appoint Plant, whom he dislikes for some obscure reason connected with the last war and who was foisted on him as a Bde Comd by Brudenell White in this.[18]

Obviously Blamey was doing his best to minimise Lavarack's prominence in the AIF, so it must have been with misgivings that he received a message several days later which requested that Lavarack go to Egypt to meet the Chief of the Imperial General Staff, Sir John Dill, who was visiting the Middle East. Lavarack recorded that Blamey simply sent him a 'cryptic wire' ordering him to Egypt with no explanation. Only on arrival did Lavarack discover that the purpose of the journey was to meet his old friend John Dill. Lavarack saw him at Wavell's residence and later in the evening at the house of Air Chief Marshal Sir Arthur Longmore (AOC-in-C, Middle East), together with Air Marshals Drummond and Tedder (the latter having been at the IDC with Lavarack).[19] That Lavarack was keeping such exalted company would have done nothing to soothe Blamey.

Nor would Blamey have been celebrating Lavarack's obvious success in preparing the 7th Division for war. In less than a year after his appointment to the AIF Lavarack had raised and trained the division under difficult circumstances, both in Australia and in the Middle East. The high standard of training attained was testament to Lavarack's professional ability and the calibre of the commanders and staff he had chosen. Brigadier Stevens wrote that during this period 'General Lavarack was always courteous, kindly and helpful. I enjoyed working under him. He had a fine military brain and extensive military knowledge'. Lavarack's training policy was realistic, especially in that he had emphasised the need for troops to treat tanks and aircraft aggressively, a necessary attribute considering the way these weapons would soon be used by the enemy in the Western Desert. He had also rightly decided, as events would soon prove, that the division must not limit itself to preparing for war in the desert alone.[20] Lavarack had shown that a Staff Corps officer, with almost no experience of field command, could raise and train an infantry division to be ready for battle. It now remained to be seen if Lavarack himself could handle a division on the battlefield.

Lavarack confidently expected that he would soon find himself in command of his division in action in Greece. When Lavarack farewelled Blamey, and his 'vast quantities of baggage', on the latter's departure for Greece on 18 March it was planned that the 7th Division also would be concentrated there by late April or early May. Blamey had failed in his attempt to prevent Lavarack going to Greece by trying to entice him to remain in Egypt with empty offers of future advancement. Without Lavarack's concurrence Blamey had no grounds which could justify his ordering Lavarack to stay behind—if there had been any, there is little doubt that Blamey would have resorted to them. The only result of his desperate bid to keep Lavarack out of the campaign had been to expose once again his loathing of a man he saw as a rival. For his part, Lavarack could hardly have been relishing the prospect of serving under Blamey in Greece, even if it did mean taking his division into action. However, events in North Africa were soon to intervene to spare them both: on 6 April, the day the German attack on Greece began, Blamey was informed that Lavarack's division was needed in North Africa and would not be joining his force fighting beside the Greek army.

9

'A bloody insult'

Tobruk, April 1941

ON 3 APRIL LAVARACK received orders that he and a small staff were to report to Alexandria for embarkation on the 6th to join 'Lustreforce', the codename given to the Allied force sent to Greece. However, events were moving fast and that same day Wavell had decided that a front had to be established immediately in the Western Desert if the enemy advance into the eastern region of Libya, known as Cyrenaica, was to be halted. German and Italian forces under General Erwin Rommel were advancing rapidly, pushing British and Australian troops back towards Tobruk and the Egyptian frontier. On the afternoon of the 3rd, after visiting the front line, Wavell cabled Churchill that to counter the enemy threat in Cyrenaica he intended to send part of Lavarack's 7th Division to Tobruk instead of Greece.[1]

The next day reinforcements began to head west to Cyrenaica, and in the evening Wavell summoned Lavarack to tell him of the change of plans for the 7th Division. In Lavarack's words:

Gen Wavell consulted me on the question of sending my 18 Inf Bde to Tobruk, together with 2/4 Aust Fd Coy, 2/5 Aust Fd Amb and a British Army Field Regt, in an endeavour to forestall the danger to 9 Aust Div's left flank and rear. This consultation was probably more formal than real, as something had to be done in any case to assist 9 Aust Div and the troops named were the only ones immediately available. I agreed. I was also informed that the move of my division to Greece would probably be cancelled and the division employed in an endeavour to stabilise the situation in the Western Desert. This information was the basis of my request, a few days later, for the addition of 7 Aust Div to the forces allotted for operations in and from Tobruk.

Lavarack pointed out to Wavell that he did not consider his division fully prepared for 'serious operations' because of the shortages in transport and other equipment, particularly artillery, and also because 'the state of training of the 25 Inf Bde could only be described as backward'. Wavell assured him that the deficiencies would rectified by the end of the month.[2]

On the 5th, after ordering Brigadier G.F. Wootten to take his 18th Brigade to Tobruk by road and sea immediately, Wavell sent the following message to Blamey:

> On urgent operational grounds have had to order 18 Aust Inf Bde to Tobruk. Owing to lack of reserves may also have to send remainder 7 Aust Div to Cyrenaica...Have cabled full details CIGS and have asked him to consult you. Am keeping Melbourne informed.[3]

When Blamey received this news 'he blew up' and cabled his protest against the arrangements to Wavell, who was sympathetic and optimistic that the 21st and 25th Brigades would still be able to go to Greece, and that they would be joined later by the 18th as soon as circumstances permitted. The reason for Wavell's optimism, as he explained to Lavarack early on the morning of the 5th, was the belief (later realised to be mistaken) that the enemy was not developing an eastwards thrust south of the coast road which ran through Tobruk to the Egyptian frontier. Nevertheless, the situation was still serious and Wavell told Lavarack that his planned departure for Greece the next day had been delayed, and that the rest of the 7th Division would probably also stay in Egypt until the crisis had passed. Having had his embarkation indefinitely postponed, Lavarack decided to go to Alexandria to see Wootten and Plant about the new role allocated to the 18th Brigade. During the remainder of that day and the next he was at Rear AIF HQ as reports arrived revealing the true gravity of the situation in Cyrenaica, which had been practically abandoned to the enemy after his troops arrived at Mechili. More unwelcome news was that the Germans had begun their invasion of Greece.[4]

At a conference in Cairo on the 6th attended by Sir Anthony Eden, Sir John Dill and the three service commanders-in-chief (Wavell, Cunningham and Longmore) it was decided that a stand against Rommel would be made at Tobruk, which might have to hold out for two months until sufficient forces could be built up to launch a counter-offensive. Wavell then decided finally that the 7th Division would not go to Greece but to Mersa Matruh, and, perhaps encouraged by Dill, that Lavarack would succeed General Neame as GOC Cyrenaica Command. Since the bulk of the fighting at Tobruk would fall upon four Australian brigades and also since the 7th Division would constitute a major part of the defence of Egypt, the official historian wrote that 'It was therefore natural that consideration should have been given to placing the force under an Australian commander'. Wavell later said that he had also considered Blamey and Mackay, but after the German invasion of Greece they were less likely candidates. Lavarack, who was still at Alexandria, received urgent orders to report to GHQ ME in Cairo by 11 a.m. the next day.[5]

When they met on the 7th Wavell explained the situation in Cyrenaica to Lavarack. The British 2nd Armoured Division had lost most of its tanks and the 9th Australian Division had been ordered to retire on Tobruk. At this stage Generals O'Connor and Neame were believed to have been either killed or captured and so Cyrenaica Command was without a commander. Wavell proposed to Lavarack that he take over Cyrenaica Command. Lavarack readily agreed, not only because he considered that there was no alternative, but also because 'Personally I regarded this as a blessed relief from control by a certain person [Blamey] and a chance of independent command'.

Arrangements were made for them to travel together to Tobruk early the next day, taking with them Lavarack's senior staff officer, Colonel Chapman, in case the whole division was eventually required to go there. Lavarack later wrote that at this meeting both Eden and Dill 'said goodbye to me as one unlikely to return'. Eden wrote of Lavarack that night: 'I was much impressed by his calm and grip of situation and readiness to take command at Tobruk'. In the evening Wavell informed the War Office and Blamey of his intentions: 'Dust storm now blowing. If weather permits am flying [Tobruk] to-morrow, and taking with me Laverack [sic] who will probably take over command of all forces in Cyrenaica.'[6]

All was in readiness for Lavarack's first taste of battle since 1918 and, although the outlook was not promising, he approached the prospect eagerly. As he worked late into the night repacking his kit for the desert, the defence was beginning to coalesce. Near Mechili, about 100 miles west of Tobruk, the headquarters of the British 2nd Armoured Division, the 3rd Indian Motor Brigade and other units, including part of the 2/3rd Australian Anti-Tank Regiment, were preparing to break through the enemy lines to join the defenders in the town. Much closer to Tobruk, Morshead's 9th Division (less the 24th Brigade, but supported by the 2nd Armoured Division Support Group) was astride the coast road with its left flank at Acroma, about 15 miles west of Tobruk. Behind them the 24th Brigade was already in Tobruk preparing the defences and had been joined during the day by the 18th Brigade. Covering the south and south-west approaches to Tobruk there was a small force at El Adem about sixteen miles from the town.[7]

At 7 a.m. on 8 April Lavarack, Wavell, Chapman and Lavarack's ADC, Wilson, left by air for Tobruk, but without fighter cover owing to the shortage of aircraft. Three hours later they landed at El Adem in the midst of a *khamsin* and were forced to wait on the airfield in the hot swirling dust for an hour before they could be found and driven away. Coincidentally, Lavarack's approaching adversary, Rommel, had himself only recently experienced a *khamsin* for the first time and described an attempt to drive in it:

> Now we realised what little idea we had had of the tremendous force of such a storm. Immense clouds of reddish dust obscured all visibility and forced the car's speed down to a crawl. Often the wind was so strong it was impossible to drive along the Via Balbia. Sand streamed down the windscreen like water. We gasped in breath painfully through handkerchiefs held over our faces and sweat poured off our bodies in the unbearable heat.[8]

Once at HQ Cyrenaica Command Lavarack spent the remainder of the morning discussing the situation with Wavell, Brigadiers Harding and Nares (the heads of the operational and administrative staffs of Cyrcom), and the local naval and air force commanders. During the conference Morshead and his GSO1, Colonel C.E.M. Lloyd, arrived and were ushered in; Morshead reported that his division had suffered few casualties and was in good order. Wavell then announced that Lavarack was to assume command in Cyrenaica and asked him if he would like written orders.

Lavarack replied that he would.[9] Wavell pencilled the following under the heading of 'Instructions to Major-General Laverack [sic] GOC 7th Australian Division':

1. You will take over command of all troops in Cyrenaica. Certain reinforcements have already been notified as being sent to you. You will be informed of any others which it is decided to send.

2. Your main task will be to hold the Enemy's advance at Tobruk, in order to give time for the assembly of reinforcements, especially of armoured troops, for the defence of Egypt.

3. To gain time for the assembly of the required reinforcements it may be necessary to hold Tobruk for about two months.

4. Should you consider after reviewing the situation and in the light of the strength deployed by the enemy that it is not possible to maintain your position at Tobruk for this length of time, you will report your views when a decision will be taken by G.H.Q.

5. You will in any case prepare a plan for withdrawal from Tobruk, by land and by sea, should withdrawal become necessary.

6. Your defence will be as mobile as possible and you will take any opportunity of hindering the enemy's concentration by offensive action.[10]

After accompanying Wavell to the airfield to begin his return journey, Lavarack made a preliminary reconnaissance of the Tobruk defences to the south and east while he considered the disposal of the forces under his command. These were situated in three areas: at Acroma, some 15 miles to the west, were the 20th and 26th Brigades of the 9th Division, the 1st Royal Horse Artillery (RHA), the 51st Field Regiment and the 1st/Royal Northumberland Fusiliers; to the south at El Adem was the 18th Indian Cavalry Regiment, there being joined by British and Australian units which had broken out of Mechili and soon to be joined by the 11th Hussars moving up from the frontier; in Tobruk was a more varied assortment of formations and units: the 18th and 24th Australian Brigades, the 104th RHA, the remainder of the Support Group of the 2nd Armoured Division, the 3rd Armoured Brigade, 1st Royal Tank Regiment, anti-tank and anti-aircraft units, service troops, three Libyan refugee battalions and three Indian pioneer companies. During the day the 3rd RHA arrived and the 107th RHA was expected the next day.

After completing his reconnaissance Lavarack instructed Morshead to withdraw his division to positions inside the perimeter the next day. Morshead demurred, not wanting to call upon his division to undertake the move at such short notice so soon after the long and tiring retreat from Benghazi, but Lavarack insisted the order be carried out, reminded by his First World War experience that 'men often surpass expectations in the way of mental and physical effort under stress'.[11]

Lavarack had decided that Morshead would be the commander of the fortress itself, and so responsible for its defence, under his own overall direction as GOC Cyrcom, and had allocated for the task the 9th Division, the 1st King's Dragoon Guards (a reconnaissance regiment), the 1st/Royal Northumberland Fusiliers (a machine gun battalion), four British artillery regiments, and the 2/1st Pioneer Battalion and other attached troops. Apart from the main force under Morshead's control, Lavarack had decided that under Brigadier W.H.E. Gott a mobile force, consisting mainly of the Support Group strengthened by the 11th Hussars (less one squadron), the 4th RHA (less one battery), and some other units, would operate outside the perimeter. Gott's force was to remain for the time being at El Adem supplying Lavarack with information about the enemy and ready to resist any hostile advance. Within the perimeter there would be a command reserve under the control of Lavarack himself, comprising Wootten's 18th Brigade, 'J' Battery of the 3rd RHA, and an improvised armoured force containing all the available tanks.[12]

However, having decided that this was how his force would be grouped, there remained the problem of organising its various components. The 9th Division, for example, did not have its artillery and so neither its CRA nor his artillery staff. Consequently, a commander had to be found, and a staff improvised, for the British artillery the division had been allotted. In the same way commanders and staffs had to be found for the anti-aircraft units and the tanks which had been reorganised in ad hoc formations and units. These problems Lavarack discussed with Harding in the afternoon after seeing Morshead; he then despatched a message to Wavell in which he stressed the necessity for accelerating tank repairs in the workshop at Alexandria.[13]

Gradually Lavarack was establishing some order from the chaos of retreat, but whether it would be possible to defend Tobruk successfully he had to determine quickly if he were not to be overtaken by the enemy's advance. Although the day had seen no offensive action by the enemy, there had been reports of large numbers of armoured vehicles moving towards Tobruk via the Derna Road, enemy activity near Acroma, and a force of tanks at Mechili. Furthermore, it was clear that the 2nd Armoured Division had suffered badly at the enemy's hands and it was unlikely that it could provide any substantial reinforcement of the garrison.[14] Apart from these reports the situation in the desert was mostly a mystery, but a decision had to be made immediately lest enemy action be allowed to force the issue.

To Lavarack's mind most factors seemed to point towards staying: Tobruk had supplies and ammunition enough to last four months, though Wavell had only asked for the garrison to hold out for two; strategically Lavarack thought it desirable that the enemy should have to reckon with a hostile force at Tobruk threatening the approaches to Egypt; also, at this stage no-one could be sure that Rommel would by-pass Tobruk and that, by abandoning it, enemy forces would not be freed immediately for an attack on Egypt. Moreover, Rommel's forces did not appear to be overwhelmingly superior to the combined strength of Tobruk and Egypt, morale was high amongst the British and Australians, and the prestige of British and Australian arms seemed to Lavarack to demand that if Tobruk was only remotely defensible, then the attempt should be made. In any case, he doubted whether a withdrawal with full fighting equipment was possible, probably because of difficulties with transport, and was certain that huge amounts of equipment and supplies would, through lack of time, remain in Tobruk undestroyed and thus available to the enemy. There was also the question of the physical condition of the troops. If Morshead was reluctant to move his men the 15 miles back to Tobruk it seemed unlikely that they would be able to endure an immediate, longer retreat to Egypt, although some could have been evacuated by sea. Also, Lavarack did not relish the idea of abandoning those men still making their way into Tobruk from the desert.[15] He summed up his situation:

> My position was that I could decide to stay and fight on my own
> responsibility, whereas if I decided that withdrawal was necessary I
> should have to consult the C-in-C. Time was short and a decision had to
> be taken that night if the alternative of evacuation were to be adopted.
> All available senior commanders and staff officers had already given

their views, and the general situation was clear, though the details were not. After weighing the pros and cons with my B.G.S., Brig. Harding, my conclusion was that we must stay and fight. Harding summed up the general feeling with the words 'Let's fight, sir', and so I decided.[16]

Lavarack rose early on the morning of the 9th to continue the preparations which were necessary if Tobruk were to withstand the blow from Rommel's forces which must soon fall. Lavarack made a thorough reconnaissance of the fortress area with Morshead, Harding and Wootten. Wavell had suggested to Lavarack during the flight from Cairo that it might not be possible to hold the 28-miles long outer perimeter with the forces available, and that he should consider basing his defence on the inner perimeter. But Lavarack soon realised that the inner perimeter existed in little more than name and was not an option. He therefore disregarded Wavell's advice and decided to base his defence on the outer perimeter:

> Though about 28 miles long, it was at any rate continuous. Here and there it [the anti-tank ditch] was filled with sand, but it was still a sufficient obstacle to prevent tank penetration on a broad front, provided the enemy were not allowed a free hand. Its length made it undesirable to do more than observe it, but I had already decided that mobile defence was the right method, since whatever we did we could not hope to prevent penetration by the enemy at his selected point. The defence was therefore to be based on fixed infantry posts, which were to be held however deeply the enemy might penetrate, distribution of all types of artillery in such a way as to cover the ditch and to break up a tank attack after penetration, and the strongest possible local and general reserves, including all available tanks, for counter-attack.[17]

Morshead disagreed, preferring to occupy the inner line, the Blue Line, arguing that he did not have enough troops to occupy the outer perimeter, but, as Wootten's brigade-major, who was present at the time, recalled:

> Lavarack, the professional, insisted that Morshead occupy the Red Line since withdrawal to the Blue Line would reduce the depth available to the garrison in which to manoeuvre and would bring Tobruk Harbour and the base installation within range of field artillery, so imperilling the only channel through which the garrison could be maintained.

Having made this decision early, the remainder of the day was taken up with allotting brigade sectors, the siting of a second line of defence based on the Blue Line (which would include switch lines), the location of Wootten's reserve brigade group, the selection of an inner 'keep' to be held by Wootten in extreme emergency, and the choice of a new site in open country for Lavarack's headquarters, which was in danger of being 'bombed out of Tobruk village'.[18]

Lavarack now wanted Morshead's 20th and 26th Brigades, both of which had until recently been part of Lavarack's division, within the perimeter as soon as possible because of reports in the afternoon of large-scale enemy activity. Morshead again demurred, this time on the ground that it was unwise to move the entire division in one night, and Lavarack noted that Morshead 'rightly feared the disorganisation that might result from such a comprehensive move'. However, enemy activity was increasing, especially to Morshead's front and on his left flank, and Lavarack decided that

> I could not take the risk that the 9 Div might be pinned on its front and attacked round its left flank at the same time. The loss of an appreciable proportion of the division, (to say nothing of its complete destruction), would obviously have been fatal. It was probable, also, that but little time would be allowed by the enemy for the organisation of the fortress area, and for this reason also it was necessary to bring the division inside with the least possible delay. I therefore insisted on compliance with the original order [of the day before] ... [19]

Lavarack had correctly assumed that the enemy would allow little time for him to prepare the defence. Rommel wrote of 9 April:

> It was now of the utmost importance to appear in strength before Tobruk and get our attack started as early as possible, for we wanted our blow to fall before the enemy had recovered his morale after our advance through Cyrenaica, and had been able to organise his defence of Tobruk.[20]

Late in the afternoon Lavarack sent a signal to Wavell explaining the decisions he had taken during the day:

> Have carried out recce and decided to hold Italian perimeter as FDLs to take advantage of existing wire and obstacles pending construction of inner and shorter perimeter. Have brought 9 Aust Div inside perimeter

to be responsible for its defence with 18 Bde and 1 R Tanks as my reserve. Role of [Support Group] remaining unchanged. Time factor makes it essential use present obstacle but to do so with present force does not give me sufficient reserve in depth and therefore strongly of opinion that remainder 7 Aust Div should be sent up without delay...

Wavell received the cable as he was about to embark for Greece. While there he would have to placate Blamey who was not pleased with the diversion of the 7th Division nor, as events were to show, with Lavarack's appointment.[21]

At about the time Lavarack's signal to Wavell was being sent, the position at Acroma came under artillery fire which lasted until after dark, but as soon as the enemy ceased firing the 9th Division commenced its move back to Tobruk. On the morning of the 10th Lavarack visited Morshead at his new headquarters, where he learnt that the withdrawal, which had been completed just before dawn, had been successful despite Morshead's misgivings.

Lavarack then returned to his own headquarters where Brigadier Gott was waiting at his request to discuss the employment of his force, which was still operating outside the perimeter. The day before Lavarack had intended to change the orders issued by Harding for Gott to retire on Sollum if hard-pressed. Instead Lavarack thought that, under those circumstances, it would be better if Gott came inside the perimeter since he considered that the Tobruk defences would be too thin without Gott's reinforcement.

However, after discussing the matter with Gott, Lavarack decided against altering the original orders, and so the force, if seriously threatened, would retire to the frontier rather than be bottled up in the fortress. As GOC Cyrcom Lavarack was not only responsible for the defence of Tobruk, but also for the defence of the Egyptian frontier, which at that time was 'practically unguarded', and so,

> as the support group was the only organised mobile fighting force available to assist in the direct defence of Egypt, its orders to retire to the East if pressed [were] confirmed.

Lavarack added one rider to Gott's orders: if landward communications with Tobruk were still open by the time an adequate mobile force were provided for the defence of Egypt, then Gott would retire on Tobruk.[22]

Although Wavell's orders had specified that the enemy's advance was to be held at Tobruk, Lavarack now realised that this was impracticable and so proceeded to plan for the defence of Tobruk against an encircling force, while establishing the main defence further east. He wrote that his 'General policy [is] to hold here and strike [the] Boche in [the] flank while establishing [a] stop at Sollum. Gott and Harding agree'. Coincidentally, later, at about midday, an aircraft arrived carrying Brigadier E.E. Dorman-Smith (BGS MEF) on a liaison mission from Wavell, who had also realised that it would not be possible to stop the enemy advance at Tobruk, although he believed that Rommel would be able to continue past Tobruk only 'with light raiding forces'. Wavell's policy was to

> hold Tobruk, to place [a] force in [the] Bardia-Sollum area with as much mobility as possible to protect communications and act against flank or rear of enemy attacking Tobruk and to build up [the] old plan of defence in Mersa Matruh area.

Understandably, Lavarack was gratified to find Wavell's policy the same as his own, although conceived on a larger scale.[23]

Dorman-Smith confirmed that Lavarack was to conduct an active defence for about two months to allow time to prepare for a counter-offensive, and also informed Lavarack that Cyrenaica Command was to be incorporated into a new command, Western Desert Command (later Western Desert Force), to extend indefinitely westwards almost from the Nile Delta. The two also discussed the question of reinforcing the garrison, and according to Lavarack it was agreed that there should be two complete divisions within the perimeter:

> I requested Brig Dorman-Smith to obtain a decision from the C-in-C on this point, and if a decision to make the garrison up to two divisions were taken, to suggest that the remainder of 7 Aust Div might be allotted.

After promising to do this Dorman-Smith departed.[24]

Meanwhile, the pressure from Rommel's German and Italian force was increasing. During the day there had been some skirmishes on the western perimeter and casualties were inflicted on both sides, but Lavarack considered that it was only to draw attention away from other forces attempting to move around the perimeter to the south. The 10th was the last day that Cyrenaica Command headquarters operated from

Tobruk township. After eating meals in a trench because of the bombing, and then having the wall of his office blown in, Lavarack decided that the time had come to move to a tented camp near Fort Peronne.[25]

The next morning (Good Friday) a patrol of the 18th Cavalry Regiment moved outside the perimeter and onto the escarpment overlooking the Derna Road, but could see no sign of enemy activity. However, part of Gott's force operating in the desert to the south of the coast road shelled an enemy column 12 miles west of the perimeter. Obviously enemy vehicles were leaving the road well to the west of the perimeter and moving into the desert to skirt the defences. Nevertheless, there was some probing of the perimeter: about mid-morning some 50 enemy vehicles appeared to the right of the 20th Brigade. These were shelled and dispersed, although about seven tanks later reappeared, but then withdrew.

To the south the main body of the Support Group had seen a column of about 40 enemy tanks approaching from the south. Just before midday these split into two groups, one maintaining the original axis of advance while the other moved eastwards in an encircling move. By mid-afternoon, after some local engagements in the eastern sector of the perimeter, this move had been completed, and the road leading east to Bardia had been cut. The siege had begun.[26]

When the news that the garrison had been isolated reached Cairo, Wavell's CGS at GHQ MEF, Lieutenant-General Arthur Smith, sent the following signal to Lavarack (Wavell was still in Greece): 'Am sure you realise that enemy force now astride road Tobruk-Bardia impedes reinforcement of Tobruk. Very desirable if practicable it should be removed'. Smith was assuming that Lavarack could use his medium (or cruiser) tanks to reopen the Bardia road. Considering the large perimeter at Tobruk and the small garrison, which had to depend heavily upon its tanks for an effective mobile defence, Lavarack regarded the suggestion as unrealistic, and observed that: 'Had I been able to comply with this fatuous suggestion I should also have been able to defeat Rommel in the open desert and win the whole campaign'.[27]

Another message shortly afterwards suggested that he might consider the proposition that the medium and infantry tanks could be better employed if they were with Gott's force outside the perimeter. Lavarack's reply to these suggestions sent the following day left little doubt as to where he stood on the issue of depleting the tank force inside the fortress:

Fully appreciate importance re-opening Tobruk-Bardia rd and will seize any opportunity doing so. Also realise advantage of having armoured units with Sp Gp but am strongly of opinion that small size of garrison and large area whatever perimeter is held makes a mobile defence of Tobruk necessary. Present armoured force in this area probably less than minimum that would be considered necessary and is subject to attrition...[28]

Egos were being bruised in other places. After the Bardia Road had been cut Gott notified Lavarack that he was retiring to the frontier since the enemy had moved between El Adem and the frontier, and also because he was short of gun ammunition. In so doing he earned Morshead's annoyance by taking with him seven anti-tank guns of D Battery, 3rd RHA which the latter obviously thought could be better used within the perimeter. Morshead raised his criticism of Gott with Lavarack who felt that Morshead was,

> evidently under a misapprehension as to Brig Gott's authority for his action. It is important that it should be clearly understood that at this time Brig Gott was under my orders, not those of Gen Morshead, and that any criticism of his action by the latter, who did not know all the circumstances, has no application.[29]

Lavarack left Morshead in no doubt who was in command, and this may have contributed to ill-feeling between the two in later years over Tobruk.

From mid-afternoon until after dusk the enemy probed the defences with infantry and armour in the El Adem sector held by the 20th Brigade. The enemy came under effective fire from artillery, tanks and infantry. From the over-confident way in which the Germans had assaulted the perimeter it was clear that they had hoped to find an unguarded approach and capture Tobruk quickly at little expense. The German armoured force commander commented afterwards that 'Reports given to the regiment had led it to believe that the enemy would retire immediately on the approach of German tanks'. But instead of retiring before the German armour the men of the 20th Brigade had held their ground, as they had been trained to do when part of Lavarack's division, and engaged the enemy infantry who had come forward, encouraged by the sight of their tanks firing with apparent impunity into the Australian positions.[30]

At one stage it was thought that some enemy tanks had broken through the perimeter and so Lavarack released the 1st Royal Tank Regiment. Although it was soon ascertained that no breach had been made by the enemy, the British tanks moved forward in the direction in which the enemy tanks had last been observed in the hope of engaging them. Clearly taking Tobruk was not going to be as easy as Rommel had hoped.

Lavarack expected a much more substantial attack, and soon. The blocking of the roads out of Tobruk, the thrusts against the perimeter during the afternoon, air reconnaissance reports that more enemy columns were approaching from the south-west, and enemy activity near the perimeter after dark all seemed to indicate that a large-scale attack was imminent. At 11 p.m. that night Lavarack, who had been at Morshead's headquarters for some time during the afternoon, ordered Wootten to move the 18th Brigade to the junction of the El Adem and Bardia Roads and to be prepared to meet a dawn attack. He also arranged to be at Morshead's headquarters at 5.30 a.m. on the 12th. During the night the three forward brigades and the engineers were to be kept busy strengthening the defences, the 2/3rd Field Company laying more than 5,000 mines in the 24th Brigade area.

After making all possible preparations, Lavarack retired late. However, the discomfort of a slight attack of dysentery and the expectation of an enemy attack conspired to prevent much rest. Twice during the night he telephoned 9th Division headquarters and spoke to the GSO1, Lloyd, who assured him that there was nothing amiss, but this did not prevent him from rising before 4 a.m. and making his way to Morshead's headquarters, 'rather too early' in his own words, as the day dawned fine and warm. There he and Morshead awaited developments, but there was none of importance; Lavarack entered wistfully in his diary that there was to be 'no first battle after all!'[31]

Nevertheless, the prospect of an attack that day had served a useful purpose. It had taken too long to move Wootten's reserve brigade from Wadi Auda to the threatened area, and so Lavarack redistributed the tanks and Wootten's battalions between Fort Airente, Fort Pilastrino and a position south of the Bardia–El Adem road junction. Thenceforth there was one battalion of the 18th Brigade astride each road leading to the port. Having given his orders, Lavarack, still unwell, rested for a couple of hours as enemy bombers attacked the town.

At midday he was roused with the news that about eight enemy tanks had attempted to locate gaps in the anti-tank ditch near Post R31 in the

2/17th Battalion's sector. He requested the RAF to bomb the 'cavorting' offenders and told Harding to arrange for more mines to be laid in the threatened sectors.

Then, for a short time, there was little further activity by the enemy, who had probably been discouraged by accurate bombing and shelling throughout the morning. But in the afternoon 'an intense, hot wind...blew up and swept clouds of thick dust across the front' under cover of which enemy infantry again advanced towards the 2/17 Battalion sector and were once more repulsed. Although no tanks had taken part in the attack, Lavarack suspected that there would be some in the vicinity. As visibility improved his suspicion was justified, and he asked that they be bombed by the RAF at about 4 p.m. This forced the enemy to withdraw from the perimeter. As the official history has recorded: 'The honours of the day had gone to the defenders, but their satisfaction was somewhat marred by news received in the evening that the enemy had occupied Bardia' close to the frontier with Egypt. It seemed that Tobruk's isolation was growing by the hour, and that it would be only a short time before Rommel would make a determined attempt to remove this thorn from his side. However, the only event of any importance that night was the movement across the 2/17th Battalion's front of some 40 enemy vehicles, which were scattered by more than 400 artillery rounds.[32]

Meanwhile, Wavell had visited Blamey at his headquarters in Greece the previous evening (the 11th) when Lavarack's request for Tobruk to be reinforced with the remainder of the 7th Division was discussed. Blamey thought that four brigades should be sufficient, but said that, if Lavarack insisted, one more brigade could be sent up on the condition that it was able to 'be passed safely in and out'. However, Blamey thought that it would be better to reinforce Tobruk with heavily-armoured infantry tanks rather than men and stressed that the defence should be based on mobility and counter-attack, with the outer perimeter being held only for observation. It seems that at this stage no-one in authority outside Tobruk had a clear idea of the state of the defences, not even Wavell who had obviously told Blamey that the inner perimeter could be used. If Lavarack suspected that this was so, then a signal he received in the evening of the 12th would have confirmed it for him. The message was not to his liking:

(1) C-in-C has discussed Tobruk with Gen Blamey. They consider 4 bdes should enable you to put up active defence and better to keep remainder

7 Div held in reserve and strengthen defence with 'infantry' tanks. Am arranging therefore send 8 more 'I' tanks to you and hope your cruisers can operate outside under Gott. (2) C-in-C and Gen Blamey suggest repeat suggest defence Tobruk should be based on mobility and counter attacks and that outer line should mainly be for observation. (3) Your comments above will be welcome.[33]

As Horner, in his book on Blamey, has observed: 'That Blamey should have felt competent to offer advice on the tactics to be employed at Tobruk while conducting his own operations across the Mediterranean in Greece seems extraordinary'.[34]

Indeed it was extraordinary and, as might be expected, Lavarack considered the advice from Wavell, but particularly Blamey, 'a bloody insult'. He only thinly disguised his feelings in a strong reply which said that he was convinced that the only way to defend Tobruk successfully was with the forces as he had organised and disposed them, and that 'any other...defence could be quickly swamped' by the enemy. He did agree, though, that the infantry tanks would be useful and suggested that once they had arrived it might be possible to release some of the lighter, faster cruisers, although they probably would have to be evacuated by sea.[35]

At about the same time as the signal informing Lavarack of the discussions between Blamey and Wavell was despatched, another was also sent confirming the conversation Lavarack had had two days previously with Brigadier Dorman-Smith, who had visited Tobruk to discuss the reorganisation proposed by Wavell under which a new headquarters, known as Western Desert Force, would be established from HQ Cyrenaica Command. Wavell had decided that, behind a screen of light forces at the frontier, he would build up his defences at Mersa Matruh, where the 7th Division less the 18th Brigade was now disposed. It had become clear that Rommel could not be stopped before the frontier, as Wavell had hoped might be possible at Tobruk, and so a commander was required in Egypt, rather than in the besieged fortress.

The signal carrying this information reached Lavarack during the evening of the 12th, and outlined the following: that a HQ Western Desert Force would be established from HQ Cyrcom; that Morshead would assume command of all forces in Tobruk Fortress; that Major-General Evetts, GOC British Troops Egypt, would assume command of all forces in the Western Desert, except Tobruk, until HQ Cyrcom arrived; and that the organisation would come into effect at one minute after midnight 13/14 April.[36] As far as Lavarack personally was concerned, the message was significant for the following passage:

> Maj. Gen. Lavarack and HQ Cyrcom will move to Maaten Bagush under arrangements to be made by Mideast and on arrival HQ Western Desert Force will assume command of all forces in Western Desert including Tobruk Fortress in relief Gen Evetts who will revert to Command of BTE less Western Desert Force.[37]

Lavarack's staff congratulated him on his appointment as the commander of Western Desert Force.[38]

No doubt he retired satisfied that his career was once more in the ascendant after the setbacks of the past two years. But as he slept under a blanket of sand driven by the wind, he was about to come under attack by his two greatest wartime adversaries, Generals Rommel and Blamey.

Map 1: The Eastern Mediterranean, 1940–41

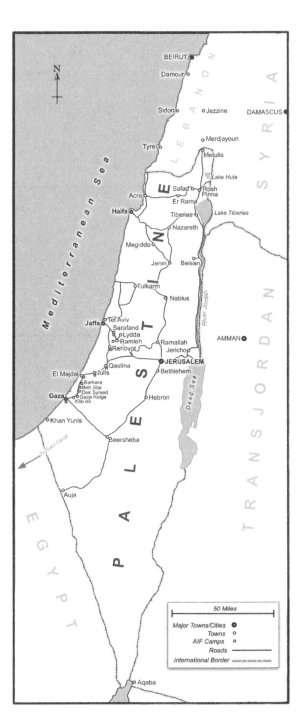

Map 2: Palestine, 1940–41

164

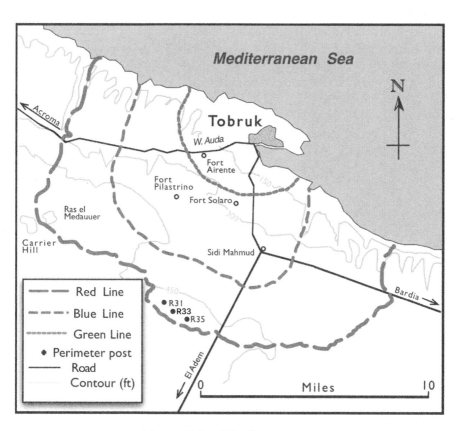

Mediterranean Sea

N

Acroma

Tobruk

W. Auda

Fort
Airente

Fort
Pilastrino

Fort Solaro

Ras el
Medauuer

150

300

Carrier
Hill

Sidi Mahmud

Bardia

Red Line
Blue Line
Green Line
Perimeter post
Road
Contour (ft)

450

R31
R33
R35

El Adem

0

Miles

10

Map 3: Tobruk Defences, 1941

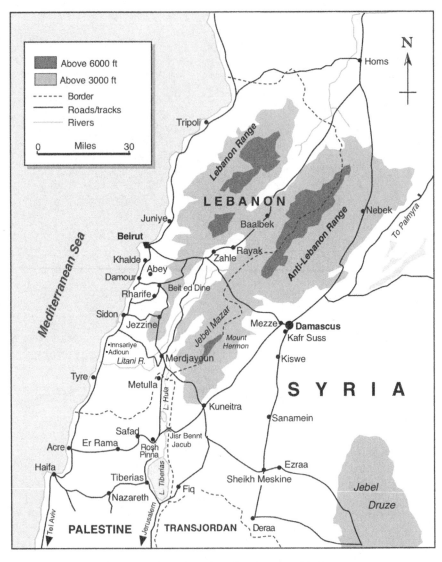

Map 4: Lebanon & South-Western Syria, 1941

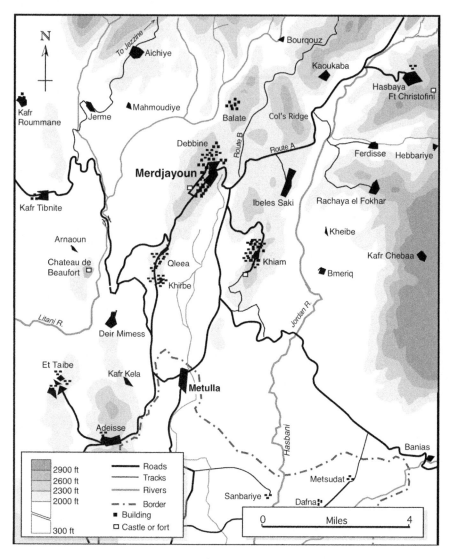

Map 5: The Merdjayoun Area, Lebanon

167

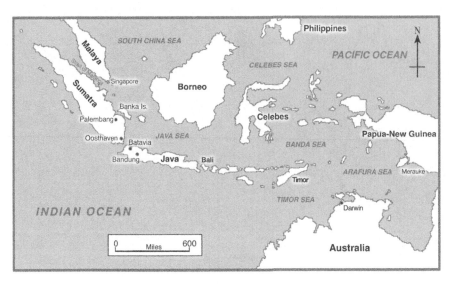

**Map 6: The Netherlands East Indies and nearby countries,
1942**

10

'I am not conscious of failure at Tobruk...'

The Easter Battle, 1941

THE GERMAN PLAN to take Tobruk was devised using the only two maps of the town which had reached them by 12 April. Rommel had decided that on the evening of the 13th, while the Italian *Brescia Division* staged a demonstration in the west opposite the 26th Brigade, the German *5th Light Division* would breach the southern defences west of the El Adem Road. The Germans intended to penetrate as far as the junction of the Bardia–El Adem Roads to form a bridgehead through which, early on the 14th, the main force would launch a dawn attack towards the harbour.[1]

Lavarack knew from aerial reconnaissance that large numbers of enemy vehicles were converging on Tobruk from the directions of Derna and Mechili to the west. During the morning of the 13th enemy motor-cyclists and a staff car were scattered by artillery fire while apparently trying to set up a headquarters in front of the 2/17th Battalion. Soon afterwards an enemy aircraft made a low-level reconnaissance of this sector and later dropped leaflets carrying Rommel's call on the garrison to surrender:

> The General commanding the German Forces in Libya hereby requests the British troops occupying Tobruk to surrender arms. Single soldiers waving white handkerchiefs are not fired upon. Strong German Forces have already surrounded Tobruk, useless to try an escape—remember

Mekhili! Our dive bombers—Stukas—are awaiting your ships which are lying in Tobruk [sic].[2]

Apart from these incidents the perimeter was quiet until mid-afternoon, when enemy armoured cars began probing the southern defences. At the same time German infantry alighted from their transport in an assembly area about 4,000 yards away in full view of the defenders, who called down artillery fire causing them to seek cover. Shortly afterwards groups of the enemy set up machine guns about 1,500 yards from the perimeter and began firing on any movement inside the wire. At the same time aircraft were apparently plotting the defences. The enemy was making no efforts to conceal his intentions, which obviously would concern that part of the perimeter held by the 2/17 Battalion.[3]

On returning to his headquarters after visiting Morshead, Lavarack found a liaison officer from GHQ in Cairo waiting to see him with various queries. Lavarack noted later that during the discussion this officer,

...let [the] cat out of [the] bag in admitting that many at G.H.Q. had believed, before hearing from me, that there was an inner obstacle at Tobruk as well as the outer one!!! Hence the absurd suggestion, made by Blamey, I think, that we should only use the outer obstacle as a Line of Observation, whatever that may mean.

The liaison officer obviously told Lavarack more than was necessary, for Lavarack continued:

There is an extraordinary amount of suggestion being made in various quarters that I am pursuing [the] wrong policy as regards Cyrcom. Above from Gen[eral] Wavell and Blamey and also two wires from [the] DCGS making suggestions as to [the] adoption of policy of mobile action outside [the] Tobruk perimeter. Have indicated my determination not to accede to such suggestions. Fully aware of [the] desirability of such a policy as soon as conditions render it possible.

Lavarack said that he did not want to attempt to reinforce Gott's force outside the perimeter while the Bardia Road still remained open, even though it might have saved Sollum, because he was not prepared to risk the loss of Tobruk by doing so.[4]

But with the Germans preparing to pounce, Lavarack had little time to brood on the unsettling meeting with the liaison officer. About an hour and a half later there began the enemy attack which had been heralded in the afternoon by the attention paid to the 2/17th Battalion's section of the perimeter. That a major assault was imminent had been confirmed by aerial reconnaissance in the evening, and at 11 p.m. a platoon-sized group of Germans (heavily armed with two small field guns, a mortar and eight machine guns) breached the wire and brought fire to bear on Post R33. These were pushed back by the defenders. Then at 2.30 a.m., despite the handicap of an incomplete reconnaissance because of the aggressive Australian defence and a lack of maps, approximately 200 German infantry established a bridgehead several hundred yards inside the perimeter near Post R33. The attackers, men of the German *8th Machine Gun Battalion*, came under heavy artillery and small arms fire but were able to maintain their position within the perimeter.

The spirited defence, though, had disrupted the attackers' plans. The majority of the Germans, who had intended to advance deep within the perimeter when their tanks attacked through the gap they had made, were obliged to remain behind to ensure that the breach stayed open. The German plan was for 38 tanks of the *5th Armoured Regiment*, followed by the *8th Machine Gun Battalion*, to penetrate deep inside the perimeter. After two miles the tanks were to divide into two groups: one to make for Tobruk itself, the other to pursue the retreating defenders to the west. However, the enemy tanks yielded the advantage of surprise when they became lost outside the perimeter and were forced to travel along it to locate Post R33. Finally, covered by artillery fire, the German tanks drove through the perimeter at 5.20 a.m. The Australian defenders allowed the tanks to pass, then engaged the German infantry following the tanks. The German foot soldiers suffered heavy casualties as the tanks advanced without them eastwards in the direction of the El Adem road. A mile short of the road they turned and drove parallel to it in the direction of the El Adem–Bardia road junction. Before reaching the junction they stopped to await dawn, and there were engaged by a battery of the British 1st RHA.[5]

The first news to reach Lavarack of the breakthrough came at 6 a.m., when Harding woke him with a report that 20 tanks had forced their way into the perimeter; this estimate was soon increased to 40 enemy vehicles. Lavarack then made his way to Morshead's headquarters so that he would be ready to take any decisions without delay. Lavarack decided to place under Morshead's command both regiments of cruiser tanks, to be used at division's discretion. The more heavily-armoured infantry tanks he allotted to Wootten's reserve, but told Wootten that they were not to be employed without his (Lavarack's) approval except in the event of a complete breakdown in communications or in dire emergency. As reports came in Lavarack was heartened to learn that the enemy tanks were facing north-east towards the El Adem–Bardia road junction as he had forecast, but he was puzzled why the enemy was 'hovering' when 'he usually hits quickly'.[6]

The explanation was that the enemy attack had, even by that early stage, lost its impetus. Having forfeited surprise before breaching the perimeter and now, because of the dogged resistance by the Australian defenders at the perimeter, the German tank attack, deprived of infantry support, was being blunted by effective artillery fire. Morshead ordered the cruiser tanks given him by Lavarack to attack the enemy tanks which were being engaged by the 1st, 3rd, 104th and 107th Regiments of the Royal Horse Artillery, and the Australian 2/3rd Anti-Tank Regiment. The leading German tank battalion was forced to retreat after losing about half-a-dozen vehicles, running into the battalion following it, causing confusion and collisions. At about this time the British cruiser tanks, which had crossed the El Adem road so as to be able to attack from the east, engaged the German tanks. The Germans then decided to break off the engagement and make for the gap in the perimeter, pursued by the cruisers and two infantry tanks, which Lavarack had ordered to join the fray so that the enemy would be aware that these heavier tanks were part of the garrison, a move he thought 'useful move in [a] war of nerves'.[7]

At the perimeter the Australian infantry, who had fought hard to overcome the infantry attackers and contain the bridgehead, were mopping up as the enemy tanks rushed for the gap to escape. One defender described the mayhem into which the German attack had descended:

> There was terrible confusion at the only gap as tanks and infantry
> pushed their way through it. The crossing was badly churned up and the
> tanks raised clouds of dust as they went. In addition, there was the
> smoke of two tanks blazing just outside the wire. Into this cloud of dust
> and smoke we fired anti-tank weapons, Brens, rifles, and mortars, and
> the gunners sent hundreds of shells.[8]

At about this time, to ensure that the enemy were sent speedily on their way, Lavarack ordered Wootten to despatch a battalion, with infantry tanks in support, to the scene of the battle.

By 8.30 a.m. on the 14th the battle was over and it only remained to subdue the small pockets of enemy which had been trapped inside the wire. A second German attack planned for later that day was cancelled. At least 400 enemy had been killed or taken prisoner and Rommel had lost 17 tanks; the defenders had sustained 80 casualties (killed and wounded) and two of the cruisers had been destroyed. 'The German commander's first major operation against the fortress had ended in complete defeat', wrote the official historian. After the battle, at 1 p.m., Lavarack issued a special order of the day in which he congratulated the defenders on their 'stern determination, prompt action and close cooperation'.[9]

Although Lavarack was not as much the commander fighting the battle in Tobruk as Morshead, he was nevertheless the overall commander and it had been his plan and orders which dictated how the defence would be conducted. His determination to ignore gratuitous advice from Blamey, and others, and to base the defence on the outer perimeter had been thoroughly vindicated. The Germans had expected, after their string of lightning victories in Europe and their hitherto rapid advance across North Africa, that once the Tobruk perimeter had been breached all resistance would collapse. So completely surprised were they when this did not happen that some German troops wept after the attempt failed.[10]

Lavarack can take some credit for this success at the tactical level as well. Almost a year before, his first training instruction to the newly-raised 7th Division had stressed the necessity for infantry in the defence to remain in position when attacked by armour, allow the enemy tanks to pass and then engage the enemy infantry following. Three of the four defending brigades were, or had been, part of Lavarack's division and so were well-acquainted with his tactics. It was these tactics which defeated the German assault on 14 April.

This appeared to be Lavarack's hour. A determined assault against the fortress by an outstanding and experienced opponent, Erwin Rommel, had been beaten off and now, as far as Lavarack knew, he was to proceed to a command which would make him responsible for the defence of Egypt, upon which hinged the British position in the Middle East. Although he had been in command of Cyrenaica and based at Tobruk for less than seven days, he had made several important decisions. The first was to fight for Tobruk and organise an aggressive defence with the forces at his disposal. Second, in spite of 'suggestions' from Wavell and Blamey, he had based the defence on the outer perimeter since it was the only real obstacle to the enemy. Third, he organised a defence in depth and ordered that work commence on constructing a second line of defence with switch lines to localise any enemy breakthrough. Finally, Lavarack maintained his aim of defending Tobruk and refused to be enticed into making decisions which would dissipate his strength, such as complying with the requests to open the Bardia Road or to despatch his cruiser tanks to the Egyptian frontier, which he felt would 'certainly have vanished in the attempt like a puff of gas in a furnace'.

While there may seem to have been an element of 'Hobson's choice' in choosing to defend the fortress and in selecting the outer perimeter as the main defensive line, they were decisions which had to be taken. Had Lavarack decided differently not only might Tobruk have been lost, but the British position in North Africa could have been seriously jeopardised. He had shown himself to be a resolute commander and a capable organiser. His nephew, Brigadier Ochiltree (at the time a junior staff officer in the 26th Brigade which was holding the western side of the Tobruk perimeter) has recalled that

> Although the situation was desperate and in many instances chaotic, he [Lavarack] was calm and completely unruffled and very much in command of a potentially dangerous state of affairs; he radiated confidence and this affected those around him.[11]

Lavarack no doubt felt doubly confident now of his ability to defend Egypt successfully as the commander of the new Western Desert Force, having defeated the German attack precisely as he had planned to do.

However, he was about to experience another of the shocks of war which could be as devastating as the loss of a battle. At 2.30 p.m. a signal arrived from Wavell informing Lavarack of his return to the 7th Division:

> Arrangements now made for Cyrcom Desert Force. On return to Egypt you will therefore assume comd 7 Aust Div less 18 Bde. Most grateful your invaluable services in stabilising situation in Cyrenaica.

A British officer, Lieutenant-General Sir Noel Beresford-Peirse, would now command Western Desert Force instead.

To Lavarack it must have been almost incomprehensible that he had been cast so unexpectedly from the pinnacle of success precisely at the moment he had attained it. It was a bitter and incomprehensible blow: only the night before, in accordance with Wavell's initial orders, Lavarack had issued 'Cyrenaica Command Operation Instruction No. 9' which, after outlining a reorganisation of forces, concluded: 'On arrival at Maaten Bagush Major General Lavarack will assume command of Western Desert Force including the forces at Tobruk'.[12]

At 6 p.m. Lavarack handed over command of Tobruk to Morshead and embarked upon HMS *Fiona* for the voyage to Mersa Matruh. Brigadier Plant wrote to Blamey three days later:

> [Lavarack] did a good job of work and was terribly disappointed when on the point of embarking for his new HQ a signal came through informing him that he was to return to 7 Aust Div. I sailed on the night 14/15 from Tobruk with Cyrcom staff to Metruh [sic] ... The BGS and other officers stated how sorry they were that General Lavarack was not to continue with them as they had every confidence in his ability to run a good show.[13]

Lavarack recorded in his diary a remark made to him as he was leaving Tobruk by a 'senior British officer':

> Why, don't you see? If they leave you in command and you are successful everyone will say that when the British Army gets into a jam they have to put in a Dominion officer to get them out.

It may be an indication of the existence of this attitude that the British official history, written by Major-General I.S.O. Playfair, mentions Lavarack's name only three times in connection with Tobruk and implies that at no time was Lavarack's appointment considered anything but temporary. Yet when Lavarack had been appointed there had been no indication that it was to be temporary. If Wavell had wanted a commander with greater experience of the desert, as he later said he did, it might reasonably be expected that he would have appointed Beresford-Peirse initially instead of Lavarack, or if that were not immediately feasible, tell Lavarack that he was to command until his replacement arrived.[14]

The Australian official history considers that British reluctance to appoint Dominion officers to senior commands outside Dominion formations probably influenced the decision not to appoint Lavarack. Blamey's biographer, Hetherington, agreed and claimed that there existed at this time an 'unofficial but powerful pressure group', dubbed by him the 'Union of British Generals', which contrived to prevent Dominion officers commanding any but their own forces. Blamey's wartime aide-de-camp, Norman Carlyon, also believes that this 'British General's Club' existed and was convinced that:

> The self-interest and prejudice of this group worked powerfully behind the scenes to exclude Dominion officers from the top operational commands.
>
> I don't think there is any doubt about the existence of this clique. Blamey...was convinced that there was a 'closed shop' policy where senior commands were concerned.[15]

There is, however, no conclusive evidence that prejudice against Dominion officers was the primary reason for Wavell's decision. Of course, this does not mean that such an unofficial policy did not exist and was not practised. Indeed, the failure to appoint Morshead to a corps command in August 1942 and the inordinately long time it took for the commander of the New Zealand Division, Major-General B.C. Freyberg, to be given command of a corps reflect what Blamey called 'the repugnance of the British Command to accept Dominion officers, however successful in higher command'.[16]

Troubled by this abrupt change in orders, on 16 April Lavarack met Wavell in private and asked him why Beresford-Peirse had been chosen to command Western Desert Force in his stead. He recorded in his diary that Wavell 'stated [that the] change [was] due to his desire to have an officer well acquainted with [the] Western Desert and [was] no reflection on [my]self at all...'.[17]

Although still disappointed, Lavarack may have let the matter rest there had it not been for a visit two weeks later to Blamey who had returned from the failed campaign against the Germans in Greece and was in hospital with suspected dysentery. Blamey told him then that not only had Wavell decided against him because an officer with more experience of the desert was desired, but also because Lavarack had 'insisted' on having two divisions in Tobruk. This, as Lavarack maintained, was a misrepresentation as he had never insisted on two divisions, although he had strongly recommended that the remainder of the 7th Division come into Tobruk, and Wavell himself had thought that, if available, two divisions would be preferable. After speaking with Blamey, Lavarack wrote: 'Obviously, from T.A.B.'s manner my supersession by Beresford-Pierce [sic] was arranged bet[ween] himself and Wavell and [the] reasons given were trumped up...Found T.A.B. very wary and uncommunicative.'[18]

Blamey's allegation preyed upon Lavarack's mind and so, about a week after visiting the hospital, he wrote to Wavell, relating to him the conversation he had had with Blamey and asking that any misunderstanding be resolved:

> As you had already assured me that there was only one reason for my removal from the higher command and relegation to my previous divisional command (i.e. your desire to have a commander with intimate knowledge of the Western Desert) I denied General Blamey's statement, but am still left with the uneasy suspicion that he believes that I was removed from the command for personal failure.
>
> I am not conscious of failure at Tobruk...I have no quarrel with your own reason for not leaving me in the command, even though the result was a personal humiliation, but am dismayed at the results that may flow from General Blamey's misapprehension, and feel that no other course is open to me but to request you to correct it.[19]

Wavell replied several days later:

> I hope you will get out of your head any idea that the changes of command made in the Western Desert during the rather critical period last month reflected on you in any way whatever...
>
> While I was considering this reorganisation I visited Greece and saw General Blamey and asked him whether he recommended leaving you in command at Tobruk. He thought you would probably be better outside. I then considered you as the Commander of W[estern] Desert Force, but decided instead to recommend Beresford-Peirse to [the] War Office since the enemy attack might come very shortly and he had dealt with the same problem last year and knew the ground and the problem.
>
> I can assure you that your recommendation of two divisions for the defence of Tobruk did not affect my decision; to the best of my recollection my opinion was that two divisions would be a suitable garrison if they were readily available...I hope this explanation will relieve your mind...I was very pleased with the way you handled the force at Tobruk and Gott's Force while in command.[20]

Wavell's letter, while ostensibly truthful, is nonetheless misleading. Blamey had indeed said that he thought Lavarack would be better outside Tobruk, and Wavell had indeed considered, if not chosen, Lavarack as the commander of Western Desert Force. However, Blamey's recommendation was not made in response to the question of whether Lavarack, as the commander of Cyrenaica Command/Western Desert Force, would be better placed inside or outside Tobruk, as Wavell implied, but whether Lavarack should remain in command at all. Wavell later wrote that:

> Blamey himself did not think Lavarack entirely suitable for high command. As it was essential to have [a] commander immediately I recommended Beresford Peirse, who had local knowledge and had done well there and in Sudan.[21]

It is clear that Wavell, who had been considering the reorganisation in Cyrenaica since at least 9 April, had indeed decided to appoint Lavarack as the commander of Western Desert Force before he went to Greece and spoke to Blamey: 'I had considered Blamey, Mackay and Lavarack for Western desert command [sic], but did not think Blamey and Mackay available during [the] fighting in Greece...'. The signal appointing Lavarack had been sent early on the 12th, probably in accordance with arrangements Wavell had made prior to leaving for Greece but before he spoke to Blamey. But after talking to Blamey, Wavell felt that he would have to reconsider, and so on the 14th Lavarack received another order returning him to the 7th Division in spite of the victory at Tobruk.

Blamey's predictable, but unfounded, opinion that Lavarack was not suited for the command by itself might not have been enough to persuade Wavell that he should find an alternative commander. But Blamey's additional argument (recounted later to Lavarack by Wavell) that the Australian Government would not approve of Lavarack remaining in command in Cyrenaica, most likely tipped the scales.[22]

Lavarack was returned to the 7th Division not because he had failed in Tobruk—indeed, he had triumphed against one of Germany's most talented and experienced generals. Nor was he denied command of Western Desert Force because Wavell wanted a commander with more experience, which ostensibly explains why Beresford-Peirse was chosen to replace Lavarack, but not necessarily why Lavarack was discounted. (Indeed, after the war Lavarack told the official historian, Gavin Long, that Beresford-Peirse had admitted 'that his desert experience was negligible, and of no more value, in his opinion, than mine in Cyrenaica'.) Prejudice against Dominion commanders may have had some effect, but if so it was of minor importance. The decisive factor was Blamey's influence.[23]

It was Blamey's duty to keep the AIF intact and he could argue that he was acting in accordance with his charter in trying to have Lavarack returned to the 7th Division. However, while Blamey's duties as GOC AIF may have played a part in his opposition to Lavarack remaining as GOC Cyrcom/WDF, and while he may have been motivated by genuine doubts about Lavarack's limitations as he saw them, given the history between the two men Blamey's most likely spur to action was his personal dislike of Lavarack. He had not wanted Lavarack in the Second AIF, had resisted him being given command of the 6th Division and, most recently, had attempted to lure him away from command of the 7th Division for the expedition to Greece. Perhaps more pertinently, it had been planned in January that Blamey, as commander of the 1st Australian Corps, would become responsible for Cyrenaica in February, but the Greek expedition intervened to prevent him taking over that important duty. Given his feelings for Lavarack, Blamey could hardly be expected to readily accept the prospect of Lavarack being appointed to essentially the same senior post which he had been required to forego—nor view with equanimity Lavarack's likely promotion to lieutenant-general which the command of Cyrcom/WDF warranted.

This had ramifications not just for Lavarack's career, but for Australia's prestige. Had it not been for Blamey's personal aversion to Lavarack's appointment and promotion, an Australian may have been the first Dominion general to occupy in the long term a senior command in North Africa comprising British as well as Dominion troops. In another ironic twist, it was Lavarack's replacement as the commander in Cyrenaica by the more junior Beresford-Peirse which contributed to the decision taken just over a week later to appoint Blamey as Deputy Commander-in-Chief, Middle East (a largely ineffectual post) in order to stave off Dominion criticism.[24]

Blamey was as at least as much a politician as a general, an aspect of his character which was of some value in trying to ensure the integrity of the AIF abroad in the face of British pressure to employ it piecemeal. But Blamey often directed his political energies to affairs within the army, with the result that several senior officers' careers were to be crippled during the war while others, who were less able, flourished because they were Blamey's favourites. That there were sometimes good reasons for the actions Blamey took affecting other officers is not doubted, but he was conscious that there were rivals for his position and as far as possible he protected himself, sometimes to the detriment of the army and the country.

The battle in Tobruk was remembered by Lavarack with satisfaction, but a satisfaction tinged with bitterness—he felt ever after that he had not received his due for the work done there. He also believed that Blamey was responsible for his not being made a 'local lieut-general' during the short time he was GOC Cyrenaica Command, as Wavell had said he would be, as well as preventing his appointment to command Western Desert Force:

> If I am right this incident confirms my previous opinion that T.A.B. is both ruthless and unscrupulous. Apparently he combines these qualities with a bad inferiority complex, which he confessed to me some time ago had been his constant companion in life. Ever since the treatment he received from senior officers on joining the cadet staff in 1906. A queer and, on the whole, unpleasant makeup.

The depth of Blamey's malevolence, and the ramifications which would flow from it, were now becoming clearer to Lavarack, for he also wrote that '[I] shall never get any parades if T.A.B. can prevent it, and yet have always been loyal to him and have not attempted to mine him'. Loyalty, even to Blamey, was a quality on which Lavarack prided himself, a quality he was soon to demonstrate regardless of his suspicions about Blamey's role in thwarting him at Tobruk and having him returned to the 7th Division at Mersa Matruh.[25]

11

'He was almost in tears...'

Egypt, April–May 1941

ONCE BACK IN COMMAND of the 7th Division at Mersa Matruh, Lavarack's orders were to observe the western approaches from Cyrenaica, maintain contact with Gott's mobile force operating between Mersa Matruh and Tobruk, and be prepared to hold Matruh against a superior force strong in tanks and well supported by aircraft. There was also much to be done to repair and develop the Matruh defences and Lavarack had made it clear that no effort would be spared, regardless of how hot, dusty and dull the work. The monotony was a burden for all, but for Lavarack personally it was aggravated by a deep disappointment at not being in Tobruk, especially since one of his brigades was still there. As General Beresford-Peirse, under whose command Lavarack now found himself, told Morshead: 'He is full of envy of 18 Bde and would like to join you en masse'.[1]

Lavarack's five weeks in Matruh were filled not just with dismay at being replaced by Beresford-Peirse, but the growing realisation that Blamey had engineered his removal from the command of Western Desert Force. Blamey was much on Lavarack's mind, as his aide-de-camp, Curtis Wilson, recorded at the time:

Lav[arack] thinks too much of TAB's animosity. Very real nevertheless, but Blamey [is] frightened of Lav[arack]. One reason why Lav[arack] thinks of TAB so much is that Lav[arack] is very active man; this inaction of our position and inaction that surrounds TAB (except in party tactics)...gets him down. Needs exercise to reduce his mental activity.[2]

If there was any consolation for Lavarack in the frustrating days immediately after Tobruk it was perhaps the discovery that there was growing dissatisfaction with Blamey at high levels within the AIF in the Middle East.

The Revolt of the Brigadiers?

Blamey's return to North Africa from the debacle in Greece had brought with it not just the knowledge that he had sabotaged Lavarack's command of Western Desert Force, but also the unsettling news that Blamey's leadership during the campaign had been deficient, both personally and professionally. Near the end of the campaign Blamey had been ordered back to Egypt from Greece and instructed to bring with him several officers who formed the nucleus of his headquarters. Among these Blamey included his son, who then held the relatively junior rank of major as a liaison officer on the headquarters of the Australian corps.

One of Blamey's aides, Wilmoth, has criticised the decision that his son should be evacuated as weak. Another ADC, Carlyon, has noted that: 'By nominating his own son for a place in the flying-boat, Blamey was giving his critics one more reason for assailing him'. And assail him they did, as George Vasey, one of Blamey's brigade commanders in Greece, wrote to his wife:

> He [Blamey] and the boy were first away and went non-stop to Egypt.
> Some excuse might be made for him but to include the boy was just too
> terrible. Taking him home to mother I suppose. He has lost a terrible lot
> of caste on account of it. Syd [Rowell] and Bill [Bridgeford] were
> terribly fed up...In a letter to me the other day he [Rowell] said he
> rarely saw him nowadays and he preferred it that way since they were
> not now attuned to the same wavelength. There is little doubt that as a
> result of this and innumerable other things, small in themselves perhaps,
> confidence in him has been lost. He was never seen in the battle area
> and, I understand, was usually to be found within a few yards of a slit
> trench.[3]

The criticism of Blamey by his chief staff officer, Rowell, was more serious. He wrote of the departure from Greece:

> I was asleep on the ground when Blamey got in. He told me he'd been ordered back to prepare a plan for the defence of the Western Desert. I said, "What can we do about the Western Desert? I don't believe you". I think he was terrified; terrified of being taken prisoner...

Carlyon has confirmed that Blamey and Rowell had 'one hell of a row' before they left Greece, after which Rowell told Carlyon that he thought Blamey had lost his judgement. Upon arrival in Egypt Rowell wrote to the Australian CGS, Sturdee, stating that he would never serve in the field again with Blamey, considering him 'unfit to command troops in the field'. After the war he described Blamey's conduct in Greece as cowardice, as did General Bridgeford (the AA&QMG on Blamey's headquarters in Greece), who said: 'Blamey had acted like a coward. While the battle for Greece was on he stayed at his headquarters and lived sumptuously on champagne.'[4]

Blamey's ability to command towards the end of the campaign also came under fire. Rowell later told the official historian of an occasion when Blamey tried to issue orders to General Mackay and his senior staff officers:

> [Blamey] was physically and mentally broken. He was almost in tears and gave Mackay, who was always a model of calm, such garbled orders that I was forced tactfully to intervene and get him straight. After it was all over, I took Mackay, Sutherland and Prior out on to the side of the hill and we went through the whole thing again in proper sequence.[5]

The aircraft evacuating Blamey from Greece had arrived in Alexandria in the afternoon of 24 April. The next day he left for GHQ in Cairo, but the officers who had left Greece with him remained in Alexandria, where Lavarack met them on the 25th, ANZAC Day, in the Union Club. It was only then that Lavarack learned from Rowell that Blamey was back with part of the corps staff, including his son, and was informed of events which had taken place in Greece.

That evening Lavarack dined with Blamey's senior medical officer, Major-General S.R. Burston, Rowell, Brigadier Andrew and Lieutenant-

Colonel C.M.L. Elliott. Talk of Blamey's conduct in Greece dominated the conversation. Afterwards Lavarack noted in his diary that Andrew stated categorically that Blamey did not control operations in Greece as he should have and that at a critical stage effective command was passed to Rowell. Andrew accused Blamey of cowardice.[6] The next day Lavarack recounted the previous evening's events to his ADC, Wilson, who recorded what he had been told:

> Senior officers are back from the Greek debacle. Brigadier Rowell said he
> wanted to resign because of events in Greece. Said Blamey showed
> white feather, ran out of the country in a plane with his son. The whole
> Australian headquarters staff is seething with more than dissatisfaction.
> Brig Andrews, [sic] who says he can see Gen Blamey for only an hour a
> week, wants an enquiry into the conduct in Greece ... [T]hey filled his
> [Lavarack's] ear talking revolt.[7]

According to Wilson, Lavarack was asked to approach the Australian government in an attempt to have Blamey recalled to Australia. Lavarack refused and shortly afterwards, on 28 April, Brigadier Andrew died unexpectedly of pulmonary thrombosis.

After attending Andrew's funeral on the 29th, Lavarack spoke once more with Rowell and several other senior officers, recording later: 'Conversations w[ith] Rowell, Allen, Bridgeford and Co. All apparently very dissatisfied with ops. in Greece. Rowell and Bridgeford non-communicative, Allen very outspoken ag[ainst] T.A.B.' However, Wilson noted that, with the death of Andrew,

> So goes the hope of an inquiry into the Greek campaign. No one else
> will have the guts to tell the Australian Government. The senior officers
> who remain are career men, but it did not stop them talking to Lavarack
> in the Union Club again. Today's paen [sic] of hate was sung by
> Brigadiers Allen, Savige, Herring, [and] Bridgeford in the bar of the
> Union Club.[8]

It is unlikely that the removal of Blamey was discussed at any meeting attended by Brigadiers Herring or Savige. Both were considered to be loyal to Blamey at that time (although less than a year later Savige would strongly denounce Herring for attempting to topple Blamey) and, as Carlyon has observed, having Savige at the meeting would be like 'having a telephone link direct to Blamey'. What seems more likely is that, at this second meeting, senior officers familiar with the disastrous Greek expedition were voicing their misgivings about the reasons for the campaign and its general conduct. Even Blamey supporters like Herring and Savige, commanding the artillery and the 17th Brigade of the 6th Division respectively, would have agreed that the campaign had failed in its objective of defending Greece against Axis aggression. In addition, Australian losses had been high, their division badly mauled and there had been regrettable incidents of ill-disciplined behaviour by some troops. The tension after Greece was evident everywhere, as the official history noted:

> At both Army and Air Headquarters during the next few days there was a hum of splenetic activity, reminiscent of an overturned beehive. Everybody was writing out reports, the Army blaming the Air Force...the Air Force blaming the Army...The atmosphere was full of acrimonious tension, which was felt even by other ranks, for there were incidents at Alexandria between soldiers just in from Greece and men of the R.A.F., some of whom had never even been there.[9]

Disaffection with Blamey was an additional matter. It is beyond doubt that those senior Australian officers who were present at the original meeting on ANZAC Day were deeply unhappy with Blamey's leadership and would have welcomed his removal. Brigadiers Rowell and Bridgeford were outspoken critics of Blamey's character and leadership and there is little reason to question their views that day as recounted in Wilson's diary—nor for that matter, the views of Brigadiers Allen and Andrew whose disillusionment and grievances were still remembered by Elliott forty years later. It is quite conceivable that these officers (who, being on the headquarters staff, were the people best placed to form a judgement of their commander) would want an enquiry which might expose Blamey's serious lapses in leadership during a difficult campaign. From there it would be a short step to touch upon the idea, as recorded by Wilson, that Lavarack, as the next most senior officer in the AIF, might be asked to approach the government to call for Blamey's removal.

On the other hand it is possible that, in recording the events relayed to him, Wilson may have confused the idea of a general enquiry into Greece with a particular submission for Blamey's replacement.[10] However, Wilson's account is supported by another officer. According to Lieutenant-Colonel F.J. Howard (who in 1941 was a captain attached to HQ

AIF Middle East), feeling against Blamey after the Greek campaign was so strong that several of Blamey's most senior officers considered requesting the Australian government to replace him in the Middle East. In a news-paper article in 1974 article Howard wrote that

> some senior AIF officers, immediately after the evacuation from Greece, planned to seek the removal of Blamey from his command. Their intended joint ultimatum to Canberra, declaring that they could no longer serve under Blamey, was never sent. A central figure in the move died suddenly, from a heart attack. In this hiatus, the plot dissolved.

Howard was emphatic that the discussions were not merely 'a gripe session' and that Brigadier B.J. Andrew (the Deputy Adjutant-General at AIF headquarters) had prepared a draft of the proposal to be sent to the Australian government.[11]

Several weeks after the article appeared in 1974 Rowell wrote to Blamey's biographer, John Hetherington, that 'I am unwilling to challenge Howard's bona fides, but I don't really think any such plot existed'. Of Brigadier Andrew he recorded: 'he was the soul of honour and is, to me at least, the last man who would become involved'. Rowell continued:

> Who else is there? The Corps Staff and 6 Div were fully engaged in avoiding captivity and the only three senior officers left in [the] Middle East were Lavarack at Matruh, Plant in Alexandria and Robbie at the training depot at Gaza. If there was a plot, then they are the only people of standing who could be involved. I can well imagine Lavarack and Robbie having less than pleasant personal feelings about TAB, the former by his persecution complex and the latter after TAB's violent smack in the face at the dinner in Benghazi when Menzies was present. But I can't conceive either of them going so far as to petition for TAB's relief.

However, not all of the corps staff officers were in Greece trying to avoid captivity—in his letter Rowell skirted the fact that he and several other members of the corps staff were in Egypt at the time also. And, undeterred by Rowell's views, Lieutenant-Colonel Howard remained adamant that Brigadier Andrew had prepared a draft document for transmission to the Australian government calling into question Blamey's leadership.[12]

Despite the equivocations decades later, and perhaps the fading of memories, the anger of the officers involved and the notion of an approach to the government hardly seems likely to have materialised out of thin air to appear in the diaries of Lavarack and Wilson, and later in Howard's article. Even Blamey's ADC, Carlyon, has admitted that such discussions 'could well have happened' given the events in Greece, but as far as he could ascertain, Blamey had no knowledge of any such move against him—he was certain that had Blamey known, he would have taken action. Regardless of whether Blamey knew in April of the strong criticisms made of him, and by whom, it seems unlikely that he could have remained unaware of them for long. However, he may have considered it imprudent to retaliate immediately lest, by so doing, the criticisms achieved a wider currency.[13]

But by July he, as Deputy Commander-in-Chief in the Middle East, was in a stronger position when dealing with his critics, for it was then that Rowell was recalled to Australia to become Deputy Chief of the General Staff. Vasey considered that Rowell had been dismissed: 'I could hardly contain myself. I feel the whole thing is thoroughly dishonest'. It is possible, too, that knowledge of the discussions may have influenced Blamey's decisions the next year when both Rowell and Allen were relieved of their commands in New Guinea. From Blamey's point of view, though, there was sufficient justification for these actions without taking into account any knowledge he may have had of the angry discussions in Alexandria.[14]

In spite of the discord between himself and Blamey, Lavarack would not consider taking part in any move to petition the Australian government in the hope that Blamey might be relieved of his command. It was Lavarack's diary entry for the day after Andrew's funeral—the day he visited Blamey in hospital and concluded that Blamey was responsible for his being relieved as the commander of Western Desert Force—which contained the remark that he could not understand Blamey's attitude towards him when he had 'always been loyal to him [Blamey]'.[15] It would be characteristic of Lavarack that loyalty to his superior officer, even if that officer happened to be Blamey, would prevent him taking part in such an enterprise.

In any case, Lavarack had not been in Greece so could not speak with first-hand authority of what had happened there and, while not doubting the stories of Blamey's failings, he may well have concluded that the talks were no more than the understandable venting of frustration and disgust

187

at Blamey's conduct. Most of the disgruntled senior Australian army officers—whether angry with the way the campaign had gone or Blamey's leadership, or both—were mature men who, as tempers cooled, would have realised that, irrespective of its merits, a request for an official enquiry (and especially a petition to have Blamey recalled) would have been rebuffed by the Menzies' government.

So in the end there was no enquiry and no call to the government to replace Blamey, though it seems that both possibilities were aired during the Alexandria discussions. Nevertheless, the commander of the AIF had been shown to have feet of clay. Blamey's personal reputation and his standing within the AIF as a military commander had suffered a significant blow, the ramifications of which would continue to felt as the war rolled on. To Lavarack's credit, neither the humiliation of being returned to the 7th Division after Tobruk, nor his fears about his future under Blamey, had pushed him to be disloyal to his commander. Neither did they distract him from the comparatively mundane 'wire and shovel' task he had been given after leaving Tobruk: strengthening the defences at Mersa Matruh.

Wire and Shovel Work

Being under Beresford-Peirse's command in Matruh was galling for Lavarack, but there is nothing to suggest that he conveyed this to the Englishman or that he was reluctant to co-operate. Indeed, it appears that he co-operated more readily than was prudent. Blamey's questionable performance in Greece may have his weakened position in the eyes of some of his senior officers, but it did not distract him from his private war with Lavarack—and perhaps exacerbated it. So even in Matruh, and despite the fact that the 7th Division was part of Western Desert Force, Lavarack was to find himself in Blamey's sights for helping Beresford-Peirse.

By the end of the first week in May Lavarack had detached his ammunition company and one of his anti-tank batteries to Gott's Support Group, and on the 9th agreed to a request from Beresford-Peirse for transport assistance, provided that the Australian troops making up the convoy remained under his control. Naturally Beresford-Peirse was pleased by Lavarack's co-operation and expressed his appreciation to the CGS in the Middle East, Lieutenant-General Arthur Smith:

I know well the 'terms of reference' under which it is difficult for
Dominion Commanders to disperse their formations in any way.

In this case he has co-operated nobly, and being bound by the secrecy
of the operation has been unable to keep his Australian Headquarters
informed.

Beresford-Peirse concluded by saying that he took all responsibility for
the detachments and for 'imposing secrecy upon Lavarack'.[16]

Smith passed the letter to the Deputy Commander-in-Chief, Middle
East, who, since his return from Greece, had been Blamey. In helping
Beresford-Peirse Lavarack had acted in a way which, in principle, struck
at the core of Blamey's charter. Blamey took the opportunity to chastise
both Lavarack and the British in a letter to Smith:

General Lavarack knows very well that he has no authority to transfer
portion of his command on loan or otherwise and that the only
authority for this is myself. He should have so informed Beresford-
Peirse, or have consulted me direct.

The Australian Government is getting very restive over the distribution
of the A.I.F. There is a growing feeling that the Army is completely
disregarding the terms of its agreement with His Majesty's Government
for the sending of Australian Forces overseas.

The episode was especially annoying for Blamey because he was facing the likelihood that soon he would have no option but to promote
Lavarack to take his place as corps commander. Blamey's new duties as
Deputy Commander-in-Chief precluded him from effectively commanding the 1st Australian Corps and a successor had to be found. Lavarack
was the obvious choice because of his seniority and availability. Blamey
would delay Lavarack's promotion as long as possible, but events were to
force his hand.[17]

On 21 May Lavarack was informed that his division had been
nominated to take a major role in an invasion of Syria and Lebanon.
Although the size of the operation (to be code-named 'Exporter') had not
yet been determined, the move of the 7th Division to Palestine was to take
place immediately. Brigadier F.H. Kisch, the Chief Engineer at Beresford-
Peirse's headquarters, praised the work done as Lavarack's men left
Matruh: 'By this work, the defensibility of the Fortress has been radically

changed from a derelict state to a state nearing completion...'. The outer perimeter anti-tank ditch had been cleared completely of sand, the inner perimeter developed, new concrete emplacements, underground dressing stations and command post constructed, and 50,000 anti-tank mines laid. Beresford-Peirse 'heartily' endorsed Kisch's views and expressed his regret that Lavarack had to leave his command.[18] Lavarack did not share his disappointment.

In retrospect, April and May 1941 had been tempestuous months for Lavarack. Although he had been GOC Cyrenaica Command for only a short time, he had shown himself capable of command at corps level and of defeating a first-class enemy under unfavourable circumstances—the lion's share of the credit for checking Rommel's advance at Tobruk must go to Lavarack. However, the subsequent few weeks had further exposed the depth of Blamey's weaknesses and the extent of his animosity. Lavarack now surely recognised, if he had not before, that Blamey would do everything possible to consign him to military oblivion.

12

'He did not want Lavarack as corps commander'

The Syrian Campaign, 1941—Invasion

WHILE LAVARACK HAD been at Matruh, British fears had been growing that the Germans were about to seize Syria and Lebanon, which were ruled by France under a mandate from the League of Nations. After the fall of France in 1940 an armistice had been signed between France and Germany, which led to the establishment of a collaborationist French government, led by Marshal Philippe Pétain, based in the French town of Vichy. This created a schism in the French armed forces. Some soldiers, sailors and airmen believed it was their duty to remain loyal to Pétain's new French government, even though it meant cooperating with the Germans and Italians. Others decided that their loyalty lay with the Free French forces led by General Charles de Gaulle who had fled to London.

It was, however, the Vichy French who controlled strategically important Syria and Lebanon. In early May 1941 General Henri Dentz, the Vichy French High Commissioner and Commander-in-Chief of the Army of the Levant, allowed the Germans to use Syria as a staging area for Luftwaffe aircraft which were supporting an anti-British coup in neighbouring Iraq. (For the sake of convenience, and in accordance with the convention at the time, the term 'Syria' can also be taken to include Lebanon.) Dentz also released equipment held in Syria for use by the new pro-Axis Iraqi Prime Minister, Rashid Ali.

Wavell was therefore being pressed by London to move into Syria, or at least support a small Free French force which General Catroux, the senior Free French officer in the Levant, wanted to lead against the Vichy troops there. His resources already thinly spread, Wavell was reluctant to commit himself to any action in Syria, but he was overruled by Churchill and the Defence Committee in London. His hand having been forced, and believing that weak action (such as simply providing the Free French with transport and some air support) would be useless, Wavell set about mustering as strong a force as he could for an invasion of Syria. The largest formation which he could spare for the operation was Lavarack's division, and even its transfer to Syria jeopardised the defence of Egypt.[1]

Ironically, when it was soon realised in Berlin that Rashid Ali's pro-Axis regime in Iraq would not last, the Germans decided to withdraw their few personnel from Syria so that the British would have no pretext to attack. At that time the significance of Syria in the minds of German planners was dwarfed by the imminent invasion of Russia which was to begin in June. However, mounting evidence that Germany was about to attack Russia and reconnaissances of Syrian airfields which yielded no proof of a German build-up were seen by British intelligence as indicating not that the Germans had no intention of establishing themselves in Syria, but rather that the German move was still in its initial stages. So Lavarack was committed to play a major role in an unnecessary operation in which political aims overruled military objections.[2] Yet, for all that, it was to be a hard-fought and bloody campaign.

On 22 May Lavarack travelled to Jerusalem to report to General Sir Henry Maitland Wilson, the commander of British forces in Palestine and Transjordan, who would also command the Syrian invasion force.[3] The British historian Ronald Lewin has described Wilson:

> An amorphous elephant of a man—hence the nickname 'Jumbo'—with a disconcerting habit of talking down his nose or trunk, Wilson later reached the rank of Field Marshal for reasons which are difficult to identify and have never been explained. His endowment for one of the most senior commands seems sparse, in retrospect, and at best run-of-the-mill. Perhaps the very absence of originality or scintillation enabled him to float upwards unimpeded.

In a letter to Menzies shortly before the campaign began, Blamey outlined his misgivings about Wilson and concluded simply: 'The grey matter is not quite adequate'. Menzies, who had already met Wilson and was not in the least impressed by him, would probably have agreed. Nevertheless, whatever doubts there may have been about Wilson's abilities, he was in command and his aim was to secure control of Syria and Lebanon south of Tripoli in order to deny its use to Germany.

The invasion was to begin at 2 a.m. on 8 June. Wilson had decided to advance on three axes, as he explained:

> The main objective was Beirut; the shortest approach was along the coast but the road could be easily blocked. I decided, therefore, to advance three-headed on a wide front.

However, as the Australian official historian has observed, 'By dividing his force into three columns each of approximately equal strength General Wilson reduced the likelihood of achieving a marked success in any one sector'.[4]

On the right, the 5th Indian Brigade Group (Brigadier W.L. Lloyd) was to advance in four columns on Deraa, Ezraa, Kuneitra and Fiq. Once Ezraa had been taken, General Paul Legentilhomme's greatly understrength Free French Division was to pass through the Indians and press on to Kiswe and then Damascus. The centre and left lines of advance were Lavarack's responsibility. The centre column was to advance through Metulla and Merdjayoun to Rayak, and the left column along the coast road to Beirut. Lavarack was responsible for the protection of his right flank, although the capture of Kuneitra by the 5th Indian Brigade Group would afford him some security. Wilson also allotted Lavarack a flight of Hurricane fighter aircraft, C Battalion of the Special Service Brigade to land on the coast at his discretion, and a naval force to operate off the coast in support of the advance on Beirut.[5]

The terrain favoured the Vichy French, who were strong in numbers and equipped with tanks. Wavell's headquarters had estimated the Vichy strength in Lebanon and Syria to be 25,000 regulars, 20,000 local troops and 90 tanks, but Australian intelligence estimated the proportion of regular troops to be greater, about 35,000. Leaving aside the Levantine troops, the Vichy French had the equivalent of two strong infantry divisions and a half-division of tanks, armoured cars and cavalry. The position in the air promised to be little better. In all, the invaders could expect to have about 50 first-line aircraft at their disposal. At the beginning of the campaign the Vichy air force consisted of about 30 bombers and 60 fighters (but during the fighting this number would be almost doubled by reinforcements from French North Africa).[6]

Despite the numerical strength of the French, senior British officers thought that resistance would not be strong and that the advance would be rapid. The outline plan for Operation 'Exporter' issued by Wavell's headquarters stated that 'the success of the operation largely depends on lack of resistance, or at least acquiescence by the French' and envisaged a

> rapid move along the coastal road to Beirut by Armoured Cars and motorised infantry with the object of seizing all important control points and high officials in Beirut before dawn.

Wilson in particular felt that the Vichy French would not put up a strong defence and that the operation was, in Churchill's words, a 'kind of armed political inroad'. Lavarack was therefore told that white flags and Union Jacks should be visible when approaching French positions to win over the defenders and that loudspeakers should be used to broadcast propaganda during the advance. A Free French or French-speaking officer was to be attached to each battalion with the task of approaching the Vichy French positions calling upon them to join de Gaulle. It was also suggested that British troops should shout for the Vichy French 'to get out of the way and let us get at the Germans!'[7] Lavarack told the official historian after the war:

> Wavell and Wilson hoped that the Vichy French would not put up even a token resistance. Wavell once expressed to me the hope that we should be in Beirut in one day, or two at the most.

General Rowell, then the BGS at HQ 1st Australian Corps, wrote that

> There was indeed some confidence that this would be very much a "pushover" and the feeling was stronger the farther away one was from the front. It was a strange idea that a mere show of force would make the Vichy French give up. Certainly the 7th Division did not share the view, nor did we at corps headquarters give it any credence.

Lavarack, unlike Wavell and Wilson, was convinced that the French would fight, even accurately forecasting the area of staunchest resistance in his diary on 5 June: 'My conclusion is that 25 Bde will be opposed at Merdjayoun, perhaps seriously...'. However, with more than a touch of hindsight, Wilson would write after the campaign that 'Wavell and myself had no illusions that our forces would be received with open arms'.[8]

Wilson had envisaged taking Syria in two phases: first the capture of

Damascus, Rayak and Beirut, and then an advance to Palmyra, Homs and Tripoli. Wilson planned that on the completion of the first phase 'or at such other time as may be decided', Headquarters 1st Australian Corps would take over operational command of 'Exporter Force'. The corps headquarters had reassembled at Deir Suneid in Palestine after the evacuation from Greece. But it was without a commander because Blamey had taken up the post of DC-in-C in Cairo, and had also resumed control of AIF administration from Brigadier Plant, to whom he had delegated his authority when he left for Greece. Clearly an Australian corps commander would have to be appointed and Lavarack was the obvious choice because of his seniority.[9] Blamey, though, baulked at appointing Lavarack, as Rowell later confirmed.

The first Rowell knew of Operation 'Exporter' was when Lavarack and Chapman arrived at his quarters in Deir Suneid on 25 May. Immediately Rowell went to see Wilson in Jerusalem to urge that the operation, which would be carried out by forces largely Australian, be controlled by an Australian headquarters. Wilson said that power to alter the arrangement rested in Cairo, so Rowell set out to see Blamey, who

> was most unhelpful. He said the Vichy French would either run so fast that we'd never catch up or the British would get stuck and we'd be handed the platter. He also said our transport and signals wouldn't cope after Greece.

Rowell 'begged' Blamey to intervene to ensure that the operations were controlled by the Australian corps headquarters, but 'To my amazement I found him dead against it, an attitude which ran counter to his whole philosophy of the command of national forces'. Blamey argued that there was no corps commander, to which Rowell replied that he could easily appoint Lavarack, but, Rowell recalled, 'it was clear that he did not want Lavarack as corps commander unless forced to appoint him'.[10]

Rowell returned to Palestine without much hope that Blamey would support the claim of an Australian headquarters to control 'Exporter'. Then on 2 June, less than a week before the operation was due to commence, Wilson received confirmation from Wavell's headquarters that HQ 1st Australian Corps would assume operational control, but only after the first phase of the operation. News that he could be given command of 1st Australian Corps in Syria reached Lavarack unofficially soon after his arrival in Palestine and was confirmed by Blamey on 4 June.

The official historian recorded that 'It was appropriate that General Lavarack should thus be promoted to a senior command' since he had been CGS before the war and his drop in rank to command the 7th Division had made him junior to British officers who had previously been his juniors.[11] Brigadier A.S. Allen would succeed Lavarack in command of the 7th Division when the time came.

Still, it was hardly an ideal command arrangement for the Syrian operation. Blamey's resistance to promoting Lavarack to command the corps and, as a consequence, his willingness to allow a ramshackle command arrangement to develop had increased the risk to Australian soldiers and undercut the principle of the command of national forces which had been clearly laid out in the charter issued to Blamey by the Australian government. Rowell had no doubts that had the Australian Corps HQ been placed in charge from the beginning the campaign could have been handled better, especially during the first phase when operations in Lebanon and Syria would be controlled from Wilson's headquarters situated many miles to the rear in the King David Hotel in Jerusalem.

Moreover, Rowell was concerned about Wilson himself who not long before had delegated command at a critical time during the fighting in Greece. Rowell believed that as long as there were no difficulties Wilson's headquarters would control operations from Jerusalem and that even once the first phase was completed the Australian headquarters might not be permitted to take over. Nevertheless, Rowell decided that he would be prepared. Before the campaign began he moved the corps headquarters to Nazareth in northern Palestine, with the aid of vehicles borrowed from the Palestine police, and ordered that, as soon as the campaign commenced, corps headquarters staff would be in the field gathering information and preparing for the moment when Lavarack would assume command.[12]

Meanwhile, Lavarack had been preparing his divisional plan, greatly hampered by a paucity of information. As late as 28 May there was still no detailed information on the order of battle, or air and naval support. The outlook was not promising for an operation which was to begin in little more than a week. Indeed, although Lavarack frequently pressed Wilson for details, it was not until 4 June, four days before the invasion, that he was at last given the dates on which most of the additional units he was to command would come under the control of his headquarters.

Even though Lavarack had only the 21st and 25th Brigades of his division (the 18th Brigade was to remain in Tobruk), on paper he had strong divisional troops at his disposal: three field artillery regiments, one anti-tank regiment, two cavalry regiments, two infantry battalions, one machine gun battalion and one pioneer battalion. However, such strength was to a degree illusory, for one of the cavalry regiments (the 9th), the 2/3rd Machine Gun Battalion and the two Australian infantry battalions (the 2/3rd and 2/5th, just returned from the debacle in Greece) were not properly equipped, and it would take some time to make good the deficiencies.[13]

Lavarack also had under his command several British units: a horsed cavalry regiment (the Cheshire Yeomanry), a composite mechanised regiment (made up of the Scots Greys and Staffordshire Yeomanry), one squadron of armoured cars (detached from the Royals), and the 57th Light Anti-Aircraft Regiment, as well as certain engineer and service troops. However, the most glaring omission from the order of battle was medium or heavy armour, and reconnaissance vehicles were scarce. The invasion force was to feel keenly the absence of tanks, as Lavarack reported after the campaign:

> Throughout the campaign the French made extensive use of their tanks, particularly for the purpose of counter attacking our troops and driving them from ground already captured; as our forces were entirely without tanks, except for the light tanks of the Div Cav Regt and for those tanks captured from the French, we had no suitable weapon to counter these tactics, and in many cases, such as at Merdjayoun, our hard won gains were completely nullified by the French in this way.[14]

The ground over which the 7th Division had to attack was difficult. The direction of advance was parallel to the two major mountain ranges which run the length of the country. Lavarack's two brigades would be separated by the Lebanon Range, with the 21st on the western side along the coast and the 25th inland to the east in the Bekaa Valley. (Beyond that, and still farther to the east on the other side of the Anti-Lebanon Range, was the desert route through Syria to Damascus being taken by the Indians and Free French who were not under Lavarack's command for the time being.)

The coast road, stretching some sixty miles from the frontier to Beirut and dominated by the western hills of the Lebanon Range, offered partic-ular difficulties: at some points it had been cut through rocky spurs reaching to the sea, thus making demolition by the defenders a simple matter. Bypassing opposition on the road itself would not be easy, as the 7th Division assessment noted:

> The mountain country that lies east of the coast r[oa]d is rugged and barren, its boulder-strewn hillsides and narrow rocky gorges offering a tremendous natural barrier to military movement. Few r[oa]ds exist, and off the r[oa]ds the country is impassable for wheeled or tracked veh[icle]s of any kind. Progress on foot is incredibly slow and exhausting, and any natural approaches that exist can be readily closed by a resolute enemy with mortars and automatic weapons.[15]

For Lavarack, controlling two widely separated brigades promised to be a difficult task, especially because of the rugged nature of the mountain range between them and the scarcity of lateral roads. If strenuously opposed by the French, Lavarack would face a potentially disastrous situation, made worse by the absence of his third brigade as a reserve. Consequently, he did not envisage a 'break-neck' pace, but rather a sure-footed advance with each bound being made from a firm base.

The day before the invasion the divisional headquarters moved forward from Nazareth to an olive grove near Er Rama, about seven miles west of Safad. After visiting Brigadiers Stevens and Cox 'mainly for reasons of morale' while the move was taking place, Lavarack returned to his headquarters and retired early, convinced that the morning would bring news of strong French opposition.[16]

Invasion

In the early hours of 8 June the Australians crossed the border into Lebanon. For Lavarack, waiting long hours for the first reports to come in, it was a day of tension, the end of which would see his misgivings about 'Exporter' realised. As the invasion force crossed the frontier at 2 a.m. the increasing volume of small arms fire from the Vichy French outposts testified to their intention to fight. The main Australian force had been preceded by small parties whose task it was to disrupt communications and prevent the demolition of the coast road near Iskanderoun. Although telephone lines had been cut it had not been possible to prevent the cratering of the road. Nevertheless, by late afternoon the leading elements of the 21st Brigade had taken Tyre and were within half a mile of the enemy's main defensive line along the Litani River.[17]

Lavarack was not so fortunate with the 25th Brigade's advance to the east. At the end of the day Cox's force had been halted before Merdjayoun, a short distance inside the frontier, as Lavarack had feared. The Vichy French had resisted strongly and 'little had been gained beyond finding the enemy's defences, sampling his strength, and learning that hard fighting lay ahead'. Lavarack gave Cox the remaining two companies of the 2/25th Battalion, held in divisional reserve, to help break the deadlock. He suggested to his brigadier that the 2/33rd Battalion mount an attack during the night to take Fort Khiam and that at dawn on the 9th a concentrated attack be made to clear the Merdjayoun area from the east to the bridge over the Litani River in the west. In that way lateral communications with Stevens' brigade on the coast might be opened up.[18]

On the extreme right flank of the invasion not under Lavarack's control, Indian and Free French troops advancing towards Damascus had taken Fiq and were in commanding positions about El Kuneitra and Sheikh Meskine. But overall the Vichy French had left the attackers in no doubt that the invasion would be hard fought. In the light of the day's events the measures proposed to induce the defenders to lay down their arms and join the Allies seemed ridiculous. Amongst the first casualties were those manning vehicles equipped with loudspeakers calling upon Vichy troops to cease resistance.

Feelings ran especially high on the Free French front where Legentilhomme's men were greeted with a 'blast of invective' from their countrymen on the other side, followed by gunfire. The Australians, who had been ordered to wear slouch hats to distinguish them from the British in the hope that they would be better received by the Vichy French, were almost immediately encouraged by circumstances to don steel helmets, leaving in the wake of their advance 'a line of felt hats about ten yards past the starting line'. It was a sad irony that the first Australian casualty of the invasion was a young non-commissioned officer of Lebanese descent whose father had migrated to Australia before the First World War.[19]

After seeing Lavarack during the day Blamey despatched a cable in the evening to Australia, addressed to the Minister for the Army, in which he reported:

Considerable fighting along frontier. R[oa]d demolitions caused considerable delay. Tyr [sic] captured at 1720 hrs. Advance continues. Penetration approx. 20 miles. Considerable fighting in centre...T[roo]ps participating British Free French Australian Indian. Enemy air action slight. Request minimum publicity of details.

Blamey's request that minimum publicity be given to the operations angered Lavarack who felt that Blamey was attempting to belittle his division's part in the invasion. The official historian noted that the order in which Blamey named the nationalities of the participating troops 'may have created an impression that the Australian and Indian forces had provided contingents to augment a mainly British and Free French force', whereas the number of Australian units was almost twice that of the other three combined. It was unusual for Blamey, normally conscious of Australian prestige, to present the Australian contribution in such a way. For Lavarack it leant weight to his suspicions that Blamey was trying to deprecate his role and was apparently willing to do it at the expense of the reputation of Australian soldiers engaged in a bloody campaign.[20]

There was little time, however, to dwell on Blamey's behaviour. With the expectation that the 25th Brigade would be attacking Merdjayoun at dawn on the 9th, Lavarack rose before first light and drove to Cox's headquarters. On arrival there he was surprised to discover that Cox had no intention of attacking as expected and also that the attack planned for the previous night had not taken place. Lavarack found his brigadier to be 'rather jittery', offering as his reason for postponing the attack the 'absurd excuse of exhaustion of men'. Not only was Lavarack angry with Cox's lack of drive, but he thought Cox's plan for an alternative attack to be so lacking in judgement that he ordered that it was not to be carried out under any circumstances. Lavarack noted in his diary that Cox's plan required the 'movement of half his artillery from end to end of his position between his own front and that of the French'. He told his brigadier to prepare sounder plans.[21] However, eventually he withdrew the artillery unit under Cox's command, the 2/6th Field Regiment, and placed it under the command of his CRA, Berryman. To Berryman he also gave the 2/5th Field Regiment and a company of the 2/3rd Machine Gun Battalion to support a three battalion attack against Merdjayoun at dawn on the 11th. Berryman later wrote:

I do not know what Lavarack told Cox but he ordered Headquarters

Royal Australian Artillery and 2/5 Field Regiment into the Merdjayoun
Sector, placed the Artillery under my command and after discussion
with me told me to get a plan for Porter [commanding the 2/31st
Battalion] to attack and take Merdjayoun.

The attack on Merdjayoun must have seemed a daunting prospect in the
absence of any medium tanks. The French were entrenched in well-prepared defensive positions sited to make best use of enfilade fire and Cox's
troops were on sparsely-covered ground so well known to the enemy that
small cairns of stones had been placed over the area to mark the range for
the French gunners.[22]

On the 10th, as preparations for the Merdjayoun attack continued,
Lavarack visited Stevens for the first time since the invasion began. The
21st Brigade had crossed the Litani River the previous day, but had been
strongly opposed by the Vichy French. Stevens felt that even the Vichy
African troops were the equal of the Australians, at least in daylight and
on the defensive:

> The Vichy troops we encountered were tough professionals of the
> French Foreign Legion, together with Moroccan and Algerian troops.
> They gave nothing away and what was envisaged by the British High
> Command as a relatively peaceful advance to Beirut turned out to be a
> bitterly contested battle throughout.

Many casualties had been suffered by the Australians and by British
commandos of the Special Service Battalion who had been landed at the
mouth of the river before dawn on the 9th. The commandos had been
unsuccessful in their mission to prevent the demolition of the ancient
bridge across the Litani, so crossings of the river had to be made by groups
of Australians in small boats under heavy Vichy fire. Despite the
determined resistance, by the afternoon Stevens had portions of two
companies on the north bank of the river. Afterwards, during the hours of
darkness, a pontoon bridge had been erected and vehicles had reached the
north bank of the river by the time of Lavarack's visit. Stevens had done
well to be able to cross against strong defences so quickly after the
demolition of the bridge. Heartened after seeing Stevens and his battalion
commanders, Lavarack returned to division headquarters with the 'firm
conviction that the 21 Bde has already made good'—it was the 'perfect
team, and Stevens the master'.

Part of the credit also belonged to Lavarack: he had instituted 'solid training' in mountain warfare in Palestine earlier in the year, the value of which was proved in the first days of the campaign, to the detriment of the defenders. The Australians' determination impressed the French, as one French colonel would remark after the fighting was over: 'Until I saw your infantry crossing the...river and fighting in the mountains, I believed the Foreign Legion were the toughest troops in the world'.[23]

The coastal plain was now in Australian hands almost to Adloun, about five miles north of the Litani River, and a track leading inland had been explored to approximately the same depth. It was obvious, however, that hard fighting still lay ahead, as the official historian observed:

> [T]he Syrian expedition, instead of a fast-moving three-pronged thrust against a half-hearted enemy, had resolved itself into a hard campaign against resolute and skilful troops. On the right the Free French had been held but were now being reinforced from Lloyd's Indian brigade which had been guarding their rear; in the centre the advance had bogged down within sight of the frontier; on the left progress had been faster but, to judge by the events of the previous days, a series of exacting fights lay ahead against an enemy who would put up a capable defence at well-chosen positions in the long defile between sea and mountain.[24]

Having decided to be on hand for the attack on Merdjayoun early next morning, Lavarack was once more on the road before midnight. One of his senior staff officers recalled that as Lavarack was about to leave his headquarters

> I...suggested he should have a rest instead, but he went off to Merdjayoun. It was my opinion at the time and still is, that his personal intervention and his presence was the major factor in Merdjayoun being taken.[25]

Lavarack believed in going forward whenever possible and he was to spend long hours travelling during the campaign visiting subordinate commanders at the front.

Lavarack hoped that the deadlock at Merdjayoun could be broken, thus allowing his inland column to keep pace with the advance on the coast. However, when he arrived at 25th Brigade headquarters at 1.30 a.m., he found Cox 'in depths of dejection'. After a long discussion with him, Lavarack felt that Cox was probably physically ill and he began seriously to consider replacing him. Berryman, on the other hand, was taking a leading role on the 25th Brigade front. At his instigation the French defences around Khirbe had been tested by a small force of Bren carriers, which sustained substantial casualties, indicating that strong resistance could be expected. The plan called for an assault by the 2/25th Battalion against Ibeles Saki to the east of Merdjayoun and for the 2/31st Battalion, supported by the 2/5th and 2/6th Field Regiments under Berryman's control, to attack Khirbe, Qleaa and then Merdjayoun itself from the south.[26]

Lavarack stayed long enough to witness the first stages of the attack, which began at 2.30 a.m., preceded by the heaviest artillery bombardment yet seen in the campaign. At dawn the 2/31st Battalion was fighting its way through Khirbe and Qleaa, and by early afternoon it was clear that Merdjayoun had been abandoned by the French. The evening of the 11th found the 2/31st Battalion in Merdjayoun, the 2/25th north of Ibeles Saki and the 2/33rd north of Khiam. With the fall of Merdjayoun a major hurdle had been overcome. Lavarack felt that the laurels of the day belonged to Berryman, who was clearly the driving force on the 25th Brigade front (during the attack on Merdjayoun he and his brigade-major had managed to take 14 prisoners). To maintain pressure on the retreating French, Lavarack immediately ordered that a column under the command of Lieutenant-Colonel Todd of the Scots Greys (to be known as 'Todforce'), pursue the enemy to harass his withdrawal and determine the next line of resistance.[27]

Meanwhile, further progress had been made along the coast road. By dawn on the 11th Stevens' troops had overcome enemy positions near Adloun and Innsariye (about halfway between Tyre and Sidon), and continued advancing until past the road junction at Es Sakiye. Here the Australians came under fire from tanks, artillery and infantry of the Foreign Legion, but the French were overcome and by mid-afternoon the leading troops had passed Khan Saada. The enemy next made a stand just south of the Wadi Zaharani at the junction of the coast road and the lateral leading inland to Merdjayoun. Despite a hard fight, the French maintained their positions for the rest of the day. Lavarack wanted Stevens to take that particular road junction as soon as possible— divisional headquarters was now too far to the rear to allow rapid communication with the two brigades and could not move forward until the road linking the two fronts was taken.[28]

Since the invasion began, every day had made it obvious that the French intended to exact a heavy price for each gain made by the attackers. Yet, despite reports of mounting casualties, those not directly involved in the fighting clung Micawberishly to the comforting theory of French non-resistance or at least an early collapse of opposition. In a signal to Sturdee on 12 June Blamey said that 'It is hoped if momentum can be maintained by constant pressure that enemy morale will break'. When Wavell visited Lavarack that day he again raised the question of using vehicles equipped with loudspeakers to persuade the enemy to lay down arms. No doubt Lavarack explained that there was little to be gained by further exploration of propaganda and political solutions to what had become a difficult military problem. Yet, from Wavell's reaction to the 7th Division's progress, it seemed clear to Lavarack that he had not reached a full understanding of what was happening in Syria and the Lebanon. Lavarack wrote in his diary:

> He seemed not at all amused at our efforts and practically refused to look at my recommendation of Stevens for the immediate award of the D.S.O., despite his magnificent work… He was (literally) querulous at our failure to provide him with frequent reports to Mr Winston Churchill, quite forgetful of the fact that we knew nothing of Mr Churchill's need of such reports. After all I am merely a Div Comdr.

Nothing Lavarack said seemed able to mollify Wavell and he departed as he had arrived, 'not amused'. He wrote after Wavell departed that 'This smacks of my Tobruk adventure. Archie [Wavell] has failed, but we may save him'.[29]

Lavarack's assessment of Wavell at this time, although somewhat harsh, was generally accurate. The Commander-in-Chief had come to the end of his tether from having to deal for too long with a war on several fronts and Churchill would soon replace him with General Auchinleck. There had been concern at the War Office in London caused by the unexpectedly slow progress of the Syrian invasion and the CIGS, Dill, already had made suggestions to Wavell about how the campaign might be more speedily concluded. When he visited Lavarack Wavell was conscious of the precarious position he was in with Churchill and held little hope that a new offensive in the Western Desert (Operation 'Battleaxe') would cause a rise in his stocks. Consequently he was disappointed when he saw that 'Exporter' had not developed more favourably. A short time later when

'Battleaxe' failed, Harding (who had been on Lavarack's staff in Tobruk) related that Wavell was distressed to the point of tears.[30]

Yet Wavell understood the position in Syria better than Lavarack thought. After his visit to the front he ordered from Egypt the 16th British Brigade and an artillery regiment, which would increase the strength of the attackers to approximately that of the enemy. He also admitted to Dill the difficulties Lavarack was experiencing:

> Progress slow as I warned you it would be if French resisted. They are doing so strongly at present. Country is difficult and favourable to defence and French are making full use of demolitions. 7th Aust. Div. is engaged in battle for first time. In circumstances I consider we have got along quite as fast as could be expected.
> [paragraphs deleted]
> On the whole I consider progress satisfactory in view of difficulties of ground and inadequate size of force.

However, it is a pity that he did not tell Lavarack that he thought that satisfactory progress was being made. 'I regret', Lavarack wrote later to the official historian, 'that he never gave me the satisfaction of knowing that this was his opinion'. Lavarack was aware of the difficult situation in which Wavell was placed and felt that it was unfortunate that 'my contacts with him all took place during the period when he was being forced to attempt more than mortal man could perform with the means at his disposal'. Nevertheless, Lavarack's recognition of Wavell's position could not ease the sting of his barbs about the slowness of the advance:

> I cannot forgive him, despite my knowledge of his troubles. He seemed to believe that I was making difficulties, whereas the fault was in himself and his advisers, who believed that the French would not resist and that the people would help. Unfortunately no franc-tireur's bullet cracked past him during his one visit to my front. He never realised, I feel sure, how difficult was the task he had given us to perform in one or two days.[31]

After his unhappy meeting with Wavell at 7th Division headquarters on the 12th, Lavarack began the two-hour drive to Merdjayoun fort, where he officially assumed control of the town and proclaimed martial law. The post-ceremony champagne reception with local dignitaries was interrupted by a Vichy French air attack, but nothing could mar Lavarack's satisfaction: despite enemy bombing, Merdjayoun was in Australian hands and a major obstacle to the 7th Division's advance had been removed.

Unfortunately, this did not mean that there would be no more problems for Lavarack on his right flank. 'Todforce', which had been harrying the French withdrawal, soon discovered that it had not far to travel before making contact with the enemy. Only a few miles from Merdjayoun the two columns into which 'Todforce' had been divided were halted by demolitions and accurate, heavy fire on both Routes A and B leading out of the town. It seemed unlikely that the enemy would withdraw further unless forced to do so, probably at no small cost to the 7th Division.[32]

Lavarack therefore decided to alter his plan of attack. In the time that it had taken the 25th Brigade to advance less than ten miles, the 21st Brigade had pushed thirty-five miles along the coast road and by late on 12 June was within three miles of Sidon. With his left flank outstripping his right, where there appeared to be little prospect of speeding up the advance, he made up his mind after dinner on the 12th to support Stevens' more successful advance on the coast by moving the 25th Brigade to Jezzine, a town on the western side of the Lebanon range not far from Sidon. There was a lateral road linking the two towns and earlier that day contact between the brigades had been established via another road further to the south. Lavarack explained that

> I decided on this movement late in the evening of the 12th June, because it had become obvious that the French were going to oppose us bitterly at Merdjayoun, and there was danger in letting 21 Bde (Stevens) on the coast, go ahead with his right flank exposed to attack from the Jezzine area.[33]

The only troops to remain in Merdjayoun were to be the 2/33rd Battalion, the 6th Australian Cavalry Regiment, a battery of artillery, and the Scots Greys. The decision met with some opposition from Lavarack's staff, but he chose to follow his own counsel, remarking that at least the idea had the merit of being 'completely original'. As preparations for the move to Jezzine continued during the 13th, French resistance north of Merdjayoun continued and harassing shellfire began falling on the town.

Such evidence of enemy intransigence seemed to vindicate Lavarack's decision to shift the weight of his attack to the coast.[34]

At 9 p.m. on the 13th the vanguard of the 25th Brigade set out for Jezzine, which lay almost due north of Merdjayoun at a distance of about twelve miles in a direct line. Only one road joined the towns, however, and that was a tortuous ribbon cut into steep hill-sides from which the French could easily launch delaying actions. It was an audacious decision considering the difficulties under which the move had to be made:

> The convoy drove all night without lights. At times the trucks had to back three times before they could get round the sharp corners and the guns had to be unlimbered and man-handled. Sometimes the trucks bogged in the mountain streams; one overturned. There was a delay of two hours at the turn from the Sidon road where no guide had been placed, and part of the convoy continued towards Sidon and had to be recalled. Just south of Jerme was a bend so sharp that the engineers had to work on it for two hours before heavy vehicles could pass; the tail of the advance-guard was still struggling round it when there arrived the head of the main column, which had set off at 1 a.m.

Not surprisingly, Lavarack too laboured late into the night: the move to Jezzine increased the tempo of his work to a level which would barely slacken before he relinquished command of the division (the only entry made in Lavarack's diary for the period 13-17 June 1941 was 'Syrian Campaign. Too busy').[35]

Early on the 14th he set out for Jezzine, calling at Merdjayoun en route to see Lieutenant-Colonel R.F. Monaghan, the commander of 'Monforce', which had been left to defend the Merdjayoun area, and Lieutenant-Colonel Todd, commanding the Scots Greys, which now became part of the divisional reserve and responsible for internal security in Merdjayoun. Lavarack gave Monaghan permission to conduct an active defence, but emphasised that his primary task was to defend the division's right flank and rear as it advanced further north. Every reasonable opportunity of harassing the enemy was to be taken, but always subject to the performance of the main task. Lavarack warned Monaghan not to be reckless.[36]

Lavarack then continued his journey to 25th Brigade headquarters, which he found at the end of a road 'jammed with vehicles' about seven miles from Jezzine—had French aircraft seen the column strung out along the road great damage could have been done, but Lavarack's gamble had paid off and Cox's force was unmolested. By dawn the brigade had reached Kafr Houn, several miles south of Jezzine and from there the advance had continued on foot towards Green Hill, which dominated the town and where there were strong enemy positions. Lavarack told Berryman 'to get Jezzine that night' and at 6 p.m. an attack was launched against Green Hill which carried the assault past the objective and into Jezzine itself, Berryman being among the leading troops when they entered the town unopposed at 8.30 p.m.

That Jezzine had fallen so quickly was welcome news, especially since the 21st Brigade had been making little ground. By late in the afternoon of the 14th Lavarack learnt that the 21st Brigade was still in the gardens south of Sidon. After initial success, which by 3 p.m. had carried the attackers past the town and to within several hundred yards of their final objective of the Wadi Abou Zare, the French counter-attacked with tanks. Without tanks of its own the 21st Brigade had no answer to the enemy armour and much of the ground taken had to be relinquished.[37]

Now, with a brigade group on the coast, one at Jezzine and the holding force at Merdjayoun, Lavarack was responsible for a front of approximately thirty-seven miles. Ordinarily he could have expected to have another brigade as his reserve, but with the 18th in Tobruk he had almost all his troops in the front line. Instead his reserve was a motley collection of units, some of which were understrength, spread out between Er Rama and Merdjayoun. And by 14 June the configuration of the line dividing the two armies favoured the French in the Merdjayoun area: on the western side of the Lebanon range the two brigades of the 7th Division were thirty miles from Beirut; in the desert the advance of the Indians and Free French had carried them almost to Kiswe, twelve miles south of Damascus; but in between these extremities was the Merdjayoun salient, where the frontier with Palestine jutted northward to within ten miles of the town. Lavarack was concerned about the unfavourable geography and the lack of a reserve, and also worried that Monaghan's impetuous nature might cause him to act rashly.[38] Should the French decide to counter-attack at Merdjayoun there would be very little between them and Palestine. Lavarack did not have to wait long for his fears to be realised.

Above: **Syria, June 1941.** Major-General Lavarack inspects the 2/31st Battalion after the capture of the key Lebanese town of Merdjayoun from the Vichy French. The Vichy French were tough, seasoned opponents who made the Australians, British, Indian and Free French forces fight hard for every objective. (AWM)

Below: **Syria, 1941.** Australian troops move over difficult country to attack enemy positions. Lavarack thought the ground over which the campaign was fought to be 'truly awful'. (AWM)

Above: **Senior officers of the 6th Division AIF in early 1941**. Soon three of them—Berryman, Allen and Savige—would be fighting under Lavarack's command in Syria. Rear, left to right: Colonel F.H. Berryman, Brigadier S.G. Savige (17th Brigade), Colonel G.A. Vasey. Front, left to right: Brigadier A.S. 'Tubby' Allen (16th Brigade), Major-General Iven Mackay (GOC 6th Division) and Brigadier H.C.H. Robertson (19th Brigade). Allen succeeded Lavarack as commander of the 7th Division when Lavarack became GOC of the Australian corps. Mackay and Savige were militia officers who enjoyed Blamey's favour. Robertson was a regular officer who early in the war attracted Blamey's wrath. Vasey, another regular, was critical of Blamey's behaviour during the Greek campaign of 1941. (AWM)

Right: **Syria, 1941.** Australian 25-pounder field guns shell Vichy positions entrenched in the mountains. Lavarack began the campaign outnumbered in men and deficient in most types of heavy weapons, particularly tanks, which the enemy possessed in considerable numbers. (AWM)

Above: **Syria, 1941.** Lavarack (once again a lieutenant-general and now in command of the 1st Australian Corps) confers with one of his division commanders, Major-General A.S. 'Tubby' Allen. At right is the Commander-in-Chief in the Middle East, General Sir Archibald Wavell. Lavarack later wrote of Wavell that 'He never realised, I feel sure, how difficult was the task he had given us...'. (AWM)

Below: **Syria, 1941.** Australian soldiers take cover as shells explode ahead of them before the final assault on the wireless mast at Khalde, not far south of their final objective of Beirut. (AWM)

Above: **Acre, Palestine, 12 July 1941.** Lavarack and the commander of Allied forces in Palestine, General 'Jumbo' Wilson, sign the armistice ending hostilities in Syria. Although nominally in command of the campaign, Wilson (who tried to control the fighting from the luxurious King David Hotel in Jerusalem) handed over to Lavarack when it became clear that the Vichy French were determined to put up a ferocious defence. (AWM)

Below: **Beirut, July 1941.** Australian troops march through the city to celebrate victory. More Australians were killed in the hard-fought campaign against the French than had been in the Greek campaign against the German army earlier in the year. (AWM)

Above: **The Victors.** Air Commodore L.O. Brown, Lavarack, General Wilson and General Georges Catroux, the Free French leader. After the defeat of the Vichy forces Catroux was appointed High Commissioner in the Levant and oversaw the transition to independence in Syria and Lebanon. (AWM)

Right: **The Vanquished.** General Henri Dentz, Vichy France's High Commissioner in the Levant until he responded to Lavarack's call for an armistice. Dentz had been the military governor of Paris in 1940 when the city was surrendered to the Germans. After the war he was tried in France for collaborating with the Axis and sentenced to death. President de Gaulle commuted his death sentence to life imprisonment. Dentz died soon afterwards, in December 1945. (GDL)

Above: **Senior officers of the 2nd AIF in Cairo, September 1941.** Left to right: Major-General S.R. Burston, Lavarack, Blamey, Major-General L.J. Morshead and Major-General E.F. Herring. All were Militia officers apart from Lavarack. Blamey's unpopularity with the British at this time would prompt Churchill to suggest that Lavarack replace him in the Middle East. (AWM)

Below: **Armistice Day, Beirut, 1941.** Lavarack and General Catroux, the French High Commissioner in the Levant, at the Beirut Armistice Service on 11 November 1941. Lavarack was acting GOC AIF Middle East at the time during Blamey's absence in Australia. In little more than two months Lavarack would leave for the Netherlands East Indies after the outbreak of war in the Pacific. (AWM)

Above: **War in the Pacific.** Smoke rises above Tanjong Priok harbour, near Batavia on the island of Java, after a Japanese bombing raid in February 1942. The speed of the Japanese advance had left Lavarack and Wavell, the commanders of Australian and British troops in the Netherlands East Indies, no time to organise an effective defence. The staff of Lavarack's headquarters left for Australia from this harbour late on 21 February. (AWM)

Right: **Singapore Harbour, February 1942.** Japanese troops celebrate victory on the waterfront at Singapore the day after the British surrender. The British naval base, upon which such high hopes had been placed in Australian pre-war defence planning, was in enemy hands. (AWM)

Above: **The Commander-in-Chief, 1942.** Blamey with four of his Staff Corps generals after the outbreak of war in the Pacific. Left to right: Blamey, Sturdee, Lavarack, Wynter and Rowell. Blamey preferred citizen officers to regulars, and while Sturdee and Wynter were able to avoid Blamey's ire, both Lavarack and Rowell suffered greatly. Three of the men had served, or would serve, as CGS: Lavarack, Sturdee (twice) and Rowell. Wynter was one of the brightest of his generation of army officers, and a possible CGS, but suffered from ill-health which curtailed his career. (SLQ)

Below: **Two Army Commanders, 1943.** Lavarack with the commander of the US Sixth Army, Lieutenant-General Walter Krueger. Unlike Lavarack (who had American troops under his command), Krueger was allowed to lead his men against the Japanese. (AWM)

Right: **Civilian–Military Relations.** The supreme commander of the South-West Pacific Area, US General Douglas MacArthur, with John Curtin, the Australian Prime Minister from late 1941. MacArthur deplored Blamey's habit of promoting his friends and supporters (such as the mediocre General Savige) over more able and experienced Australian generals. Curtin, though aware of Blamey's personal and professional failings, protected him from his critics. Curtin was also no fan of Lavarack, who he rebuked over his advice on the diversion of Australian troops to Burma in 1942. Thus, with Blamey in charge of the army and without political allies of his own, Lavarack's fighting career was over before the war ended. (NAA)

Below: **Blamey and Lavarack at First Army Headquarters, Toowoomba.** Blamey's reluctance to move Lavarack's First Army HQ to New Guinea to control operations against the Japanese allowed the Americans to substitute a command arrangement which effectively ended control by Blamey (as Commander, Allied Land Forces) over any but Australian troops. By early 1944 Blamey had arranged Lavarack's posting to the military mission in Washington. Several months later First Army HQ was moved to New Guinea. (AWM)

Above: **Washington, 1944.** Despite the smile, Lavarack (centre) was unhappy as the Head of the Australian Military Mission in Washington, a posting which proved to be a 'sadly inactive' end to his military career. On Lavarack's right is Field Marshal Lord Alanbrooke, the Chief of the Imperial General Staff. At the extreme right is Lavarack's old friend Field Marshal Sir John Dill, Chief of the British Joint Staff Mission in Washington. (The two naval officers, one British and one American, are unidentified, though the former on the extreme left is most likely Admiral of the Fleet Lord Cunningham.) (SLQ)

Right: **Homeward bound, 1946.** John and Sybil Lavarack left Washington in 1946 to return to Australia. The journey did not go according to plan, with passenger shipping problems delaying their departure from the United States. On return, with Lavarack's time in the army coming to an end, they faced an uncertain future in Australia until he was offered the post of Governor of Queensland. (SLQ)

Above: **The Governor of Queensland.** Sir John and Lady Lavarack in the grounds of Government House, Brisbane c.1947. Lavarack would occupy the post from 1946 until shortly before his death in late 1957. During this period the official histories of the war were being written. In correspondence with the historians he would do his best to redress Blamey's attempts to downplay not only his own achievements but also those of the 7th Division during the fighting. (SLQ)

Left: **Governor of Queensland.** Lavarack soon after taking office. Lavarack's 11 years as Governor from 1946 marked the last, but welcome, phase of an otherwise frustrating career. His duties were varied, from officiating at the opening of parliament to laying the foundations of outback hospitals. (SLQ)

Below: **Royal Visit.** Lavarack escorts Queen Elizabeth II during her visit to Australia in 1954 (Lady Lavarack and the Duke of Edinburgh follow). (SLQ)

Above: **ANZAC Day.** Lavarack inspects a new generation of Australian troops, in this instance soldiers of the 11th National Service Battalion, during a post-war ANZAC Day commemoration. (SLQ)

Below: **Australia, 1966.** The Prime Minister, Harold Holt, opens Lavarack Barracks in Townsville on 29 July. Holt was an appropriate choice. Not only was he the country's head of government, but 30 years before, as a young parliamentarian during Lavarack's time as CGS, he had criticised the effects on the army of a defence policy based on the Singapore strategy. After the outbreak of war in 1939 Holt joined the AIF and was posted as a gunner to the 2/4th Field Regiment, which was part of Lavarack's 7th Division. (NAA)

13

'We have Damascus in our pocket...'

Syria, 1941—The French Counter-attack

WITH JEZZINE IN Australian hands Lavarack could move his headquarters forward, and on the 15th established himself about 10 miles south of the town in a fig orchard near Nabatiye. Just as the 25th Brigade had occupied Jezzine without opposition, on the coast the 21st Brigade occupied Sidon at 3 p.m. that afternoon—the French had abandoned their positions during the night and made a long withdrawal towards Beirut 30 miles to the north. However, hopes that the advance would continue at a good speed were soon dashed. At 4.30 p.m. Lavarack heard that Allied troops on the desert flank south of Damascus had been counter-attacked by the Vichy French. Late in the afternoon of the 14th enemy infantry, armoured cars and artillery had driven two squadrons of the Transjordan Frontier Force out of Ezraa, and another column was advancing on Kuneitra.[1]

The French counter-attack was not confined to the desert flank—once more Merdjayoun was to demand Lavarack's urgent attention. During the night of the 14th, Lieutenant-Colonel Monaghan left one company of his battalion at Merdjayoun and began a wide flanking movement to the east with his other three companies towards Fort Christofini, Hebbariye and Ferdisse. When the French attacked at 3 p.m. on the 15th Monaghan and the bulk of his unit were some miles from Merdjayoun. After shelling positions north of the town the French pushed down Routes A and B with infantry and tanks, causing great confusion, which led to panicky withdrawals by the defenders, some even crossing back into Palestine.

223

The French, however, did not pursue and instead halted at Merdjayoun at dusk. Nor did they drive westwards along the lateral road linking Merdjayoun and Sidon, a move which would have cut the 7th Division's lines of communication. Lavarack later concluded that one of the reasons for the French hesitancy was that their intelligence had estimated there was a second Australian division in reserve. Another reason, of which he was unaware at the time, was the Vichy plan for defending Syria and Lebanon, which was criticised by one of Dentz's staff officers, Captain Le Corbeiller:

> This plan of defence precluded all idea of manoeuvre or mobile defence. The enemy will be held back wherever he attacks, he will be stopped by a position ... set up in advance, we will counter-attack him. The outdated notion of a front ... was retained. The plan was rigid in its conception. No variation was foreseen.

The spirit of initiative in the Vichy defenders had been curtailed. Consequently, having counter-attacked successfully and re-established the front, they stopped and did not exploit their advantage.

Even so, the French thrust threatened lateral communications in the 7th Division area and, more serious, the enemy was now in a position to launch an attack into Palestine. The gravity of the situation was described by Berryman:

> The loss of Merdjayoun endangered the whole campaign. An enemy advance to Rosh Pinna [in Palestine] would split our front whilst should he cross the Litani and advance on Sidon our 21st and 25th Brigades would be threatened.[2]

The inexperience of the troops in Merdjayoun when faced by enemy tanks contributed to the loss of Merdjayoun, but Lieutenant-Colonel Monaghan, commanding 'Monforce', must bear a large proportion of the blame: his wide circling movement on the right gave the French the opportunity to sweep into the town. He had spent most of his military service in light horse units and had not adapted to infantry tactics. (Apparently, though, Monaghan profited by his experience for he remarked later to General Allen: 'I've learnt one thing—one infantryman has two legs not four'.) Lavarack was critical of Monaghan, but he was not blind to his own part in the debacle. He felt that he made an 'error of omission' in not placing either Todd of the Scots Greys or Monaghan in command at Merdjayoun when the move to Jezzine was made:

> Probably I should have appointed either Monaghan or Todd to command...However, neither of them had a staff suitable for the control of even a small mixed force. I trusted to their ability to co-operate and told them both that this was what I relied on. However, it would probably have been better to have placed one or the other in command, staff or no staff. To say this is to be wise after the event, like other critics. In any case the nett result was that there was no co-ordination, and as Monaghan chose to depart from the strict line of military virtue, there was no co-operation either, and the result was, to say the least about it, unfortunate.[3]

Of course, the situation might have been avoided had Lavarack not decided upon the move to Jezzine at all. Yet, when it became obvious that the French were in strong defensive positions north of Merdjayoun after it was first taken by the 25th Brigade, he was faced with two possible courses of action: to stay in the Merdjayoun area and fight it out on ground of the enemy's choosing or to attack at a key point where the enemy was probably unprepared. Wanting to maintain the momentum of the advance, Lavarack decided that it was the time to shift the weight of the 25th's advance to the left. His bold decision was justified, as General Allen observed: 'Joe's idea of moving to Jezzine was good, over dreadful country, where we surprised them'. To the official historian Lavarack wrote:

> It should be understood that this surprise was deliberate. We were fairly certain that the French had not yet put in a sizeable garrison, but they were at least as strong in numbers as we were, and could easily have afforded to do so if alarmed. Dentz himself stated to me, when staying, as a P.O.W., in my house in Aley just after the Armistice, that I had 'surprised' him at Jezzine, and that he had intended to put two good battalions there on the very morning after we seized the place.[4]

The Vichy French general, Pierre-Georges Arlabosse, the deputy military commander in the Levant whom Dentz had placed in command of the defence of southern Lebanon, also admitted that the move to Jezzine came as a surprise to him. However, Lavarack did not consider the success to be his alone. He felt that the credit for actually occupying the town belonged to Berryman, as he also told the official historian in generous terms:

> I believe that it was due to the initiative of Berryman, who as Artillery Commander was as usual well up where things were happening, that the Infantry, who had been poised on the brink for part of the day, eventually took the plunge, and occupied Jezzine.[5]

It was unfortunate that some of the advantage of this bold move was offset so quickly by the French counter-attack at Merdjayoun. Throughout the night of the 15th there was feverish activity at 7th Division Headquarters as reports arrived and Lavarack's orders went out in response to the French move. He ordered the 21st and 25th Brigades to halt and placed strong detachments from his scratch reserve on the roads from Merdjayoun. The 25th Brigade had not been attacked by the French in the strength that troops in other areas had been and so, lacking a reserve brigade, Lavarack had little choice but to reinforce Merdjayoun with troops from Jezzine. The 2/25th Battalion, the 2/5th Field Regiment (less one battery already at Merdjayoun), and one troop of the 2/6th Field Regiment were ordered to reinforce Merdjayoun that night. This left only the 2/31st Battalion and Cox's headquarters in Jezzine. The reinforcements for Merdjayoun were placed under the command of Berryman, who recalled the orders he received from Lavarack at about midnight on 15-16 June:

> I was to proceed to the area, take command and stop the enemy from crossing the Litani River so as to prevent him threatening the rear of our forces on the coast and at Djezzine [sic].[6]

While the move of the 25th Brigade units back to Merdjayoun took place, the 2/3rd Machine Gun Battalion, under the command of Lieutenant-Colonel A.S. Blackburn, and an anti-tank battery were to cover the crossing over the Jordan River at Jisr Bennt Jacub, south of Lake Hula. It was at this bridge on 27 September 1918 that the Australian Mounted Division overcame strong opposition by German and Turkish forces during the advance to Damascus by Chauvel, an irony which would not have been lost on Lavarack. Other possible crossings had to be held as well, and a proportion of the anti-tank guns and machine guns were ordered north towards Metulla. Lieutenant-Colonel N.F. Wellington, the commander of the 2/2nd Pioneer Battalion near Merdjayoun, was ordered to contact

Monaghan if possible and to prepare for demolition the bridge across the Litani which gave access to the rear of the 25th Brigade at Jezzine.[7]

As more information about the night's events began to come in during the morning of the 16th, Lavarack learned that at dusk the day before his troops had still been in control north of Merdjayoun, despite some hasty withdrawals brought on by panic, but in the early hours of the 16th the last troops had abandoned their positions to the French and concentrated north of Qleaa. At daybreak the detailed dispositions around Merdjayoun were clearer: the Scots Greys, an attached squadron of the Staffordshire Yeomanry, and a recently-arrived company of the 2/5th Australian Battalion were forward of Qleaa; one company of Monaghan's battalion was south of Merdjayoun with the remainder in the hills east of the town near Rachaya el Fokhar; and the 6th Cavalry Regiment covered the Banias–Merdjayoun road junction. By evening Monaghan would have two companies at Bmeriq and two south of Fort Khiam, but such was the disruption caused by the enemy attack that even the next day his exact dispositions would still not be known to Lavarack.[8]

Berryman had arrived at the Litani River west of Merdjayoun at dawn on the 16th and immediately took steps to prevent any further advance by the French from Merdjayoun. Throughout the day, as more units arrived from Jezzine, the defences of Merdjayoun were probed. Some Australians even entered the outskirts of the town, but French tanks forced them to withdraw. It was clear that the fort at the southern tip of Merdjayoun was strongly held. At 3 p.m. Lavarack arrived and gave approval for an attack against Merdjayoun the next day and extended Berryman's command east of the Litani to include all troops in the Merdjayoun area, the whole being known as 'Berryman Force'.

The troops under Berryman's command formed the strongest force in any area under Lavarack's command, comprising two infantry battalions, a pioneer battalion, a regiment of field artillery (plus one troop), a composite mechanised regiment, a cavalry regiment (less two squadrons), and sub-units of machine-gunners, field engineers and anti-tank and anti-aircraft artillery. Meanwhile, at Jezzine, as vehicles streamed southwards throughout the day towards Merdjayoun, Cox and his remaining battalion, the 2/31st, defended the town against enemy thrusts along the roads from the north and from Machrhara to the east.

The 16th had been a hectic day for Lavarack leaving him no time to visit the 21st Brigade, which had consolidated its position four miles north of Sidon. He had intended to declare martial law there himself, but instructed Stevens to make the declaration instead. The day also confirmed suspicions that Wilson would control the invasion as long as it went smoothly and Lavarack received a message that he would take over command as GOC 1st Australian Corps within two days. As Rowell had predicted, when the enemy struck his first severe blow against the invasion, Wilson decided to hand over command to Lavarack.[9]

On the morning of the 17th, his last full day in command of the 7th Division, Lavarack went to Berryman's headquarters. The attack against Merdjayoun failed, one battalion being unable to reach the objective and another being pinned down in front of the fort, suffering heavy casualties. In the afternoon, as Lavarack watched from Kafr Tibnite across the Litani valley, a 'terrific artillery bombardment' fell upon the fort. The French magazine within exploded and the 'place lifted skywards', but by then Berryman was short of ammunition and could not launch another attack until he had replenished his stocks.[10]

That evening, after returning to his headquarters, Lavarack received more worrying news. A message from Cox informed him that at Jezzine he was opposed by three and a half French battalions and that if reinforcements were not received it would be necessary to withdraw. Cox was facing a force of fresh Vichy troops, the nucleus of which was the *6th Foreign Legion Infantry Regiment*, a unit which had until then been held in reserve because its loyalty to Vichy was thought to be suspect. However, despite the Free French leanings of its officers, the regiment had launched a determined attack to retake the town.[11]

Lavarack told Cox to hold on and immediately instructed Stevens not to advance any further until the 25th Brigade's position could be stabilised. He also ordered Stevens to send the 2/14th Battalion, and detachments of anti-tank artillery and machine guns, to reinforce Cox at Jezzine. Half the battalion moved that night, the remainder the next morning.[12] This left two battalions on the coast, two at Jezzine and the bulk of Lavarack's forces at Merdjayoun, which was the place he had hoped to bypass a few days before—the French counter-attack had even halted the coastal advance, which had been making good progress.

Brigadier Stevens was unhappy to have his advance checked and later wrote of Lavarack's decision to halt the coastal thrust:

With the greatest respect to those above me, I believe that this decision was wrong, that it broke a vital principle of war—to reinforce success and not failure—and prolonged the campaign.

Such an opinion is understandable when Stevens' brigade was advancing steadily on the coast and when he felt that he was close to reaching Beirut. Yet his views and Lavarack's were not substantially different. It was precisely because Lavarack wanted to reinforce Stevens' success that he had moved the 25th Brigade to Jezzine, from where it would be better able to support the 21st Brigade on the coast. Despite Stevens' view, Lavarack had little choice but to halt the coastal advance while the French had control of Merdjayoun. With no real reserve to guard the rear of the division and the approaches to Palestine, Lavarack had to take units from Jezzine to reinforce Merdjayoun, and then, once Cox announced that he was in trouble, from the coast to reinforce Jezzine.[13]

The 7th Division was in effect fighting on a three-brigade front, which would have been a risk even had it possessed three brigades. General Wilson later noted in his post-campaign report that Lavarack

was continually faced with having to improvise some form of reserve without having a Bde H.Q. to control it. Moreover, this reserve had to be formed from units which belonged to one or other of the two existing brigades and this in turn handicapped the operations of the Bdes.[14]

To offset this shortcoming, just after midnight on the 17th Lavarack telephoned Wilson in Jerusalem to ask him for the 2/3rd and 2/5th Australian Infantry Battalions, which had been promised before the campaign began, to bolster his dangerously thin defences. He told Wilson of the steps he had taken to alleviate the growing problem in the Jezzine sector, but that he expected more pressure from the French. Initially Wilson gave him not the two Australian battalions, but the 2nd King's Own of the 16th British Brigade, which Lavarack decided to attach to Stevens' brigade on the coast to replace the 2/14th Battalion he had sent to reinforce Cox at Jezzine. The Australian battalions would follow.[15]

So ended Lavarack's last day in command of the 7th Division. After a few hours' rest he was up at 5.30 a.m. on the 18th. Nothing had changed at Merdjayoun, but at least Cox had held his ground and the 2/14th Battalion was in contact with him. At 9 o'clock Lavarack handed over command to Allen and began the drive south from Tyre to Nazareth where HQ 1st Australian Corps had been established.[16]

Lavarack's brief, but eventful, stint as a division commander in action was over, and even the most partisan militia officer would have to admit that that for a Staff Corps officer had handled the operation as adroitly as could be expected in the circumstances. He had shown his prescience as a planner and had fought the first part of the campaign well, if not faultlessly. Now he would be tested as corps commander, but given his performance in Tobruk at a similar level, it was a task he was more likely to relish than approach with any trepidation.

Corps Commander

The official British view was that Lavarack took over at a time when Wilson was faced with the additional task of co-ordinating the advance of the main force with that of 'Habforce' in the eastern desert and columns to be provided from Iraq. According to Rowell, however, French resistance was the main reason that 1st Australian Corps was allowed to take over from Wilson's headquarters:

> It is doubtful if we would have been allowed to take over unless the thing had got stuck—it had not gone as they thought it would go. After the first week the decision was arrived at that fighting the battle from the King David Hotel was not the way to do it.

The nature and location of Wilson's headquarters many miles to the rear in Jerusalem hampered effective control of the operation. His staff worked peace-time hours in luxurious surroundings, as Brigadier J.D. Rogers recalled:

> The King David is probably the most expensive hotel in the Middle east. At this time British Force HQ under General 'Jumbo' Wilson was established in many of its palatial rooms and a perfect galaxy of beautifully groomed staff officers with wives and/or pet dogs in attendance created a very ornamental if not a completely utilitarian atmosphere in the place.[17]

The invasion had developed into a hard fought campaign which required a more mobile and efficient headquarters than Wilson's overblown officers' mess which was so far from the fighting, as much in attitude as distance, that effective control must have been all but impossible. Blamey wrote to Sturdee in late June about Wilson: 'he was fighting the battle from Jerusalem and I found a grave lack of grip on the part of his staff in the early stages of the operation'. Part of the responsibility for that situation lay squarely with Blamey, who had resisted putting Lavarack in charge of the 1st Australian Corps and denying him the advantage of commanding from the beginning. Still, Wilson's determination to show that modern war could be waged without compromising comfort had ensured that Lavarack succeeded Blamey as the commander of the Australian Corps even earlier than planned.[18]

Lavarack's arrival at his new headquarters was marred by an accident: en route to Nazareth the car containing his baggage struck and killed a Palestinian civilian. This put Lavarack in poor humour and prompted Rowell to recall that although 'Lavarack had great gifts, patience was not his outstanding characteristic and we all had a pretty edgy day'. At 11 a.m. on 18 June, half an hour after Lavarack's arrival, corps headquarters assumed control. Lavarack was then responsible for all operations from Damascus westwards to the sea. (The only formation fighting in Syria not under Lavarack's command was 'Habforce', consisting of a cavalry brigade and other units, including the 350-strong Arab Legion, which was advancing from Iraq on Palmyra, north-east of Damascus.)

The situation at the time was, in Rowell's words, 'pretty confused' and rumours that Vichy French reinforcements were being despatched from North Africa appeared to promise hard fighting. Lavarack's first task was to ascertain the location and condition of the formations and units now under his command. Not surprisingly Wilson's headquarters was of little assistance, but Rowell's unofficial policy of having corps headquarters treat the operations as its own during the first phase of the campaign proved its worth immediately—from the beginning of the campaign liaison visits to the forward formations and other preparations had been made by the corps staff to facilitate a smooth transition to control of the campaign.[19]

On the right flank, the Free French, whose morale was low, and the 5th Indian Brigade, which had suffered heavy casualties, were south of Damascus and preparing to attack, and the 2/3rd Australian Infantry Battalion was now moving from Palestine to guard the lines of communication at Sheik Meskine and Deraa. At Kuneitra one battalion of the 16th British Brigade held the town, but between there and Damascus the position was obscure, although it was known that the Vichy French were astride the Kuneitra–Damascus road at some point.

In the centre and on the coast, the dispositions of the 7th Division were as Lavarack had ordered after the French counter-attack several days before. The small detachments of machine-gunners and artillery from the divisional reserve remained between Metulla and Rosh Pinna, where there was also the headquarters and another battalion of the 16th British Brigade. At Merdjayoun there was 'Berryman Force', and at Jezzine Cox held on with his remaining battalion and the battalion transferred from the coast, where Stevens was consolidating his position around Sidon. But Lavarack was on the defensive at Merdjayoun and Jezzine and there remained practically nothing in reserve. Fortunately, naive hopes of an easy victory with token forces had evaporated and British policy now was to build up the force in Syria as fast as possible in order to increase the pressure on the Vichy French. Coincident with this realisation was the abandonment of the unsuccessful Operation 'Battleaxe' in the Western Desert which had deprived the Syrian operations of equipment.

General Wilson arrived in Nazareth shortly after Lavarack to hand over command formally. Wilson told Lavarack to regard the operations against Damascus as being of secondary importance and to concentrate his efforts on the coastal advance against Beirut. Lavarack thought, however, that Damascus deserved a little more attention. The French counter-attack had made him especially sensitive to the vulnerability of his right flank and neither he nor Allen wanted to risk the loss of a substantial proportion of the 7th Division in a French outflanking movement. In any case, the capture of Damascus would make possible an advance on Beirut from the east as well as from the south. After the campaign Lavarack wrote that

> I also expressed the view that if 16 Infantry Brigade (Brig Lomax, DSO, MC), which had just arrived in the forward area, was used against Damascus, the result would probably be decisive. I was, however, ordered to incorporate 16 Inf Bde in 7 Aust Div and proceed with preparations for an advance on Beirut.[20]

Wilson had in mind Wavell's strongly-expressed views that the advance on Beirut via the coast must have priority. Lavarack could do little but pass on the instructions. He told Allen that the 7th Division would be concentrated on the coast for a decisive drive against Beirut with the 16th British Brigade replacing the 25th Brigade at Jezzine. The 6th British Division under Major-General J.F. Evetts would replace Berryman's force at

Merdjayoun and assume responsibility for the area from Merdjayoun to the east.[21]

This plan was to last little more than twenty-four hours. As it was being formulated, hard fighting continued in most areas, but it was operations on the Damascus front which were to strengthen Lavarack's hand in his attempts to have the inland areas secured before again attacking up the coast. Brigadier Lloyd, commanding the 5th Indian Brigade, had decided to press on to Damascus with Indian and Free French troops in an attempt to cut the Damascus–Beirut road, the main Vichy lateral route.

Although Lloyd's troops had been held at Mezze near Damascus and the Free French, advancing on the right of the 5th Indian Brigade, had been forced back to their start lines, Lavarack was tempted by the near success of Lloyd's endeavours. So, on the 19th, he turned a blind eye towards the instructions he had received from Wilson the day before and relieved Evetts of responsibility for Merdjayoun. Instead he placed at Evett's disposal all British troops in the Damascus–Rosh Pinna–Deraa–Kuneitra area and gave him two tasks: to defend the desert flank of the invasion force and to control operations around Damascus. Lavarack noted in his diary that he was 'very anxious to go for Damascus and clean up [the] situation there with [a] view to solving problems of rear area defence and of relations with Druses' (a minority group with separatist political aspirations inhabiting parts of Syria and Lebanon).[22]

On the 19th Blamey arrived at Lavarack's headquarters and the two discussed the advantages of taking Damascus as soon as possible. Lavarack still wanted Wilson to alter his decision that the 16th British Brigade brought in from Egypt would be used at Jezzine so that it would be available, if necessary, for operations against Damascus. As soon as he arrived in Jerusalem late that night Blamey telephoned Wilson and then drove immediately to see him to urge him to support Lavarack's plan for throwing additional weight against Damascus. As a result, Lavarack received a telephone call from Wilson soon after midnight agreeing to the transfer of the 16th Brigade to operations against Damascus. There seemed a good chance that Damascus would soon fall, and if Berryman could also quickly take Merdjayoun, Lavarack would feel secure in resuming the coastal advance.

However, although Berryman's second attempt to retake Merdjayoun had reached the outskirts of the town, enemy tanks forced him to give the order to withdraw. Lavarack's concern about the stubborn defence at

Merdjayoun was growing. He also had problems of a different type. On the 19th General Allen reported that Brigadier Cox was too ill to carry on. Lavarack ordered Allen to relieve him, something which he probably should have done earlier himself. A more agreeable task for Lavarack that day was to don the rank of lieutenant-general, for the second time in his career.[23]

Early on the 20th Lavarack ordered the 2nd King's Own, the British battalion attached to the 21st Brigade, to move to the Merdjayoun area to act as a 'backstop' near Metulla in the event that more troops were transferred to the Damascus front. Soon after he received an urgent request from Evetts that the 16th Brigade be despatched to Damascus as Free French morale was low and the 5th Indian Brigade was almost worn out. Evetts said that General Legentilhomme had reported that the enemy force between Damascus and Kuneitra had withdrawn to the north-west, thus leaving the way clear for the 16th Brigade to reach the city. He told Lavarack that 'we have Damascus in our pocket except for a few rear guards'.

Lavarack thought it likely that if the Vichy French were withdrawing from Damascus they would be reinforcing Merdjayoun. If he were to accede to Evetts' request he had to be confident that Allen could hold his ground at Merdjayoun. Allen was emphatic that he could hold the line and continue with active patrolling, and so Lavarack ordered the 7th Division to go on the defensive. He told Evetts that he could have the additional troops which, as the enemy were apparently withdrawing, he considered sufficient to give a 'final push to rear guards'. Lavarack later elaborated upon his decision to move the 16th Brigade to the Damascus front:

> No-one knew how the Druze would jump, just at this time, and Wilson was compelled...to guard his right rear against them...Finally, it must be remembered that the effect of a complete failure at Damascus upon the Arabs generally would have been disastrous.
>
> It was for these reasons, but mainly on account of the military complications, that I agreed to the temporary use of the British 16th Bde which was all the reserve we had, and the 2/3 Battalion, on this flank, as a temporary measure, in order to stabilise the situation before launching the main attack on the Western flank.[24]

Lavarack's attention was now focused on Damascus. By mid-afternoon on the 20th aerial reconnaissance had confirmed Evetts' report that Vichy troops were withdrawing from the city to the north-west. Lavarack told Evetts that with the transfer to his command of the 16th Brigade Group, and the 2/3rd and 2/5th Australian Infantry Battalions, he expected Damascus to be captured soon. Indeed, it was essential that Damascus be taken quickly because it was possible that the enemy were about to reinforce Merdjayoun and by giving Evetts the additional troops he had denuded the centre and coastal sectors of practically all reserves of infantry.

The final push for Damascus seemed an uncertain business at first— the Free French south of the city were making little headway and in the afternoon of the 20th the Indians in Mezze were overwhelmed by the Vichy French. The attack was continued, however, with the Australian 2/3rd Battalion which had been diverted from its defensive role at Deraa. During the night a company of the 2/3rd cut the Damascus–Beirut road, just as the 5th Light Horse Brigade had done in 1918. During the morning of the 21st the attack was resumed by the Free French, bolstered by Australian machine-gunners and artillery which Lavarack had made available. Fighting continued in the suburbs of Damascus and at the Barada Gorge to the north-west until late in the morning when the city was formally surrendered.[25]

Lavarack, intent on being in Damascus for the surrender, left Nazareth in the morning. He called at Evetts' headquarters on the way, but found he had already left. He kept going in an attempt to beat Legentilhomme to the city at least, but on arrival at Free French headquarters found him absent as well. Eventually he arrived at Damascus just as Legentilhomme was preparing to enter the city accompanied by cavalry. Lavarack realised he was beaten, as he wrote in his diary that night:

Le Gentilhomme entered Damascus at 1600 hours on the 21st. I was there at the time, having come to Damascus via Quoneitra and Sheikh Meskein [sic] to try to enter before him. However, being hampered by an armoured car escort, forced on me by Wavell's orders, I arrived just too late, having had to abandon the escort...I had spoken to Le Gentilhomme, congratulated him, and told him to take over the duties of Military Commander, Damascus. It was too late to perform the formal entry myself, and would have been in the nature of an anti-climax to go in with him and his Circassian escort, who looked very ornamental.

Lavarack entered Damascus quietly for the satisfaction of being there so soon after its capture, but noted ruefully: 'I received no formal luncheon and heard no polite speeches, being there, as it were, incog[nito]'.[26]

The credit for taking the city, and the effect its fall had on the campaign, has been spread broadly. Blamey's biographer, Hetherington, has given the impression that Blamey's visit to Wilson in the early hours of 20 June was the hinge upon which victory in Syria turned because he had persuaded Wilson to allow Lavarack to use the 16th Brigade on the Damascus front. Blamey's ADC, Carlyon, holds similar views:

> It may seem strange to talk of the stocky Blamey standing over the mountainous Jumbo; but that is virtually what happened. One of the staff then got through by telephone to Lavarack's headquarters, and Wilson ordered a switch in the weight and direction of the main attack, as Blamey had recommended.
>
> The outcome was the turning-point of the campaign. Damascus fell quickly after Lavarack reinforced Evetts' sector, and this forced the Vichy French to abandon their strong stand in front of Beirut.[27]

Carlyon has even gone so far as to suggest that Blamey mentioned to Lavarack that he should concentrate on taking Damascus, but it is clear that Lavarack already had decided on that course before he spoke to Blamey. It was helpful that Blamey convinced Wilson that he should allow Lavarack to concentrate on Damascus, but hardly vital—even before Blamey's arrival at his headquarters on the 19th Lavarack had already begun to take matters into his own hands in order to give Evetts a freer hand. The forces made available as a result of Blamey's visit had a minimal effect on the fall of the city, which was taken by troops who already had been allocated by Lavarack (although Wilson agreed to allow the use of the 16th Brigade at Damascus, it took no part in the fighting for the city).[28] Indeed, it is conceivable that had Blamey been unsuccessful in convincing Wilson the result would have been the same. Lavarack recognised that Damascus was within his grasp and he was determined to take it, even if it meant not immediately carrying out Wilson's orders to concentrate on the coast.

With Damascus out of the way, Lavarack's next most pressing problem was Merdjayoun. On the 21st the Vichy French had abandoned Fort Khiam, and during the night they withdrew from the villages of Khiam and Bmeriq. They were dependant upon Routes A and B leading out of the town to the north and north-east as their lines of communication, but had ceased using Route B from the time it could be fired upon by Australian artillery situated south of Jezzine. Berryman proposed to cut Route A by taking the high ground near Ibeles Saki, from where the road could be covered by fire, while a diversion created the impression that the objective was Merdjayoun instead. After examining the ground with Allen, Lavarack approved the plan.[29]

On the 22nd Wilson and Wavell arrived to discuss the progress of operations and witness Berryman's attack. Lavarack told Wavell that he intended to push forward along the coast and inland at Jezzine and Merdjayoun, as well as continuing the advance from Damascus with a view to cutting the roads leading north-east from Merdjayoun to the Damascus–Beirut road. He also outlined some of the deficiencies within the corps, especially in the 7th Division, pressing Wavell for tanks. To his surprise, Wavell now observed that he thought a battalion of infantry tanks would have been a better investment in Syria than in the Western Desert, where the failed Operation 'Battleaxe' had deprived 'Exporter' of much equipment.

This admission was cold comfort for Lavarack, and, in any case, despite Wavell's opinion, Lavarack was to receive no tanks, nor much of anything else. He had been requesting 3-inch mortar ammunition since planning for the campaign had begun, but with little result. There were serious shortages in the 7th Division (the 21st Brigade, for example, had only seventy-six mortar rounds, yet it was estimated that 7,000 rounds would be needed for an attack on the Damour defences in front of Beirut). In addition, ammunition for anti-tank rifles had never been sufficient to meet first line requirements. Allen told Lavarack that

> as the forward troops have been continuously held up by tanks, many casualties no doubt have been caused owing to the lack of means for these men to defend themselves.[30]

Wavell stayed the night at corps headquarters and early on the 23rd he was taken to the Merdjayoun area to see part of the attack on Ibeles Saki, where, as Lavarack related, he apparently gained a better understanding of the problems facing the advancing troops:

> I believe that he had not the least comprehension of the differences between the Lebanon and the African desert. On one occasion he asked

me 'Are you doing this?' meanwhile making semi-circular gestures with his right arm [alluding to an outflanking movement]. He must have thought us complete mutts. He knew nothing of the rough, rocky slopes over which our turning movements had to struggle. Of course, we were 'doing this', with infinite pain and exhaustion. Eventually he came up and looked at our truly awful theatre of war. Before this visit he had been rather contemptuous, using the word 'sticky'. During and after it he was silent.

Lavarack added that 'Thereafter I had no more complaints, though we still got neither tanks nor trench mortar ammunition despite the notes he took about them'.[31]

After seeing Wavell off for Cairo, Lavarack returned to Nazareth and the news that Berryman's attack had enjoyed some success, but that he had failed to take the most important objective of Ibeles Saki itself.[32] However, progress was still being made on the Damascus front. Instead of removing the extra troops from Evetts' command as he had planned to do after the fall of Damascus, Lavarack had decided to make up the 16th Brigade to full strength and leave it with Evetts. (Thus, the Australian 2/3rd Battalion from Lavarack's reserve could be ordered west to Merdjayoun, though the other reserve battalion, the 2/5th, would remain on the Damascus front at Deraa to guard the southern right flank.)

Lavarack had also decided that the 16th Brigade would move westwards from Artouz, about twelve miles south-west of Damascus, to capture Qatana and then advance northwards in attempt to turn the right flank of the enemy defences at Dimas, about ten miles to the west of Damascus on the road to Beirut. The remainder of Evetts' understrength division faced north-west and the Free French had extended their area of occupation to the east and north of Damascus, rendering the city reasonably secure against a Vichy counter-attack.[33]

The original Vichy plan for the defence of Syria was to make a stand in the quadrilateral Tripoli-Baalbek-Merdjayoun-Sidon. But the south-west corner of the quadrilateral, Sidon, had already been taken by the 21st Brigade. Now with Damascus in his hands Lavarack therefore faced two possibilities. First, that the Vichy French would attempt to hold at Merdjayoun and to regain Sidon; or second, that Merdjayoun would be abandoned and that the base of the quadrilateral would be adjusted to a line further north between Damour and Beit ed Dine.

The course of action the Vichy French had decided upon became clear the next day. Just before 9 a.m. on the 24th Australian patrols found that Ibeles Saki had been abandoned. Later Merdjayoun itself was entered and positions occupied to the north and east of the town. The Vichy French defenders had withdrawn during the night. Although he received the news of the re-occupation 'with bated breath', Lavarack must have been confident that its abandonment was part of a general withdrawal and, consequently, that it was unlikely that the Vichy French would attempt to retake it. Despite Berryman's failure to seize Merdjayoun, Lavarack was convinced that the 'persistent pressure' to which it had been subjected forced the enemy to withdraw to new positions covering the roads leading northward from the town.[34] With Merdjayoun back in Australian hands, Lavarack at last had regained the ground lost in the Vichy counter-attack.

Lavarack remained eager to throw the weight of his force behind the coastal drive, but he was also determined to consolidate the inland flank first, given the disruption caused earlier by not taking sufficient precautions in this sector. He impressed upon Allen that his division's role was still a defensive one and would remain so until further notice. On the Damascus front, however, Lavarack authorised more attacks. He gave Evetts permission to try to take the Dimas position west of Damascus in the hope that it might cut the lines of communication of enemy troops in the Merdjayoun area and allow a breakthrough to the Zahle–Rayak area, where there was a Vichy French airfield. Lavarack ordered the Free French to continue guarding Damascus against the possibility of attack from the desert while making preparations for an advance towards Homs, to be undertaken if Evetts' division could reach Rayak.

To facilitate these moves, Lavarack told Legentilhomme on the 25th that in future he would take orders directly from corps headquarters, no longer through Evetts. Apart from the divergence of the lines of advance of the Free French and the 6th Division (by this time part of Legentilhomme's force had occupied Qastal, about six miles south of Nebek), placing Legentilhomme under HQ 1st Australian Corps was probably indicative of Lavarack's growing dissatisfaction with Evetts who, he noted in his diary, was, 'as usual, bellyaching' about the lack of aerial artillery reconnaissance. Lavarack's ADC, Curtis Wilson, described Evetts as 'an extraordinary creature. Emaciated, nervous, drives his car while his driver sits in the rear seat'—he was certainly not the kind of subordinate likely to be appreciated by Lavarack, either professionally or personally.[35]

Evetts' attack on the Jebel Mazar that night failed and prompted Lavarack to reconsider his position. The French opposition confirmed that the enemy intended to fight delaying actions in front of the main line of defence, which, it appeared, would be along the length of the Lebanon Range. If this were the case, any operations Lavarack ordered from Merdjayoun or Damascus would only overcome delaying forces in the Anti-Lebanon. Once that had been accomplished, he would have to face the task of crossing another mountain range, the Lebanon, to take Beirut. On the other hand, the distance to Beirut from his forward positions on the coast was much shorter and operations in that sector had the advantage of being able to be supported by the navy. Once Beirut, the main French base and the seat of government, was taken it was likely that Vichy resistance would collapse in other areas. So Lavarack decided that it was time once more to concentrate on the coastal advance.[36] Coincidentally, Wilson had come to the same conclusion: at 4 p.m. on the afternoon of the 26th he arrived at Lavarack's headquarters with instructions that the coastal advance to Beirut was to be resumed.

14

'What he fears above all things is my success'

Syria, 1941—The Final Assault

ON THE 28TH the operation instruction for the concentration of the 7th Division in the coastal and Jezzine sectors was issued. As Lavarack later wrote to the official historian:

> The plan to make the main advance by the coast had never been abandoned...The return to the original plan was dependant upon the security of the communications of the force appointed to advance along the coast, and this could not be guaranteed until [the] Merdjayoun situation was stable. In other words the Vichy counter-stroke on Merdjayoun had been most successful, and I must still maintain that I was right in insisting on removing this menace to our communications before pressing on. Another reason for making sure of the actual occupation, (as distinct from masking,) [sic] of the Merdjayoun area was the fact that this would give us, at last, a short lateral road to and from the coast road.[1]

Evett's 6th Division would go on the defensive and control the Damascus and Merdjayoun sectors with the 16th Brigade, plus the 23rd which would come forward to take over from 7th Division troops at Merdjayoun. The 7th Division could then concentrate on the coast, with its order of battle augmented by the 17th Australian Infantry Brigade commanded by Brigadier S.G. Savige.[2]

On the 29th an extensive redeployment of troops began across almost the entire width of the corps front. Generally, Australian units moved westwards to the coast while British units moved east towards Merdjayoun and Damascus. This was to continue for several days and was especially difficult as nearly all units which had to be moved were in contact with the enemy. To give the impression that the Merdjayoun and Damascus sectors, not the coastal sector, were being reinforced, Lavarack ordered all eastward movement be done in daylight, while movement to the west take place under cover of darkness; in addition a number of armoured vehicles were to drive through Damascus continuously. However, the plan to prevent French reinforcement of the coast was to little effect since enemy agents were reporting the nightly movement of vehicles towards the west.[3]

Lavarack soon realised that the enemy was strengthening defences about 12 miles south of Beirut along the line Damour–Beit ed Dine. The civilian population of Damour had been evacuated and tanks, armoured cars and trucks could be seen in the streets. Additional machine gun strong points were being constructed, and more wire and mines were being positioned on roads, in wadis and to cover possible detours the Australians might take to avoid road blocks and other obstacles. Moreover, the bridge spanning the Damour River had been demolished, which indicated that the defenders expected an attack soon. Information from prisoners of war, which was considered reasonably reliable, placed the first line of defence at Damour, the second at Khalde, and the third along the line Choueifat–Aley–Bhamdoun.[4] The French military historian, Henri de Wailly, succinctly captured the mood when he wrote:

> In an increasingly tense atmosphere, everyone was getting ready for battle. Each person knew that it was there, on the Nahr ed Damour, only 18 km [sic] from Beirut, that the war was going to be decided. If Damour fell, Beirut would inevitably fall afterwards. It was the last rampart.

To Lavarack it was clear that the enemy was going to fight hard, but still he hoped that a final battle might be avoided. In the afternoon, with Wilson's approval, he sent the following message to Dentz through the United States Consulate:

> The Commander of the Australian Forces in Syria, General Lavarack, feeling that to both Frenchmen and Australians the idea of comrades of the last war fighting against one another is repellent and distasteful and

a useless waste of good men, suggests that he send an envoy by air to Rayak or to some other mutually convenient airport to meet the representative of General Dentz and to deliver to him a message from General Lavarack which may lead to a solution of the unpleasant conditions which today exist and thus avoid unnecessary bloodshed.

Lavarack's words were heartfelt and reflected the views of many older Australian soldiers in the 7th Division who had seen action in France just over twenty years before (some of whom, like Lavarack, wore French decorations from *la Grande Guerre*). Indeed, Lavarack's appeal to stop fighting was being extended not just to a former member of a friendly army, but to a man he knew: he and Dentz had met during the First World War when they had been allies fighting the Germans. Lavarack, though, doubted the likely efficacy of his message since Dentz's residence had been bombed the day before just as the Frenchman had received a message from Wilson calling upon him to declare Beirut an open city. Dentz happened to absent in Aleppo at the time of the bombing, but five of his guards were killed and the building severely damaged. Although antagonised, the Frenchman resisted the urgings of some of his staff to retaliate by bombing Wilson's HQ in the King David Hotel in Jerusalem. Independently Dentz, too, had become convinced that there was little point in continuing to waste men and equipment and had already asked permission to negotiate a ceasefire, but had been ordered to continue the fight.[5]

Failing a positive response from the Vichy French, there was nothing to do but push on with the advance. On 2 July Lavarack approved in principle the plan for the attack on Damour. The 21st Brigade was to force crossings over the Damour River and then secure an east-west line just south of Damour itself; it would also protect the right flank of the assault from any counter-attack down the Beit ed Dine road from the heights in the east. The 17th Brigade would then move through the hills to the right of Damour and block the road leading north out of the town, while the 25th Brigade was to attack from Jezzine and Rharife towards Beit ed Dine. The date for the operation was tentatively fixed for the 5th or 6th, depending on further reconnaissances of likely points of entry into the defences and the success of a preliminary attack on the 4th. As the French awaited the Australian assault, the situation was relatively quiet on all sectors of Lavarack's front, both sides limiting their activities to patrolling and shelling.[6]

Having under his command the strongest force in Syria to that time, Lavarack felt confident of cracking the Damour defences. With the gradual build-up of Allied strength in Syria, he now had eight field artillery regiments under his command, and although the formations to be used in the Damour attack were in some cases understrength, the French were in worse straits, as a 'steady trickle' of deserters from the French army was showing. Also, there was evidence that the enemy were evacuating some positions in the Jezzine area and the enemy garrison at Palmyra in the north-east had surrendered early that morning to 'Habforce'. Lavarack had to be careful, however, that he did not permit the enemy to launch another large-scale counter-attack. In particular, should either Evetts or Legentilhomme leave Damascus uncovered it was likely that the French would make the most of the opportunity, perhaps forcing the advance on the coast to halt once again. Consequently, a close rein on both was needed.[7]

On 2 July Lavarack had issued a tactfully-worded operation instruction to Legentilhomme. He reminded the Frenchman that a previous instruction had defined the task of the Free French force as being the security of Damascus against attack from the north-east, east, and south-east. It continued:

> While the Corps Comd does not desire unnecessarily to restrict your liberty of action in your interpretation of the above task, he wishes to make it clear that, for the present, he does not approve of any advance in force beyond Nebek.

To ensure more effective control of the Free French, Lavarack also intended that a senior Australian liaison officer be attached to Legentilhomme's headquarters.

The arrangement which placed the Free French not under command, but acting in co-operation, was a nuisance to Lavarack. He wrote that one of the main points to emerge from the fighting around Damascus was 'the difficulty of having at any time co-ordination of effort with allied forces without unified Command', a view supported by the official historian. But, with tact, and the benefit of his First World War experience of fighting in France, Lavarack was able to exercise effective control of the Free French throughout the campaign.[8]

On the 4th Lavarack went to Damascus to finalise arrangements with Evetts and Legentilhomme. Lavarack ordered that they were to create, by patrolling and the use of artillery, the impression that an attack was to be launched by them, but stressed that no major action was to be taken. Although he had already made it clear to Evetts that his role was defensive and diversionary, Lavarack was worried that his divisional commander would not be content to restrict his activities while the main assault was made by the 7th Division, and true to his irrepressible nature Evetts admitted to Lavarack that he was planning to attack the Jebel Mazar again on the night 7/8 July. Lavarack made it clear that any such operation would depend on the success or otherwise of the coastal attack.[9]

The Final Assault

Soon after midnight on 5-6 July the attack on the Damour positions began. The 21st Brigade attacked across the river (the 2/27th Battalion on the right and the 2/16th Battalion on the left), supported by most of the 7th Division's artillery, with the addition of a medium battery and naval and air force co-operation. By 7.05 a.m. the 2/27th had captured El Boum, about half a mile north of the river, although progress was slower on the 2/16th Battalion's front. Soon after receiving the news that El Boum had been taken, Lavarack left for 7th Division headquarters. When he arrived just before midday the situation had not altered—the 2/27th was still making progress, but the 2/16th had only two of its four companies across the river. A tenacious defence by French troops established in olive groves with heavy artillery support was hampering the advance, particularly the work of engineers who were trying to bridge the river, but Lavarack was not worried. He thought it more important that the right flank of the attack, through which the 17th Brigade would pass to block the road behind Damour, made good progress. The other encouraging news was that elsewhere on the corps front there had been no significant change, indicating that for the time being there would have to be no diversion of effort from the coast to meet an enemy counter-stroke inland.[10]

In the evening the news from the 7th Division front was still favourable and by the next morning the 17th Brigade had also crossed the river and moved forward to a wooded area south-west of El Boum. The advance by the 25th Brigade towards Beit ed Dine from the south had made slow progress, but by midday on the 7th troops of the brigade had taken several intermediate objectives and were north of Niha which lay between Jezzine and Beit ed Dine.

Lavarack telephoned 7th Division headquarters in the morning and again in the afternoon, but it was difficult to obtain reliable information about the forward troops. Nevertheless, by late in the day he knew that there was heavy fighting in the Wadi Daquon area east of Damour and that the 17th Brigade was in position, ready to pass through the 21st during the night, and take over the advance. He was disappointed, however, that there was little chance of a 'big bag' of prisoners because he suspected the enemy was slipping away to the north along the coast road and through the rocky olive groves.[11]

That night Lavarack reflected once more on the advantage given to the French by the ground over which he had to attack and the apparent failure of Wavell and Wilson to appreciate the significance of this handicap. In his diary he wrote:

> Incredibly difficult country, and French, with perfect fore-knowledge, are making fullest advantage [of it]. Slow progress by 25 Bde in Jezzine and Rharifa [sic] sections, where country is even more difficult than East of Damour. I wish Sir Archie [Wavell] and Sir Henry [Wilson] could have had a look at it. The word 'sticky' sticks in all our gizzards.[12]

The French were continuing to fight hard for every piece of ground, but by this time the threat of large-scale reinforcement of the Vichy forces from outside the country, about which Lavarack had been most concerned, was diminishing. Intelligence from Vichy prisoners indicated that promises of reinforcements from overseas were largely intended to boost morale among French troops and that by the time of the attack on Damour the defenders were giving up hope of being reinforced. Nevertheless, while reports indicated that Vichy morale was flagging, for the time being most troops would continue to resist.[13]

During the morning of the 8th Lavarack was obtaining a clearer picture of operations. Latest reports placed the leading troops of the 21st Brigade a mile east of Damour and the forward battalions of the 17th Brigade two miles north-east of the town. Further inland the 25th Brigade's advance on Beit ed Dine was making some progress: two battalions were north of Bater, but an attack on the heights north-east of Rharife had been unsuccessful. At about midday the 17th Brigade blocked the road north of Damour, which was thus encircled and it remained only to mop up the French isolated in and around the town. Lavarack went forward on the 8th to see Allen, who was convinced that his troops desperately needed a rest. He told the official historian that 'After we took Damour it was physically impossible to go on without a week's spell—the troops on the coast had had a lot of battles'. However, Lavarack gave Allen only 24-48 hours to secure the ground he had won, to reorganise and to prepare for the next stage of the advance.[14]

By about 11 a.m. on the 9th the occupation of Damour was complete and Lavarack was en route to Damascus to see Legentilhomme and deal with Evetts, who wanted to make a second attempt that night to break through the French defences around Dimas, situated on the heights 11 miles west of Damascus. Although Lavarack was confident that the attack would be successful, he was just as certain that Evetts' troops 'will not hold position for long as I do not think his b[attalio]ns. will stand French counter-attack which is certain to come'. Lavarack approved the operation in spite of this, probably reasoning that it would prevent some Vichy troops being transferred to the coast. He also approved a small operation proposed by Legentilhomme to clear Vichy forces from the road leading north from Damascus through Nebek.[15]

While Lavarack was at Damascus he received the welcome news that possibly the Vichy French wanted an armistice. He wrote that it 'Looks as though [the] Damour battle was [a] harder knock for Vichy than we have so far realised'. Naturally, Lavarack was elated with the prospect of an end to the campaign, but his pleasure was tempered by the information that the news apparently had already been broadcast in Australia by Sir Frederick Stewart, the Minister for External Affairs. He was to pursue the matter of Stewart's announcement later, but in the meantime Allen, Evetts and Legentilhomme were warned to expect plenipotentiaries.[16]

During the afternoon of the 9th the coastal advance was resumed. The next day, however, was one of 'waning hope'. The Vichy French were still offering strong resistance as the advance continued beyond Damour and Lavarack had seen no 'firm signs of intention to parley'. He suspected that the alleged approaches by the French for an armistice 'were [a] trap into which we fell'. Fearing that such a move was designed to reduce the willingness of his troops to take risks near the end of the campaign, he ordered his commanders to maintain the fullest pressure on the French. However, Lavarack's fears were beginning to appear groundless: intelligence reaching corps headquarters pointed to a collapse of the French defences in the coastal area and at Merdjayoun. It was still possible that diminishing opposition on the coast after the fall of Damour, and the enemy's withdrawal from the Jezzine and Merdjayoun areas, presaged a move to new defensive positions on the western slopes of the Lebanon Mountains and the eastern slopes of the Anti-Lebanon. But the heavy casualties inflicted upon Vichy troops and reports of falling morale made it more likely that the defenders would cease resistance rather than carry the fight into the hills.[17]

Meanwhile, the attack by Evetts, which Lavarack had authorised the day before, had commenced at 2 a.m. that morning. Reports coming in early on the 10th were sketchy, but indicated that initially Evetts had been successful, although a Free French battalion 'did not go a yard' and some Vichy outposts on the right flank had not been taken. The problem was compounded by the reluctance of French Foreign Legion units to fight other legionnaires. For some of them politics were immaterial: 'Legion did not fight Legion'. To relieve Evetts of the responsibility for the Merdjayoun area while he prepared to continue the attack, Lavarack placed the 23rd British Brigade directly under his own command from 3 p.m. on the 10th and, as the French were withdrawing from the area around Merdjayoun, he ordered the brigade to pursue them.[18] In a letter to the official historian after the war he expanded upon his reasons for removing the Free French and the 23rd Brigade from Evetts' command:

> Evetts...was continually belly-aching about his long front and seemed
> incapable of realising what his role was. He wanted a short front,
> completely integrated, like the sort of thing Wellington's divisionnaires
> were used to in Spain. Eventually, to avoid trouble and friction, I gave
> him his short front, and assumed direct command of the other groups.
> However he did no more good that way than any other and the attacks
> of the 6th Div. were no more impressive than their support of the 2/3rd.
> Bn. had been earlier in the piece.[19]

Berryman also did not think that Evetts' had done a good job in keeping Vichy troops engaged on the right flank while the final attack was launched in July 'as [the] French withdrew a battalion and sent it to Damour'. Evetts had a penchant for independent action and has admitted that on at least one occasion he disobeyed orders. It is not surprising, therefore, that Lavarack wrote that Evetts 'was a difficult subordinate and there are several bits of background that must be left out of the picture' (which was probably a reference to Evetts' apparent relationship with a Druze princess who was eventually ordered from Syria for spying).[20]

Events soon confirmed Lavarack's prediction of the 9th that Evetts' advance would not be able to withstand a Vichy counter-attack. The summit of the Jebel Mazar near Dimas had not been reached when determined Vichy attacks regained most of the ground Evetts had taken. At 9.30 a.m. on the 11th Evetts telephoned Lavarack to tell him that the French had launched a counter-attack and that he was experiencing severe administrative difficulties. He said that he proposed to order a withdrawal. Although Lavarack told Evetts to be guided by his own discretion, he was in no doubt that withdrawal was inevitable. (News of an armistice, however, was to ensure that Evetts gained the heights that night, just as he was contemplating issuing the order to retire.)

Further east the news was better—the Free French were advancing past Deir Aatiye, north-east of Damascus, encountering no opposition and contact had been established with 'Habforce' in the north. The 23rd Brigade was advancing also, following up the Vichy withdrawal from Merdjayoun. As far as the 7th Division was concerned, although the 25th Brigade was mostly static (some minor engagements were continuing south of Beit ed Dine with limited success), the coastal advance had reached Khalde about eight miles south of Beirut, and Abey, on the heights above Damour, had been occupied.[21]

The Cease-fire

Throughout the 11th rumours of a possible armistice had circulated amongst the advancing troops and Lavarack, mindful that the infantry in all areas was very tired, was eager to end the fighting. The day before he had strongly urged Wilson to accept the 'apparent offer' of the French to negotiate an armistice. On the 8th Dentz had approached the United States Consul at Beirut, who transmitted to him the British conditions for a ceasefire. Dentz accepted the conditions on the 9th and asked that hostilities cease at midnight 11–12 July.

However, Wilson's view was that such a matter was for politicians and that the most that he and Lavarack could do was parley on the issue of declaring Beirut an open city. Lavarack had disagreed and had maintained his view that as soldiers they could approach Dentz to arrange a meeting. Nevertheless, Wilson had stood firm. Lavarack then sent what he considered to be a 'strongly worded' signal to Wilson urging that he 'make a concrete proposal for Dentz to dispatch [an] envoy at [a] time and place to be definitely stated to negotiate [a] purely military armistice'. Wilson replied that he intended to warn Dentz that Beirut should be declared an open city because it would be within range of Lavarack's artillery by the next night. Wilson's wireless message to Dentz also said that unless Vichy plenipotentiaries presented themselves at a British position on the Beirut-Haifa road by 9 a.m. the next morning, hostilities would continue.

At about 6.15 p.m. on the 11th a message from Dentz was intercepted in Cairo announcing his conditional agreement to parley and stating that he would cease hostilities that night. Wilson was informed of the message and that a reply was being considered at a meeting of political and military leaders in Cairo.[22] The meeting in Cairo decided to tell Dentz that if his representatives were not at the British outpost on the Beirut–Damour road by 9 a.m. on the 12th hostilities would be resumed.

At 7 p.m. Lavarack informed his subordinate commanders to be prepared for a ceasefire during the night at a time to be advised. At 7.55 p.m. Wilson's senior staff officer telephoned Lavarack with the news that at one minute past midnight all troops were to cease firing and to stand fast, and that Lavarack's representative was to be prepared to meet the Vichy envoy on the Beirut road late in the morning. Lavarack passed on the orders, emphasising that full military precautions were to be taken and there was to be no fraternisation. The Vichy envoy was to be met at 9 a.m. at an Australian outpost on the Beirut–Haifa road and then taken to Acre.[23]

The armistice was something about which Lavarack felt strongly. Had the decision been his, he would have taken steps to bring about an earlier end to the fighting and he was incensed that the news that Dentz had proposed an armistice had been made public in Australia. As he waited for the French envoys he wrote to Blamey criticising the Australian government's decision to broadcast the news, which had reached Lavarack's troops early the day before via a BBC bulletin, because·

> ... it is not unreasonable to assume that with the knowledge of the
> possibility of an early armistice the troops would be disinclined to
> produce that small amount of extra effort which so often means the

difference between success and failure. No man is likely to risk his life unnecessarily if he feels the campaign is virtually over...[24]

Although the time available to inform forward troops of the cease-fire was short, all Australian units but one ceased operations at the appointed hour. The exception received the news at 1.30 a.m., when it immediately ceased hostilities. On the other hand, the French appeared to have greater difficulty in reaching forward positions with the news, possibly in part because Dentz had just moved his headquarters from Beirut. Consequently, shelling of 7th Division positions continued after midnight. Although most enemy activity ceased at 4 a.m., there was spasmodic shelling in the 2/25th Battalion area until 9 a.m., forty minutes after the Vichy envoys had reached the Australian positions. The troops facing Evetts, however, strictly observed the timing of the cease-fire.[25]

The failure of the French to observe the cease-fire prompted Allen to telephone Lavarack, which in turn has led to severe criticism of Lavarack by one of Blamey's biographers. Hetherington wrote in his second book on Blamey that events such as the one reproduced below may account for Blamey's determination to retard Lavarack's career.

> While negotiations for an armistice in the 1941 Syrian campaign were in progress the Vichy French in one sector had gone on shelling Australian front-line positions after the agreed time of the ceasefire, 12.1 a.m. on 12 July. The impetuous and somewhat irascible General Allen, GOC of the 7th Division, rang up Lavarack's headquarters and said he was going to order his gunners to fire back. The duty officer, Lieut-Colonel Wills, told him some Vichyist local commander must have misunderstood the ceasefire orders and there must be no reprisal, but Allen was in no mood to listen. Fearful that the armistice negotiations would be jeopardised, Wills hurried to Lavarack's bedside, woke him, explained the trouble in a few words, and said, 'Will you speak to General Allen on the telephone, sir?' 'No, I won't,' Lavarack snapped back and flounced over in bed, pulling the blankets about him. Wills had to solve the crisis unaided by telephoning Allen's headquarters and saying that Lavarack had issued orders forbidding the Australians to reopen fire in any circumstances.[26]

Hetherington's account creates a thoroughly misleading impression. Notes made by Lavarack on the 12th, and entries in his diary and the war diary of the 7th Division, present a very different view of events. Lavarack recorded that Allen telephoned his headquarters at 1 a.m. to report that the enemy 'were firing harder than ever'. This is confirmed by the 7th Division war diary, in which it is recorded also that Allen asked Lavarack 'whether the war was on or off'. Allen also asked Lavarack what action he was to take, but 'insisted that if the French wanted a fight he would direct it and our troops would give it to them'. Lavarack promised him an answer on what he should do within half an hour, after he had spoken to Wilson. Allen assured him that if the French 'were still firing after a reasonable time had elapsed' the division would retaliate strongly.[27]

At 1.03 a.m. Lavarack told Brigadier McConnel at Wilson's headquarters of the conversation he had just had with Allen. McConnel promised to see Wilson and then to telephone Lavarack with his instructions. In the meantime, Lavarack instructed his staff to contact the 6th Division and the 23rd Brigade to discover if Evetts and Brigadier Galloway had experienced difficulties similar to Allen's. At 1.20 a.m. Wilson himself spoke to Lavarack who wrote:

[He] is desirous of holding off if possible. Situation to be watched without retaliation for [the] present taking all precautions. Particular care to be taken to let plenipotentiaries through if they present themselves.[28]

Lavarack waited until he had heard from Evetts and Galloway before he once more spoke to Allen. Although Galloway himself could not be contacted, it was reported that no firing could be heard in the area, and Lavarack assumed that this 'probably means nothing [is happening] as there has been nothing all day'. A few minutes later, at 1.35 a.m., Evetts telephoned Lavarack with the news that there had been complete silence on his front since midnight. Lavarack called Allen immediately and told him not to retaliate unless it was 'absolutely necessary for protection'. His orders to Allen, as recorded in the 7th Division war diary were:

Your orders are not repeat not to retaliate unless absolutely necessary for protection—that is unless it appears that the enemy is about to launch an attack. Every military precaution is to be taken. No attack is to be mounted. Every endeavour will be made to help plenipotentiaries when they present themselves...

Lavarack explained that it appeared that the enemy on the right flank, facing Evetts and Galloway, were observing the armistice, but that there were Vichy troops opposite the 7th Division who did not wish for an armistice and that they may be causing the trouble. According to the 7th Division diarist, Allen told Lavarack that 'he was very concerned as to whether there was an armistice or not, as he objected to our being shelled without retaliating'. Lavarack promised to telephone Allen as soon as he received any more information.[29]

Lavarack wrote that he had found Allen 'very recalcitrant' and inclined to repeat, senselessly in Lavarack's opinion, the statement that he was 'peeved'. Allen also said more than once 'What do we want a ---- armistice for?' Lavarack formed the opinion that his divisional commander 'had had too many drinks and was not in a fully responsible state of mind'. Co-incidentally, Wills felt it his duty to inform Lavarack that he too was of the opinion that Allen had taken too much alcohol. Lavarack noted that Wills offered the information without any suggestion from himself, and that Wills and another member of Lavarack's staff 'had been treated to a tongue-lashing by Allen'.[30]

At 2 a.m. Lavarack again telephoned McConnel at Wilson's headquarters to discuss plans for what should be done if the French did not desist in front of the 7th Division. At 3 a.m. he spoke with the duty officer at 7th Division headquarters, who told him that there had been no firing since 2.20 a.m. At 4.05 a.m. a signal from GHQ Middle East was received at corps headquarters which confirmed that the Vichy envoys would be at the rendezvous as directed later in the morning. At 5 o'clock Lavarack warned Allen to expect the Vichy representatives in half an hour. After that Lavarack may have gone to bed—he makes no reference to any further telephone calls either to or from 7th Division headquarters until 7.10 a.m. when he again telephoned the duty officer at Allen's HQ who told him that there had been no firing later than 4 o'clock.[31]

It is just conceivable that the incident as recounted by Hetherington in his book may have happened after 5 a.m., but it is highly improbable given that firing had ceased on Allen's front for some time by then and Vichy envoys were about to arrive. In any case, to give the impression that Lavarack took no interest in ensuring that the cease-fire was maintained is a most unjust distortion of events. Not only Lavarack's own notes and personal diary, but also the war diary of the 7th Division, verify that he was awake most of the night in order to keep Allen in check.[32]

The Armistice

At 8.20 a.m. Dentz's envoys, led by General de Verdilhac (the senior military commander under the High Commissioner, General Dentz), arrived at the forward posts of the 7th Division and were taken to Allen's headquarters where they were entertained for a time by him in the officers' mess. From there the Frenchmen were escorted south to Sydney Smith Barracks at Acre in Palestine where they were met by Lavarack, Wilson, Catroux and representatives of the other services. The 12th was to be a tiring day of proposing and re-proposing armistice terms punctuated by frustrating incidents.

The first of these arose as soon as the delegates entered the conference room when de Verdilhac expressed his displeasure at being forced to sit at the same table as the Free French representative, Catroux, and throughout the day the two were to be seen at various times 'engaged in heated argument'. According to Rowell, the 'proceedings opened with a blast from Wilson addressed to the French commander General de Verdilhac' the gist of which was that Wilson threatened to call off the truce because the French had continued firing after midnight. De Verdilhac replied that there had been difficulty in reaching all troops by midnight. Rowell handed a note to Wilson that this was not surprising as the French had relied heavily on civil communications and consequently Arabs had been paid one piastre for each telephone pole they cut down.[33]

At lunch there was another disturbance when a Vichy political representative objected to being served by a Jewish waiter and an Australian chaplain threatened to punch the Frenchman. During lunch Catroux's gold-embroidered kepi was stolen from his car. The blame was attached to the Australians and light-heartedly Catroux wrote after the war:

> The incident delighted Wilson, and made Lavarack smile. Lavarack was
> commander of the Australians and well knew what his soldiers were
> likely to get up to. When the incident became known to the Vichy
> delegation the whisper went round that I was a deserving victim of the
> bad company I kept.

In fact, the incident did not amuse Lavarack in the least. He wrote that the accusation caused the only disagreement between himself and Catroux with whom 'on every other occasion I had the most agreeable relations'. It was the type of incident which was bound to cause Lavarack to flare up. His ADC wrote that when a British major later accused Australians of having stolen the cap, 'Lavarack fiercely assailed him'.[34]

After a weary day spent arguing over terms, a draft agreement was ready to be initialed at about 11 p.m. Lavarack's ADC, Curtis Wilson, recorded the scene:

> Just as the draft terms were to be initialed at 11 p.m. the electric lights failed. There were no candles, no lanterns to be found. A motor cycle was wheeled into the room, its motor started and its light shone on General Wilson. The noise was too much. A car was driven to a window and its headlights shone through the window to dimly light the conference room. Finally a few lanterns were found. Kenneth Slessor, war correspondent for Australia, was a bit high and had words with Wilson's aide, Chapman Walker, a loose mouthed, supercilious streak of effete Englishman. In the room, hushed after the motor cycle had been stopped, Slessor was heard to say [to Walker] 'I'll knock your block off'.[35]

Despite the pandemonium, Lavarack appreciated the atmosphere generated by signing the armistice late at night in a room illuminated by lanterns and wrote later that the scene 'Might have been after Blenheim'. On the whole, he was satisfied with the draft terms of the armistice, but not with the fact that apparently de Verdilhac was to submit them to Dentz who would in turn pass them to Vichy for ratification. Another displeasing aspect was that at the conference Lavarack felt that Australia was regarded as little more than an appendage to the British delegation:

> Order of importance of those attending (to the Press) was quite obviously British generals, Vichy French ditto, Free French ditto, and the only Australian one present, nowhere. Natural but unfortunate in view of fact that Australians have done 9/10 of the fighting.

Nevertheless, nothing seemed able to mar victory for Lavarack that night. He returned to his billet half an hour after midnight where he had a late dinner of sandwiches and whisky before turning in 'very tired, but happy'.[36] Lavarack had won his first campaign. Although the strategic value of ousting the Vichy French was marginal, the effect of victory in Syria was for those in Australia an exciting and encouraging feat after the disasters in Greece and Crete. The Sydney Morning Herald quoted an official communique from GHQ in Cairo:

Allied forces, under the terms of the convention, have occupied selected strategical points in central and south-east Syria. English and Indian troops are now occupying further positions in the northern area. The occupation of Beirut has been completed. A cordial reception was accorded the Allied forces, particularly the Australian troops.

Elsewhere, however, Australia appears to have gained little prestige for a hard-fought campaign conducted mostly by an Australian general, controlled by the Australian corps headquarters and one in which Australians, while providing just over half the number of troops, had twice the number of killed and wounded as the British, Indians and Free French combined. General Allen told the official historian:

> It wasn't a walkover. It hasn't got the publicity because the heads will not admit they underestimated [the] fighting spirit of [the] French. The country was ideal for defence. A[rlabosse] said: 'We had an idea the British thought we didn't fight in France and we were determined to show we could fight. Petain was our commander, we were permanent soldiers and we fought for France'. They were not pro-German, but they would not join the Free French whom they despised.[37]

In part, British censorship during the fighting may have contributed to the lack of publicity, but the major reason seems to have been the British tendency to regard Dominion forces as available to be used, and described, as British forces. That Australia did not receive more credit after the campaign was also partly the fault of the Australian government which had not been alert enough during the preparations for Syria to ensure that Australian interests were voiced effectively. As GOC AIF, Blamey, too, must share some of the blame because initially he minimised the Australian role in his cables to the government in an attempt to diminish Lavarack's prominence.[38]

Lavarack recounted for the official historian the practical effects of Australian troops being regarded as some form of indentured manpower as far as the ceremonial entry into Beirut on 16 July was concerned: 'As usual this was regarded as a British function and the Australians, who had done practically all the real fighting, were ignored.' Lavarack was part of the official party (led by Wilson and including the Free French general, Catroux) to be greeted by Syrian and Lebanese dignitaries. It was a colourful event full of pomp, as an Australian war correspondent described:

Escorted by Australian mechanised cavalry on Bren carriers, the Allied commanders, General Sir Henry Maitland Wilson, Lieutentant-General J.D. Lavarack, and General Catroux, made a formal entry into Beirut yesterday amid further scenes of enthusiasm.

They were welcomed by a large crowd in the Place des Martyrs—Beirut's big central square—where a guard of honour of mounted Lebanese gendarmes greeted them with a flashing salute with drawn sabres. British planes dipped in salute overhead

The Tricolour and the Lebanese flag, with its green cedar tree to the centre, flew on many buildings. A few flew the Free French flag.

[Paragraph omitted]

...As the Generals alighted from their cars [at the Grand Serail, the French High Commission], little Lebanese girls came up, curtsied, and presented each with a posy of flowers. The Generals were received by a guard of honour of British Yeomanry, French marines, and steel-helmeted cavalrymen.

In a big marble reception room, the Generals received colourfully dressed and bearded notables from the surrounding districts. Fifty representatives of all the Churches in Syria made a striking picture in their full vestments. They included dignitaries of the Orthodox Church, carrying heavily-jewelled ikons, shaven-headed monks, and leading members of the Moslem faith.

Lavarack may have been in the official party for the entry into Beirut (as he had failed to be after the fall of Damascus), but that was all. From the victor's point of view it was a British event, as Lavarack noted in his diary that night: 'Wilson met all and sundry. No Australians need apply, whatever the Corps has done. Was completely ignored. They treat us as a dependent nation, or perhaps as mercenaries'. Brigadier Stevens wrote that at the victory parade 'Wilson appeared and with his usual thorough-ness congratulated the wrong Brigadier for his capture of Beirut!!'.

Lavarack was even unable to renew his personal acquaintance with General Dentz, who had refused to carry out the handover of power to Wilson. He had surrendered Paris to the Germans the year before and, according to one French historian, he could not endure another capitula-tion: 'To surrender Beirut after Paris was probably beyond his strength, and to recognise the authority of the Free French was forbidden.'[39]

The fighting in Syria may have been over, but Lavarack's war with Blamey continued unabated. The day before the ceremonial entry into Beirut Blamey had reminded Lavarack that his command of the corps was only temporary. Blamey said that eventually he would resume command of the corps himself and Lavarack would return to command the 7th Division. Lavarack was shaken:

> This becomes ridiculous. Why should these people play battledore and shuttlecock with me? A repetition of Tobruk when TAB saw to it that I was removed from what was more than a corps command and relegated back to 7 Div at Mersa Matruh. What he fears above all things is my success. To him Tobruk was bad enough, but Syria has put the lid on.

Lavarack's ADC recorded that this news resulted in a 'Black Day' at corps headquarters.[40]

There was nothing in Lavarack's conduct of the campaign against the French which would have justified Blamey relegating him again to a divisional command. On the contrary, if victory in Syria can be said to belong to any one man, it is Lavarack. He had shown himself to be an accomplished commander capable of flair when required, in spite of the sparseness of his practical experience. Although he had made errors, he possessed an intuitive grasp of command and, considering the difficulties of the campaign, it was appropriate that he was rewarded for his efforts in Syria and Tobruk with a knighthood. Indeed, he would not settle for less. When Blamey told him in late 1941 that the new Labor government in Australia was not in favour of knighthoods being awarded to senior officers, he wrote to the Governor General's secretary putting the case in favour of such honours, especially for himself and Morshead who he knew had been recommended some time before. He wrote that 'I have set this honour before myself as an objective all my service, and cannot help a feeling of discouragement at the prospect of failure at the moment of apparent success'. He said he would refuse a lesser award.[41]

In his recommendation for Lavarack's knighthood Wilson referred to his earlier commands in the Western Desert and then turned to his role in Syria:

> [H]e proved himself a Commander of high ability. It was due largely to his leadership and inspiration that the momentum of the attack was sustained in [the] face of difficult terrain and with limited resources. He

showed throughout the campaign a clear idea of the tactical picture which contributed considerably to its final success.

In support of Wilson's recommendation Wavell wrote that 'Gen Lavarack showed abilities of a high order both in the Western Desert where he organised the original defence of Tobruk, and during the Syrian campaign', and in another place reported that Lavarack 'commanded the 7th Australian Division, and later, the whole of the forces in Syria most ably'. Yet, despite Lavarack's success, it was not until October, that Blamey finally relented and recommended that he be retained as the Australian corps commander in the substantive rank of lieutenant-general.[42]

For his part, Lavarack did not agree with the way in which Blamey had allowed AIF units to be fed into the campaign, as he told the official historian Gavin Long in 1952:

[O]wing to difficulty in getting hold of records, I did not write a 'reasons for decisions' report for Syria, as I had done for Cyrenaica. Perhaps it was just as well, as I was bitterly angry, during and after Syria, about the ruination of 7 Div., caused by Blamey's juggling with Brigades and Battalions, and would probably have said too much. I need not have bothered, for he made sure that I never had another chance.[43]

Despite Lavarack's view, it was the limited number of troops who could be spared for Syria and the shortage of equipment after the operations in Greece and Crete which dictated the way in which Australian units were employed in Syria. To be fair, Blamey was aware that because of the way the force in Syria was being reinforced there was some mixing of units, and attempted, not always successfully, to have it rectified.[44]

Nevertheless, a tough campaign had been won, morale had been boosted at home and the 7th Division had gained valuable experience which would stand it in good stead for its next campaign against the Japanese in New Guinea. For Lavarack personally, the invasion of Syria had shown that, despite his limited command experience as a regular officer of the Staff Corps, he could successfully command a division and a corps against a determined and skilful enemy under difficult conditions. Perhaps the greatest accolade came from a French officer who had been chief of staff to the Vichy commander-in-chief, General Dentz. After the campaign, when discussing the Australian move to Jezzine (the tactical importance of which had eluded the French during their planning), he is reported to have said: 'Whoever conceived that move, and appreciated the importance of Jezzine, and moved so quickly was indeed a great soldier'.[45]

Having won an unexpectedly difficult campaign in Syria soon after defeating Rommel in the Easter Battle at Tobruk—and been knighted for both achievements—Lavarack had proved himself as a commander at a time when there serious doubts about Blamey's abilities on the battlefield. And Lavarack's rank as a lieutenant-general in the Australian Imperial Force had been confirmed, making him second only to Blamey. Lavarack's stocks may have risen, but his battles with Blamey, and with politicians and civil servants in Australia, were far from over.

15

'It may be necessary to take risks'

The Netherlands East Indies, 1942—

Race Against Time

ONCE THE CAMPAIGN in Syria was over, Lavarack's primary concerns became the implementation of the armistice and safeguarding the hard won victory in Syria against a possible German counter-attack through Turkey and Iraq. As far as the former was concerned, he had problems both with the Free French, whose 'arrogance' had to be curbed despite their poor fighting record, and the Vichy French, who breached the terms of the armistice by sending some Australian, British and Indian prisoners to France and other destinations outside Syria. In retaliation Lavarack arrested a number of Vichy French generals to ensure the return of Allied prisoners.

The military situation, though, remained stable during the second half of 1941. As more troops moved into the Levant, General Wilson took command of the newly-created 9th Army, which incorporated all troops in Syria and Lebanon, including Lavarack's 1st Australian Corps. At about the same time that 9th Army was being formed the Germans and Italians suffered severe reverses in the Middle East and the Russians checked the Germans on the Eastern Front, so the possibility of a large-scale Axis operation being launched against Syria seemed remote by the end of the year.[1]

For Lavarack the months of consolidation after the armistice were personally satisfying: he had won a difficult campaign, he wore the rank of lieutenant-general again and he had earned the knighthood which had been one of his goals. However, such success could do little but aggravate Blamey's dislike and fear. In late 1941 Major-General C.E.M. Lloyd recalled being told by Blamey, who was preparing to return to Australia for a short time, to see that Lavarack did not get control of the AIF during his absence. For once, Blamey had some cause to be worried about Lavarack.

Blamey's relationship with Wavell's replacement as the British Commander-in-Chief in the Middle East, General Sir Claude Auchinleck, had deteriorated dramatically in the latter half of 1941 because of Blamey's insistence that the Australian troops in Tobruk be relieved. Blamey had written to the Minister for the Army, Percy Spender, on 8 September 1941 that 'I am becoming personally the most unpopular man in the Middle East over the matter', but that he was forcing the issue 'because I am convinced I am right'. By the end of the year the relationship between Blamey and Auchinleck was so bad, because of the Tobruk episode and other matters, that the British Minister of State in the Middle East, Sir Oliver Lyttelton, suggested to Churchill in December that Blamey should be replaced because 'He is now very little short of being insufferable'. As for his replacement, Lyttelton suggested that:

> Laverack [sic] would probably be an adequate substitute, but as he is a professional soldier he will possibly not find favour with the Australian Government. I am satisfied, however, that if Blamey remains, it will be most prejudicial to the conduct of the war in this theatre and that Auchinleck will be hampered at every turn.[2]

A short time later Churchill drafted a cable to Curtin, in which he suggested Lavarack as Blamey's successor in the Middle East:

> In the circumstances, I feel that to ensure harmonious command in the Middle East it would be wise to transfer Blamey to some other sphere. It may be that in view of the turn the war has taken and the impending withdrawal of two out of three Australian Divisions to the Far Eastern theatre, you may desire the benefit of his knowledge and experience in Australia. If you agree, I naturally leave it to you to choose his successor, but from what I hear of him Laverack [sic] would be suitable.

The cable, written while Churchill was in Washington, was never sent, but it was shown to Australia's Minister to the United States, R.G. Casey, who suggested that mention of Lavarack be omitted. One of Churchill's staff remarked, 'not (I gathered) because he does not have a high opinion of Laverack [sic] (quite the contrary) but because to make such a suggestion might give offence'. Casey was right: such a suggestion would have found little favour in Australian political circles and certainly would have outraged Blamey.[3]

Perhaps the British felt that Lavarack, as a regular army officer, would get along better with Auchinleck. Perhaps Lavarack was considered more cooperative than Blamey, a view which may have been reinforced in November and the early part of December when Lavarack was Acting GOC of the AIF in the Middle East during Blamey's absence in Australia. Whatever the reason, although Lavarack did not accept without question British doctrine and practice, he certainly viewed the military relationship between the British and Australian armies differently from Blamey. After his arrival in the Middle East Lavarack had shown that, as far as the employment of Australian troops was concerned, he was more likely to see a problem from a purely military perspective than Blamey, an attitude which would certainly have made Auchinleck's life easier. There seems little doubt, for example, that if he had been GOC AIF instead of Blamey the Australians in Tobruk would not have been relieved—after the war Lavarack told Gavin Long that 'in this controversy I agreed with Auchinleck, for several reasons' (which unfortunately he did not share with Long). So it is not surprising that he was viewed favourably by the British as a successor to Blamey, who Churchill characterised as being 'a more ardent politician than soldier'.[4] Lavarack was the opposite: a career soldier who, though possessing a keen appreciation of the political dimension, was not one to pander to politicians, as he had made clear during his time as CGS before the war.

However, the issue of Blamey's possible replacement by Lavarack was rendered irrelevant by the outbreak of war with Japan in the Pacific—soon neither Blamey nor Lavarack would be in the Middle East. The Japanese invasion of Malaya, which began on 8 December 1941, proceeded so swiftly and with such success that on 18 December representatives of the United Kingdom, the United States, Holland, Australia and New Zealand, meeting in Singapore, called on the British chiefs of staff to send substantial air and ground reinforcements. The senior Australian representative at the conference, Major-General H.G. Bennett (GOC AIF Malaya and commander of the 8th Division) urged the Australian authorities to transfer another Australian division from the Middle East. By early January it was proposed that, as well as reinforcements for Malaya, two divisions would be transferred from the Middle East to the Netherlands East Indies. On 5 January 1942 the Australian government consented to the despatch to the Far East of the largest experienced formation in the Middle East not involved in operations: Lavarack's 1st Australian Corps, comprising the 6th and 7th Divisions, plus corps troops.[5] Lavarack's appreciation of the situation in the Netherlands East Indies as the Australian national commander there would profoundly affect his subsequent career.

Lavarack first learned of the proposed move to the new theatre of war on 8 January when Wilson told him that General Wavell, now Supreme Commander of the ABDA (American, British, Dutch, Australian) area encompassing both Malaya and the Netherlands East Indies, hoped to use Lavarack's corps for a counter-offensive against the Japanese. As well as having the obvious advantage of using more experienced troops from the Middle East to meet the Japanese, the plan had the added merit that the 6th, 7th and 8th Australian Divisions would be concentrated.[6] While Lavarack would once again come under the command of Wavell, this time he would not simply be a subordinate formation commander, but also the senior Australian commander in the area. Such a position carried with it responsibilities more wide-ranging than those associated with purely operational considerations: Lavarack was about to assume a quasi-diplomatic role similar to that of Blamey's in the Middle East.[7]

It was assumed that Blamey would eventually follow Lavarack and take command of the AIF in the ABDA area. Probably with that likelihood in mind, Blamey was adamant that Lavarack should have sufficient powers to protect the AIF in the Far East in the meantime. He cabled the Prime Minister, John Curtin, on 8 January:

> On arrival 6th and 7th Aust Divs Far East three Aust Divs in two or
> more groups will be within area of British Far Eastern Command.
> Essential there should be one supreme Australian authority in command
> AIF with same powers and authority as GOC AIF Middle East to ensure
> proper regard for Australian interests and co-ordinate administrative
> requirements.

> From military point of view Australian commitment for some time
> apparently greater proportionally to British than it has been in Mideast.

Australian Commander should be given status that will admit him to full consultation all operational and administrative plans. Particularly should be member any War Council that may be formed.

Regard this as particularly important in view of British propensity for dispersing organisations.

However, despite the importance of this matter, little urgency appears to have been attached to it in Canberra and Blamey again raised the issue with the Prime Minister on 19 January:

Reference departure General Lavarack for Far East it will be appreciated that I have no power to give him any instructions since my authority is limited to Mideast. Consider essential he be given definite authority and powers similar to those of GOC AIF ME. Otherwise he will face many difficulties from outset which will tend to hamper AIF. Most important that policy laid down for AIF ME should be continued Far East.

Blamey referred Curtin to his cable of 8th January and reminded him that an 'Early decision and issue of instructions to Lavarack [is] of greatest importance'. The matter was passed to the Military Board for advice, but nothing was decided before Lavarack's departure for the Netherlands East Indies.[8]

Lavarack left the Middle East by air on 21 January accompanied by key officers of his staff, including his BGS, Brigadier Berryman. Six days later he reported to Wavell at his headquarters near Bandung in Java. Wavell explained to Lavarack that originally he had intended to use the Australian corps to counter-attack in Malaya, but the situation there was worsening and it now seemed likely that at best only Singapore Island could be held. Therefore he had decided instead that Lavarack's troops would have to be deployed in Java and Sumatra to bolster the local defence forces. Wavell intended to use one of the Australian divisions to protect important airfields in southern Sumatra, while the other formed the core of the defence in central Java.

Naturally Lavarack was unhappy with the arrangement—not only would his two divisions be deployed on separate islands, but there was to be a Dutch division between them in western Java. Since the army of the Netherlands East Indies (comprising about 25,000 men) had no experience and their dependability was questionable, it made sense to keep the

Australian divisions together to provide the backbone of the defence. Lavarack was in no doubt that the fighting quality would be

> at least doubled if the Divs. are able to fight side by side, or even back to back, if necessary, in one area allotted to the Corps as a whole, and in one of the main islands.

In addition, there would be administrative, command and communications difficulties if the divisions were separated.[9]

Lavarack protested to Wavell about the splitting of his corps, as well as the 'extreme dispersion' of troops in the divisional areas, and strongly urged him to maintain the integrity of the corps. However, after Wavell explained his position, Lavarack 'could only agree that present circumstances make concentration impossible'. As he later explained to the CGS in Australia, General Sturdee, not only were the Netherlands East Indies land forces inexperienced, but they were ill-trained, probably unreliable and, most significantly, almost totally static: 'They rely very largely on civil sources for their supply, transport, repairs, signals, provost and other services and are consequently not mobile'. Because Wavell 'literally cannot move the NEI land forces' he was compelled to plan to use 1st Australian Corps to plug the gaps in his defence, which happened to be in Sumatra and central Java.[10]

The outlook was not promising and Lavarack felt no more encouraged after talking to the Dutch commander of the Allied land forces, Lieutenant-General H. ter Poorten. When he asked ter Poorten about conditions in Sumatra the Dutchman replied 'We don't know much about Sumatra'. Frustrated, Lavarack wrote in his diary: 'In that case who does?' It was clear to him that the 'Dutch [are] obviously determined [to] wish centre belt of Java onto Aust Corps'. He was becoming increasingly concerned, but consoled himself with the thought that it would be several weeks before the corps arrived and the situation could easily change before it reached the Netherlands East Indies—he could bide his time before making a stand on the matter.[11]

Indeed the situation would change, but perhaps more rapidly than expected. During the night 30/31 January British and Australian troops abandoned the Malayan mainland and withdrew to Singapore Island. Nevertheless, in Java confidence was still relatively high and on the 31st, after setting up his headquarters in a hotel in Tjisaroea, Lavarack cabled an outline of Wavell's plan and dispositions to Australia. He told Sturdee that Wavell intended to hold southern Sumatra, Java, Timor and Darwin, with his main strength in Java, where there would be Dutch formations in the east and west, and an Australian division (with a British armoured brigade) in the centre of the island. The other Australian division would defend aerodromes and oil supplies in southern Sumatra. Lavarack said that he had made it clear that Australian policy was not to split the corps but Wavell, while eager to comply, felt that operational commitments necessitated that the two divisions operate separately.[12] As the days passed and the situation worsened, the employment of the Australian corps would assume increasing importance.

In the meantime, Lavarack's first task was to reconnoitre the areas he would be defending and to draw up his plans. The first three days of February were spent mostly in the air on a sometimes hazardous reconnaissance of southern Sumatra where a Japanese attack was soon expected. On the 4th Lavarack reported to Wavell that the protection of the airfields and oil refineries around Palembang, the port of Oosthaven 200 miles to the south, and the line of communication between those two centres had to be the primary aim. He recommended several measures to bolster the defence until the Australian division arrived in Sumatra, which Wavell ordered to be put into effect.

However, even at this early stage it seemed as if time may have run out. One of Lavarack's intelligence officers, Lieutenant-Colonel K.A. Wills, noted in an appreciation written during Lavarack's absence that the Japanese could capture Sumatra as early as 2 March. The appreciation contained three important opinions: that the corps could not arrive and establish itself in time to prevent the loss of Java and Sumatra; that if part of the corps arrived before the Japanese attack it would be lost; and, considering all the circumstances, the defence of Australia would be jeopardised by trying to bring the 1st Corps to the Netherlands East Indies.[13]

Lavarack, well aware of the perilous predicament of the Allied forces in the Netherlands East Indies, was by now not optimistic about future operations. He wrote to Sturdee on 6 February, the day which saw the first Japanese air raid on Palembang airfield, that the 'general situation in the South Western Pacific Command can only be described as grim'. The first brigade of the 7th Division would not arrive until 1 March and the division would not be complete until two weeks later. The 6th Division was due to sail from the Middle East between 19 and 29 March, and so Lavarack could not expect to have his corps on the ground before late

April—more than enough time for the Japanese to launch a successful offensive.

However, while he felt there was little chance that there would be time to move an Australian division into southern Sumatra, he told Sturdee that there was a remote possibility of holding at least part of the island if the Japanese did not move as quickly as expected. Even so, by the time the first Australians arrived it was likely that the Japanese would hold southern Sumatra. Since it would be impossible to land and retake Sumatra given the balance of air and naval forces,

> I envisage the possibility that before the arrival of the first flight a decision may have to be taken to alter its destination, either to Java or some other vital area. I will, of course, keep in touch with the situation and ensure, as far as may be possible, that the Corps is not misused. You know that it is not always a simple matter to judge situations exactly, and that it may be necessary to take risks. I will certainly endeavour to avoid another campaign like that in Greece...I have represented to him [Wavell] very strongly that this distribution of the Corps is not in accordance with the desires of the Australian Government and not what I would have chosen myself, but have had to agree that the concentration of the Corps in one area is not in the circumstances practicable. He thoroughly understands our views on this subject.[14]

Lavarack was also worried about his position vis-à-vis Wavell. On 5 February, still with no written instructions from the Australian government, he agreed to a request from Wavell's headquarters that AIF personnel might be used for tasks other than those concerned purely with the operation and maintenance of the Australian corps. However, this was to be only until they could be replaced, and he made it quite clear that

> the command of AIF personnel arriving in S.W.P.C. from the Middle East must remain with GOC 1 Aust Corps and all orders and instructions affecting such personnel, whether as units, detachments or individuals, should be issued through 1 Aust Corps.

Nevertheless, he obviously felt the need for more guidance, as he also told Sturdee in his communication of 6 February:

> This brings me to another most important point, which is that I have had no instructions from the Government. Blamey assured me that I should

find these awaiting me upon my arrival here, but there has been nothing so far. Presumably the Government possesses knowledge of future intentions which is denied to me, and in default of which I must act in the dark. I should be glad to have instructions from the Government, even if they are simply a repetition of those previously given to other commanders.[15]

The next day Curtin sent a cable to Blamey in which he outlined the probable command structure in the Netherlands East Indies after the arrival of the 6th and 7th Divisions and Blamey himself. Curtin was not entirely happy with the arrangements, particularly as Blamey, who was Deputy Commander-in-Chief, Middle East, would not occupy a similar post in the ABDA area. The cable showed that Curtin was more concerned with future arrangements than with Lavarack's role in the meantime. In his reply, Blamey made it clear that he, on the other hand, was very much concerned about the present situation in the Netherlands East Indies. After his experience in the Middle East, a tight rein would have to be kept on the AIF by Lavarack if Australian troops were not to be 'scattered in penny packets' by the British. He felt that the arrangement already existing between the United Kingdom and Australia regarding the AIF in the Middle East carried sufficient authority and could also be applied in the ABDA area.

Unfortunately Lavarack would still have to wait to be informed of the details of such an arrangement and given instructions on precisely what powers he wielded to ensure that Australian interests were safeguarded. Not everyone in Australia had been dilatory in the matter: as early as 28 January Sturdee had recommended that Lavarack be given a charter and powers similar to those given Blamey as GOC AIF, Middle East. Three days later the Minister for the Army, F.M. Forde, had approved a charter for Lavarack. But it was still to be a further two weeks before he received it.[16]

In the meantime, planning continued on the assumption that some form of defence could be established. On the 8th Lavarack, accompanied by the commander of the British 7th Armoured Brigade, left on his second reconnaissance, this time to central Java where the other AIF division was to be employed. When he returned to his headquarters the next morning it was to receive the worrying news that the Japanese had landed on Singapore Island in the area defended by the Australian 8th Division. Also waiting for him was a signal from Curtin. It contained superfluous advice to Lavarack on how he might conduct any future campaign and was an indication of the alarm being experienced by the Australian government:

> War Cabinet wish you to be aware of views on strategic policy in Malaya and Singapore which have been received from a responsible quarter [Major-General Gordon Bennett]...They are to the effect [that the] best policy is a strong counter offensive as soon as reinforcements [of] aircraft and troops can be arranged; that a purely defensive policy cannot succeed but an offensive cannot fail...It is desired to have your views on this opinion after consultation [with] Wavell.[17]

On 9 February Lavarack replied to Curtin. Naturally he agreed that a counter-offensive was the answer (an imprudent hint of annoyance being his comment that 'this is fundamental and obvious'), but that until the necessary troops and equipment were assembled there was no alternative to conducting an active defence. He also made a suggestion which would antagonise Curtin: that troops in Australia be used to reinforce Wavell's command and that the air force be bolstered to wrest air superiority from the Japanese. Lavarack felt that the enemy was taking risks and over-stretching himself, thereby increasing his vulnerability.[18]

The Japanese may have been taking risks, but their vulnerability hardly seemed high the next day as more reports arrived from Singapore recounting their relentless advance across the island. The situation was becoming increasingly desperate for the defenders and a Japanese victory seemed imminent. Moreover, the build-up of Japanese forces in the Anambas Islands north-east of Singapore was continuing—enemy convoys were moving south from there in greater strength than expected and Japanese flying boats had been sighted east of Banka Island off the coast of Sumatra. Major-General Lloyd (the Australian Deputy Intendant-General on Wavell's Staff) regarded the prospects as so uninviting that when Colonel H.F.H. Durant (another Australian attached to Wavell's HQ) left to visit Darwin on the 11th he told him to stay there and not be foolish enough to return to Java. Like Lloyd, Durant was pessimistic and so was told by a senior British officer to keep his views to himself while in Australia.[19]

By 12 February it was clear to Lavarack that the situation in Singapore was about to exercise a 'dominating influence' on the defence of the Netherlands East Indies. He was certain that the Japanese force in the

Anambas Islands was 'obviously about to pounce', probably on Banka and southern Sumatra, and was disconcerted that officers at Wavell's headquarters seemed unperturbed at the prospect of committing the 7th Division to southern Sumatra in such ominous circumstances. Lavarack was 'by no means calm' about the possibility, but, although Lloyd and several other Australian officers were pressing him to refuse to permit the landing of the 7th Division in southern Sumatra, he still felt there was time enough to delay the decision until the division was closer and the situation clearer. There was an immediate concern, though—one transport, the *Orcades*, sailing ahead of the main convoy, was due at Oosthaven in two or three days. The *Orcades* carried 3,400 Australian troops, including the 2/3rd Machine Gun Battalion (Lieutenant-Colonel A.S. Blackburn, VC) and the 2/2nd Pioneer Battalion (Lieutenant-Colonel J.M. Williams). Lloyd, Durant and Wills were pessimistic and urged Lavarack not to land the 7th Division, but Berryman supported Lavarack's view that there was no need to make the decision immediately. Nevertheless, it was obvious that unless the situation changed dramatically action would have to be taken soon and so Lavarack again pressed for a reply to his request for the powers of a GOC AIF abroad.[20]

The next day Curtin cabled Wavell, drawing his attention to the agreement between the governments of Australia and the United Kingdom governing the use of the AIF in the Middle East. Curtin then added:

> These are of course equally applicable to the AIF in the ABDA Area as in the Middle East. The Government desires to emphasise that the concentration of the AIF in one Force under its own commander is a principle of cardinal national importance.

Lavarack also received a cable on the 13th from Sturdee, who told him that documents outlining his authority had been despatched by safe hand on 7 February, adding that

> Commonwealth Government has cabled General Wavell regarding your status in the following terms:- Begins. Having in view the very considerable Australian contribution to fighting resources under your command the G.O.C. A.I.F. should be accorded the right of direct access to you and senior officers, your staff and plans, especially those affecting A.I.F. in order to provide effective Australian representation and suitable

status for G.O.C. A.I.F. ABDA area. This would entail the fullest consultation in regard to all operational administrative and other plans and proposals in so far as they affect A.I.F. ends.[21]

The cable was encouraging, but not all that enlightening as to how far Lavarack was authorised to go to protect Australian interests.

Meanwhile, the prospect of large numbers of Japanese troops being released for an attack on Sumatra and Java after Singapore fell had filled Lavarack's mind during the night of 12/13 February and at 2.15 a.m. he began writing a cable to Curtin. It contained a depressingly realistic appreciation in which he said that the situation in the Far East would be altered drastically when Singapore fell and the chances of holding the Netherlands East Indies would be reduced considerably. Once Malaya was under their control, the Japanese could re-direct their military resources to an attack against Sumatra. Northern and central Sumatra would fall easily, and if the enemy moved quickly enough they could attack southern Sumatra before the arrival of the main body of the 7th Division:

> In any case one Australian division plus [the] few N.E.I. troops available will delay very superior enemy only for short period. Length of this period not calculable. Am unable to judge whether such delay would justify probable loss of Seven Div equipment and possible loss of large proportion personnel. In any case Seven Aust Div without equipment would be of little further value for defence N.E.I.[22]

In his opinion the Netherlands East Indies army would not offer strong resistance, so the addition to the defence of Java of the 6th Australian Division, wedged between Netherlands East Indies formations, would not greatly prolong resistance on that island either. It was therefore most unlikely that 1st Australian Corps would be able to prevent the fall of the Netherlands East Indies to the Japanese. Lavarack did not have enough information to enable him to judge whether the sacrifice of the corps in the Netherlands East Indies could be justified by the influence such a stand might have on future developments, but he reminded Curtin that the corps was the only trained and experienced formation within striking distance of the Far East. The implication was clear: the corps should not be committed to a campaign in which it would most probably be destroyed. And, since the 7th Division could not be ready for operations until the third week in March and the 6th Division until mid-

April, Lavarack told Curtin that 'very earnest consideration needed regarding future role One Aust Corps [sic]' should Singapore fall.²³

After the morning conference at GHQ Lavarack showed his cable to Wavell and declared that he intended to send it to the Australian Prime Minister. In Lavarack's words it caused an 'immediate commotion, which lasted all day' and his ADC recorded that GHQ was 'in a flap'. At 6 o'clock that evening Wavell, lying in bed as a result of a back injury sustained during his last visit to Singapore, read his own appreciation to Lavarack and other senior officers. This assessment, prepared for the Combined Chiefs of Staff in Washington, was very similar to that prepared by Lavarack, although Wavell's conclusion was marginally more optimistic:

> The situation does not at present demand change in plans but it may be forced on us. If that were so the destination of the Australian Corps would be first consideration for it contains the great majority of fully trained and equipped Australian troops. From purely strategic aspect there are advantages in diverting one or both divisions to Burma or Australia. But any abandonment of the Dutch East Indies would obviously have most serious moral and political repercussions. We must reinforce Sumatra until it is clearly useless to do so, subsequent reinforcement of Java would probably be unprofitable. We shall continue with present plans until the situation enforces change. This message gives warning of serious change in situation which may shortly arise necessitating complete reorientation of plans.

During Wavell's reading, news arrived that Japanese convoys bound for Banka Island included forty-five transports. Lavarack wrote that 'this settled [the] matter'. Wavell then asked Lavarack to postpone the dispatch of his appreciation until Wavell had sent his own. Lavarack, as he recorded, 'agreed, though certainly not in my own interests, as originator of [the] whole matter'. So ended what he called a 'tiring and interesting and momentous day'.²⁴

The following morning, the 14th, Lavarack sent his appreciation to Australia, at about the same time that he learned that Japanese paratroops had landed near Palembang. Nevertheless, at the morning conference Wavell told Lavarack that it was still intended to disembark the *Orcades* at Oosthaven. Despite the danger involved, Lavarack agreed to the landing of the Australian troops, partly because without heavy equipment they could easily be re-embarked. At the same time he hoped that the Japanese advance would be so rapid as to forestall such a move. Perhaps, if he felt that disembarkation was such a dangerous move that he hoped it would not be possible, he should not have agreed and taken an immediate stand on the matter. The difficulty for him, though, was that at that stage he still had not received from Australia details of his charter which could bolster him in such a confrontational course of action with his commander.[25]

At midday the next day, 15 February, the *Orcades* and another vessel arrived at Oosthaven and disembarkation of Blackburn's troops began. The 15th also saw the arrival from the Middle East of the 7th Division's commander, Major-General 'Tubby' Allen and his GSO1, Colonel C.M.L. Elliott, neither of whom were confident about future operations against the Japanese. At a conference of senior commanders on the afternoon of the 15th, Lavarack stressed the futility of disembarking more troops in the Netherlands East Indies. However, Wavell's chief of staff, General Pownall, dissented, arguing that the Allies should fight, even if it were to the last. Lavarack retorted that from a military point of view one should fight to best advantage after which, he noted, 'Pownall agreed, as a sensible man'. Pownall wrote afterwards:

> It looks as if the days of A.B.D.A. were numbered and we must start at once to consider the problem of getting this massive H.Q. away if we are ordered to clear out. Another Dunkirk in fact.

Lavarack, though, still had doubts that Wavell could be persuaded to cut his losses.[26]

However, that evening there was a dramatic, if not unexpected, change in the strategic situation: Singapore fell to the Japanese, who were now free to throw more weight behind the attack on Sumatra. Wavell ordered the re-embarkation of the troops landed from the *Orcades* (and the embarkation of some already in Sumatra) and the ship sailed for Java immediately. That night the first Japanese troops reached Palembang. All that Lavarack had feared had come to pass, but it was small consolation that his forecast had been correct. Nevertheless, if southern Sumatra had to fall Lavarack was grateful that at least it had happened, as he had hoped, with such speed as to forestall the permanent landing of troops from the *Orcades*.[27] His next step was to ensure that his corps was not disembarked in Java.

On the 15th Lavarack at last received a cable specifying in detail the powers given to him as the Australian commander in the area—finally he had the means to protect his troops.[28] Why it took so long for the government to ensure that it reached Lavarack is perplexing since the instructions were markedly similar to the charter given to Blamey when he took the AIF to the Middle East and Bennett's directive when he took the 8th Division to Malaya:

(a) The Force to be recognised as an Australian force under its own Commander, who will have a direct responsibility to the Commonwealth Government, with the right to communicate direct with that Government. No part of the Force to be detached or employed apart from the Force without his consent.

Questions of policy regarding the employment of the Force to be decided by the United Kingdom and Commonwealth Governments, in consultation; except that, in an emergency, the Commander of the Force may, at his discretion, take a decision on such a question, informing the Commonwealth Government that he is so doing.

(b) The Force to be under the operational control of the Commander-in-Chief of the theatre in which it is serving.

(c) Administration of supply services, and such other questions as are amenable to the adoption of a common system, to be controlled by the Commander-in-Chief of the Forces in which the Force is serving—subject to a financial adjustment between the respective Governments concerning the cost of such administration incurred by the British Government. All major financial questions, arising from the service of the Force abroad, to be reserved for direct discussion between the Commonwealth and United Kingdom Governments.

(d) Administration of the Force in domestic matters to be your prerogative, subject to general control by the Minister for the Army.

Forde also attached a copy of an Order-in-Council defining Lavarack's powers in matters of internal administration.[29] Lavarack now had the authority to keep his command intact.

Meanwhile, in Australia Sturdee had been preparing an appreciation based on Lavarack's letter to him of 6 February on the future employment of the AIF, in which he argued that the Allied aim should be to hold not small and isolated localities, but a continental area from which an offensive against the Japanese eventually could be launched. To Sturdee's mind, Australia provided a more suitable strategic base than either India or Burma. The immediate problem was to ensure the security of the country until sufficient American forces arrived. Although the army in Australia was being built up, it was short of equipment and not fully trained. The return of the AIF from abroad, however, would more than double the security of Australia. To lose Australia, but hold Java, would achieve little; even if Australia were not lost, to lose most of the Australian corps in Java would greatly weaken Australia's ability to participate in an eventual offensive.

Therefore, Sturdee strongly recommended that the government consider the diversion to Australia of that part of the AIF en route to the Netherlands Fast Indies and the early recall to Australia of the 9th Division and other AIF personnel still in the Middle East. Soon after he had finished, another appreciation of the situation by Lavarack arrived. Sturdee attached a copy to his own, noting that it 'endorses the basis of the views I have expressed'.[30]

As Wigmore pointed out in the official history, although the disaster in the Far East had been largely unforeseen by the United Kingdom and the United States, Australia was in a different position:

> Sturdee and Lavarack had the advantage, when preparing these and
> later appreciations, that they were reproducing proposals and
> arguments which they had been expressing during the last decade,
> whereas the British and American Ministers and their advisers were
> viewing calamities which they had not foreseen and which were
> occurring in areas about which they knew little. The Australian leaders
> belonged to a school of thought which had long contended that the
> situation of February 1942 would come about: Singapore fallen; the
> British and American fleets temporarily impotent against Japan; and
> Australia, the only effective base, being required to hold out until British
> or American reinforcements could arrive in strength.[31]

Perhaps Lavarack derived some satisfaction from knowing that his far-sighted criticism of the Singapore strategy in the 1930s had been proved well-founded, but considering the circumstances it would have provided little comfort.

Curtin, acting on Sturdee's advice, and fortified by Lavarack's latest appreciation, cabled Churchill on the 15th that (since the defence of the Netherlands East Indies was becoming impracticable):

It is a matter for urgent consideration whether the A.I.F. should not proceed to N.E.I. but return to Australia. The defence of Australia in short term period must largely rest on Australian forces and the degree to which they can be supplemented by forces, and to a large degree equipment, from U.S.A. The question of large scale assistance to Australian defence by American and Canadian forces has been raised but regret cannot be of assistance as quickly as Australian Imperial Force.

Curtin concluded by stating that the aim of such a strategy was 'to ensure as far as possible the certainty of ultimate victory by defending Australia as a base even though ground may be given to the enemy'. Wavell also sent a cable to Churchill on the 15th in which he warned of just such a message as Curtin's, adding that

although Lavarack is entirely willing to undertake any task with his corps I know that he has felt it his duty to warn his government of [the] danger involved to [the] Australian Corps.[32]

Despite warning Australia of the dangers, however, Lavarack had angered the Australian Prime Minister. In the early hours of the 15th he had received a cable from Curtin in reply to his of 9 February (in which he had suggested that troops in Australia be used to reinforce ABDA Command):

It is not understood on what grounds you feel yourself in a sound position to put forward a recommendation to Govt. for reinforcement of General Wavell's forces from those allotted to local defence of Australia. The C. of G.S. is responsible for the defence of Commonwealth and disposition of Australian military forces. The machinery for the total strategical view is Pacific War Council in London which is advised by Chiefs of Staff Committee.

Lavarack replied that when he had written in his earlier communication strongly urging 'reinforcement of General Wavell's forces from forces now allotted local defence in Australia if politically possible', he 'intended to refer to minor local reinforcement such as that now taking place at Koepang' and that he regretted any obscurity on his part. Lavarack had also criticised the disposition of the 8th Division in Malaya, and Curtin asked whether his criticism was aimed at its commander, General Bennett, or at Malaya Command. He made it clear that he had not criticised General Bennett and that he was fully aware of the importance of protecting Australian 'interests' with regard to the disposition of the corps in the Netherlands East Indies.[33]

It was churlish of Curtin to rebuke Lavarack at such a time. Lavarack had offered an opinion with suitable caveats: it was entirely up to Curtin whether he took the advice or ignored it, but it hardly called for him to remind an ex-CGS of the duties of that particular post. On the other hand, perhaps it was precisely because of Lavarack's perceived attitude to politicians when he was CGS before the war, which had made a bad impression on Curtin, that the issue arose at all. In any case, it was a pointless exercise on Curtin's part: whether Lavarack had suggested taking troops from Australia to reinforce the Netherlands East Indies or whether he had criticised Bennett or Malaya Command had become academic. With the fall of Singapore the whole complexion of the problem facing Lavarack and the Australian government was altered. It was clear that a successful defence of the Netherlands East Indies was now impossible and that any troops committed to such an endeavour would almost certainly be lost. As the AIF commander on the spot Lavarack would now have to ensure that he protected Australian interests, in particular as far as the landing of any troops was concerned. Unfortunately, although he finally knew officially, and in detail, the extent of his powers, it was clear that he did not have the support of the Prime Minister. The next few days would be harrowing and would seal Lavarack's professional fate.

16

'Emphatically a bad business'

The Netherlands East Indies, 1942—
Where Next?

THE DAY AFTER Singapore fell to the Japanese, Wavell sent a message to Churchill. The general's assessment of 16 February painted a gloomy picture of the prospects for holding Java, especially since Lavarack's Australian corps would not be ready for action until mid-April. Wavell recommended that no attempts be made to reinforce Java which might compromise the defence of either Burma or Australia, both of which he considered vital in the war against Japan. If Lavarack's corps were to be diverted, Wavell suggested that at least one of its divisions, preferably both, should go to Burma, the only theatre in which a land offensive could be launched against the Japanese in the near future. Australia could be reinforced by US troops if necessary instead of the corps.[1]

Lavarack, too, was 'firmly convinced' that the correct employment of the corps would be in Burma and had told Wavell so. Lavarack had received a copy of Curtin's cable to Churchill of the previous day arguing for the corps' return to Australia, but he felt that Curtin's appreciation was 'Rather ex parte and leaves out [the] question of Burma, from which [a] C.A. [counter-attack] on Japan can most effectively be launched'. Wisely, though, in a cable he also despatched on the 16th, Lavarack refrained from telling Curtin that he favoured Burma, but did stress that a decision about the destination of the corps had to be made urgently, since he considered it could not be usefully employed in the NEI. He also referred to a more immediate problem: what to do with the troops in the *Orcades* now that the strategic situation had taken a turn for the worst.

After the morning conference on 16 February Lavarack had again pressed Wavell not to disembark the *Orcades*, this time in Java. But Wavell would not be moved. He did not want to jeopardise relations with the Dutch or lower British prestige. He also wanted the troops for airfield protection and labour on the wharves. Lavarack cabled Curtin of Wavell's determination to disembark the Australians, but before despatch he had shown his message to Wavell's chief of staff, Pownall, 'who read [the] cable, amended and assented'. When sent the signal contained no reference to Wavell's wish to use AIF troops as wharf labour. The fact that Australians might have been used not only for military purposes, but also for labouring may have strengthened Curtin's hand in not having the men on the *Orcades* disembarked. And, if it were indeed still intended that the men would be used on the wharves, it is difficult to understand why Lavarack, as the Australian commander, would submit to such apparent censorship.[2]

Nevertheless, the next day Lavarack continued to protest to Wavell that the troops on the *Orcades* should not be disembarked. General Lloyd at Wavell's HQ was also doing what he could to prevent a landing. Lavarack wrote in his diary: 'This can't continue. Ship must be unloaded or sent away. Possibly greater danger in retention [in] Batavia (Tanjong Priok) harbour than in disembarkation'. Lavarack therefore also urged Wavell, whatever his decision on the *Orcades*, that as many ships as possible be sent away from Batavia. But again Wavell refused because of the possible detrimental effect on the Dutch, which prompted Berryman to write in his diary that 'Rome burns while Nero fiddles'.[3]

Lavarack was by now disillusioned with the operation of Wavell's headquarters. After the morning and evening conferences on the 17th Lavarack thought the meetings to be so out of touch with reality that they 'ought to be held in Bedlam'. He was not the only disenchanted senior officer: even Wavell's Chief of Air Staff and Commander of the Allied Air Forces, Air Marshal Sir Richard Peirse, had ceased to attend conferences regularly because he considered them futile.

Given such chaos perhaps it came as no surprise to Lavarack that at 10 p.m. in the evening of the 17th he was told by Wavell that the AIF troops in *Orcades* were to be landed to guard aerodromes in the Batavia and Buitenzorg areas. To rub salt into the wound, Wavell's decision to land the Australians was taken at the same time as plans were being made for the evacuation of his own headquarters from Java. As a precaution Lavarack ordered that arrangements be made to evacuate HQ 1st Australian Corps if necessary—and it seemed that it would be: the main evacuation from Sumatra took place that day and few doubted that Java would also eventually fall to the Japanese.[4]

On the morning of the 18th Lavarack again spoke to Wavell about the *Orcades*. He felt bound to 'disagree flatly' with Wavell's decision and pressed for the ship to be sent away immediately since the disembarkation had not yet begun. However, Wavell's position remained unchanged and that afternoon orders went out that those troops with personal arms—unit weapons were not available—were to leave the ship. Although 2,920 people were disembarked, Wavell told the War Office that only 'about 1,200 Australian troops' were being landed. Lavarack sent a cable to Sturdee and Curtin in which he outlined what had been ordered by Wavell and told them that he had strongly opposed the move.

At about that time Curtin and the other members of the War Cabinet were considering Lavarack's earlier message of the 16th in which he told them that it would be pointless to disembark the troops on the *Orcades*. However, instead of backing Lavarack unreservedly, the War Cabinet decided to present Wavell with Lavarack's opinion and so Curtin cabled Wavell that day asking what he intended to do with the Australians.

There was little to be gained from such a move—Wavell was hardly likely to have a change of heart because he had been confronted once more with Lavarack's views on the matter, as Lavarack observed: 'General Wavell can only disagree with my view, as he has already done'.[5] Referring the matter back to Wavell did nothing to help the men in the *Orcades*, but it did serve to highlight Curtin's lack of trust in Lavarack, as well as seal the fate of the men disembarked.

Lavarack's next message to Curtin would undermine still further his position with the Prime Minister. On the 18th Wavell suggested to Lavarack that he volunteer his views in favour of Burma as the destination of the corps to the Australian government. Misjudging the political mood in Australia, Lavarack agreed and asked Wavell to quote him in his own cable. Thus, Curtin received the following message from Wavell:

> I have been in close touch with Lavarack throughout and you may like
> to know that he agrees with my view that Australian Corps if diverted
> from N.E.I. should be used to reinforce Burma.[6]

Lavarack then sent his own cable to Australia:

> First. Reference my opinion quoted by supreme commander regarding
> best employment Aust Corps desire submit explanation as follows.
> Second. This opinion based on strategic conditions present situation and
> subject normal reservations in view possible major deterioration Burma
> or elsewhere. Third. Opinion based on following considerations. Believe
> future success dependent on retention of and action from main bases
> Australia and Burma. Future safety NEI no longer possible by direct
> defence and must depend on indirect influence operations from
> Australia and Burma. All Australian troops should be withdrawn from
> NEI immediately for use in Australia or Burma. Best method imposing
> our initiative on Japanese territory by air action. At present such threat
> or attack most feasible by land and air from Burma into China and then
> against Japan from Chinese air bases. Believe establishment land and air
> forces Burma adequate repeat adequate strength will compel Japan
> conform to our initiative. This would tend to draw Japanese forces from
> Australian and NEI regions. Fourth. Nearest available strong land and air
> forces possibly available are those in and approaching NEI present time.
> Not personally in position judge Australia's home defence position
> owing considerable absence. If this reasonably satisfactory believe
> Australia's best interest served by course suggested. This despite natural
> desire Aust Corps assist direct defence own homeland if considered
> necessary.[7]

This cable was to do Lavarack great harm, despite the provisos he had
stipulated and the fact that the Australian High Commissioner in London,
S.M. Bruce, also told Curtin on the same day that it was 'essential' that the
7th Division be diverted to Burma. The Pacific War Council (comprising
Churchill, the UK chiefs of staff and representatives of Holland, New
Zealand and Australia) had met in London to consider Wavell's
recommendation in his cable of the 16th that at least one Australian
division go to Burma. The Council recommended to the Combined Chiefs
of Staff in Washington that, while resistance in the NEI should be
continued by forces already there, the Australian corps should not be
landed. It also recommended that the Australian government be asked to
agree to the diversion of the 7th Division to Burma where it would be
joined by two brigades of the British 70th Division, while the remaining
AIF divisions, the 6th and the 9th, returned immediately to Australia.

At the time the Pacific War Council made its recommendations, the 7th Division was in ships spread out from west of Bombay to Batavia and was not tactically loaded, which would necessitate the unloading of almost the whole convoy before the troops could go into action with their supporting arms and transport. It seems unlikely that the corps could have undertaken operations in Burma any sooner than it could have in Sumatra, which Lavarack estimated would not be until the last week of March.

At a meeting of the Australian Advisory War Council on the 19th the non-government members recommended that the 7th Division be diverted from Java to Burma, but the government would not be moved from its request that all three divisions be returned to Australia, despite urgings from Australia's Special Envoy to the United Kingdom War Cabinet, Sir Earle Page, that Curtin change his mind. Notwithstanding offers of United States troops for Australia, General Sturdee's advice was that the home defence situation was not satisfactory.[8]

In a letter to Sturdee on the 19th Lavarack explained his intentions, revealing too that he was, to some extent, aware of the political disfavour into which he was falling in Australia:

> General Wavell asked me yesterday to cable the P.M., my views on the subject of the future employment of 1 Aust Corps, knowing that, from the purely strategical point of view, they coincided with his own. I demurred because, having made the mistake of offering suggestions the other day, without making the minor nature of them clear, I had been reproved by the P.M. I suggested however that he might quote me in a cable he intended to send to the P.M. Afterwards I felt that an explanation of my position was necessary and sent you my cable of yesterday. One gets out of touch with things at home after an absence of nearly 18 months, and I have no idea of the extent of your present preparations for defence, or of the amount of help likely to be received from the U.S.A. So I hope my expression of views will be accepted in the spirit in which it was made.

Lavarack warned Sturdee that if orders for the diversion of the convoys and the evacuation of Java were not received soon more troops could be lost when the Japanese attacked, probably in a week's time. His *sang froid* had not deserted him, though, and he told Sturdee that if the Japanese attacked before a decision to withdraw Australian troops was made 'you may perhaps have to include this letter in the category of "last words", though not, I fear, in that with the designation of "famous"'.[9]

By the time Lavarack was writing to Sturdee the island of Bali, at the eastern tip of Java, had been occupied by the Japanese, which meant that air communication with Australia was all but cut. Air raids on Batavia and Bandung had begun and the aerodrome near Lavarack's headquarters came under attack as he watched. Yet, that morning, the 19th, the troops from the *Orcades* finally left the ship as Wavell had ordered. Lavarack wrote that 'the situation round Java is now so serious that the units that have landed may well, in the end, be a total loss', so it was imperative, as he had pointed out to Sturdee, that no more troops be wasted in the defence of Java. Early on the 20th he received a cable from Curtin on the AIF diversion and the *Orcades*. Curtin told Lavarack that he was 'greatly concerned' that the units landed from *Orcades* had only rifles, and asked him to speak to Wavell about having the troops evacuated. The cable also contained a curt paragraph on the destination of the corps:

> You are being informed that I was against diversion to Burma. You will note that we have been influenced by your own opinion that condition precedent to diversion to Burma is that our home defences must be reasonably satisfactory. Our home defences are far from satisfactory. You will please explain situation to Wavell and ask for his sympathetic co-operation.[10]

Lavarack received nothing more tangible than a considerate hearing from Wavell who was not prepared to co-operate on the question of the diversion of the 7th Division to Burma. Neither would he countenance the immediate evacuation of the AIF troops landed from *Orcades*, for reasons he had already put forward. Nevertheless, Wavell promised Lavarack that he would make arrangements for an evacuation later, if it became necessary and were possible, and said that he had already spoken to Rear-Admiral Palliser, his Deputy Chief of Naval Staff. Later, however, when Lavarack spoke to Palliser, he discovered that no definite arrangements for evacuation had been made, although the latter promised to do what he could. A signal received that evening from the Combined Chiefs of Staff in Washington confirmed that there would be no withdrawal of combatant troops already landed regardless of nationality and there would be no surrender. Wavell was also told that attempts were still being made to obtain Australian consent for the diversion of the 7th Division to Burma.[11]

There was little more to be done in the Netherlands East Indies except prepare to leave. Lavarack obtained Wavell's permission to evacuate the staff of the 1st Australian Corps and the 7th Division headquarters in Java. Preparations for the move began immediately. The *Orcades* was to be used to take them away while Lavarack flew to Australia to report to the government. On 21 February Lavarack cabled Curtin:

> Adv parties Aust Corps 7 Aust Div and HQ AIF embarking Orcades for Colombo pending decision destination Corps. Lavarack flying to Australia report situation. Wavell not prepared modify views about employment 7 Aust Div. Total Australian tps in Java 2920 being retained for defence aerodromes. Arrangements in train for their embarkation when final decision taken about Java.

At this stage Lavarack was still under the impression that eventually the 1st Australian Corps would probably go to Burma, and so told the commander of the 7th Division, General Allen, to assume command if it went into action before he returned (Berryman was to command the 7th Division).[12]

Lavarack also issued instructions to Blackburn, who had been promoted to brigadier to command the Australians remaining in Java, adding in a personal letter:

> I deeply regret that events have forced me into the position of having to leave you stranded here in this island with a mere handful of Australians. I did everything possible to prevent your disembarkation, but General Wavell was determined to have you ashore to guard the aerodromes and for reasons of prestige and morale. In fact you are the equivalent of the force that was sent to Greece in the late campaign. However I have hopes that the parallel will end there. Urgent representations about your position have been made, both by General Wavell to London, and by myself to Canberra, (still earlier and several times). Sea transport arrangements are being tentatively made, and generally I feel hopeful that you will not be called upon to do the desperate and stupid things that were done in Greece and Crete.

Lavarack went on to explain the safeguards he had put in place for Blackburn's force. He had arranged with Pownall that Blackburn would be under direct operational control of Lieutenant-General ter Poorten and told Blackburn:

Remember that this means that you have direct access to the general himself and need not take orders from his staff. He reports twice a day at least to Sir Archie himself, and I think this is the best safeguard I can arrange, in the absence of an Australian Command.

He advised Blackburn to contact General Lloyd, the Australian at Wavell's headquarters, and the officer commanding the Australian 2/3rd Reserve Motor Transport Company, which was under Blackburn's administrative control only. Lavarack had been making arrangements to ensure that if Blackburn's force had to be evacuated, then the Australian motor transport company would get it to the ships in an emergency. He told Blackburn:

> I cannot order this to be done, having no actual command, but have asked the staff at Supreme H.Q. to see to it. In any case it would be advisable that you make contact with the commander and concert arrangements with him. After all they are Australians and it is proper that they should help you, and incidentally themselves, to make a get-away at the proper moment. In case of real need I think you should step in and take the unit, but of course I can't put that in orders. Don't forget that you wield A.I.F. powers.

Lavarack concluded: 'However, my real hope is that you will be out of this…before you have time to do these things'. By 2 p.m. on the 21st Lavarack and his ADC had left by air for Australia. Two hours later most of the Australian corps staff left by road for Tanjong Priok, from where they sailed at 11 p.m. aboard the *Orcades*. Four days later ABDA Command was dissolved and Wavell left for India.[13]

Lavarack flew all night after leaving Java and arrived in Broome, Western Australia at about 6.30 a.m. on 22 February. (In passing, it should be noted that subsequent allegations by Major-General Gordon Bennett, who had escaped from Singapore without authorisation and had reached the Netherlands East Indies, that Lavarack had refused him a place on an aircraft to Australia are groundless.)

The next day Lavarack continued his journey in an American bomber, crossing Australia to Melbourne, where he was met by General Sturdee. He asked Sturdee how soon it would be before he had to leave again, because at that stage:

I still believed that 7 Div was en route for India and Burma, as it had been when I left Java, and that my visit to Australia was only for consultation before returning to my command.

Lavarack was astonished when told that the 1st Australian Corps was returning to Australia and that he was to remain in the country. He noted in his diary: 'So we are to adopt the false strategy of head-on defence, instead of attacking the Jap flanks, communications, and home bases (latter through China). Parochialism run mad!!'[14]

It was not to be a pleasant homecoming: Lavarack would soon discover that his opinion that at least the 7th Division should go to Burma, and his earlier suggestion that troops in Australia be used to reinforce ABDA Command, had firmly established him as unreliable in Curtin's eyes. This was hardly reasonable since, as Wigmore pointed out in the official history, Lavarack had been overseas with the AIF for more than a year, so it was to be expected that he was out of touch with defence developments in Australia.

The destination of the corps was a sensitive issue for Curtin, especially after support for the diversion of Australian troops to Burma had come from the non-government members of the Advisory War Council and an old political opponent in London, Sir Earle Page. The issue had been made even more emotive by the discovery that on 20 February Churchill had imperiously ignored the wishes of the Australian government and ordered that the ships carrying the 7th Division to alter course for Burma. Despite Churchill's manoeuvrings and a message from Roosevelt promising United States troops, Curtin stood firm and was eventually able to have the AIF diverted to Australia on the 23rd.

Given the political storm the destination of the corps had generated, perhaps it was to be expected that Curtin resented Lavarack's expression of the same view as Churchill, Wavell and others. Lavarack had been the odd man out: both Sturdee and Blamey had opposed the diversion to Burma, but Lavarack had given it qualified support. Curtin had made up his mind about Lavarack, but that did not prevent him, when arguing for the return of the division to Australia, citing Lavarack's view that the diversion to Burma of the 7th Division should take place only if Australia's home defence preparations were satisfactory.[15]

Lavarack had taken the broader view and it went against him in Canberra where the perspective on the Pacific war was different. At a meeting of the Advisory War Council in Canberra on 24 February Lavarack gave an account of events in the Netherlands East Indies and offered his views on the broader strategic situation. Although he was impressed by the courtesy and respect extended to him by the members, he came away feeling that their discussions were unrealistic and that the rift between Curtin and Churchill was both unnecessary and unfortunate. He felt that too much emphasis was being placed on local defence, by which he meant 'the defence of the mainland on the mainland', rather than keeping open lines of communication with the United Kingdom to the west and the United States to the east.

However, as soon as Lavarack fully appreciated the inadequacy of the Australian defences, he supported the decision to return 1st Australian Corps to Australia. With hindsight, little would have been gained by sending part of the AIF to Burma. It would probably have had minimal influence on the campaign, but would most likely have had to remain there, preventing it participating in the New Guinea campaign later in the year. Even so, Lavarack believed that if his plan for the formation of extra divisions in 1940 had been adopted, the defence of Australia in 1942 would have been adequate, which in turn would have permitted part of the corps to go to Burma.[16]

On the day Lavarack met the Advisory War Council in Canberra, Curtin made a last attempt to have Blackburn's troops evacuated from Java. He cabled Sir Earle Page in London, referring to Wavell's statement that to evacuate them would violate orders from the Combined Chiefs of Staff, and insisted that Wavell be given authority to ensure that the Australians eventually returned to Australia:

> The Government instructed Lavarack on 19th February that if worst comes to worst some chance of withdrawal should be afforded our men. In view of present position in Java the Government insists that the necessary authority be given to Wavell to ensure that these troops are evacuated, their ultimate destination being Australia.

A copy of this cable was also sent to R.G. Casey, Australian Minister in Washington, and to Wavell. Curtin also cabled General Wavell in a separate message:

> Should the situation deteriorate before the receipt of orders for evacuation, the Australian Government requests that you should act in

accordance with the instruction to Lavarack to provide for evacuation of Australian Troops.

The issue was settled, however, when Page replied from London that the Pacific War Council had already recommended to the Combined Chiefs of Staff that the resistance in Java be continued by the troops already there.[17] Lavarack, who by then thought it impracticable to evacuate Blackburn's force, was not surprised when Frederick Shedden told him several days later that the troops still in Java would not be relieved and that if an evacuation were ordered they had no special priority. In Wigmore's words: 'Curtin, probably impressed by the undesirable moral effects of withdrawing troops already deployed on the soil of an ally, did not persist, and the 3,000 Australians remained in Java'. Lavarack wrote that it was

Emphatically a bad business, mainly because the troops should never have been sent to Java so far ahead of their convoy and should never have been disembarked. Wavell's criminal obstinacy!

Wavell later told Lavarack that he had 'always regretted' having to land the troops from the *Orcades*, but felt that in the circumstances 'I do not feel that we could have acted otherwise'. But Lavarack felt that he had been let down by both Curtin and Wavell, as he told Gavin Long in 1953:

Curtin had sufficient determination to force the return of 7 Div. to Australia, but not enough to save the 3,000 men in Java. He did not support me, and even referred my advice to Wavell, who of course disagreed, as he had done in Council. You can see also that action to evacuate Blackburn's force was also promised [by Wavell]. Can you see any reason why I should distrust both Wavell and Curtin?[18]

There is no doubting Lavarack's concern for Blackburn's men and his desire to see them remain aboard the *Orcades*. As he told Sturdee on 19 February before he left the NEI: 'I have been doing my best to prevent their disembarkation, going so far as a direct disagreement with General Wavell on the subject.' Unquestionably Lavarack was attempting to protect Australian interests, as he made clear to Sturdee:

[Wavell] will be thinking of immediate and transient utility, whereas I was thinking of ultimate advantage and was desirous of forwarding the Government's policy of maintaining the integrity of the A.I.F.

Unfortunately, although Lavarack was convinced that he was right, he seemed to feel that if he could not persuade Wavell to leave the troops on the ship, then there was little he could do but disagree before eventually complying with the order to disembark. Indeed, he even nursed the forlorn hope that the Japanese would resolve the problem by advancing so rapidly that there would not be time for disembarkation.[19]

Wielding the powers of GOC AIF in the Netherlands East Indies, Lavarack had more authority than a British general commanding a corps under Wavell and was in a position to take a robust stand on the issue of the *Orcades*. Perhaps Lavarack's advice to Curtin could have been stronger, urging that under no circumstances should the AIF be split by allowing 3,000 men to land with only small arms, largely as a diplomatic gesture. Lavarack might even have referred to the first paragraph of his charter as GOC AIF, refused to permit the disembarkation and then appealed for Curtin's support on a matter of national importance (which, given Curtin's political persuasion, could well have been forthcoming, despite his dislike of Lavarack).[20]

The fate of the *Orcades* should have been inextricably linked with the remainder of the convoy carrying the AIF—if the AIF were to be diverted, so should the troops aboard the *Orcades* have been diverted. General Lloyd later said that if Blamey had been in Java, AIF troops on the *Orcades* would not have been landed. On the other hand, General Berryman strenuously defended Lavarack:

> As Chief of Staff to Lavarack, I wrote the reports and signal messages with strong recommendations against our troops being landed in Java, and I consider the part we played was our most important contribution to our army during the war. Furthermore, I submit, no General could have done more than Lavarack.
> [paragraphs deleted]
> ...I submit that Blamey could not have done more than Lavarack, and whilst credit is due to Curtin and Sturdee, great credit should go to Lavarack for the strong recommendations and reports which we forwarded to our government, and for Lavarack's refusal for any of our troops to be landed until told by our government to obey Wavell's orders.[21]

It is impossible to say whether Blamey would have prevented the troops being landed. He had more experience than Lavarack in such matters and was more politically astute, but, possibly most important, he was more likely to be supported by the government. If Blamey had been in command, perhaps the government would have followed his advice instead of referring the matter back to Wavell. Lavarack felt that this had been a mistake which gave the supreme commander the opportunity to disembark the troops, as he later told Curtin:

> In my opinion at the time no useful military purpose could possibly be served by landing these almost helpless units and I represented this strongly to the Government. The Government, unfortunately in my opinion, referred the matter back to General Wavell, with whom I had already disagreed, and he decided to land the men, the only concession being that those completely unarmed, i.e. not even having rifles, should not be disembarked.

Lavarack did fight hard for Blackburn's men and probably no other Australian army officer except Blamey might have done more, but even that is not certain—Blamey had not been consistently successful in preventing the AIF being broken up in the Middle East by British commanders. For his part, Curtin made an error in placing the matter in Wavell's hands instead of taking a stand on the issue after receiving Lavarack's opinion.[22] It is with the Prime Minister that the ultimate responsibility for the fate of the men aboard the *Orcades* lies: those who were not killed fighting the Japanese endured years of brutal captivity, during which more died. To Lavarack's credit, he at least managed to have another ship, the *Mt Vernon* conform to the movements of the main convoy.

The disembarkation of the *Orcades* was an important national issue, but it was the broader question of the employment of the Australian corps (first in the NEI and then its ultimate destination after the defence there collapsed) which claimed most attention and which became the real stumbling block for Lavarack's future. In February 1942 the fate of the corps was an issue which extended beyond the purely military into the realms of politics and diplomacy.

Lavarack had been aware of Australian interests and had done his best to protect them, but perhaps as a regular officer he was so imbued with the tradition of loyalty to his military superior that he found it difficult to wear comfortably the mantle of national commander. Of course, he disagreed with Wavell on several occasions, as he told Sturdee in February:

naturally I do not always see eye to eye with the Supreme Commander and his Chief of Staff [Pownall]...The differences of opinion that have arisen have all had to do with the employment of Australian troops.

Nevertheless, Lavarack could be influenced by Wavell and Pownall in areas affecting Australia's interests. Lavarack's ADC, Curtis Wilson, recalled of Lavarack that 'His cables were scrupulously shown to the Supreme Commander or his Chief of Staff before despatch' and he had delayed sending his appreciation of 13 February to Curtin at Wavell's request.[23] That Lavarack could readily take the Imperial view of events should not be too surprising. Although he had exhibited a distinctly Australian point of view as CGS, it had been always within the context of Imperial defence. In the letter he wrote to Sturdee on 6 February he had made quite clear his priorities as the Australian commander in the NEI:

> You will understand, I imagine, that in all decisions I may take in [the] present circumstances there will be two guiding considerations; first the probable effect on the general war effort, and second the fact that an Australian division is cooped up in Singapore, and relies largely on our efforts for its eventual relief.

Lavarack's ADC, Wilson, later wondered whether Lavarack had advocated Burma as the destination for the AIF in part because Wavell favoured it or, if by going to Burma, Lavarack hoped to escape Blamey's command. Lavarack may have been encouraged to work as closely as possible with Wavell in case the latter harboured any doubts about Lavarack's performance in Tobruk or because of their misunderstanding during the Syrian campaign (when Wavell unfairly criticised the 7th Division's progress in the early stages of the fighting).

However, while Lavarack would almost certainly have welcomed being independent of Blamey, there is little doubt that he genuinely believed that Burma was the proper destination for the Australian corps, regardless of Wavell's opinion. As far as the British were concerned, Lavarack was no cipher: General Lloyd noted after the Netherlands East Indies episode that 'Wavell had just about had the difficulties of employing Dominion troops in Imperial battles'. Wavell's chief of staff, General Pownall, was more specific and hoped that he would never have to deal with Australians again.[24]

Lavarack could not know in February 1942 that he would never again have to fight alongside the British. His appreciation of the situation in the Netherlands East Indies had been realistic and valuable to the Australian government, and Menzies later told Lavarack that he had made a good impression at the Advisory War Council meeting after his return from Java. Unfortunately, political naiveté had allowed him to offer advice on the destination of the corps which had fuelled Curtin's distrust of him, a distrust possibly reinforced by the opinions of Shedden whose relationship with Curtin was excellent. Support for Lavarack in Australian political circles, which had never been great, had been further diminished. That lack of political backing, combined with Blamey's antipathy, would have a profound effect on Lavarack's prospects as a battlefield commander in the war against the Japanese.[25]

17

'There is no generosity in Blamey'

GOC First Army, 1942-1944

LAVARACK'S FIRST WEEKS back in Australia were clouded with uncertainty about his future. It seemed that there was no role for him. His report to the Advisory War Council and a meeting of the Defence Committee the next day were the only two official meetings he attended for several weeks after his return. Being excluded from discussions on the defence of the country was a turn of events about which he had 'mixed feelings':

> After all [it is] not my responsibility, but feel [I] could have something to say, especially in view of [the] Government's obvious tendency to draw in all Australian forces to home defence, which may be fatal.

He began to speculate on his future position in the army and made discrete enquiries, coming to the conclusion (a correct one, as events were to show) that probably he would be given command of an army. Nevertheless, he remained anxious until it was decided on 11 March that he was to be acting Commander-in-Chief pending the return of Blamey, who the War Cabinet had decided to recall from the Middle East on 18 February.[1]

Lavarack was not considered for the post of C-in-C himself. Gavin Long noted after interviewing Curtin in April 1942:

> Curtin said that for years he had seen the present situation coming. He felt in his bones that Singapore could not stand. Army men, Lavarack

particularly, predicted what had happened but nothing was done to build army, airforce or industrial machine to meet the danger. Curtin appeared to harbour lack of faith in Lavarack because, in September 1939, Lavarack gave him the impression of being a man in despair because the long-expected war was on him and we were not ready.[2]

Curtin seems to have conveniently overlooked the role of politicians in laying down defence policy. It was hardly Lavarack's fault that the army had been starved of funds during the inter-war years. He had done his best within the constraints of a defence policy (accepted by successive governments) which had been based on the flawed Singapore strategy favouring the navy—and all but crippling the army and the air force in the process. If looking for individual scapegoats, Curtin might have done better to blame Shedden, whose wholehearted support for the Singapore strategy had helped deny the other services the men and equipment necessary to be ready for war.

Curtin's poor opinion of Lavarack had then been exacerbated by his advice while the Australian commander in the Netherlands East Indies. So Lavarack could scarcely have been considered a serious candidate for Commander-in-Chief in February 1942—with Curtin in power and Shedden in the shadows, it had to be Blamey. Nevertheless, Lavarack was to do useful work during the brief period before Blamey's return. Although he was cautious about making decisions which might be overturned later by Blamey, the plans he prepared in collaboration with Sturdee formed the foundation of the reorganisation of the army in March.[3]

However, in the meantime, three senior officers, Major-Generals Edmund Herring and George Vasey, and Brigadier Clive Steele, not knowing that Blamey had been recalled and fearful that either Lavarack or Bennett (who had made an unauthorised and controversial escape from Singapore) would be made C-in-C, approached the Minister for the Army, F.M. Forde, on 18 March with the proposal that Major-General Horace Robertson be appointed to the post. They also suggested that all generals over the age of 50 should be retired. Herring recalled:

Clive Steele was the moving spirit. I attended a meeting, with Steele and Vasey, one night with Forde. Clive did most of the talking. To us earlier, Steele had said that Robbie would deal with the Government all right.

Speaking of our fear that Lavarack or Bennett would be appointed, Clive said, "We've got to do something about it".

Herring said that they did not want Lavarack because of his 'unpredictable moods and bad temper'. Blamey's biographer, Hetherington, recorded that in December 1970 Herring added:

Perhaps I have told you all this before, but I think when we arrived [in Australia] we found a great deal of despondency and alarm about and we felt that Lavarack could not possibly lift the Australian people in the crisis that had arisen. One of his problems was that he was temperamental and when he was down, he was terribly far down...

Another major concern of the conspirators was to have a commander-in-chief who would not pander to politicians which, reportedly, was one of their criticisms of Lavarack. If true, this seems unfair to Lavarack considering the stands taken by him when he was head of the army in the difficult pre-war years and, more recently, his advice that the 1st Australian Corps be diverted to Burma, which certainly had not ingratiated him with politicians. But Herring, Vasey and Steele had little cause to be concerned. By the time Robertson told Forde that he was prepared to accept the post of C-in-C, Blamey had already arrived in Perth.[4]

Lavarack had been told by Berryman and Rowell of the move to have a younger officer appointed Commander-in-Chief and to have all generals over the age of 50 retired, which would, of course, include him. Berryman wrote in his diary that he had been told:

Steele, Herring, Vasey, [and] Harold Luxton, were intriguing to get Robbie as Commander-in-Chief. There is not much loyalty on their part especially as most of them were very ingratiating to TAB and JDL.

Lavarack was unimpressed by the so-called 'revolt of the generals' and made it clear to Forde, when the minister raised the names of Steele, Vasey and Robertson as potential division commanders, that there were 'many others who are in my opinion both more efficient and more loyal'. He warned Forde that

I think it very necessary to stress the loyalty aspect in assessing an officer's value. Without this quality in its officers an Army must eventually break up into cliques. Therefore, other things being equal, I place an officer whom I know to be reliable in this respect above one of whom I am not sure.[5]

Three days later Lavarack, Steele and Mackay met Blamey at Essendon airport in Melbourne. His arrival left Lavarack, who in the previous two weeks had been privy to all important matters of army policy, once again unsure of his position: 'arrival of Blamey leaves me at [a] loose end pending formation of Armies. Presume my present position is GOC 1 Aust Corps AIF...' He did not have to wait long, however, to be given his new command. Blamey submitted to the War Cabinet his proposals, based on the plans prepared by Lavarack and Sturdee, for a reorganisation of the army, in which Lavarack would command the First Australian Army with its headquarters in Toowoomba, Queensland. Shortly after the official announcement of his new appointment Lavarack asked Blamey about the possibility of being promoted to full general, but from Blamey

> received [the] answer, apparently foreseen and well-prepared, that 'the Government was not willing to commit itself'. Apparently I am to be cast into the pool with all the new promotions. Such is fate with watchful jealousy ever on the lookout above me. There is no generosity in Blamey.

After asking Forde if Blamey had ever mentioned the matter to him, Lavarack wrote that Forde replied that it was 'never referred to [the] Govt in any shape or form'. Lavarack regarded the affair as a 'typical instance of TAB's unreliability'. The incident was a foretaste of the frustration Lavarack would have to endure for the remainder of the war.[6]

As the commander of the First Australian Army, Lavarack was responsible for the defence of the north-east coast of Australia at a time when it was possible that the Japanese might indeed be planning to attack that part of the mainland. Thus the First Army area encompassed Queensland, including the Torres Strait islands, and New South Wales. The force under Lavarack's command was substantial: 1st Corps (3rd and 7th Divisions) in northern NSW; 2nd Corps (1st, 2nd and 10th Divisions) in the Newcastle-Sydney-Port Kembla area; 5th Division in Queensland; and 1st Motor Division in reserve in NSW. If a Japanese attack had materialised, Lavarack would have been the commander controlling the campaign, at least initially, and so for a while at least it seemed as if Blamey had given him an important command.

However, naval battles in the Coral Sea in May and at Midway in June removed the immediate threat to Australia. Thereafter Lavarack could only hope that Blamey would either give him command of New Guinea Force or place Headquarters First Army in control of operations in New Guinea.[7]

As Lavarack waited in Toowoomba, hoping for the call which would take him to New Guinea, his First Army began to wither. On 14 July 1942 he wrote that:

Both Berryman and self envisage possibility of gradual reduction of 1 Aust Army to vanishing point, when it will be in same position as 2 Aust Army now is. Personal hostility of T.A.B. to self is very bad for 1 Aust Army. No place for this in time of war. Have done my best to eliminate it, but fear that it is part of T.A.B.'s makeup. Patience!

In August Lavarack pressed Blamey on the possibility of placing HQ First Army in New Guinea, but Blamey was not receptive, arguing that the troops in New Guinea comprised a 'task force' not an army. Lavarack even broached the matter with General Douglas MacArthur, the new Commander-in-Chief, South-West Pacific Area, but to no avail. He suspected that Blamey had foreseen the eventuality and had already spoken to MacArthur about HQ First Army.[8]

Blamey thought that Lavarack might also be pursuing other avenues in his efforts to get to New Guinea. In September 1942 he challenged Lavarack about meeting Sir Keith Murdoch, chairman of the Herald and Weekly Times newspaper company, who Blamey suspected was working to have him replaced as Commander-in-Chief. During the First World War Murdoch had played a part in Sir Ian Hamilton being recalled from command of the Allied forces in the Dardanelles and later had taken against Blamey when he was police commissioner in Victoria. Lavarack wrote in his diary on 18 September:

T.A.B. intimated that he had been informed that I had 'seen Murdoch and took a poor view of the situation'. Informed him positively that I have not seen Murdoch and that I do not take a poor view of the situation. Am naturally anxious, but have not said so to anyone, even Murdoch, (presumably Sir Keith Murdoch). Looks like usual effort to give this dog [a] bad name with view to subsequent hanging. T.A.B. took my denial quite calmly. Called me 'Johnnie' for first time for two years.[9]

The incident seems to have been a case of mistaken identity provoked by Murdoch's recent invitation to Berryman, Vasey, Hopkins and Brigadier J.D. Rogers to dine with him and a friend of Lavarack's, William Dunstan, the General Manager of the Melbourne *Herald*. Berryman declined, hoping 'to choke them off tactfully' and warned the others to be careful. He noted later that 'Afterwards Murdoch told P.M. Curtin he did not worry about generals because he could get all the information he wanted from the Brigadiers'. Hopkins wrote that Murdoch's invitation

> was aimed, I always thought, at establishing... cordial relations with the "medium-senior" echelon of army officers. There had been a lot of new faces after the return of the AIF but things were settling down by September 1942 and it was the start of a new campaign.

As for plans Murdoch may have had for unseating Blamey, Hopkins wrote in 1983:

> My ear couldn't have been very close to the ground in those days! I doubt if I ever heard that Murdoch was angling to unseat Blamey. At least I have not retained any memory of Murdoch criticising Blamey at that dinner.[10]

However, one of Blamey's ADCs, J.A. Wilmoth, maintained that Murdoch had vowed to bring Blamey down and Lieutenant-Colonel F.J. Howard, Assistant Director of Public Relations (New Guinea Force) at LHQ, has said that Murdoch would call and see him 'for information which he could use against Blamey after his return from the Middle East'. Whether Murdoch had placed unseating Blamey high on his list of priorities was essentially immaterial: Blamey was suspicious of him and viewed with alarm any senior army officer's association with him.

Lavarack had dined with Murdoch on several other occasions (they had met twice in March and again in July, accompanied by Generals Sturdee and Cannan), but Hopkins felt that Lavarack's character 'would be too strong to join in such a disloyal movement', and that he was more likely to confront Blamey face-to-face than go behind his back on any issue. Indeed, earlier Lavarack had assured Blamey that 'I have no hand in any intrigues that may be taking place'. But Lavarack's association with Murdoch, regardless of intent, would have done nothing to improve the chances of HQ First Army going to New Guinea, especially when Blamey himself felt under threat because of the army's failure to stem the Japanese advance there.[11]

As a result of criticism by MacArthur of Australian progress, Blamey went to New Guinea a few days later to supervise operations, a move which precipitated the well-known clash between himself and General Rowell, commanding New Guinea Force. Initially Lavarack wondered if this presaged a change for HQ First Army. Had the decision been left to Rowell, Lavarack's headquarters would have been in New Guinea: by mid-September 1942 he felt that New Guinea Force was becoming too big to manage effectively with the resources at his disposal. Rowell wrote that, as a way of easing the tension between himself and Blamey,

> I suggested that the First Army Headquarters should be brought in from Toowoomba, but Blamey dismissed this by saying, "To do that would be to bring in a commander I don't want". He meant Lavarack.

Rowell warned Blamey that if he did not 'take some action on these lines' he was sure the Americans would: 'And they did, bringing in General Kruger's [sic] Army Headquarters, which spelt the end of effective control by Allied Land Forces Headquarters of any forces other than Australian.'

After Rowell had been sacked by Blamey for largely personal reasons, Major General J.M.A. Durrant and the war correspondent Chester Wilmot told Lavarack of Blamey's response to Rowell's suggestion that HQ First Army come to New Guinea:

> Durrant informed me at Queensland Club that Rowell had asked TAB why he did not put First Army in charge of N.G. ops instead of coming himself and that TAB had replied 'You know I can't do that for personal reasons'. Later met Chester Wilmot who said that the actual words were 'That would involve putting in someone I don't want to put in'. Deplorable! And nice for me!!...Rowell is the sacrifice, to a very unworthy god.[12]

Once again Blamey had chosen to place a personal grudge above the best interests of the Australian army.

In the last week of October Lavarack was himself in New Guinea on a visit when he discussed Rowell's dismissal with Blamey, as he noted in his diary:

Welcome by C.-in-C. not better than cool. Had talk with him after dinner, when he stated categorically that could never again entertain any esteem for Rowell. Said that he 'really believed he thought I was lying',[sic] when he (Rowell) was informed by T.A.B. that the Govt had requested him to go to P[ort] M[oresby] Could make no comment. Obvious dilemma for Rowell. How could he know!? Funny if not tragic.

Lavarack could also see the implications for himself and noted later that night:

> Feel certain now of TAB's definite personal hostility towards myself. He is shifty and uncommunicative and the frankest approaches meet with no response. I literally never know whether or not he is telling the truth in all personal matters, e.g. his attitude towards Plant whom he accuses (still) of refusing a Bn command in 1918, 'When he was Gellibrand's D.A.Q.M.G.'

Lavarack defended Plant against Blamey's accusations, and pointed out Plant's 'excellent work' in the Syrian campaign after he had appointed Plant to replace Cox as commander of the 25th Brigade. Plant later told Lavarack that he had indeed refused the command of a battalion because he expected to be GSO1 of the 3rd Division—Lavarack thought that it was 'perfectly legitimate for Plant to refuse Bn command for GSO1, as latter much the best experience from his point of view'. Although he did not say so, Lavarack regarded Blamey's long-standing charges against Plant as 'trumped-up', writing in this diary that 'this is typical of TAB's methods'. He continued:

> My own case, Rowell's, and Plant's, are all instances of the influence of personal considerations on Blamey's actions. These personal considerations exercise a malign influence on important operational decisions. Rowell was undoubtedly doing excellent work at Moresby, (Allen supports this and so do many others, e.g. Morris), and there is now an atmosphere of unease and suspicion.

Blamey's accusations against Plant caused Lavarack to wonder what

> stories he repeats about myself. Probably the lie about Archie Wavell's attitude after Tobruk last year. Fortunately if this is ever brought up I

can produce Sir Archie's letter. Sir Archie told me that he had shown my letter and his reply to Blamey, but latter has probably forgotten this.

Lavarack was sure that he and Plant were targets for Blamey's antagonism because they had both been appointed to the AIF in spite of Blamey's opposition.[13]

Blamey was under great stress at the time he and Lavarack met in Port Moresby. Lavarack saw this reflected in Blamey's physical state: 'Noticed T.A.B. hiccuping in the old familiar way; his memory seems bad and he constantly repeats prejudiced stories which can easily be proved untrue. What complex?' Whatever else may have been ailing Blamey, there is no doubt that Lavarack's arrival in New Guinea had a bad effect on him. But Blamey was about to take action to rectify that particular problem.

The next day, the 30th, Lavarack left on a visit to Milne Bay. Before departing he told Blamey that he intended to return to Australia in the early hours of 1 November. When he returned to Port Moresby after the visit Lavarack was surprised to discover that Blamey had arranged that his departure for Australia be brought forward a day. 'This is very nice,' wrote Lavarack in his diary. 'Chucked out. He can't remember my name in conversation and obviously *hates* it. Shall have to be more wary than ever.' Before his departure Lavarack and Blamey talked for some time during the night, but reached no understanding. Lavarack wrote that Blamey

informed me that his reasons for turning me out of N.G. a day earlier than I intended was that (1) I am accused (by Canberra) of being absent too much from my H.Q. Pointed out that I have a large area to cover. T.A.B. then shifted ground and said I had visited Melbourne four times in three months. Consider myself best judge of need for visits but pointed out that my diary shows three visits in four months, the first being in first week in July, ordered by himself, and that I had never gone without his authority. T.A.B. then shifted ground again and said it was during a previous three months, but did not offer to produce the alleged complaint (hopeless). (2) He also said that he had only approved my visit to Port Moresby on condition I came from Horn Island direct. Replied that his own staff had made the transport arrangements and that there was no transport from Horn Island during my visit to Torres Straits command. Informed him also that Gen MacArthur is anxious that senior officers shall see as far as possible, the conditions in N.G. Does T.A.B.

regard a visit to N.G. as a joy ride? I went as a matter of duty. Personal again! Any stick will do to beat a dog with!! Hopeless!!!

On the question of his headquarters coming to New Guinea, Blamey told Lavarack that he had come to New Guinea at the request of the government and that while he remained there was no scope for Lavarack, and then said that his stay was indefinite. Lavarack returned to exile in Toowoomba early the next morning.[14]

Lavarack did not believe, as Blamey had said in Port Moresby, that the government was concerned about the time he spent away from his headquarters. Recalling that Wavell had not confirmed Blamey's allegation that he had been removed from Tobruk because Wavell was dissatisfied, Lavarack wrote: 'I am justified in regarding him as capable of lying'. He was not critical of Blamey on the personal level alone. Turning to his performance as C-in-C he wrote:

> The Army in Australia and neighbouring territories is now suffering from his gross mismanagement as witness the incident of 21 Aust Bde on the Kokoda track, due to Potts' inexperience...the Rowell incident, caused by the fact that Rowell, as Blamey admits himself, suspected him (Blamey) of lying, as it happens in this case unjustly...To these must be added the immense waste of trained staff officers and other personnel brought about by his establishment of Landops in Brisbane to perform the functions properly appertaining to First Aust Army.[15]

Lavarack was angry that now Blamey was in New Guinea it appeared as if he were going to form a new headquarters for himself there:

> It looks as though yet another subsidiary headquarters for himself is to be established in New Guinea. All that he really needs, apart from the main H.Q. in Melbourne, is a small group including his personal staff and one or two others which can accompany him whenever he decides to go forward and take temporary personal control in a particular area. This should not often be necessary. It was not really necessary on the present occasion, but his hand was forced...The result of his action in forming a large H.Q. in Brisbane has been the emasculation of existing H.Q., especially that of First Army, and to a less extent that of 2 Corps. Landops, in its present form, is a monstrous growth, expensive,

(particularly in accommodation), and immovable. It could be abolished without loss of efficiency if existing H.Q.s were properly employed.

Lavarack's assessment of Blamey's organisational inefficiency was accurate. General Vasey, who was DCGS at Landops, admitted to his wife that there was not much routine work for the staff at Landops and Blamey was later criticised by the Minister for the Army for the excessive number of headquarters.[16]

Lavarack considered his treatment at Port Moresby, which included being allocated sub-standard accommodation, was 'the last straw':

> After deep consideration have come to conclusion that T.A.B.'s attitude leaves me no alternative but to take my own way. Despite bad treatment in past, (from the moment when I became a candidate for selection for command of an A.I.F. Div.) I have remained consistently a good supporter of his, but he has not given me the loyalty which is due even by seniors to juniors.

Lavarack, however, could give that loyalty. He wrote to Blamey defending Plant once again and asking that he be appointed to HQ First Army. He had even defended Blamey at a meeting with MacArthur, as he recorded:

> McA inclined to make suggestions savouring of teaching one's grandmother to suck eggs, such as importance of filling up units to W[ar] E[stablishment] and of training. Couldn't stand this and pointed out that T.A.B. is about as keen on training as anyone in any army. McA took this very well. Gives one impression that [he] is feeling his way and that Americans are slightly conscious of our superior experience.[17]

A loyal subordinate Lavarack may have been, but, as events were to show, it made no difference to Blamey. HQ First Army stood little chance of being transferred to New Guinea while Lavarack was in command, no matter how many senior army officers thought it to be the best and obvious command arrangement.

In November 1942 General Northcott, by then CGS, told Lavarack that he had pressed Blamey more than once to place Lavarack in command of operations in New Guinea, but Blamey gave the proposal only lip-service. Brigadier Sir Frederick Chilton, who was GSO1 Operations at HQ First

Army until June 1942 when he was transferred to HQ New Guinea Force, has written:

> It was generally accepted that it [First Army] was a very effective HQ
> and later there were many who expressed regret that it was not sent up
> to control the N.G. operations.

Similarly, when Brigadier Sir Charles Spry was transferred from the post of GSO1 Staff Duties and Training at HQ First Army to GSO1 on the 7th Division headquarters in August 1942 he wrote that:

> I paid my respects to General Lavarack before leaving. I asked him why
> H.Q. 1st Army was not sent direct to New Guinea. It seemed a sensible
> thing to do. He said that Blamey would never have allowed that and
> somewhat ruefully said ultimately he would be left with nobody. It was
> obvious that there was little relationship between Blamey and
> Lavarack.[18]

By late 1942, whenever he was summoned by Blamey Lavarack expected to be told that his headquarters, which was being bled of experienced officers, was to be disbanded. (In four months Lavarack's H.Q. had lost 25 staff officers.) On 12 November 1942 Lavarack was told that Blamey had ordered that the First Army Signals School, which had been established by Lavarack to replace personnel already transferred to New Guinea, was itself to be transferred in its entirety to New Guinea. Lavarack was furious, but not surprised:

> The sabotage of First Army proceeds apace, but the process of robbing
> Peter to pay Paul cannot go on indefinitely if the part of the Aust forces
> still in Australia is to be maintained at any reasonable standard of
> efficiency. Looks as though TAB is striving to re-constitute the original
> AIF under himself while leaving out of it those elements to which he is
> passionately hostile, e.g. Rowell, Plant, and self, not to mention lots of
> others.[19]

At the same time Blamey told Forde that it was necessary for HQ First Army to remain in Queensland in case 'circumstances necessitate a rapid re-grouping of formations in Northern Australia'. On the other hand, Lavarack had been made responsible for Merauke in Dutch New Guinea at the beginning of 1943, but so suspicious was he of Blamey by then that he wrote:

I have no troops to send there. In any case I have no transport at my disposal and no aircraft, also no air liaison staff. Query—Has Merauke been placed under my command so that I may be blamed if the Japanese occupy it?[20]

Although Blamey did not limit Lavarack's area of responsibility to the mainland, he nevertheless kept a tight rein on him, limiting his freedom of movement and powers as much as possible. If Lavarack wished to visit that part of his command outside Australia, Landops would infuriate him by referring the matter to Blamey for approval. Moreover, orders were being issued to formations under Lavarack's command without going through First Army headquarters. General Berryman, Lavarack's MGGS, astounded General Northcott in August 1942 by telling him that Lavarack had learnt only indirectly that one of his divisions had been ordered to New Guinea. This was not an isolated incident. In October Lavarack discovered that, without his knowledge, orders had been issued to Lieutenant-General R.L. Eichelberger, commanding the 1st US Corps, and in April 1943 he had to tell General Morshead (GOC 2nd Corps) to stop communicating directly with Blamey's headquarters.[21]

It was clear that Blamey was isolating Lavarack, who noted after dining with Curtin in January 1943, that the Prime Minister

appeared to think that I am consulted about various policy matters and I was compelled to make clear the fact that this is not so as I am not consulted at all.

A few days later Curtin asked Blamey who would be his successor should he fall ill or become a casualty; the minutes of their conversation noted:

He [Curtin] understood that Lieut.-General Lavarack was the next senior officer, but he asked General Blamey for his views as to whom he would recommend as his successor.

General Blamey stated that he had not placed the operations in New Guinea under Lieut.-General Lavarack, who was the Commander of the First Army, as he did not consider he possessed all the attributes of a first class Commander. He felt that, after further experience in a higher Command, Lieut.-General Morshead was the officer possessing the best qualifications and personal attributes for this post.[22]

Lavarack was not widely regarded as a possible C-in-C, as William Dunstan, the General Manager of the Melbourne *Herald*, confirmed in late September 1942. Dunstan wrote to Rowell that at one stage Curtin had admitted that the government was not entirely satisfied with Blamey and that there

> has been a canvas of names. You, Northcott, Herring, Morshead. Joe [Lavarack], as far as I can ascertain, never. And I may say, since I had a long talk to him a few nights ago, quite rightly so. I never heard such childish stuff as he talked.

Brigadier Denzil Macarthur-Onslow gave his opinion to Gavin Long in October 1942:

> You cannot go past Robertson, Berryman and Herring when looking for a C-in-C. None have the strength, brains and integrity to surpass these...Lavarack, temperamental, too old.

The question of age was a red herring: Blamey was nearly two years older than Lavarack, MacArthur almost six and Lieutenant-General Walter Krueger, one of the most successful American army commanders in the South-West Pacific Area, was four years older than Lavarack. Still, Lieutenant-General Sir Ragnar Garrett told Blamey's biographer, John Hetherington, that as a commander-in-chief

> Lavarack would never have done. He was an appallingly bad loser, at tennis, golf, bridge, anything you care to name. He would have been unforgiving. His judgement would have been warped by that weakness.

General Lumsden, Churchill's special military representative to General MacArthur, summed up Lavarack's situation when he reported to London that 'General Lavarack is not so popular with the politicians, nor does he appear to receive very strong backing from his own officers'.[23]

Blamey, of course, was in a different position, as Hopkins observed: 'I think it is true to say that TAB had the wider experience and that he found it easier to understand, and work with, politicians.' In Menzies' view:

> It was Blamey's very toughness that was one of his most valuable qualities. He will take on anything or anybody. He can see the big picture. I still think that at no stage of the war could we have found a better man for his job.

Menzies thought that if Blamey had been killed only Morshead or Herring could have replaced him as C-in-C. Lavarack was not a possibility. Even General Hopkins felt that Lavarack was no competition for Blamey: 'Although I could be counted as one of JDL's admirers, I am quite sure he would not have made a better C-in-C than TAB'. The key to Blamey's success was that he was a politician in uniform, something that Lavarack, a proud career soldier, never wanted to be.[24]

As a soldier Lavarack would never cease trying to get into the fighting while there was a chance. After his meeting with Curtin in January 1943 it was obvious that he could expect no support from the Prime Minister in getting First Army into New Guinea. Still, he was not prepared to give up and invited Sir Keith Murdoch to dine with him a few weeks later, when they discussed Lavarack's predicament, as he noted in his diary:

> From Keith Murdoch's remarks he is very well aware of the static position of First Army and in sympathy with any moves that might be made in the higher commands.

However, the discussions at this meeting, and another a week later, appear not to have concentrated on Blamey's replacement, but rather on the transfer of Lavarack and his headquarters to New Guinea. (Lavarack's personal assistant and aide-de-camp were also present, which they would hardly have been if Lavarack and Murdoch were conspiring to have Blamey replaced.) That is not say that Lavarack did not relish the idea of Blamey being replaced as C-in-C, but there is no evidence that he actively sought to bring it about.

Rather, he seems to have been most concerned to take his army headquarters to New Guinea. Murdoch's motives, however, are more obscure than Lavarack's. Perhaps he was sounding out Lavarack as a possible successor to Blamey, or perhaps he thought by entangling Lavarack he could force Blamey to act rashly, possibly precipitating his downfall. At the least he wanted information.[25]

If Lavarack could not get his army headquarters into New Guinea, he was prepared to drop to the command of a corps in order to be posted to the front. Not long after his meetings with Murdoch he wrote that he had told Blamey that

> [I] would be glad of turn in command in N.G. C-in-C expressed surprise, averring that he had thought I would regard this as a downgrading. On

my assurance that I would not do so he promised to consider me when possible. Do not regard his attitude as ingenuous...

Lavarack was right: Blamey would not allow him to command any formation in New Guinea. As 1943 wore on Lavarack's command, and his morale, diminished. Not only was the number of troops under his command falling, but the area for which Lavarack was responsible was shrinking. By August 1943 the First Army area still included Queensland, but incorporated only a portion of northern New South Wales. Gavin Long attended a press conference given by Lavarack in September:

> Lavarack gave a quiet but pregnant talk, the upshot of which, put into plain language, was: He is disappointed at the way in which his army has steadily lost troops until it now has two militia and two American divisions, a motor brigade and a corps H.Q. His area has been reduced until it includes Queensland and a bit of New South Wales. Shouldn't 1st Army now be facing north not east, he asked...
>
> After the conference Lavarack spoke to me about the way in which his staff, the old 1 Aust Corps staff in the main, was being robbed to supply qualified staff men for other formations, especially Advanced LHQ.[26]

In late 1943 Lavarack made one last, desperate attempt to get back into the war. On 21 September he wrote to Blamey:

> Not long ago I sent you by signal an appeal for the more active employment of this HQ in a role in which its still high potential could be of greater value to the common cause. This signal was the result not of a sudden impulse, but of a long period of observation of the members of the HQ, at the end of which I have come to the conclusion that under present conditions of service morale and therefore efficiency cannot much longer be kept at their present high standard.
>
> Until lately I have found that hope still sprang eternal in the breasts of most of them—just as it has done in mine—but the results of hope long deferred are, I believe, beginning to make themselves felt. After all they belong to an AIF Headquarters, a large number of them have had service overseas, and feel that they belong to the AIF. I can only say that when this HQ was formed it was certainly among the best organised, trained, and experienced HQ in the British Empire, and that it has not lost all its

quality by any means. Its present employment is not adequate to its capacity.

Lavarack told Blamey that he was 'sitting here and eating my heart out' for an active role for HQ First Army.[27]

Even this frank approach met with no hint of appreciation or conciliation. Blamey would not be moved and replied:

> In regard to your request that First Army HQ should be utilised as a HQ oversea [sic], I am afraid it is not possible to accede to this. The continuity of control would be broken by a complete reorganisation, and First Army HQ layout does not entirely fit in with New Guinea Force.
>
> I will endeavour, however, to give as many of your staff a turn in New Guinea as possible, and indeed I think this policy has been pursued for some time.

In response to Lavarack's claim that HQ First Army was not being fully utilised Blamey offered to reduce Lavarack's staff still further.[28]

Nothing Lavarack could say or do would secure him a fighting command. Blamey was determined that he would take no further part in operations. Hetherington wrote that Blamey ignored Lavarack's requests (and those of another other exiled general, Gordon Bennett) because

> He ranked Morshead at least equal to Lavarack and ahead of Bennett in technical military skill, and far above either of them in personality.
>
> While recognising the 59-year-old Lavarack's technical ability, Blamey disliked him personally and considered him too 'precious' for a command in which life was often physically trying for the GOC and his staff, even though far less wearing than for the front-line officers and men.[29]

Leaving personalities aside, there is no evidence that Lavarack's physical health would have been an unusual liability on operations. But, if Blamey had placed Lavarack's First Army headquarters in control of operations in New Guinea instead of trying to control them himself as well as fulfilling his administrative duties as C-in-C, AMF, he risked Lavarack equalling, or perhaps even surpassing, him in influence and importance. There is no doubt that Blamey regarded Lavarack as a rival. Blamey's ADC, Norman Carlyon, wrote:

I know that Lavarack frequently pressed his claims for a more prominent share of the action. I also recall Blamey's comment to me after receiving one of these many requests. 'Norman, the man has command of 1st Army in the rank of lieutenant general. What more can he want? There is only my job left. Perhaps that is what he is after...'.

Blamey did something about it. He arranged for Lavarack to become head of the Australian Military Mission in Washington, changing places with General Vernon Sturdee.[30]

The exchange between Lavarack and Sturdee was discussed at a Prime Minister's War Conference in September 1943. Blamey told Curtin that Lavarack was dissatisfied as GOC First Army and that he did not cooperate well with Morshead who commanded the 2nd Corps, nor with Herring who Blamey was withdrawing from New Guinea and replacing with Morshead. Both Lavarack's and Sturdee's records were considered and both were criticised, as recorded in the conference minutes:

> There was a discussion regarding the past records of Lieutenant-Generals Lavarack and Sturdee. In the case of General Lavarack, it was recalled that he had agreed with General Wavell's recommendation that the A.I.F. should be diverted to Burma. The Prime Minister thought that Lieutenant-General Sturdee had not been very alive to preparations for the defence of Australia from the North and had persisted in the appointment of Major-General Blake to Darwin and Major-General Morris to Port Moresby.

Not surprisingly, Blamey came only to Sturdee's defence:

> General Blamey agreed that the appointment of Major-General Blake had been an error, though he thought that Major-General Morris had not done badly in the light of the resources made available to him.

It was obvious from the minutes of the meeting that Lavarack had no military or political champion: Curtin agreed to Lavarack going to Washington 'provided that there was no implication in these moves of further advancement'. As usual, Lavarack was *persona non grata* politically. Curtin's antipathy for Lavarack ensured Blamey's control over him and sealed his fate.[31]

Lavarack's association with Murdoch, which had goaded Blamey's paranoia, probably also counted against him with Curtin: the previous month Murdoch had been criticising Curtin in newspaper articles over his decision not to reinforce Burma with troops diverted from the Netherlands East Indies. On 3 August 1943 he had written:

> Mr. Churchill was the first to suggest the return of the A.I.F. to fight the Japanese. While they were on the water, he asked that the 7th Division should go to Burma, and, although the request was pressed by President Roosevelt, by the British and American Chiefs of Staff, and by at least some sections of the Australian Command, Mr. Curtin refused.[32]

The matter was especially annoying for Curtin because Murdoch's repeated references to the matter appeared during the 1943 election campaign. The phrase 'some sections of the Australian Command' clearly was a reference which included Lavarack, and Blamey no doubt informed Curtin that Lavarack had been seeing Murdoch. On 15 August Curtin released a statement to the press, in which he said:

> Lieutenant-General Lavarack, who had been G.O.C. of the A.I.F. in Java, stated that the ships carrying the A.I.F. from the Middle East had not been tactically loaded, and that, if the first convoy was diverted to Burma, the troops could not be landed as an effective fighting force and many units would be without complete fighting equipment.[33]

Lavarack was disturbed to read this in the newspaper and on 17 August he cabled the CGS to say that, to the best of his knowledge, his advice referred to Java, not Burma. Concerned that Wavell would see the newspaper reports, Lavarack told Curtin in a letter written on 5 September:

> The matter is important to me personally because General Wavell, and all his commanders and staffs, knew that my view coincided with his. They also knew what my advice to the Government was, since I made a point throughout of showing General Wavell all my messages. It would naturally seem dishonourable to General Wavell and these others if it should appear, as it must, that I had departed from this view and advice after leaving his command.

He felt that it now appeared to anyone reading the report that on his advice the AIF had not been diverted to Burma because the transports had not been tactically loaded, not because the Australian Government had decided that the AIF was needed for home defence. Lavarack wanted to see Curtin and discuss the matter personally, as he was convinced that he had been misrepresented.[34]

Curtin refused to meet him, however, because to his mind there was nothing to discuss—Lavarack had made the statement at a meeting of the Advisory War Council, and it was a matter of record. This was a little unfair to Lavarack as Curtin had made it appear in his statement to the Press that this advice had been given while Lavarack was still in Java and that it had greatly influenced the decision to insist on the return of the AIF to Australia. However, when he replied to Curtin, Lavarack pointed out that although he could not remember clearly his statement to the Advisory War Council, it did not matter since the meeting was held a few days after the government's decision to have the AIF returned to Australia was announced. He added:

> My chief concern is that your statement in Perth may have come to the notice of Field-Marshal Lord Wavell and the members of the staff he had with him in the Far East, many of whom knew of the advice I was giving the Government when in Java, and that they may be led to believe that I was secretly giving you contrary advice at the same time. I wished to assure Lord Wavell that this was not so, but not before referring the matter to you.[35]

Still, as Lavarack told Curtin, there was little point in pursuing the matter further if his statement at the Advisory War Council could have had no effect on the government's decision. Even so, he did write one more letter, this time to Wavell explaining his situation. Wavell replied:

> I very much appreciate your writing as you did. The statement you mention had not come to my notice, but I have never doubted your perfect straightforwardness and loyalty to me. That was a very difficult decision for everybody. I have often tried to wonder what would have happened if the convoy had been diverted and the Australian troops landed in Burma... Anyway, it is never profitable in war, or in anything else, to look back on what might have been, the thing is to keep on looking forward.[36]

However, by September 1943 Lavarack had very little to look forward to. Blamey's position was unassailable. When it was later alleged in the press that Lavarack had been sent to Washington because of a personality clash with Blamey, the Army Director of Public Relations, Brigadier J.H.

Rasmussen (who had Blamey's support) stated that 'There is no grain of truth in the allegation. Lt.-Gen. Lavarack was, in fact, chosen for the Washington post by the late Prime Minister (Mr Curtin)'. Publicly Lavarack said that the appointment to Washington was a happy release from an intolerable situation, but in private as Berryman noted, he 'seemed to be anything but happy'. Washington was exile—it had been for Sturdee and for the former Chief of the Air Staff, Air Marshal Richard Williams, who had been despatched there in 1942 as the RAAF representative (and would remain until 1946).

Sturdee replaced Lavarack as GOC First Army on 1 March 1944. On 11 August Blamey announced that HQ First Army would move from Queensland to Lae and from there control all Australian forces in Australian New Guinea.[37]

18

'He has not had a good war'

Washington, 1944–1946

THE WORK LAVARACK had to do in Washington was different from anything he had been called on to do before, but it was not the battlefield command he so fervently desired. His disappointment at the way his war had turned out was evident in a letter he wrote to the official historian from the US capital:

> Am having quite a pleasant though sadly inactive stay here, but fear that my present activities will not occupy a very large part of your records of this war—nor my previous ones, for that matter, I imagine.

Most of Lavarack's work was routine liaison, although there were several highlights. In September 1944 he represented Australia at the Quebec conference which dealt with Allied strategy for the war against Japan, and from April to June 1945 he attended the United Nations Conference on International Organisation in San Francisco. Later that year he also became involved in planning for the role and organisation of the British Commonwealth Occupation Force (BCOF) for Japan. According to Sir Paul Hasluck, who was a member of the Australian delegation at San Francisco, where he worked with Lavarack on the committee dealing with enforcement measures, Lavarack was

> a most agreeable colleague and an effective committee man. He had mastered the documents in this new field of study. In the course of my

life I have met most of the top ranking men in the Australian services. To speak with the brashness of a civilian who knows nothing of military operations, I found Lavarack to be the first of a very small number who could think as well as command.[1]

For the most part, however, Lavarack was in Washington to provide Blamey with information on matters affecting the Australian army. The brief was broad and included the civil affairs plans for the South-West Pacific Area (SWPA) and South-East Asia Command (SEAC); post-hostilities planning; agencies and functions of the Combined Chiefs of Staff and Joint Chiefs of Staff; political aspects of the United States armed forces; and proposals for BCOF.

Unfortunately, the poor relationship between the two men hindered Lavarack's effectiveness. In mid-1945 the British Joint Staff Mission in Washington was collaborating with Lavarack and the Minister for the Army, Forde, in presenting a case to the Combined Chiefs of Staff dealing with the reduction and regrouping of Australian forces in SWPA and consideration of future roles for the army. 'Jumbo' Wilson, who had been Lavarack's superior in Syria and now, as a field-marshal, was head of the British mission, wrote to the CIGS on 12 June:

> What struck me as being lacking was an appreciation from Blamey as to the implication of the reduction of the Australian forces on future operations. There was no forecast of what could be completed, what may have to be abandoned, what, if any, forces would require relief, and what base and L of C troops would remain. Lavarack asked him for information on some of these points and only got a snub in return. The trouble is that Blamey and Lavarack dislike each other intensely, which is going to make things difficult when Australia passes out of MacArthur's command and their problems come up for discussion here.[2]

Blamey's reply to Lavarack's request for information had been:

> These matters are determined by C-in-C SWPA [MacArthur] and presumably are communicated to US Joint Chiefs of Staff by him. Australian plans are part of SWPA plans and entirely under control of C-in-C SWPA. In these circumstances it is regretted that they cannot be communicated as you request.

Having been rebuffed by Blamey, Lavarack asked Forde for information, adding that 'I have no detailed knowledge of the military and strategic factors underlying the government's decision in the matters under discussion and no channel of communication to [the] Defence Department'. Forde, however, replied that the 'objectives of Government policy have been communicated to us and we must support this policy irrespective of the basis on which it has been determined'. He said that he was not prepared to accede to the request for more information because he felt that 'it might be misunderstood in Australia'.[3]

As might be expected, Lavarack was deeply frustrated in Washington. Sybil Lavarack, who had followed her husband to the United States, wrote to Jessie Vasey in April 1945:

> John of course is very sad to be over here and wants to get back to active service again—he has not had a good war—too full of frustration and disappointment.

Lavarack wanted another battlefield command, as he had told a reporter from *The Washington Post* in an interview earlier that month. But it would not happen with Blamey in charge.

Blamey, however, did not go uncriticised for his treatment of Lavarack and other senior officers. On 10 February 1944 Senator H.S. Foll claimed in parliament that Blamey had shelved Lavarack (as well as Rowell, Mackay, Wynter and Morshead). Two weeks later Mr. A.G. Cameron raised the same matter in the House of Representatives, mentioning again Lavarack, Mackay and Rowell, but adding Herring and Clowes. In early 1945 Blamey's treatment of his generals was raised once more in the Senate by Foll, who said that, amongst others (this time including Bennett and Robertson), Lavarack had been exiled in Washington:

> There is scarcely a man in the Australian Army who had more money devoted to his training, and who came through that training with higher honours and a greater reputation ... Yet, because of a personal disagreement, apparently, between General Lavarack and the Commander-in-Chief, that man had to be sacrificed. He was sent to Washington to a job that he should not have been called upon to take, to a work that was not of the type for a fighting soldier of his qualifications.

In a letter to Menzies, who was in political opposition at the time, Blamey denied Foll's allegations, claiming:

> There was no personal disagreement between General Lavarack and me, nor is there one now... [N]or was he removed from active participation in military operations. He was at the time commanding First Australian Army, then located in Australia.

Menzies told Blamey to ignore Foll's criticism, and that as far as he, and several of his colleagues were concerned, Blamey would still be their choice to lead the army, even though Menzies himself was not blind to what Blamey was doing (in February 1944 Menzies himself had noted the shelving of some generals by Blamey, in particular Lavarack, Rowell, Herring, Mackay and Morshead).[4]

Support for Blamey, regardless of his personal vendettas, ran deep. Shedden also had earlier defended Blamey to the Prime Minister, Curtin:

> If one point has impressed itself on me regarding General Blamey's character since the outbreak of the war, it has been the magnanimous way in which he has treated officers who were strongly opposed to him and who resorted to all sorts of devices to discredit him. On more than one occasion he has mentioned to me that war is such a grave business that personal interests must be entirely subordinated to it. I mention this fact for the reason that I do not think that he would bear a grudge towards another officer and seek to 'take it out of him'.

As Blamey's most recent biographer, David Horner, has observed:

> This was an extraordinary assessment from Curtin's key adviser, and one wonders how Shedden concluded that Blamey would never bear a grudge. Lavarack, Bennett, Robertson and Rowell would have had a contrary view.[5]

Indeed, it was an astonishing message which inevitably elicits the question of how Shedden, who had a deep and unparalleled knowledge of the services, could not have been alive to Blamey's true character. Did Shedden, a longtime supporter of Blamey, lie to his political leader to safeguard Blamey? If there are other possibilities to explain Shedden's action they are obscure, unless he was naive enough to believe Blamey's self-burnishing assurances, as he had credulously accepted Hankey's worthless guarantees about the Singapore strategy years earlier. If nothing else,

Shedden's letter to Curtin, for whatever reason it was written—and none of the obvious explanations are encouraging—shows how high the political and bureaucratic odds were stacked against Lavarack and the other generals Blamey disliked.

Lavarack's frustrating predicament fostered a desire for recognition and in May 1945 he asked Forde for promotion to full general:

> To put the matter shortly I have now been a substantive Lieutenant-General for well over five years. During this period I have twice commanded Australian troops together with British, French, Indian and other forces, in active and successful fighting in North Africa and Syria. To this may be added my experience in the Nederlands [sic] East Indies early in 1942, when the situation was by no means easy, and my command, later, of the First Australian Army.
>
> I am now, as you know, in Washington, where I am in constant contact with very senior British and American Service officers and other officials, and have had the experience of seeing numerous American generals, junior in rank to me on my arrival, rise to my own rank and then above it...
>
> Many of these officers have considerably less service and experience than myself, but are usually unaware of the fact, which can only be made evident if I am given the necessary rank. This would also enable me to speak with more authority... and be good for my own prestige with Service officers of other nations, and thus also for that of Australia.
>
> For the above reasons, both Service and personal, I request that you consider my advancement to the temporary rank of full general.

Forde refused, telling Lavarack that 'I have... thoroughly looked into this question, and regret that it is not practicable at this juncture to provide for your promotion...'.[6] It was probably expecting too much to believe that Blamey would allow Lavarack to be promoted to the same rank as himself. The war finished with Lavarack still a lieutenant-general and still in Washington—Blamey had succeeded in depriving him of a fighting command and promotion for the last three-and-a-half years of the fighting.

Nevertheless, Lavarack would not give up his career without a battle, even after the war had ended and Blamey had been unceremoniously shoved from power by the government. Indeed, it may have been that

Lavarack contributed to Blamey's rapid retirement soon after hostilities ended. In May 1945 he had written to Forde, re-stating a view he had expressed verbally a short time before, that the control of the AIF should no longer rest with Blamey but should revert to the Military Board:

> This opinion is based on the fact that the replacement of the Military Board by a Commander-in-Chief was merely an emergency measure, designed to tide Australia over the period when the outer territories were being invaded by the Japanese, and there was a real danger of invasion of the mainland.
>
> These dangers are now past, and it seems reasonable that Australia should revert to the normal system of control by a Military Board, with a Commander abroad of the forces actually engaged in active offensive operations against the Japanese, i.e. practically a reversion to the original system under which we had a General Officer Commanding, A.I.F.[7]

Blamey, who was shown Lavarack's letter, disagreed. He was in favour of replacing the Military Board after the war with an Army Council, which would be chaired by the minister and whose members would include the GOsC Eastern and Southern Commands, one of whom would be a citizen officer, thus ensuring militia representation. Blamey argued that the Military Board system had been ineffective in preparing for war, that it alienated the militia, and that 'over a long period of years, it formed a battleground of clashing personalities', an assertion which was challenged by Mr J.T. Fitzgerald, who had been Finance Member when Lavarack was CGS.

Despite Blamey's urgings, it was decided to re-establish the Military Board: his influence was waning and with Curtin's death in July 1945 he had lost a vital political ally. Blamey's relationship with Curtin's favoured successor, J.B. Chifley, was not good. Blamey later wrote: 'My experience of Chifley is that there is nothing he hates quite so much as a soldier.'[8] Perhaps it was simply that there was no soldier the highly-principled Chifley hated so much as Blamey, who on 14 November 1945 was given two weeks notice to vacate the post of Commander-in-Chief.[9]

When it was announced in November 1945 that Sturdee would be acting Commander-in-Chief vice Blamey, Lavarack immediately approached the Minister for External Affairs, Dr H.V. Evatt, who was in the United States, to put his case. Three years earlier the Leader of the Opposition, Mr. A.W. Fadden, told Lavarack that at one stage while he was in the

Middle East the government had been so displeased with Sturdee as CGS that it had considered recalling Lavarack to the post, so the idea of Sturdee succeeding him once again was particularly galling. Evatt told Chifley:

> Lavarack saw me yesterday and expressed great concern lest his own name was overlooked and Sturdee, who is his junior, given preference to him. I need not tell you that both in London and Washington Lavarack's campaign in Syria and other achievements are regarded as of the highest quality. I can hardly express an opinion from this distance. His interview with me was quite informal, but I told him that I felt sure that his claims would certainly not be overlooked by the Government at the proper time.

Chifley assured Lavarack that he would receive due consideration.[10]

However, the matter reached the press almost immediately, with reports that Lavarack was surprised that he had not been consulted about the appointment even though he was the most senior regular officer. He was also reported to be dissatisfied with his posting to Washington. The day after the first of these articles appeared Lavarack emphatically denied making any public comment on Sturdee's appointment: 'I made no protest and have no intention of making one'. One newspaper reported that

> He is angry about the reports published in Australia, which not merely embarrassed him but put him in a false position.
>
> Lieut.-Gen. Lavarack declared that he strongly disapproved of soldiers carrying their troubles to the public and has not the slightest idea how the reports that he protested over Lieut.-Gen. Sturdee's appointment originated.[11]

When a journalist remarked to Lavarack that he had been unlucky in his career, Lavarack replied 'grimly' that 'I can take it'.[12]

It is unlikely that Lavarack complained to the press. He had not resorted to that tactic before to further his career and there was little to be gained from such a move, but much to lose, considering he had already spoken to Evatt who was sympathetic. The source was probably to be found amongst his staff. One of the reports said that 'several other officers at the Australian Military Mission have been dissatisfied with the treatment that he [Lavarack] has received'.

In any case, there was no question that Lavarack would be appointed as acting C-in-C or CGS. The choice was to be one of Sturdee, Rowell,

Berryman or Robertson. At the War Cabinet meeting in December 1945 when the matter was discussed, it was noted that in choosing a new CGS it would have to be borne in mind that 1946 was an election year. Strategy in SWPA and service administration were likely to be controversial issues during the campaign and so the government wanted an officer who had not suffered at Blamey's hands, and therefore would 'not seek personal retribution by embarrassing the Government on matters of strategic policy in the Southwest Pacific Area, with which General Blamey has been associated.' Clearly Blamey's conduct and decisions—and the government's support of them—had become electoral liabilities with voters who, even if not ex-service men and women, had been affected by the war and were still deeply concerned with how it had been fought.

The government wanted Rowell as CGS, but of course he had been sacked by Blamey and so Sturdee (who was considered to be independent) was appointed and Rowell became Vice-Chief of the General Staff. Lavarack was never a serious contender, in part because of his relationship with Blamey and his volatility, but also because the government wanted younger generals with recent experience of modern war. Consequently, on 6 February 1946 Lavarack's retirement, to take effect later that year, was approved by the Cabinet.[13]

Lavarack's military career reached its unsatisfying conclusion on 17 September 1946, his last day of service in the Australian army. The letter of farewell he received from Forde the next month, while complimentary, would have done little to assuage his disappointment:

> It is not given to many officers to have served as you have done with such distinction in such senior commands and appointments, embracing two major wars, and you cease active duty with the Australian Military Forces with the assurance that your service has been well and faithfully rendered.
>
> I would like you to know that the forces and your country have always benefited by your commission and that your fellow officers will remember with pride and gratification the exemplary standard and comradeship you have always exhibited.

A pro forma farewell to an ultimately disappointing career it may have been, but at least Lavarack had outlasted Blamey, if that could provide any consolation.[14] In any event, Lavarack still had battles to fight against Blamey's lingering influence over the past.

19

A Rearguard Action

State Governor, 1946–1957

AFTER LEAVING THE ARMY Lavarack took up the post of Governor of Queensland. When he was sworn in at State Parliament House on 1 October 1946 he became not only the first Queenslander to hold the post, but the first native-born Australian.

The road to Queensland had not been smooth. John and Sybil Lavarack had left Washington in May 1946 to travel across North America by car and train, visiting old friends en route, before taking a ship home to Australia from San Francisco. However, shipping problems meant that they became stranded on the west coast of the United States for several weeks before eventually finding a cabin on a 'very poor Swedish ship'. On arrival in Australia in July the Lavaracks had begun the search for somewhere to live. Finding few houses for sale, or even to let, they had considered building a house, but became frustrated by local restrictions. However, the problem, and their 'despondency', evaporated with the unexpected news that Lavarack had been appointed Governor of Queensland.

Although pleased to accept the appointment, Lavarack at first found it difficult to adjust to the pace of a somewhat parochial, peacetime role back in his home state:

> I feel, as I expected, rather out of things here in Queensland. It is hard to settle down to the humdrum life of a State Governor after having had some slight experience of international affairs.[1]

That would change over time and he would settle well into in the role he was to perform for 11 years before retiring after his tenure had twice been extended.

In the meantime, that posterity should see him as a major figure in the Australian army was important to Lavarack and so his fight to secure his place, and that of the 7th Division, in the army's history would continue during his service as Governor of Queensland. Throughout his governorship a steady stream of correspondence passed between him and the official historians in preparation for the publication of the volumes dealing with Tobruk, Syria and the Netherlands East Indies. It was essentially a battle against Blamey's influence, the effects of which extended beyond his time as Commander-in-Chief. Lavarack was particularly anxious that the Australian official history deal fairly with his role. After reading drafts of the section on Tobruk he told Gavin Long in 1952:

> I should like it to be mentioned here that I was also sent to command in Cyrenaica when Generals O'Connor and Neame were captured in April, 1941, was appointed, after winning the Easter Battle in Cyrenaica, to command Western Desert Force, and replaced by Beresford-Peirse within 24 hours. In these days a soldier who does not advertise is lost indeed.[2]

By then Lavarack's campaign for recognition had been going for a decade: his growing anxiety that he would not be given his due had prompted him to begin to 'advertise' soon after his return to Australia in 1942. One of his first concerns was that he be given credit for his work in Tobruk. He began to feel 'uneasy about Libya' in mid-1942 after an article was published in *Active Service*. He wrote that it was 'Quite clear [my] own name and that of 7 Div deliberately expunged from record'. The chapter on Tobruk contained no reference to Lavarack at all, but said that

> With the appearance of Ninth Division, the defence coalesced on the line of the old Italian perimeter system. Command of all forces in the area was assumed by General Morshead on 14 April.

That may have been an oversight, but it was extraordinary that a similar chapter on Syria made no reference to Lavarack, the 7th Division or 1st Australian Corps. Lavarack wrote:

An account of the campaign was published in the Christmas A.I.F. magazine 1941 without having been referred to myself or, so far as I have been able to discover, any other member of 1 Aust Corps or 7 Div HQ. The account was very, very incorrect, in fact, some of the most important statements made were the exact reverse of the actual facts. The 7 Div was not mentioned once in the account nor anywhere in the whole book, I think. Certainly my own name wasn't mentioned anywhere. Neither, by the way, was it in 'Soldiering On' except in connection with an unfinished portrait.

Lavarack made arrangements to see Lieutenant-Colonel J.L. Treloar, who commanded the Military History Section at Land Headquarters, noting in his diary that it was 'obviously necessary to see that records are made accurate and that [the] official history, at any rate, does justice to 7 Div and self'.[3]

A week later Lavarack was told that Blamey had censored other articles referring to his role in Tobruk. Indeed, the proof of an article dealing with events in Cyrenaica in March-April 1941 read, when it was submitted to Blamey for perusal:

> On the disruption of Cirenaica [sic] Command during the German breakthrough, General Blamey's senior commander, Lieut-General J.D. (later Sir John) Lavarack, was given control of the forward area. To him, on General Wavell's orders, fell the task of planning a stand at Tobruk and of supervising the hasty organisation of defences there... General Lavarack's plan for manning the old Italian perimeter... was developed with speed and ingenuity.

After several changes by Blamey (all made in his own hand) the passage read:

> On the disruption of Cirenaica [sic] Command after the German breakthrough, and in General Blamey's absence in Greece, Lieut-General J.D. (later Sir John) Lavarack, was given control of the forward area for a short period, but before the investment of Tobruk was complete, command devolved upon Maj-Gen Morshead. The task of planning a stand at Tobruk and of supervising the hasty organisation of defences there was energetically put in hand... The plan for manning the old Italian perimeter... was developed with speed and ingenuity.

This was most unfair to Lavarack, but he was resigned to Blamey's antagonism: 'So the war goes on. Patience seems [the] only policy.'[4]

Although Lavarack refused to allow his papers on Tobruk to be published, in December 1942 he began writing his account of the episode, when he was especially keen that Curtin develop a good opinion of him, and took every opportunity to remind people that he had established the defence there. In May 1943 the army journal *Salt* published an article on Tobruk (written under a pseudonym by Morshead's ex-GSO1, C.E.M. Lloyd) which disturbed Lavarack because his part in establishing the defence there and directing the Easter Battle was dismissed as being of little or no importance. He was given permission by Blamey to put his case to the editor of the journal to correct any misapprehensions. He said in an interview with a member of staff of *Salt* that 'my feeling is that if this had been the only week of action in the whole of my military career, I should have justified my existence'. However, after reading the interview and speaking to Morshead (to whom Lavarack had written about the matter), Blamey told Lavarack that

> in view of the fact that *Salt* is an official publication for the troops, it is
> in my view undesirable that it should print matter for the information of
> the troops in which there might possibly be disagreement and even
> controversy between higher Commanders of the Army.[5]

Lavarack drafted a reply to Blamey which, although never sent, reveals his resignation to the impotent position in which he found himself:

> Your letter did not surprise me, nor did it disappoint me, because I knew,
> as soon as my answer to Lloyd was submitted to you, that it would be
> refused publication.

For a short time Lavarack continued to correspond with Morshead about Tobruk, but there remained several points on which they could not agree, such as the purpose in reconnoitring the perimeter on 9 April. But in essence their disagreements were matters of emphasis rather than fact. Lavarack was pleased, however, with the drafts of Chester Wilmot's account of Tobruk which he was reading at about the same time.[6]

Obviously, as well as denying Lavarack a fighting command after 1942, Blamey was just as determined to deny him any recognition for past achievements. Consequently, apart from amending official army publications where necessary, Blamey was also anxious that journalists not get too close to Lavarack, who told Long after the war: 'Correspondents seldom came to me and one of them once informed me, in an expansive moment, that he had been ordered not to.' One of Lavarack's senior officers has written: 'At First Army, Blamey had been at no pains to disguise his intention to keep Lavarack out of the public's eye.'

Blamey disliked and feared the press, especially after his battle with the newspapers while police commissioner in Victoria before the war, and was ever mindful of its potential to do him damage. In July 1942 he invoked a War Cabinet decision made in March, to the effect that members of the services were not to make public statements, to rebuke Lavarack who had been quoted in a newspaper article. Blamey also used the decision later in the year against another exile, Lieutenant-General Gordon Bennett. The official historian, Long, observed that

> it seems that the Cabinet decision was never once invoked in the interest of security or even public morale but always, whether by a Minister or a general, to silence or rebuke someone lower down in the chain of command, and not because he had said something harmful, but because he had said anything at all.[7]

In April 1943 the war correspondent Kenneth Slessor visited Lavarack, who was 'very affable and pleasant' and wasted no time in telling Slessor about his time in Tobruk. Afterwards Slessor noted that Lavarack also 'spoke ruefully of Chester Wilmot's dis-accreditation and Rowell's exile, inferring that he too had come up against Blamey'. Blamey had had Wilmot's accreditation as a war correspondent revoked after a dispute with him in 1942 and Slessor also had problems with Blamey for writing a series of articles on AIF generals which gave too much prominence to Lavarack, amongst others.[8]

Lavarack's fight to be recognised was protracted and extended beyond Australia. While in Washington he had again felt it necessary to beat his own drum to receive credit for his work in Tobruk and wrote to enlist the help of Lieutenant-General E.K. Smart, the Australian Army Representative in London. He admitted to Smart in 1944 that

> I fear that my eight days in Tobruk which ended at the end of the battle of Easter Monday, 14 April, 1941, are not on record in England, though I have seen to it that "the Easter Battle"...is fully on record in Australia.

In 1949 he wrote to Lieutenant-General Lord Ismay asking him to remind Churchill of his week in Tobruk so that it could be included in Churchill's memoirs. After seeing drafts of the Australian official history, even 'Jumbo' Wilson suspected that Blamey was trying to exert his influence to deny Lavarack credit for his part in Syria or at least to cast him in a poor light. Wilson wrote in December 1950 after reading one of Long's chapters that 'he has evidently taken his cue from Blamey who did not like Lavarack who therefore comes in for criticism', citing as an example that 'It is omitted that General Lavarack represented the Australian forces at the Acre armistice conference'.[9]

It was unlikely that Gavin Long could be influenced in this way—others, like Gordon Bennett who had commanded the 8th Division in Malaya, had tried to do so without success. In any case, it is doubtful that an attempt to influence the official history to his detriment would slip past Lavarack who by then was well-attuned to Blamey's attempts to distort history to his liking. Referring to the Middle East, Lavarack told Long in September 1952 that

> Blamey was most averse from the publication of any references to the 7th Division. At one time an Australian Army publication contained accounts of two campaigns in which the 6th and 7th Divisions were employed. References to the 6th Division in its campaign were almost nauseatingly numerous, while in the account of the Syrian campaign, neither the number of the Division nor the name of its commander was mentioned even once. No wonder the 7th Division was annoyed...It wasn't a question of militia versus A.I.F., but of the 7th Division versus the rest.

At the time Long was uncertain about how much substance there may have been in Lavarack's allegation, but the facts spoke for themselves and eventually it was noted in the official history that the soldiers of the 7th Division 'felt aggrieved that so little was printed about the campaign both during it and afterwards'.[10]

Blamey had denied thousands of Australian soldiers the simplest acknowledgement of their success, the risks they had taken and the casualties they had suffered, because of a personal grudge against their commander. The suppression of news about the 7th Division had exposed in the army's leader a deep vein of self-interest and disloyalty to troops who deserved far better in their supreme commander. As Blamey's most recent biographer has noted: 'He was ruthless—not just in his willingness to crush opponents but in his readiness to bend the truth'.[11]

Lavarack would always feel dissatisfied with the treatment meted out to the 7th Division and the degree of recognition he had received personally. Blamey's ADC, Norman Carlyon, wrote that

> Lavarack never quite seemed to get the appointments which he felt he deserved. His sense of grievance and his touchiness were in evidence throughout the war. Even when he became an Army commander, after his return to Australia, his attitude was unchanged.

Lavarack's own ADC, Curtis Wilson, confirmed Lavarack's sensitivity after returning to Australia in 1942, when he became increasingly 'touchy about his own dignity, the treatment given him, and insisted on respect due to his rank'. Rowell felt that Lavarack had a persecution complex, the primary reason for which was Blamey's treatment of him. The effects of that treatment never abated: even as Governor of Queensland he still resented the fact that he was not a full general. When he asked Menzies why he had not been promoted, Menzies simply replied 'Lavarack, I think you have answered that question yourself'.[12]

There was no reason why Lavarack should not have posed the question. Indeed, Blamey had obliquely suggested to Menzies the same advancement for himself while in the Middle East and was promoted a short time later. Admittedly, there was some advantage from Australia's point of view in that promotion, but even so Lavarack's request had merit. He had commanded an army, which warranted the rank, after successfully commanding a division and a corps on the battlefield. And as a former Chief of the General Staff Lavarack had some precedent on his side: in 1929 Sir Harry Chauvel had been promoted to full general before he retired as CGS and in 1940 Sir Brudenell White had received the promotion when he was recalled to be CGS less than a year after Lavarack had left the post. But with Blamey's champion, Menzies, firmly holding the political reins in Australia after returning as Prime Minister in December 1949, Lavarack stood little chance. Hence he remained a lieutenant-general while Blamey's promotion to field-marshal in June 1950 was quietly engineered by Menzies, with Shedden's able assistance.

In March 1950 Shedden noted the 'confidential nature of the proposal' to promote Blamey. Consequently, the Australian CGS at the time, Rowell, was not consulted until the decision had already been made in concert with reluctant authorities in London who had resisted the promotion on several grounds, one of which being that Blamey did not fulfil the requirement of being on the active list of the army.[13] As one historian, a former deputy director of the Australian War Memorial, has observed of Blamey becoming a field-marshal:

> He was not popular there [in Britain], had not been so during the war. As it was in Australia, too; there was no public clamour for any further recognition for the retired general. Menzies pushed hard. Tom Blamey was brought out of retirement, briefly, placed on the active list and promoted. What was it between Menzies and Blamey, people wondered.[14]

Whatever awkward questions may have been asked and contrary opinions uttered, they counted for little. Blamey's old ally, Menzies, had decided on favouring Blamey and, in concert with Shedden, presented the country with a field-marshal of dubious reputation.

Lavarack's reaction to Blamey's promotion can readily be surmised, as can the reactions of a number of other senior Australian army officers. It may well have seemed a travesty that a man considered by some to be more a politician than a soldier—and not least a commander who had been accused of cowardice and failing on the battlefield in Greece by senior members of his own staff—would become Australia's first field-marshal. Blamey's critics might have wondered why, if someone of Monash's calibre had not deserved such elevation, the honour should be accorded to Blamey, a commander-in-chief whose troops had openly ridiculed him, as well as accusing him of squandering Australian lives and removing competent commanders from the battlefield.[15]

Which raises the question of how many Australian soldiers might have survived the war had they always fought under the best commanders the country had to offer instead of being pawns in the game of favourites played by Blamey. Instead of promoting senior officers on merit (whether friends or not) and welding the army's disparate factions into a cohesive whole, with old wounds between citizen and regular mended, Blamey stoked division when it suited him and sidelined competent officers he feared or disliked, such as Lavarack. His prejudices descended as far as personally censoring official publications to erase or minimise the successes of the men of the 7th Division because he did not like their commander. It was unfortunate that, although Blamey commanded the army, he seemed unable to rise far enough above his biases and fears to lead it by example. Despite his considerable achievements over a career spanning two world wars, the high regard in which he was held by influential politicians, and his grasp of wartime strategy and politics, regrettably he was not an individual who could be held up as the indisputable personification of military virtue for future generations of young Australian soldiers to emulate.[16]

Perhaps, then, the positive aspect of Blamey's promotion lay not with the man, but with the symbol: Australia's first field-marshal represented the country's growing military independence from Britain. Such symbolism could hardly have been lost on Lavarack who had fought so tenaciously against detrimental British influence on Australian defence policy before the war.

Still, for Lavarack promotion to full general would have eased the disappointment of years on the shelf and the fact that the man who had placed him there was now a field-marshal. It would have been a public declaration that he had not deserved the obscurity which Blamey had consistently foisted upon him, that he had succeeded as a soldier, that it was personal animus which had crippled his military career. Later, though, Lavarack enjoyed a measure of success in redressing for posterity the years of Blamey's inimical influence, especially with the publication in 1953 (two years after Blamey's death) of the volume of the official history covering the campaign in Syria and Lebanon. More would follow as the official historians continued to balance fact and hearsay, to weigh opinion against evidence, in order to piece together Australia's war and Lavarack's part in it.

Meanwhile, Lavarack continued to serve as the governor of his home state, performing official duties as varied as laying the foundation of a new hospital and visiting outback schools, to officiating at the opening of state parliament. The highlight of his years in the post was the royal visit of 1954 when the new monarch, Queen Elizabeth II, and her husband, the Duke of Edinburgh, toured Australia. During their six days in Queensland the royal couple stayed with the Lavaracks at Government House. In 1954 Lavarack added another knighthood (KCVO) to his KBE of 1942, and then the next year was awarded his third (a KCMG), which was presented to him by the Governor-General, Viscount Slim, a former commandant of the Imperial Defence College and past Chief of the Imperial General Staff.

By late 1957 Lavarack had served two full terms as governor and was in the first year of his third when ill health forced him to relinquish the post. On 4 December of that year, two months after he had retired,

Lavarack collapsed in his home at Buderim, Queensland. His obituary in Brisbane's *Courier-Mail* newspaper praised his governorship, reflecting that Lavarack had 'impressed all who met him with his soldierly sense of duty, his friendly accessibility... and his desire to be of service to people in all parts of the State'. Survived by his wife and sons (all three of whom had served during the war) he died two weeks before his 72nd birthday. Fellow old-soldier, Field-Marshal Slim, sent the following message to Lavarack's family:

> My wife and I send you and your family our deepest sympathy on the death of your husband. Sir John served Australia long, and faithfully, with the greatest distinction in war and peace. He was an example of unselfish duty to all of us.[17]

Lavarack did not live long enough to see the final tangible evidence of the country's appreciation of his 'unselfish duty'. Certainly, during his years as Governor of Queensland, he had succeeded in setting straight the record of the 7th Division's campaign in Syria and Lebanon. Gavin Long's scrupulously fair 1953 account of the fighting had officially lifted the curtain of Blamey's obfuscation so that the men of Lavarack's division could finally receive long-delayed credit for their sacrifices and victories. But not until 1966 was the volume of the official history dealing with Tobruk published. Written by Barton Maughan (who had served at Tobruk as a junior officer) that volume gave Lavarack, the 'able soldier and patriot who in peace had reached the summit of professional eminence', long overdue and uncensored acknowledgement of his short but crucial work at Tobruk while in command in Cyrenaica and his victory over Rommel in the Easter Battle of 1941.[18]

Also in 1966 the Australian Prime Minister, Harold Holt, inaugurated a major new army base bearing Lavarack's name. Holt was an appropriate choice. Not only was he the country's head of government, but 30 years before, as a young parliamentarian during Lavarack's time as CGS, he had criticised the effects on the army of a defence policy based on the impracticable Singapore strategy. After the outbreak of war in 1939 Holt joined the AIF and was posted as a gunner to the 2/4th Field Regiment, which was part of Lavarack's 7th Division. Lavarack Barracks, situated at Townsville in north Queensland, would become the largest Australian Army base in the country.

Conclusion

LAVARACK'S LONG TENURE as Governor of Queensland from 1946 to 1957 had been a success, and a welcome counterbalance to the frustrating final years of his military career. After Blamey had returned to Australia in 1942 to become Commander-in-Chief, Lavarack could see the writing on the wall:

> Blamey's return [from the Middle East], of course, meant my complete suppression, since he uses the most dictatorial power ever granted to an Australian, for purely personal advantage, with a heavy and ruthless hand—I should have added 'and dishonest'.

In 'suppressing' Lavarack, Blamey had not only brought to an end the career of a rival, he had allowed personal considerations to influence him to the detriment of Australian interests. The official historian, Gavin Long, wrote to Syd Rowell in 1948: 'Lavarack and Blamey—a difficult topic, yet it cannot, in justice, be disregarded as being merely a personal affair that did not affect events.'[1] Indeed, the animosity between Australia's two most senior generals had a considerable and escalating effect on several major events during the war, beginning with the selection of division commanders for the AIF early in 1940 and culminating with the delayed deployment of First Army Headquarters to New Guinea in late 1944.

Blamey's dislike of Lavarack meant that, although Lavarack had been recommended to command the 6th Division, Mackay was given that formation and thus the first Australian general to lead troops in battle in the Second World War was a citizen soldier. This, and the number of command appointments which went to part-time army officers in the 6th Division, aggravated the rift between citizen and regular soldiers. As one senior Staff Corps officer wrote: 'We were to be the hewers of wood and the drawers of water. We, the only people who really knew the job, were to assist these militia fellows.'[2]

Blamey was also keen to keep Lavarack from playing any part in the expedition to Greece the next year, which probably influenced his decision to alter the order of departure of the 6th and 7th Divisions after he had failed to persuade Lavarack to stay behind in Egypt. As it was, by delaying the departure of 7th Division from Egypt, Blamey had ensured that Lavarack was available to take command in Cyrenaica when Rommel attacked. It was the first time that such a senior post had been given to an Australian, and a significant concession on Wavell's part. But Blamey wasted no time in ensuring that Lavarack was removed from the command despite the prestige it granted Australia and its positive ramifications for Dominion commanders in general.

The affair, in turn, influenced the British decision to appoint Blamey as Deputy Commander-in-Chief to Wavell in the Middle East. Perhaps, as Long implied in the official history, when Blamey was appointed DC-in-C, Middle East he ought to have been replaced as the commander of the AIF because of the conflict of interests between the two positions.[3] In that case, it is most probable that Lavarack would have succeeded Blamey as GOC AIF and there can be no doubt that Blamey would have opposed such a move. As it was, he stubbornly resisted the suggestion that Lavarack replace him as the commander of the 1st Australian Corps even when there were sound operational reasons for it in the invasion of Syria and Lebanon.

Similarly, once back in Australia, Blamey refused to place Lavarack's First Army Headquarters in control of operations in New Guinea, despite the obvious military and political benefits of doing so. General MacArthur was so determined to ensure that American formations did not remain under Australian command in the Pacific theatre that it was doubtless inevitable that he succeed eventually, but Blamey made it easier for him by not placing an Australian army headquarters in New Guinea earlier.[4]

Had Blamey been less ambitious or less paranoid about Lavarack, and other generals, the command organisation of the Australian army after 1942 could have been more effective. A better arrangement which has been suggested would have been to have Blamey as C-in-C and Chairman of the Chiefs of Staff Committee and Lavarack as Commander, Allied Land Forces. Blamey would have been Curtin's principal adviser on defence policy and could have retained control of the administration and training of the army, as well as having an influence on operations through his presence at the Prime Minister's War Conferences. (Incidentally, an arrangement similar to this had been proposed in principle by Lavarack as early as 1935.)[5] However, Blamey was never going to allow Lavarack to get so close to the seat of power by agreeing that he should command the army in the field. Blamey's ADC, Carlyon confirmed that Blamey felt threatened by Lavarack:

> I remember Blamey's comment in one of his thinking-aloud sessions with me: 'I wonder what some of these people actually want. The only other job left is my job; perhaps that's what they want. That was true of Robertson and Lavarack.[6]

While some army officers may have wanted to oust Blamey, Lavarack was not one of them (though, in the unlikely event that Blamey became a casualty and the position of C-in-C were offered to him, there is little doubt that he would have accepted). Certainly he was not without ambition and he resented the fact that Blamey, despite having left the permanent army and become a militia officer, was his superior in the AIF. Nevertheless, Lavarack was no palace conspirator and, while Blamey was C-in-C, Lavarack was prepared to serve under him and give him the loyalty that his position demanded.

In return, Lavarack wanted that loyalty reciprocated, above all in the form of a fighting command. There are numerous references in Lavarack's diary to his disappointment and his desire for the command of an army in New Guinea (or even a corps—an effective demotion he would have been happy to accept), but none to any wish to overthrow Blamey. And it seems unlikely that the impulsive Lavarack was so cautious as to omit any such reference when he was prepared to commit so many other feelings and ambitions to paper. Lavarack may not have liked Blamey or his methods, but Blamey was a superior officer and Lavarack would not try to usurp his position. As General Hopkins observed with supreme understatement:

'They were very different types of men. Blamey had a touch of the larrikin. Lavarack might be thought to have greater integrity'.[7]

However, that Lavarack was not a serious rival to Blamey was not as important as the fact that Blamey regarded him so and, as a result, was determined to cripple his career. There was little that Lavarack could do or say which would allay Blamey's suspicions or diminish his antagonism (and certainly Lavarack's connections to powerful people like the newspaper magnate Keith Murdoch did not help). In addition, Lavarack's battlefield successes in North Africa and Syria had done nothing to thaw relations when Blamey's own performance on the battlefield had drawn criticism. General Lloyd said that Blamey 'loathed' Lavarack and, once earned, Blamey's enmity was a hard thing to be rid of—as the Prime Minister, John Curtin, remarked of Blamey over the Rowell affair: 'This man is a great hater'.

Curtin, though, seemed willing to overlook that aspect of Blamey's character. Indeed, Curtin was crucial to Blamey's style of running the Australian army from 1942. The Prime Minister protected his C-in-C so frequently and effectively that Blamey could write that, with Curtin behind him, he had 'no need to bother about rear armour'. Although Blamey's bacchanalian personal behaviour on an official mission abroad with Curtin in 1944 soured the Prime Minister's opinion of him, and even annoyed Shedden, Blamey was virtually able to deal as he wished with Lavarack and other subordinate generals, making and breaking careers according to his own criteria and whims, something which Lavarack could not fathom. General Hopkins wrote: 'Blamey had a few toadys whom he was inclined to treat as favourites. I could never imagine JDL in such a position.'[8]

Blamey's favourites were generally citizen officers, not regulars. Hopkins also recalled that 'there was a strong anti-regular influence surrounding the C-in-C and sometimes it succeeded in convincing him to appoint the man who had risen through [the] CMF and AIF'. Perhaps contrary to expectations, that tendency did not necessarily curry favour with all citizen officers: Major-General J.H. Cannan (a militia officer and Quartermaster-General) told Lavarack that the 'men selected by TAB for his assistants and advisers, [were] men with whom he would personally have nothing to do', and in one instance refused to work with one of Blamey's appointees.

Nor had Blamey's choices of senior commanders escaped the attention of General MacArthur, who observed that the Australian Commander-in-Chief

> was surrounding himself with his own special selections, and even when General Blamey might ultimately retire, the Government would find itself saddled with a dynasty of the same type of officer.

As an instance, MacArthur thought it 'outrageous' that Savige (a militia officer of limited military and intellectual abilities, but a friend of Blamey), who had commanded a division in only one successful campaign, should be promoted and given command of a corps in preference to Vasey, a relatively young regular officer who had successfully commanded a division in two campaigns.[9]

In such circumstances, Lavarack stood no chance, especially with Curtin set against him, Shedden hovering in the background and Blamey claiming to have professional misgivings about Lavarack's character, as Norman Carlyon related:

> It was his misfortune that Blamey, while respecting his high professional talents, disliked him personally and believed that his moody, temperamental nature could be a serious handicap in a critical appointment.[10]

Yet Lavarack's temperament had not prevented him becoming Chief of the General Staff, nor had it proved to be a handicap on the Middle Eastern battlefields. And Blamey was hardly on firm ground when he criticised Lavarack's fitness to command. Lavarack had succeeded in North Africa and Syria, while there were serious and credible doubts about Blamey's character and ability after the Greek campaign. And Blamey's own extensive catalogue of character foibles raises questions about his suitability as a commander. His unsavoury reputation, and his sometimes ill-judged comments to Australian soldiers (such as his derogatory address to the 7th Division's veteran 21st Brigade in New Guinea which left the officers and men 'almost molten with rage and indignation'), all contrived to undermine respect for him amongst his troops.[11]

It was perhaps inevitable that Blamey's style of command, personal reputation and selection of commanders would have an effect on the morale of the army as a whole. A senior American officer, Major-General J.A. Doe, observed in mid-1944, that the Australian army was 'riddled with politics', a criticism which echoed General Lumsden's report to the Chief of the Imperial General Staff in London in November 1943:

The Australian Army is unfortunately not as happy as it should
be...there appears to be three or four factions in the Army, which is a
pity.
[paragraphs deleted]
The regular officers of the Australian Army are certainly not in the
ascendant at the present time. Whether this is a good thing or not I am
not yet in a position to offer an opinion.[12]

If it appeared that regular officers were 'not in the ascendant' in late
1943 it was not because they had shown themselves to be inferior to their
militia counterparts as commanders. In truth, they had shown that,
despite theories to the contrary, they were able successfully to command
formations in battle. Of the regular generals, Lavarack had been the first
to expose the myth of citizen officer superiority on the battlefield. His
victories at Tobruk and in Syria at division and corps levels, despite his
almost total lack of experience in command, were a foretaste of successes
to come for regular officers. Although he was the only Staff Corps officer
to command at division level or higher in the Middle East, soon other
senior regular officers, such as Rowell, Berryman, Vasey and Milford,
were to show in the South-West Pacific that Lavarack's success was not
an isolated case and that they too were suited for senior commands—if
and when Blamey allowed them the opportunity.

As one of the shelved generals, Lavarack was unfairly treated. He had
succeeded as a commander (which Bennett had not); he had no intent to
usurp Blamey's position (unlike Bennett and Robertson); and, although he
did not like Blamey, he had been loyal to him, treating him with the respect due to his superior rank (something which Rowell had failed to do).
Lavarack, though, was not entirely blameless for the predicament in
which he found himself. At the root of significant problems was his personality, as Menzies told Gavin Long: 'Lavarack's temperament always
went against him'.

Blamey may have been Lavarack's greatest antagonist, but he was not
the only one. Lavarack's propensity for tackling problems head-on (no
matter whether his opponent was a government minister, a powerful civil
servant or a senior officer of the services), his ill-advised flashes of violent
temper and a demeanour which was at times condescending were aspects
of a personality which alienated prominent figures who might otherwise
have been helpful. On the other hand, he was popular in certain circles, as

well as intelligent, capable, honest and loyal. But the scales were not balanced from the perspectives of key people in Australia's conduct of the Second World War, people who had largely made up their minds about Lavarack before 1939: Blamey, Menzies, Curtin and Shedden. And events during the war did little to soften their attitudes. Indeed, if anything, attitudes against Lavarack hardened regardless of his successes.[13]

For Lavarack the end of the war had not brought satisfaction, but immutable disappointment at the setbacks he had endured during the years of conflict. When Lavarack left the army in 1946 it was with the knowledge that he would never again have the opportunity to test himself on the battlefield. But if he had failed in any way, it was not as a soldier.[14]

Lavarack's contribution to the Australian army and to the defence of Australia should not be undervalued simply because Blamey managed to consign the last years of his military career to professional obscurity. He was an educated, articulate officer eminently suited to the post of Chief of the General Staff, even allowing for undiplomatic outbursts. He found it difficult to achieve much progress towards a balanced defence policy in the years preceding 1939, but in the political climate of the time it is inconceivable that any army officer could have done more (his predecessors had tried since the end of the First World War without success). Lavarack's was the most spirited and coherent criticism of the bankrupt Singapore strategy expounded by the army, but in offering it he indirectly contributed to his fate by alienating politicians and bureaucrats who might otherwise have championed his cause after 1939.

When war came he showed himself to be a determined and capable battlefield commander, one who was eventually posted far from the frontline not because of any shortcomings in military skill and leadership, but because of his superior's dislike and fear. Blamey may have been able to keep Lavarack from the fighting for the last years of the war, but he could not bury the truth. Lavarack, despite the quirks of personality which hampered him at times, had been one of the army's most perceptive and far-sighted pre-war leaders. Once the war started, he became a trailblazer for regular army officers who—after his battlefield successes in the Middle East—could no longer be regarded merely as staff officers fit only to serve their citizen officer commanders. The essence of Sir Paul Hasluck's assessment of Lavarack is a fitting epithet for the man: an exceptional Australian soldier who could think as well as fight.

Endnotes

Preface

1. Shafer, Jack, 'Who Said It First? Journalism is the "first rough draft of history"', *Slate*, 30 August 2010.

Introduction

1. Brigadier Sir Charles Spry to author, 27 July 1981. Also correspondence from Major-General R.N.L. Hopkins, 15 May 1981; Lieutenant-General Sir Thomas Daly, 4 July 1980; Colonel M.C. Morgan, 3 June 1980; Brigadier D.R. Jackson, 12 June 1980; and interviews with C.H. Wilson, 12 May 1980; General Sir John Wilton, 24 June 1980; Brigadier F.W. Speed, 6 August 1980; Mr E.S. Eyers, 18 February 1981; Dr. J.O. Lavarack, 3 May 1981; Mr A.J. Hill, 9 May 1984.

2. Hopkins to author, 15 May 1981. See also Norris, *No Memory for Pain*, p.105. Many correspondents referred to Lavarack's quick flashes of anger.

3. Letter, Brigadier Sir Charles Spry to author, 27 July 1981.

4. Rowell, *Full Circle*, p.30.

5. Brigadier Sir Frederick Chilton to author, 6 September 1983.

6. Norris, *op cit*, p.105. Lady H. Wilton interview, 10 August 1983.

7. Letter, Hopkins to author, 3 September 1983.

8. Letter, Hopkins to author, 15 May 1981.

9. Letter, Hopkins to author, 15 May 1981.

10. Letters to author from Brigadier J.G. Ochiltree, 31 August 1981 and C.H. Wilson, 1 March 1981; and Gavin Long Notebooks and Diaries N11/38, AWM. Albany Creek Memorial Park Cemetery and Crematorium Bridgeman Downs, Brisbane City, Queensland, Australia. Columbarium 1 Section 23, 188974431.

11. Letter, Major-General R.N.L. Hopkins to author, 30 January 1983. 'Ek Dum' [M.H. Ellis], 'Lavarack', *Bulletin*, 18 December 1957, p.36.

12. Shedden manuscript, Chapter 81, p.8, CRS A5954, Box 1294.

13. Hetherington, *Blamey: Controversial Soldier*, p.121; see also p.84.

14. In Greece Australian casualties were 320 killed and 494 wounded; in Crete, 274 killed and 507 wounded; in Syria the 7th Division lost 416 and 1136 respectively. However, in Greece and Crete more than 5,000 Australians were taken prisoner. See Gavin Long, *Greece, Crete and Syria*, pp.183, 316, 526. During its time in Tobruk (April to October 1941) casualties suffered by the 9th Division amounted to 749 killed and 1,996 wounded. See Barton Maughan, *Tobruk and El Alamein*, p.401. The recipients of the Victoria Cross were Lieutenant Arthur Roden Cutler and Corporal James Hannah Gordon.

15. The only other Staff Corps officer to be appointed to the command of a division before 1942 was Major-General H.D. Wynter, who relinquished the post because of ill health before seeing action. See Warren Perry, 'Lieutenant-General Henry Douglas Wynter', *Victorian Historical Magazine*, vol.43, no.2, p.865.

1 - The Foundations of Controversy

1. Military Board Proceedings, 5 May 1905, CRS A2653, vol. 1905-07, p.64. Certificate of commission, 7 August 1905, Lavarack papers. See Warren Perry, 'Lieutenant-General Sir John Dudley Lavarack. Australia's 14th Chief of the General Staff', *Victorian Historical Journal*, vol.46, no.2, p.366. Dr Peter Lavarack, 'My Grandfathers Were Both Heroes to Me', *Sunshine Coast Daily*, 22 April 2018.

2. Military Board Proceedings, 27 February 1911, CRS A2653, vol. 1908–11, p.377. 'Application to Attend the Examination for Admission to the Staff College to be held in June 1911, Lieutenant John Dudley Lavarack', CRS A289, item 1862/3/298 (see also item 1862/3/114). 'Biographical Details. Lieut.-Colonel J.D. Lavarack', 16 April 1919, AWM 183.

3. 'Result of the Examination for admission to the Staff College, Camberley, June-July, 1912. Captain J.D. Lavarack' MP 133/2, item 91/4/97. See memorandum, Chief of Operations to CGS, 5 January 1912; minute, Acting CGS to Secretary Department of Defence, 5 March 1912, MP 133/2, item 91/4/97); and documents in CRS A289, item 1952/6/150.

4. Letters, Lavarack to Director of Military Training, 17 October 1913 and Director of Military Training to Lavarack, 18 December 1913, MP 133/2, item 91/4/25; Governor-General to Secretary of State for the Colonies, 12 June 1914, MP 133/2, item 91/4/97; CGS to Commonwealth Representatives, Dominions Section, Imperial General Staff, 29 June 1914, CRS A289, item 91/4/63. Lavarack Papers loaned to author by Dr J.O. Lavarack (some of the Lavarack papers are now held in State Library of Queensland: see 7571, Lavarack Family Album, John Oxley Library).

5. *Gradation List of Officers of the Australian Military Forces*, Active List, vol.1, 18 January 1945, p.2. John Hetherington *Blamey: Controversial Soldier*, p.32.

6. War Diary, HQ Royal Artillery 22nd Division, 8 September 1915, Appendix A; 1–7 November 1915, WO 95/2166, PRO. War Diary, HQ Royal Artillery 22nd Division, 12 February 1916, WO 95/4843, PRO. War Diary, HQ Royal Artillery 16th Corps, 15 July 1916, WO 95/4825, PRO. See also Perry, 'Lieutenant-General Sir John Dudley Lavarack. Australia's 14th Chief of the General Staff', *op cit*, p.373. Stuart Sayers, *Ned Herring: A Life of Sir Edmund Herring* (Hyland House, Melbourne in association with Australian War Memorial, Canberra, 1980), p.44; B.H. Liddell Hart, *History of the First World War* (Book Club Associates, London, 1973), pp.206–207; Hugh Gilchrist, 'The Australians in Macedonia', *Sabretache*, vol.23, July/September 1982. His rank in the AIF at that time is

not clear. His statement of service in the AIF (in his personal papers) records that he was enlisted in the AIF in the rank of major, but the *Gradation List of Officers of the Australian Military Forces*, gives 1 December 1915 as the date of his promotion from captain. It is clear, however, from the 22nd Division and 16th Corps artillery war diaries (of which Lavarack was the diarist in both cases) that he held the rank of captain until 12 February 1916.

7. 'Biographical Details. Lieut.-Colonel J.D. Lavarack', 16 April 1919, AWM 183. War Diary HQ Royal Artillery 5th Division, September 1916 - May 1917, 13/14, AWM. C.E.W. Bean, *The Official History of Australia in the War of 1914–1918*, Volume III, *The Australian Imperial Force in France 1916*, pp.899–902, 916, 953; and Volume IV, *The Australian Imperial Force in France 1917*, pp.26, 422, 491, 527–535, 749–781, 833–901, 932, 934–935, and Volume V, *The Australian Imperial Force in France During the Main German Offensive,1918*, p.16n. *Gradation List of Officers of the Australian Military Forces*, *op cit*, pp.1, 2. David Horner in *Blamey: The Commander-in-Chief* cites personal correspondence with Captain John Rogers who said that the 'feud' between Blamey and Lavarack began at this time (see Chapter 2, footnote 80).

8. Bean, *The Australian Imperial Force in France During the Main German Offensive,1918*, pp.16n, 160–173, 643, 644; vol.6, pp.251, 307, 492–493, 902–907.

9. *Gradation List of Officers of the Australian Military Forces*, *op cit*, p.2. See also documents in CRS A289, item 1954/1/58. Lavarack Papers.

10. The other army officers were Wynter, Sturdee, Northcott, Rowell and Bridgeford. Defence Committee Minute, 4 November 1926, CRS A2031, vol.1, item 34/1926 (see also items 26/1927 and 31/1927). Brigadier T.I.G. Gray *The Imperial Defence College and the Royal College of Defence Studies 1927–1977*, p.78. Gavin Long, *To Benghazi*, p.50n; *Gradation List of Officers of the Australian Military Forces*, *op cit*, pp.2, 3, 4, 6, 12. Military Board Proceedings, 22 May 1928, CRS A2653, vol.4, 1928, item P&S 543.

11. Department of Defence, Historical Listing, May 1976. D.M. Horner, *High Command*, pp.6–7. See Warren Perry, 'Sir Frederick Shedden', *Victorian Historical Magazine*, vol.42, no.3.

12. 'Confidential Report on Lieut. Colonel J.D. Lavarack, C.M.G., D.S.O., Australian Staff Corps', 14 December 1928, CRS A5954, Box 46.

2 - 'A brilliant thinker'

1. The Military Board was established in 1905. The Board, primarily composed of three or four senior military members and a civilian finance member, was subject to the control of the relevant minister (for defence or for the army). Military Board Proceedings, CRS A2653, item P&S 610/1928. Rowell, *Full Circle*, pp.30-31. (see CGS Periodical Letter No. 2/1938, Lavarack to Gort, 12 May 1938, CRS A6828, item 2/1938). As well as Chauvel, he served under two other Chiefs of the General Staff as DMO&I, Major-General W.A.Coxen (1 May 1930 to 30 September 1931) and Major-General J.H.Bruche (1 October 1931 to 20 April 1935).

2. Margot Simington, 'The Southwest Pacific Islands in Australian Interwar Defence Planning', *Australian Journal of Politics and History*, vol.23, no.2, August 1977, p.175. Horner, *High Command*, pp.3,15. Minute, CGS (Coxen) to Secretary, Military Board, 27 September 1930, Military Board Proceedings, CRS A2653, item Agenda 105/1930. Rowell, *op cit*, p.31. Letter, Major-General R.N.L. Hopkins to author, 15 May 1981. Preparations for the despatch of an expeditionary force had begun in 1922 and were known as Plan 401. See Claude Neumann, 'Australia's Citizen Soldiers, 1919–1939: A

Study of Organisation, Command, Recruiting, Training and Equipment', MA Thesis, UNSW, 1978, pp.69–70.

3. 'A Brief Narrative of the Organization, Strength and Training of the Australian Military Forces Since Federation', Proceedings of the Military Board, Military Board Proceedings, CRS A2653, item vol.1, 1928. A.J. Hill, *Chauvel of the Light Horse*, pp.212–217. 'Report for the Inspector-General of the Australian Military Forces by Lieut.-General Sir H.G. Chauvel', Part 1, 31 May 1929, p.8, *Commonwealth Parliamentary Papers*.

4. 'Defence Policy...Statement by PM at interview by Chiefs of Staff', CRS A5954, Box 1012. Hill, *op cit*, p.216. 'Defence of the Suez Canal', p.1, 30 July 1929, Minutes of Defence Committee Meeting, 31 July 1929, CRS A2031, item vol.1. See 'Extract from Report by Lt.Colonel H.D.Wynter, on the Second Term of the 1930 Course at the Imperial Defence College', CRS A5954, Box 39.

5. Defence of the Suez Canal', *op. cit.*, p.2. Minute, Defence Committee to Minister, 2 August 1929, Minutes of Defence Committee Meeting, 31 July 1929, CRS A2031, item vol.1.

6. See Paul Hasluck, *The Government and the People 1939–1941*, p.64. T.B. Millar, *Australia's Defence*, p.17. 'Estimated Savings in Permanent Staffs (Other than Civil) Possible Consequent Upon Suspension of Compulsory Military Training', CRS A5954, Box 1012.

7. 'A Brief Narrative of the Organization, Strength and Training of the Australian Military Forces Since Federation', Proceedings of the Military Board, Military Board Proceedings, CRS A2653, item vol.1 1928 (the paper originally was prepared in June 1928, was updated in December 1929, but remained with the 1928 minutes). 'Summarized Proceedings of a Meeting held at Commonwealth Offices, Melbourne, on Tuesday 5th. November, 1929', p.1, and 'General Meeting of the Council of Defence held at Commonwealth Offices, Melbourne, at 2 p.m. on Tuesday, 12th November, 1929. Summary of Proceedings', p.4, CRS A5954, Box 1012.

8. Memorandum (with notes attached), Green to Scullin, 4 February 1930, CRS A5954, Box 841. 'Defence Policy...Statement by PM at interview by Chiefs of Staff', CRS A5954, Box 1012. Shedden (then secretary of the Defence Committee), in a paper submitted to the Secretary of the Department of Defence (M.L. Shepherd) on 25 November, had advocated clearly that the final responsibility for determining policy must be civil. See 'The Determination of the Principles of National Defence', pp.3–4, CRS A5954, Box 841.

9. Letter, Hopkins to author, 15 May 1981.

10. Memorandum, Richmond to Shedden, 8 September 1929, quoted in CRS A5954, Box 38. Letter, Shedden to Richmond, 30 December 1929, Richmond papers RIC/7/2, NMM. Minute, Shedden to Secretary, 20 December 1929, CRS A5954, Box 38.Quoted in Horner, *High Command*, p.250. 'An Outline of the Principles of Imperial Defence with Special Reference to Australian Defence', 7 March 1930, CRS A5954, Box 38 (hereinafter referred to as 'An Outline of the Principles of Imperial Defence....').

11. Memorandum, Richmond to Shedden, 9 September 1929, quoted in CRS A5954, Box 38. Admiral Sir Herbert Richmond, *Statesmen and Sea Power*. Minute, Shedden to Secretary, 20 December 1929, CRS A5954, Box 38.

12. See Horner, *High Command*, pp.1–2, 3. Long, *To Benghazi*, pp.7–9. Neil Gow, 'Australian Army Strategic Planning 1919–1939', *Australian Journal of Politics and History*, vol.XXIII, No.2, August 1977, p.170. Minute, Chauvel to Secretary, 5 March 1930, CRS A5954, Box 39. Chauvel did think, however, that Shedden's view of the

limited capability of air forces was eminently sound. "

13. 'Comments on Paper: "An Outline of the Principles of Imperial Defence with Special Reference to Australian Defence"', 7 March 1930, paras 1–2, 4 CRS A5954, Box 39.

14. *Ibid*, p.2, paras 3, 5. Lavarack defined Australia as a heaven-left area for Asiatic expansion (p.8).

15. *Ibid*, p.4.

16. *Ibid*, pp.4–6. 'An Outline of the Principles of Imperial Defence with Special Reference to Australian Defence', p.36, CRS A5954, Box 38. Lavarack did not think that the supply of food would present a problem and the reduced supply of fuel, chemicals and industrial commodities could be offset by stocks already in the country and the expansion of local production. The internal transport system of Australia could be kept efficient, although there would have to be reversion in some areas to horsed transport. He also foreshadowed the production of fuels by methods such as shale oil distillation.

17. 'An Outline of the Principles of Imperial Defence with Special Reference to Australian Defence', pp.35-36, CRS A5954, Box 38. 'Comments on Paper: "An Outline of the Principles of Imperial Defence with Special Reference to Australian Defence"', 7 March 1930, p.3, CRS A5954, Box 39.

18. 'Comments on Paper: "An Outline of the Principles of Imperial Defence with Special Reference to Australian Defence"', pp.1, 3, CRS A5954, Box 39.

19. 'An Outline of the Principles of Imperial Defence with Special Reference to Australian Defence', p.47, CRS A5954, Box 38. 'Comments on Paper: "An Outline of the Principles of Imperial Defence with Special Reference to Australian Defence"', pp.6–7 CRS A5954, Box 39.

20. 'An Outline of the Principles of Imperial Defence with Special Reference to Australian Defence', pp.38–40, 45, 47, CRS A5954, Box 38. 'Comments on Paper: "An Outline of the Principles of Imperial Defence with Special Reference to Australian Defence"', p.7, CRS A5954, Box 39.

21. 'Comments on Paper: "An Outline of the Principles of Imperial Defence with Special Reference to Australian Defence"', pp.8-9 CRS A5954, Box 39. Shedden's paper was criticized also by the Controller-General of Munitions Supply, A.E. Leighton. See 'Notes on a Memorandum ("Principles of Defence") dated 20th December, 1929 by Mr. F.G. Shedden', CRS A5954, Box 39.

22. Letter, Lavarack to Shedden, 31 March 1930, Shedden papers CRS A5954, Box 39. See 'Appreciation: Australia's Position in Case of War in the Pacific by D.M.O.&I. (Australia). March 18th., 1930', CRS A5954, Box 39.

23. 'Principles of Imperial Defence. Comments on a paper dated 7/3/30 prepared by the General Staff', p.3, CRS A5954, Box 39.

24. Annotation on 'Comments on Paper: "An Outline of the Principles of Imperial Defence with Special Reference to Australian Defence"', paras 2(a), 7 (see also para.11), CRS A5954, Box 39. 'Comments on Paper: "An Outline of the Principles of Imperial Defence with Special Reference to Australian Defence"', p.3, CRS A5954, Box 39. See 'An Outline of the Principles of Imperial Defence with Special Reference to Australian Defence', CRS A5954, Box 38, pp.34–35.

25. 'Principles of Defence' (handwritten notes by Shedden), CRS A5954, Box 39. Minute, Lavarack to CGS, 6 March 1930, CRS A5954, Box 39. Handwritten notes by Shedden on 'Comments on Paper: "An Outline of the Principles of Imperial Defence with Special Reference to Australian Defence"', p.1, CRS A5954, Box 39. Note by Shedden regarding queries put by him to Richmond in a letter, probably 24 April 1930. Letter Richmond to

Shedden, 21 May 1930, CRS A5954, Box 39.

26. 'Comments on Paper: "An Outline of the Principles of Imperial Defence with Special Reference to Australian Defence"', p.1, CRS A5954, Box 39. Letter, Richmond to Shedden, 21 May 1930, CRS A5954, Box 39.

27. 'Review of the Strategical Appreciation Governing Defence Policy', minute by Minister, ?/3/30, CRS A5954, Box 1012. 'Appreciation - War in the Pacific, 9 August 1928', MP1185/5, Item 1846/4/363. See also Defence Committee Minute No.9/1930, CRS A2031, 1930, vol.1.

28. Minute, Chauvel to Secretary, Defence Committee, 26 March 1930; minute, Lavarack to Secretary, Defence Committee, 19 March 1930, CRS A5954, Box 1012.

29. 'Combined review by the Army and Air Force Members of the Sub-committee appointed by the Defence Committee on 6th. March, 1930', pp.1–3, CRS A5954, Box 1012. Defence Committee Minute No.9/1930, pp.6–7, 6 March 1930, CRS A2031, 1930, vol.1. As a counter to the suggestion made by the CNS that funds for the field army should be transferred to coast defences Lavarack wrote that 'Mobile land and air forces extra to those required for passive Coast Defence will continue to be required to supplement the Naval forces in providing for Local Security'.

30. Defence Committee Minutes Nos.11/1930, 20 March 1930, 12/1930 and 13/1930, 26–27 March 1930, and No.19/1930, 11 April 1930, CRS A2031, 1930, vol.1.

31. Defence Committee Minute No.19/1930, *ibid.* The CNS, on 26 March, stated that it is the business of the Government to indicate what wars are so possible or probable that preparations should be made to meet them and for the Services to recommend what preparations should be made accordingly (Defence Committee Minute No.12/1930, 26 March 1930, *op cit*, p.2). The CGS thought that it was the government's task to decide what contribution it was prepared to make to naval defence (which encompassed the difficulties of dividing naval resources between local and imperial defence and the consequent ramifications for defence of Australia against invasion) (Defence Committee Minute No.13/1930, *op cit*, p.2).

32. 'Appreciation: Australia's Position in Case of War in the Pacific by D.M.O.&I. (Australia). March 18th., 1930', p.1, CRS A5954, Box 39.

33. Robertson, *op cit*, pp.267–274. Minute, Maguire to Secretary, Military Board, c.June 1930, Military Board Proceedings, CRS A2653, item vol. 1930. 'Information for the Prime Minister on His Visit Abroad, 5 June 1930', MP729/2, item 1855/1/131; also CRS B197, item 1855/1/131; Military Board Proceedings, CRS A2653, item vol. 1930, Ag.56/1930. Although Lavarack did not sign the paper there is no doubt that he is the author. All his papers have the letters DMO:AK as a reference on their first pages (DMO being the initials for his appointment; AK are the initials of his typist). Major-General R.N.L. Hopkins, who was on Lavarack's staff during his appointment as DMO&I, has confirmed that any paper bearing these letters was written by Lavarack (interview, R.N.L. Hopkins, Canberra-Adelaide via telephone, 29 August 1984).

34. 'Information for the Prime Minister on His Visit Abroad, 5 June 1930', *ibid.*, pp.1, 4.

35. *Ibid*, pp. 5, 10–11.

36. *Ibid*, pp.10–11. See 'Comments on Paper: "An Outline of the Principles of Imperial Defence with Special Reference to Australian Defence"', p.8, CRS A5954, Box 39.

37. Minute, Maguire to Secretary, Military Board, c.June 1930, *op cit*. See also 'The Royal Australian Navy and Australian Naval Policy', CRS A5954, Box 10. The RAAF paper also touched upon policy considerations, but not to the same degree as Lavarack; for example, it stated that provision must be made against invasion as well as minor

attacks such as raids on cities and trade. See 'Memorandum for the Prime Minister on the Royal Australian Air Force and the Australian Air Force Policy', p.5, CRS A5954, Box 10.

38. Letter, Chauvel to Minister, 14 April 1930, CRS A5954, Box 890. Chauvel suggested that if neither Jess nor Lavarack were chosen then Coxen should be appointed, although he had not attended staff college. See Council of Defence Meeting, 8 July 1929, Summary of Proceedings, CRS A5954, Box 762.

39. The other proposals were that the army and air force be amalgamated; that the question of raid versus invasion be resolved; and that the financial organization of the department be examined. See Letter, Shepherd to Shedden, 25 February 1931, CRS A5954, Box 39. Letter, Hopkins to author, 30 January 1983.

3 - 'A bit of an "invasionist"'

1. See letters Brogan to author, 26 May 1980 and Pulver to author, 25 February 1981; 'Annual Report of the Commandant, Royal Military College 1933', 23 January 1934, Military Board Proceedings, CRS A2653, item vol.1, 1934.

2. 'Memorandum by the Headquarters Promotion and Selection Committee. Changes in Command and Staff Appointments', 3 October 1932 and Military Board Minute P&S 952/1932, Military Board Proceedings, CRS A2653, item vol.3, 1932. Military Board Agenda No.151/1930, Military Board Proceedings, CRS A2653, item vol.2 1930. 'Memorandum by the Headquarters Promotion and Selection Committee, Changes in Command and Staff Appointments', 3 October 1932, Military Board Proceedings, CRS A2653, item vol.1 1932. Personal notes, Lavarack Papers. Letter, Colonel E.L. Cook to author, 1 June 1980

3. Letter, Lieutenant-General Sir Thomas Daly to author, 4 July 1980.

4. Lavarack, 'The Defence of the British Empire, with Special Reference to the Far East and Australia', *Army Quarterly*, vol. XXV, No.2, January 1933. See Admiral Sir Herbert Richmond, 'An Outline of Imperial Defence', *Army Quarterly*, July 1932, pp.207, 209. Lavarack was not the only Australian regular officer to publish his views on defence, usually in the British *Army Quarterly*: for example, in 1925 Major A.R. Selby had suggested the establishment of an Imperial General Staff with representation of the dominions; in 1927 Lieutenant-Colonel H.D. Wynter published an article entitled 'The Strategic Inter-Relationship of the Navy, the Army and the Air Force: An Australian View'; and Major H.C.H. Robertson published articles in 1933 and 1935 entitled 'The Empire and Modern War' and 'The Defence of Australia'. See Horner, *High Command*, p.5.

5. John McCarthy, *Australia and Imperial Defence 1918–1939: A Study in Sea and Air Power*, pp.54–55. See Bruche's analysis of CID Paper 372C 'The Defence of Australia, 23 Mar 1933', CRS B197, item 1855/1/165. Also, Defence Committee Minute No.6/1934 (Agendum 7/1934), Defence Committee Meeting 2 March 1934; and Defence Committee Minute No.48/1934, Defence Committee Meeting 9 October 1934, CRS A2031, item vol.3, 1934.

6. Lavarack, 'The Defence of the British Empire, with Special Reference to the Far East and Australia', *op cit*, pp.209–213, 216.

7. *Ibid*, pp.213–217. E.M. Andrews, 'The Broken Promise - Britain's Failure to Consult its Commonwealth on Defence in 1934, and the Implications for Australian Foreign and Defence Policy', *Australian Journal of Defence Studies*, vol.2, no.2, November 1978, pp. 103,108–109. N.H. Gibbs, *Grand Strategy, Volume I, Rearmament Policy*, p.375.

8. Admiral Sir Herbert Richmond, 'Imperial Defence', *Army Quarterly*, October 1933, p.7, typescript copy in CRS A5954, Box 1025. Richmond also replied to criticisms made by 'Canuck' in 'Canada and Imperial Defence', *Army Quarterly*, July 1933. See Richmond's *Statesmen and Seapower*, pp.289–290, 294.

9. Letter, Shepherd to Minister, 31 January 1934, CRS A5954, Box 890. Although Bruche did not reach retiring age until 6 March 1935, it was the practice for retiring officers to take their furlough before leaving the service. Bruche's was ten months and two weeks, hence he would have vacated his post on 20 April 1934. Letter, Chauvel to Minister, 14 April 1930, CRS A5954, Box 890.

10. 'Army Administration', n.d., CRS A5954, Box 890. The date of the paper can be established as being late 1933, probably December. Jess attended staff college at Camberley in 1920 for one year only and in the paper it is noted that almost thirteen years had elapsed since his return.

11. *Ibid.* Jess had risen from staff captain to the command of the 10th Infantry Brigade while Lavarack had risen from the rank of captain to GSO1 of the 4th Division. (see minute, unsigned to Minister, c. August 1934, titled 'Appointment of C.G.S', CRS A5954, Box 890).

12. *Ibid.* Letter, Pearce to Bruce, 18 December 1933, CRS A5954, Box 890.

13. Minute, Shepherd to Pearce, 31 January 1934, CRS A5954, Box 890.

14. Cable, Bruce to Pearce, 1 February 1935, and minute, Secretary to Secretary, Military Board, 6 February 1935, CRS A5954, Box 890. See minute, Shepherd to Pearce, 31 January 1934, *op cit.* Also 'Army Higher Administrative Posts and Commands, Draft Memorandum for Cabinet by the Minister for Defence', January 1935, CRS A5954, Box 890. Hankey diary, 27 October 1934, Hankey papers CAB 63/67, PRO.

15. Gibbs, *op cit*, p.376.

16. Letter, Hankey to Baldwin, 23 August 1934, Hankey papers 4/26, Churchill College, Cambridge.

17. John F. Naylor, 'Hankey, Maurice Pascal Alers, first Baron Hankey (1877–1963)', *The Oxford Dictionary of National Biography* (2004).

18. 'Statement of the Government's Policy Regarding the Defence of Australia', Sydney, 25 September 1933, copy in CRS A5954, Box 828. See also letter, Hankey to Baldwin, 23 August 1934, Hankey papers 4/26, Churchill College, Cambridge and Baldwin papers, vol.1). For a discussion of Hankey's manoeuvrings to obtain the assurances he desired before leaving Britain see Trotter, *op cit*, pp.322–324 and McCarthy, *op cit*, pp.56–57.

19. McCarthy, *op cit*, p.58. See letters, Hankey to Sir E.J. Harding, 28 November 1934, Hankey papers CAB 63/71; Hankey to Howarth, 13 October 1934, CAB 66/71, PRO.

20. Hamill, *op cit*, p.262. Hankey diary, 24, 27 October 1934, Hankey papers CAB 63/67, PRO. Letter, Hankey to Dill, 30 November 1934, Hankey papers CAB 63/70, PRO. David Horner, 'Shedden, Sir Frederick Geoffrey (1893–1971)' *Australian Dictionary of Biography*, Vol. 16.

21. McCarthy, *op cit*, pp.56–57. See Hankey papers CAB 63/74, PRO; Stephen Roskill, *Hankey. Man of Secrets, vol.3, 1931–1963*, p.128. 'Notes of Meetings of Defence Committee for Discussions with Sir Maurice Hankey, G.C.B., G.C.M.G., G.C.V.O. Secretary of the Committee of Imperial Defence', CRS A5954, Box 1016. Hankey requested a statement of assurance to be delivered to the Australian government, see Roskill papers 7/124; CAB 21/398, 21/386, 21/385, and PREM 1/174, PRO.

22. 'Report by Sir Maurice Hankey, Secretary to the Committee of Imperial Defence, on Certain Aspects of Australian Defence', 15 November 1934, p.10, CAB 63/76, PRO. See

also Minutes of Defence Committee Meeting, 21 March 1935, Ag.4/1935, CRS A2031, item vol.3.

23. Letter, Hankey to Dill, 30 November 1934, CAB 63/70, PRO. See Minutes of Defence Committee Meeting, 21 March 1935, Ag.4/1935, CRS A2031, item vol.3. Andrews,'The Broken Promise...', *op cit*, p.110. For a more detailed assessment of Hankey's visit see E.M. Andrews, *The Writing on the Wall: The British Commonwealth and Aggression in the Far East, 1931–1935*, pp.162–165. Letter, Hankey to Dill, 30 November 1934, CAB 63/70, PRO.

24. Letter, Hankey to Baldwin, 17 November 1934, Baldwin papers vol.1, Cambridge University Library.

25. Letter, Hankey to Dill, 30 November 1934, CAB 63/70, PRO. Defence Committee Meeting, 9 October 1934, Minute No.(48), CRS A2031, item vol.3 1934. McCarthy, *op cit*, p.166, note 56. See Ian Hamill, *The Strategic Illusion: The Singapore Strategy and the Defence of Australia and New Zealand, 1919–1942*, p.255. Letter, Lieutenant-Colonel Farlang to Hankey, 19 November 1934, Hankey papers CAB 63/75, PRO. Letter, Hankey to Shedden, 12 December 1934, CRS A5954, Box 45. See W. David McIntyre, *The Rise and Fall of the Singapore Naval Base, 1919–1942*, p.127 where it is implied that not even a veneer of consensus between the services existed. Letter, Hankey to Baldwin, 17 November 1934, Baldwin papers vol.1, Cambridge University Library.

26. Letter, Hankey to Baldwin, 17 November 1934, Baldwin papers vol.1, Cambridge University Library. McCarthy, *op cit*, p.59.

4 - 'The fullest co-operation is expected'

1. Shepherd to Parkhill, 22 January 1935, CRS A5954, Box 890. Peter Dennis et al, *The Oxford Companion to Australian Military History*, p.456.

2. 'Appointment of Chief of the General Staff. Confidential Notes for the Use of the Minister', 22 January 1935, p.1, CRS A5954, Box 890. Attached to Shepherd's paper were records of service headed 'X' and 'Y'. There is no doubt that X's service record is that of Jess and Y's that of Lavarack, who, although sixth on the seniority list of lieutenant-colonels, held the ranks of brevet colonel and temporary colonel. Horner, *Blamey*, Chapter 5, footnote 31.

3. 'Higher Army and Air Force Appointments and Salaries. Memorandum for Cabinet by the Minister for Defence', 24 January 1935, CRS A5954, Box 890. Newspaper clippings, 3 January 1935, CRS A5954, Box 890.

4. 'Army Higher Administrative Posts and Commands. Supplementary Notes for Minister' (by M.L. Shepherd), 11 December 1934, p.1, CRS A5954, Box 890. Cabinet Meeting, 2 February 1935, (No agenda), CRS A2694/XM, item vol.13, Part 1, 1311. 'Press Announcement by Minister for Defence - 6th February, 1934', CRS A5954, Box 890.

5. 'Urgency of Changes in Higher Army Posts', Shepherd to Secretary, Military Board, 6 February 1935, CRS A5954, Box 890.

6. 'Army Higher Administrative Posts and Commands. Supplementary Notes for Minister' (by Shepherd), 11 December 1934, CRS A5954, Box 890.

7. Minute, Shepherd to Parkhill, 7 March 1935, CRS A5954, Box 890. Shepherd did not mention Hyde by name, but as Parkhill obviously was not at the meeting and Hyde was the senior officer present (and a critic of Lavarack) it is reasonable to assume that he was chairman on this occasion.

8. Minute, Minister to Secretary, Defence Committee, 8 March 1935, CRS A5954, Box 890.

9. Note by Shepherd attached to minute, CNS to Minister, 14 February 1935, entitled 'The Invasion Bogey', CRS A5954, Box 1018. Hankey's visit had also generated papers by Shepherd and Shedden: see 'Australian Defence Policy. Outstanding Questions and Their Background', by Shepherd, 8 February 1935, CRS A5954, Box 841; 'Co-operation in Imperial Defence', by Shedden, 16 November 1934, CRS A5954, Box 840.

10. Minute, CNS to Minister, 'The Invasion Bogey', 14 February 1935, pp.7–8, CRS A5954, Box 1018.

11. 'Memorandum by the Chief of the General Staff on Report on Certain Aspects of Australian Defence by Sir Maurice Hankey, G.C.B., G.C.M.G., G.C.V.O., Secretary, Committee of Imperial Defence', 5 March 1935, pp.1, 11–13, Defence Committee Meeting, 21 March 1935, Minute No.20/1935, Appendix A, CRS A2031, item 1935 vol.3. Copies of this memorandum are in CAB 21/397, PRO and CRS A5954, Boxes 909 and 1016.

12. 'Memorandum by the Chief of the General Staff...', *ibid.*

13. 'Memorandum by Colonel J.D. Lavarack, CMG, DSO, Chief of the General Staff Designate, on Report on Certain Aspects of Australian Defence by Sir Maurice Hankey, GCB, GCMG, GCVO, Secretary, Committee of Imperial Defence', pp.1–2, Defence Committee Meeting, 21 March 1935, Ag.4/1935, Appendix B, CRS A2031, vol. 3; Lavarack to CGS, 6 March 1930, CRS A5954, Box 39.

14. *Ibid*, pp.1-2.

15. *Ibid*, pp.2–3, 4, 5.

16. *Ibid*, pp.4-6.

17. McCarthy, *op cit*, pp.59, 61. Hamill, *op cit*, p.263. The only CNS to question the Singapore strategy was Grant (1919–1921); see Horner, *High Command*, p.4. 'Comments by the Chief of the Naval Staff on Memorandum by the Chief of the General Staff, on Sir Maurice Hankey's Report', 21 March 1935, pp.2,5, Defence Committee Meeting, 21 March 1935, Minute No.20/1935, Appendix D, CRS A2031, item vol. 3. Also in CRS A5954, Boxes 1015 and 1016.

18. 'Comments by The Chief of the Naval Staff on Memorandum by Colonel J.D. Lavarack...' *ibid*, pp.1–3, 6, 9.

19. Shepherd to Parkhill, 10 April 1935, CRS A5954 Box 909. Hankey to Dill 30 November 1934, CAB 63/70, PRO.

20. 'Notes by the Minister for Defence on the Political Aspect of Draft Council of Defence Agendum No.1/1935', p.1, 30 May 1935, CRS A5954, Box 909.

21. McCarthy, *op cit*, p.132. McCarthy also points out that Bruce may have neglected to report this to the Australian government in December 1934.

5 - *'Treat our part of the business as strictly confidential'*

1. C.J. Lloyd, 'Parkhill, Sir Robert Archdale (1878–1947)', *Australian Dictionary of Biography*, Vol.11, 1988.

2. W.J. Hudson and Christine Steele, 'Shepherd, Malcolm Lindsay (1873-1960)', *Australian Dictionary of Biography*, Vol.11, 1988.

3. 'Defence Personnel and Equipment: Army', minute, Military Board to Secretary, 3 September 1935, CRS A5954, Box 887. Minute, Military Board (initialled by Lavarack) to Secretary, 23 January 1936, Military Board Proceedings, Ag.18/1936, A/3/1936, CRS A2653, vol.1 1936. Senior to Lavarack when he was appointed on 21 April were Brigadier E.M. Ralph, Honorary Brigadier-Generals C.H. Jess and O.F. Phillips,

Brigadiers J.L. Hardie and A.M. Martyn, Lieutenant-Colonel F.M. de F. Lorenzo, Brevet Colonel E.M. Williams, Brigadier J.T. McColl and Lieutenant-Colonels P.M. McFarlane and J. Bilton. When Lavarack's rank of major-general was made substantive on 1 June 1935 he became the most senior permanent officer on the active list. (See 'Appointment of Chief of the General Staff. Confidential notes for the use of the Minister', Shepherd to Parkhill, 22 January 1935, CRS A5954, Box 890. *The Army List of the Australian Military Forces*, Parts 1 & 2, 1 June 1940).

4. *Ross, Armed and Ready, p.139.*

5. Minutes of Defence Committee Meeting, 19 July 1935, Minute no.37/1935, Annex 8, 'Australian Coast Defences. Re-consideration of Revise of CID Paper 249C (DC Paper 35/34). Memorandum by the Chief of the General Staff', CRS A2031, item vol. 3.

6. Lavarack suggested that the phrase from CID paper 249C stating that the fleet would arrive at Singapore 'with a minimum of delay after the outbreak of war in the Far East', which had been reckoned to be within forty-two days after hostilities commenced, be altered to read: 'Whilst it is intended that the Main British Fleet should arrive at Singapore with a minimum of delay after the outbreak of war in the Far East, possible complications in Europe concurrent with a war in the Far East may cause the despatch of the Fleet to be delayed for a prolonged period.' Minutes of Defence Committee Meeting, 19 July 1935, CRS A2031, vol. 3, pp.8–9. See also Minutes of Council of Defence Meeting, 19 June 1935, AA1971/216. Five years earlier Chauvel had suggested that the difficulties in moving the fleet to Singapore and the possibility that the base there might not be completed be placed on the agenda for the next imperial conference (minute, CGS to Secretary, 6 March 1930, CRS A5954, Box 39).

7. Council of Defence Meeting, 24 August 1936, Summary of Proceedings, p.8, AA1971/216. Letter, Hankey to Dill, 30 November 1934, CAB 63/70, PRO.

8. Letter, Minister for Defence to Minister for External Affairs, 28 August 1935, CRS A5954, Box 909. 'Defence Personnel and Equipment: Army', minute, Military Board to Secretary, 3 September 1935, CRS A5954, Box 887. Minute, Military Board (initialled by Lavarack) to Secretary, 23 January 1936, Military Board Proceedings, Ag.18/1936, A/3/1936, CRS A2653, vol.1 1936.

9. Annotation by Parkhill on minute, Military Board to Secretary, 22 April 1936, CRS A5954, Box 887. 'Cabinet paper, Proposals for Improvement in Voluntary Enlistment', p.3, 21 April 1936, Military Board Proceedings, Ag.18/1936, A/3/1936, CRS A2653, vol.1, 1936. Minute, Military Board to Secretary, 22 April 1936, CRS A5954, Box 887.

10. 'Cabinet paper, Proposals for Improvement in Voluntary Enlistment', p.3, 21 April 1936, Military Board Proceedings, Ag.18/1936, A/3/1936, CRS A2653, vol.1, 1936. Minute, Shedden to Shepherd, 26 May 1936, CRS A5954, Box 887.

11. Minute, Secretary to Military Board, 30 December 1935. Letter, Lavarack to Parkhill, 17 January 1936. 'Special Note for Secretary' by Shedden, 17 & 23 February 1936. Minute by Minister, 27 February 1936. Letter, Shedden to Hankey, 17 March 1936, CRS A5954, Box 891.

12. 'Defence Committee Agenda. Priorities Under New Army Programme', 2 October 1936; and minute, Military Board to Secretary, 24 June 1936, CRS A5954, Box 887. Minute, Military Board to Secretary, 1 July 1936, CRS A5954, Box 887. 'Army. New Programme. Minute by Minister', 23 July 1936, CRS A5954, Box 887.

13. Minute, Military Board to Secretary, 12 August 1936, CRS A5954, Box 887.

14. Minute, CGS to Secretary, 18 August 1936, CRS A5954, Box 887. Defence Committee Minute no.48/1936, 29 October 1936, CRS A2031, item vol.4, 1936. Minute, Shedden to

Secretary, 'Priorities Under New Army Programme', 9 November 1936, CRS A5954, Box 887. See also minute, Shedden to Bruce, 27 November 1936, CRS A5954, Box 71.

15. Letters, Lavarack to Piesse, 7 August 1935 and 20 September 1935, Piesse papers 9/40 & 9/71, NLA MS882. Horner, *High Command*, p.12. See 'Albatross' (Piesse), *Japan and the Defence of Australia*. Lavarack later told Richmond that 'I do not by any means agree with "Albatross" on all points'. Letter, Lavarack to Richmond, 27 March 1936, Lavarack papers.

16. *Argus*, 20 February 1936. Minute, Parkhill's secretary to Military Board, 24 February 1936, CRS A5954, Box 888.

17. 'Memorandum for the Minister for Defence by the Military Board on National Service', 5 March 1936, pp.1, 7; and minute Lavarack to Parkhill, 5 March 1936, Military Board Proceedings, Ag.A/2/1936, CRS A2653, vol.1 1936.

18. 'Memorandum...', *ibid*, p.2.

19. *Ibid*, pp.3, 5, 6.

20. *Herald*, 3 March 1936. Annotation by Parkhill on minute, Military Board to Secretary, 6 March 1936, CRS A5954, Box 888.

21. 'Statement by the Military Board on Comments by Mr Holt, MHR (The *Melbourne Herald*, 3 Mar 36)', minute Military Board to Secretary, 9 March 1936, CRS A5954, Box 888. 'Press Criticism - Mr A.G. Cameron. Additional Comments by the Military Board' (with annotation by Lavarack), 9 March 1936, CRS A5954, Box 888.

22. Minute, Parkhill to Military Board, 10 March 1936, CRS A5954, Box 888.

23. *Age*, 10 March 1936. See minute (initialled by Lavarack), Military Board to Secretary, 23 January 1936, *op cit*. Similar articles appeared in the *Argus* and *Sun News-Pictorial* newspapers on the 10th.

24. Minute, Military Board (initialled by Lavarack) to Secretary, 10 March 1936, CRS A5954, Box 888.

25. Minute, Minister to Secretary, 11 March 1936, CRS A5954, Box 888.

26. Minute, Military Board (initialled by Lavarack) to Secretary, 16 March 1936, CRS A5954, Box 888.

27. *Age*, 23 March 1936. Minute, Parkhill's secretary to Military Board, 24 March 1936, CRS A5954, Box 888. Minute, Military Board to Secretary, 26 March 1936, CRS A5954, Box 888. Minute, Adjutant-General to Secretary, 26 March 1936, CRS A5954, Box 888.

28. Minute, Parkhill to Military Board, 27 March 1936, CRS A5954, Box 888. *Commonwealth Parliamentary Debates*, House of Representatives, 31 March 1936, vol.149, p.684.Minute, Shedden to Shepherd, 9 April 1936, CRS A5954, Box 887. There was another article on defence in the *Melbourne Herald* on 20 April, but the Board advised Parkhill that it did not warrant a reply (see minute, Military Board to Secretary, 22 April 1936, CRS A5954, Box 887).

29. B.B.J., 'Defence-or What?', *Bulletin*, 22 July 1936. Minute, Parkhill's secretary to Military Board, 27 July 1936, CRS A5954, Box 888. Minute, Military Board (initialled by Lavarack) to Secretary, 5 August 1936, CRS A5954, Box 888.

30. 'Newspaper Criticism. Draft Statement for the Minister', attached to minute, Military Board (initialled by Lavarack) to Secretary, 5 August 1936, CRS A5954, Box 888. Minute, Secretary to Minister, 12 August 1936, CRS A5954, Box 887.

31. Minute by Minister, 'System of Training "*Bulletin*" Article', 25 August 1936, CRS A5954, Box 888.

32. *Ibid*. Parkhill saw as inconsistent the facts that on 5 March the Board had

recommended that the peace nucleus of the AMF be raised to 130,000 by the introduction of national service; on 28 April it said that an increase of numbers in the militia could be deferred until the number of commanders and staff could be increased and more material provided; and on 5 August the Board argued that voluntary service was not working and implied that the reintroduction of compulsory service would be necessary.

33. 'System of Training- *"Bulletin"* Article', minute, Military Board (initialled by Lavarack) to Secretary, 3 September 1936, CRS A5954, Box 888.

34. *Ibid.*

35. *Ibid.*

36. Minute, Shepherd to Parkhill, 15 September 1936, CRS A5954, Box 887.

37. Minute, Minister to Military Board, 22 September 1936, CRS A5954, Box 888.

6 - 'Your luck is out'

1. Minute by Minister, 27 November 1936, CRS A5954, Box 886. Wynter's lecture, entitled 'Defence of Australia and its Relation to Imperial Defence', was in fact delivered twice, first to the USI in Melbourne (3 July) and then in Sydney (22 August). His earlier lecture, 'The Strategical Inter-Relationship of the Navy, Army and Air Force', was given on 1 September 1926 in Melbourne and published the next year in the *Army Quarterly* (vol.XIV, no.1, April 1927). Copies are in CRS A5954, Box 886.

2. Letter, Wynter to Lavarack, 11 December 1936; 'The Case of Lieutenant-Colonel (Temporary and Brevet Colonel) H.D. Wynter, C.M.G., D.S.O., Australian Staff Corps', Cabinet submission by Parkhill, 8 February 1937; and 'Case of Lieutenant-Colonel (Temporary and Brevet Colonel) H.D. Wynter', Cabinet paper, 7 April 1937, CRS A5954, Box 886.

3. Minute by Minister, 16 December 1936, CRS A5954, Box 886. Letter, Wynter to Lavarack, 11 December 1936; 'The Case of Lieutenant-Colonel (Temporary and Brevet Colonel) H.D. Wynter, C.M.G., D.S.O., Australian Staff Corps', Cabinet submission by Parkhill, 8 February 1937; and 'Case of Lieutenant-Colonel (Temporary and Brevet Colonel) H.D. Wynter', Cabinet paper, 7 April 1937, CRS A5954, Box 886. Minute, Military Board to Secretary, 9 April 1936, CRS A5954, Box 886.

4. Minute, Military Board to Secretary, 9 December 1936; and 'Colonel Wynter's Case. Special Notes for the Minister which may be of use in the Cabinet discussion', n.d., CRS A5954, Box 886. Minute by Minister, 15 January 1937, CRS A5954, Box 886. (Original emphasis). Minute by Minister, 16 December 1936, CRS A5954, Box 886.

5. Minute, Shedden to Shepherd, 27 January 1937, CRS A5954, Box 886. Minute by Minister, 16 November 1937; letter, Deverell to Parkhill, 22 June 1937, CRS A5954, Box 886.

6. Minute, Parkhill to Lyons, 27 January 1937, CRS A5954, Box 886. Minute, Shedden to Shepherd, 18 January 1937, CRS A5954, Box 886.

7. 'Speech in Parliament on Defence Estimates on 5th November, 1936 by the Honourable J. Curtin, M.P.', minute by Minister, 27 January 1937, CRS A5954, Box 886. Letter, Wynter to Lavarack, 15 January 1937, CRS A5954, Box 885. Letter, Wynter to Lavarack, 26 January 1937, CRS A5954, Box 885. Colonel L.E. Beavis was also moved to a more junior post after expressing views which the Government found unacceptable (Horner, *Crisis of Command*, p.3). See also B.N. Primrose, 'Equipment and Naval Policy 1919–1942', *Australian Journal of Politics and History*, vol.23, no.2, August 1977,

p.163–164 and Sir Richard Williams, *These Are Facts*, p.225 for brief discussions of the implications of service officers speaking on matters of government policy.

8. Warren Perry, 'Wynter, Henry Douglas (1886–1945)', *Australian Dictionary of Biography* (Melbourne University Press, 2002) Volume 16.

9. 'Speech in Parliament on Defence Estimates on 5th November, 1936 by the Honourable J. Curtin, M.P.', minute by Minister, 15 January 1937, CRS A5954, Box 886. Letter, Lavarack to Parkhill, 18 January 1937, CRS A5954, Box 885.

10. Minute, Minister for Defence to Prime Minister, n.d.; and minute by Minister, 15 January 1937, CRS A5954, Box 886. Minute, Parkhill to Lyons, 27 January 1937, CRS A5954, Box 886. Minute, Shedden to Shepherd, 18 January 1937, CRS A5954, Box 886.

11. Letter, Lavarack to Parkhill, 18 January 1937, CRS A5954, Box 885. Minute by Minister, 16 November 1937, CRS A5954, Box 886. Shedden manuscript, Chapter 98, 'A New Defence Programme and Labor's Re-Statement of Policy—1936–1937', p.17, CRS A5954, Box 1276.

12. Stephen Roskill, *Naval Policy Between the Wars*, vol.2, p.347. See James Neidpath, *The Singapore Naval Base and the Defence of Britain's Eastern Empire, 1919–1941*, pp.138–139. Council of Defence Meeting, 17 December 1937, Agenda No.4/1937, 'Imperial Conference 1937. Questions raised by Australian Delegation on Empire and Australian Defence Policy', pp.15–16, AA1971/216. See Periodical Letters No. 3/1936, Lavarack to Deverell, 21 July 1936; No. 4/1936, Lavarack to Deverell, 15 October 1936; No. 1/1937, Lavarack to Deverell, 5 February 1937; No.4/1937, Lavarack to Deverell, 15 October 1937, CRS A6828, item 4/1937. McIntyre, *op cit*, p.131.

13. Quoted in Horner, David. "Sir Frederick Shedden: The Forerunner" in Furphy, Samuel (ed.)*The Seven Dwarfs and the Age of the Mandarins: Australian Government Administration in the Post-War Reconstruction Era*, p.118

14. Council of Defence Meeting, 17 December 1937, Summary of Proceedings, quoted in Horner, *Blamey*, Chapter 5, footnote 38.

15. Note, CGS to AG and QMG, 31 December 1937. Ministerial minute, 24 December 1937. 'Notes for QMG on MB Agendum 113/1937: Coast Defence Works, Newcastle', CRS A2653, vol.1 1937, Ag.113/1937. H.V.C. Thorby, 'I Saved Our Little Ships', *Sydney Morning Herald*, 22 December 1957, p.13. Lloyd, C.J., 'Parkhill, Sir Robert Archdale (1878–1947)', *Australian Dictionary of Biography*, Vol.11, 1988. Carnell, Ian, 'Thorby, Harold Victor Campbell (1888–1973)', *Australian Dictionary of Biography*, Vol.12, 1990.

16. Council of Defence Meeting, 24 February 1938, Summary of Proceedings, pp.2–3, AA1971/216. See also pp.4,7,8. Hughes had questioned the efficacy of naval defence for Australia in a book entitled *Australia and War Today: The Price of Peace*.

17. Council of Defence Meeting, 24 February 1938, Summary of Proceedings, pp.5, 6, 13, AA1971/216. Lavarack was fully aware of the need for adequate stocks of ammunition but there were liaison problems between the Military Board and the Munitions Supply Board. See Ross, *Armed and Ready*, pp.141–4.

18. Council of Defence Meeting, 24 February 1938, Summary of Proceedings, pp.8,13, 17, AA1971/216. Horner, *Blamey*, Chapter 5.

19. Council of Defence Meeting, 24 February 1938, Summary of Proceedings, pp.9, 20, *AA1971/216*. See Ross, *op cit*, pp.118 (note 131), 126 (note 153). Minute, Military Board (initialled by Lavarack) to Secretary, 23 January 1936, Military Board Proceedings, Ag.18/1936, A/3/1936, CRS A2653, vol.1 1936. Memorandum for the Minister for Defence by the Military Board on National Service', 5 March 1936, p.7, Military Board Proceedings, Ag.A/2/1936, CRS A2653, vol.1 1936. Squires would refer to the liaison

between the MSB and the Military Board in his report as Inspector-General (pp.291–292).

20. Long, *To Benghazi*, p.26. See minutes, Military Board to Secretary, 7 January 1937, CRS A5954, Box 888; Minister to Military Board, 18 October 1937, CRS A5954, Box 911. 'Public Criticism of Defence Policy and Administration by Officers of the Services', Council of Defence Agenda No. 8/1937, 15 December 1937, AA1971/216, item 8/1937. Minute, Secretary to Military Board, 3 June 1938, CRS A5954, Box 888. Council of Defence Meeting, 24 February 1938, Summary of Proceedings, p.23, AA1971/216. Herring to Hetherington, n.d., Hetherington Papers, Box 2, 3DRL 6224, AWM. Hetherington, *op cit*, pp.83–84.

21. Minute, Jess to Secretary, Military Board, 9 May 1939, CRS A5954, Box 890 and interview, Mrs Margaret Lodge (daughter of General Squires), 23 April 1983.

22. CGS Periodical Letter No. 3/1938, Lavarack to Gort, 29 July 1938, CRS A6828, item 3/1938. Text of telegram, Lavarack to Squires in letter, Smart to Squires, 24 May 1938, Squires papers. Minute by Shedden, 16 May 1938, CRS A5954, Box 890. Rowell later wrote that after Squires' appointment 'soon the Army realised that, for the first time in many years, it had a leader, not merely a figurehead'. It detracts in no way from Squires undoubted ability to observe that this comment was most unfair to Lavarack, Bruche and Chauvel who had worked hard to protect the army's interests. Rowell also claimed that Squires was appointed because of a personality clash between Lavarack and Jess (who had hoped to be CGS). Rowell, *op cit*, p.39. The Finance Member the Military Board at this time, J.T. Fitzgerald, said that although there may have been differences, Board meetings 'were conducted with decorum' (minute, Fitzgerald to Sturdee, 4 March 1936, CRS A5954, Box 1506).

23. Military Board Minute, 24 May 1938, quoted in Defence Committee Minutes, 16 August 1938, Ag.45/1938, CRS A2031, item vol.5 1938. Letter, Hughes to Lyons, 13 May 1938, CRS A816, item 14/301/88.

24. Defence Committee Meeting, 16 August 1938, Ag.45/1938, CRS A2031, item vol.5 1938.

25. Hasluck, *The Government and the People, 1939–41*, p.98. Minutes of Defence Committee Meeting, 16 August 1938, Ag. 45/1938, vol. 5, CRS A2031. Gavin Long Diaries, D11/22–23, AWM. McIntyre, *op cit*, p.140. Council of Defence Meeting, 24 February 1938, Summary of Proceedings, p.18, AA1971/216. McCarthy, *op cit*, pp.82–83.

26. Telegram, Secretary to Minister, 29 September 1938, and message, Secretary to Minister, 28 September 1938, CRS A5954, Box 890.

27. Telegram, Secretary to Minister, 29 September 1938, and message, Secretary to Minister, 28 September 1938, CRS A5954, Box 890. Interview, Mrs Margaret Lodge (daughter of General Squires), 23 April 1983. Minute, Lavarack to Secretary, Military Board, 2 February 1939; 'Comments by the Military Board on the First Report by the Inspector-General of the Australian Military Forces dated 16th December, 1938', 3 February 1939; 'Revised Report by the Military Board on the First Report by the Inspector-General of the Australian Military Forces dated 16th December, 1938', 10 February 1939, Military Board Proceedings, CRS A2653, item vol.3 1939. Rowell, *op cit*, p.40.

28. Minutes, Army Liaison Officer to Secretary, 10 October 1938, and Lavarack to Shedden, 30 January 1939, CRS A816, item 30/301/6. 'Defence Programme—Army Appreciation for resistance to major attack', minute, Lavarack to Shedden, 28 February 1939, CRS A816, item 14/301/108. Letter, Squires to Minister, 19 February 1939, CRS A5954, Box 894.

29. Quoted in Roskill, *Naval Policy Between the Wars*, p.435. 'The Basis of the Defence of Australia', Naval Board minute, 7 March 1939, CRS A816, item 14/301/108.See Malcolm H. Murfett, *Fool-proof Relations: The Search for Anglo-American Naval Cooperation During the Chamberlain Years, 1937–1940*, pp.210–211. Letter, Secretary of the Committee of Imperial Defence to Minister, 18 March 1939, CAB 21/893, PRO. For a more detailed account of this episode see B.N. Primrose, 'Australian Naval Policy, 1919–1942: A Case Study in Empire Relations', Ph.D. Thesis, ANU, 1974, p.303f. Neidpath, *op cit*, pp.149–150.

30. Arthur J. Marder, *Old Friends, New Enemies: The Royal Navy and the Imperial Japanese Navy. Strategic Illusions, 1936–1941*, p.40. Neidpath, *op cit*, p.150. See Michael Howard, *The Continental Commitment*, pp.138–139. 'Defence Programme', Minute by Minister, 8 May 1939, CRS A816, item 14/301/108.

31. Andrews has remarked that 'It is...difficult to escape the conclusion that the army in Australia was acting independently of the government...and was not sufficiently under the control of its political "masters"'. See Andrews, *The Writing on the Wall*, p.173. Although most of the problems naturally occurred between the army and the government, the opposition would not have been so naive as to imagine that they would not face similar difficulties on different issues. A decade earlier the Labor Prime Minister, Scullin, had issued instructions to the services that public criticism of policy was to cease. See Primrose, 'Australian Naval Policy, 1919–1942'. p.193. McCarthy, *op cit*, p.91. Letter, Major-General R.M. Downes to Shedden, 13 July 1939, CRS A5954, Box 44.

32. Letter, Squires to Minister, 20 February 1939; and 'Establishment of the Australian Staff Corps', p.4, CRS A5954, Box 894.

33. CGS Periodical Letter No.1/1939, 20 February 1939, CRS A6828, item 1/1939. Long, *To Benghazi*, pp.33, 36–39.

34. Lieutenant-General E.K. Squires diary, 4 February, 12–16 August 1939, Squires papers (hereinafter referred to as 'Squires diary'). Personal notes, Lavarack papers. C.E.W. Bean, *Two Men I Knew*, p.205. Long, *To Benghazi*, p.43. Horner, *High Command*, p.43. For the reasons why Bennett was not appointed see Lodge, *The Fall of General Gordon Bennett* (Allen & Unwin, Sydney, 1986), pp.1–5, 21–24. Horner, *Blamey*, Chapter 5. Dennis, *The Oxford Companion to Australian Military History*, p.101.

35. 'Organization of Special Infantry Division of 20,000 and Intensive Training of Militia Forces', broadcast by the Prime Minister, 15 September 1939, p.2, CRS A5954, Box 828. Sir Robert Menzies, Foreword to Hetherington, *op cit*, p.vii (see also pp.83–84).

36. Gavin Long Notebooks and Diaries, D11/21–22, AWM. Long, *To Benghazi*, p.44.

37. Letter, Lavarack to Long, 8 May 1946, Gavin Long Correspondence, J.D. Lavarack, Part 2, AWM. Squires diary, 25–27 September 1939, Squires papers. Letter, Squires to Lavarack, 22/24 September 1939, Lavarack papers 2 (original emphasis). Hetherington wrote that 'It is hard to believe that Menzies ever said anything of the kind' and attributed the beginning of the 'legend' to Squires' remarks to Lavarack (*op cit*, p. 89). This is clearly not the case, however, as there can be no doubt that Menzies made the statement. Gavin Long Notebooks and Diaries, D11/23, AWM.

38. Letter, Lavarack to Long, 8 May 1946, Gavin Long Correspondence, J.D. Lavarack, Part 2, AWM. Squires diary, 25, 27, 28 September 1939, Squires papers. Long, *To Benghazi*, p.45.

39. Letter, Lavarack to Long, 8 May 1946, Gavin Long Correspondence, J.D. Lavarack, Part 2, AWM. Squires diary, 25–27 September 1939, Squires papers. Gavin Long Notebooks

and Diaries, D11/23, AWM. Horner, *Blamey,* Chapter 6.

40. Letter, Squires to Lavarack, 22/24 September 1939, Lavarack papers. See War Cabinet Minute No. 2, CRS A2673, item vol. 1. Long, *To Benghazi,* p.45. After his appointment as GOC Southern Command Lavarack's salary dropped from £2000 to £1500 per annum. However, since he had been told that his appointment as CGS would be for five years, he submitted that he be paid the higher salary until the expiration of that period in March 1940. As might be expected, such a gesture was in vain and his request was refused by the Prime Minister. See Proceedings of the Military Board, CRS A2653, vol.2, 1939, Ag. 248/1939. Letter, Lavarack to Long, 8 May 1946, Gavin Long Correspondence, J.D. Lavarack, Part 2, AWM.

41. Letter, Lavarack to Dill, 9 June 1936, Lavarack papers 1. Some progress was made, however, such as the establishment of the Command and Staff School (see Military Board Proceedings, Ag.84/1938, CRS A2653, item vol.1 1938; and related papers in CRS A5954, Box 888) and the Darwin Mobile Force (see 'Army Development Programme— Permanent Force of Mobile Troops, Darwin', CRS A816, items 31/301/1 and 6). See also Lavarack's 'Organization of Tank Units and Formation of an Australian Tank Corps', 16 April 1937, Military Board Proceedings, Meeting 5 May 1937, CRS A2653, item vol.1 1937.

42. Notes, 'Minister Interviewed by CGS in presence of DMO&I on 19 June 1934', CRS A5954, Box 1026. Letter, Lavarack to Richmond, 27 March 1936, Lavarack papers 1.

43. Letter, Lavarack to Dill, 9 June 1936, Lavarack papers 1.

44. Quoted in Horner, David. "Sir Frederick Shedden: The Forerunner" in Furphy, Samuel (ed.) *op cit,* pp.117, 121.

7 - 'The Crown of any officer's career'

1. Rowell *Full Circle* p.44. Hetherington *Blamey: Controversial Soldier* p.88. See also Horner, *Crisis of Command,* p.12; Long, *To Benghazi* pp.61-63; J.E.S. Stevens, 'A personal story of the service, as a citizen soldier', unpublished manuscript, 3DRL 3561, AWM. Horner, *Blamey,* Chapter 6.

2. Long, *To Benghazi,* pp.35,39,42-43, 65, 69, 82-4. The possible formation of a second division is also mentioned in a Cable, Northcott to Squires, 6 November 1939, CRS A816, item 52/302/135, in John Robertson and John McCarthy, *Australian War Strategy 1939—1945: A Documentary History,* pp.34-35. Squires Diary, 14 January 1940. War Cabinet Agendum 22/1940, CRS A2670, item 22/1940. War Cabinet Minute No.186, 28 February 1940, CRS A2673, item vol.2 See also MP 729/7, item 42/421/166.

3. Memo, Street to Menzies, 8 March 1940, War Cabinet Agendum 67/1940, CRS A2670, item 67/1940. Long, *To Benghazi,* p.84. Drake-Brockman was the other militia officer considered.

4. War Cabinet Minute No.207, 21 March 1940, Ag. 67/1940, CRS A2673, item vol.2. Letter, Rowell to Long, 11 October 1948, Rowell papers, File 11, 3DRL 6763, AWM. See also Herring to Hetherington, n.d., Hetherington papers, 3DRL 6224, AWM. Hetherington *Blamey: Controversial Soldier* p.101. Chapman, *Iven G. Mackay: Citizen and Soldier,* p.155. Gavin Long Diary No.11, p.23, AWM. Letter, A.J. Sweeting, Assistant Director AWM, to Hetherington, 11 February 1972, Hetherington papers, Box 2, AWM.

5. War Cabinet Minute No.207, 21 March 1940, Ag. 67/1940, CRS A2673, item vol.2. Letter, Rowell to Long, 11 October 1948, Rowell papers, File 11, 3DRL 6763, AWM. See also Herring to Hetherington, n.d., Hetherington papers, 3DRL 6224, AWM. Hetherington *Blamey: Controversial Soldier* p.101. Chapman, *op cit,* p.155. Gavin Long Diary No.11,

p.23, AWM. Letter, A.J. Sweeting, Assistant Director AWM, to Hetherington, 11 February 1972, Hetherington papers, Box 2, AWM. Horner, *Blamey*, Chapter 6 (for an account of Blamey's time as Commissioner of Police, see Chapter 4).

6. Letter, Rowell to Long, 11 October 1948, Rowell papers, File 11, 3DRL 6763, AWM. There is some confusion over when this incident occurred. When Hetherington was preparing his second biography of Blamey (published in 1973) Rowell recounted the incident to him, but said that it occurred in 'April 1940, on the day War Cabinet appointed Lavarack to the 7th Div.' He also said that Blamey was stopped at Wangaratta and that it was a Friday (Rowell Notes, Hetherington papers, Box 2, AWM). This later version is obviously incorrect as far as the date is concerned (War Cabinet made its decision on 21 March), whereas his earlier letter to Long (11 October 1948) is accurate to the extent that it places the incident 'just before Easter' which began the following day, 22 March. The first account by Rowell was written twenty years closer to the events, and is taken to be the more accurate. Blamey's official diary (Blamey papers, 3DRL 6643, AWM) is also incorrect, stating that Blamey left for Wagga after discussing the divisional appointments with War Cabinet on 24 April. It is obviously referring to the 21 March meeting because it further records that Blamey 'stopped en route to telephone Army HQ,[and] was informed that Major-General Iven Mackey [sic] had been appointed to command 6 Aust Div, and Major-General J.D. Laverack [sic] to command 7 Aust Div'. However, from these varying accounts it is apparent that Blamey attended the 21 March meeting of War Cabinet when the two new divisional commanders were discussed, that he left before the decision was made, and was travelling by road to either Sydney or Wagga when he was summoned back to Melbourne to be given the news of Lavarack's appointment.

7. *Argus*, 23 March 1940.

8. Herring to Hetherington, n.d., Hetherington papers, Box 2, 3DRL 6224, AWM. Letter, Brigadier J.G. Ochiltree to author, 31 August 1981. Major-General C.H. Finlay interview, 6 April 1982. Lavarack diary, 30 April 1941. Horner, *Blamey*, Chapter 5.

9. Long, *To Benghazi*, p.84. Hetherington *Blamey: Controversial Soldier* pp.101, 112-113. Commander-in-Chief's Diary, 12, 15 19 April 1940, Blamey papers, 3DRL 6643, AWM. War Diary HQ 7 Div, G Branch, 4 and 11 April 1940, 1/5/14, AWM. Rowell to Hetherington, n.d., Hetherington papers, AWM.

10. Letter, Birdwood to Lavarack, 17 December 1941, Lavarack papers 2. Hetherington, *Blamey: Controversial Soldier*, p.25. War Cabinet Agendum 22/1940, Appendix B, CRS A2670, item 22/1940.

11. As instances, the DAQMG reported for full-time duty on 18 April; the AAQMG reported on 29 April; the GSOI was working full-time by 30 April; and the DAAG began full-time duty on 29 May, but was recalled from 7th Division on 14 June. Other officers withdrawn included the DADOS and the DAAG. See War Diary HQ 7 Div, AQ Branch, 18 April, 29 May, 14 June 1940, October-December 1940, Appendix A, 1/5/15, AWM. War Diary HQ 7 Div, G Branch, 29–30 April 1940, 1/5/14, AWM.

12. Appointed from 4 April were: Col J.A. Chapman (GSO1), Maj H. Wells (GSO2), Capt T.W. White (GSO3), Col A.J. Boase (AA&QMG), Maj E.E. Grant (DAAG), Maj S.F. Legge (DAQMG), Brig E.J. Milford (CRA), Maj H.G.F. Harlock (BMRA), Lt-Col V.C. Secombe (CRE), Lt-Col B.T.R. Chadd (CO Div Sigs), Lt-Col H.M. Frencham (CASC), Col F.K. Norris (ADMS), Lt-Col A.H. Hellestrom (DADOS). War Diary HQ 7 Div, G Branch, 24 April 1940, 1/5/14, AWM. War Diary HQ 7 Div, AQ Branch, April 1940, Appendix A, 1/5/15, AWM. Stevens, unpublished manuscript, p.35. Dean, Peter J., 'The Making of a General: Lost Years, Forgotten Battles. Lieutenant General Frank Berryman 1894-1941',

Ph. D. Thesis, UNSW, 2007. When war broke out Chapman was again at Camberley as an instructor. Two weeks later he was appointed GSO1 of the British 'Lowland' Division, a post he held for two months before returning to Australia, where he became GSO1 (MT) of G Branch at Army Headquarters, his last appointment before joining Lavarack's division. During the 1930s Boase had twice been posted as chief staff officer to a militia division, and before joining the 7th Division had been commandant of the Command and Staff School (which Lavarack had established while CGS). *Gradation List of Officers of the Australian Military Forces*, vol.1, pp.8–9. p.11.

13. *Gradation List of Officers of the Australian Military Forces*, vol. 1, pp.9–11. Long, *To Benghazi*, p.83.

14. War Diary HQ 7 Div, G Branch, 18–20 April 1940, 1/5/14, AWM. Long, *To Benghazi*, p.83.

15. War Diary HQ 7 Div, G Branch, 1 April 1940, 1/5/14, AWM. War Diary HQ 7 Div G Branch, 18 April 1940, 1/5/14, AWM. Stevens, unpublished manuscript, pp.28, 30. Rowell, *Full Circle*, p.44. War Cabinet Agendum 22/1940, Appendix B, CRS A2670, item 22/1940. One of the foremost critics of the Staff Corps was Lieut-General H.G. Bennett who wrote that the First World War 'had proved that they [citizen officers] were more suited for high commands than were Staff Corps officers' (letter, Bennett to G.A. Street, 10 March 1939, Bennett papers, ML MSS 807, item 2, Folio 235). Another Staff Corps critic was Lieut-General Sir S.G. Savige, whom Major-General G.A. Vasey described as a 'shooter' of the Staff Corps (letter, Vasey to wife, Vasey papers, NLA MS 3782). Long, *To Benghazi*, p.52. See Horner, *Crisis of Command*, pp.4–5.

16. Originally the HQ was located in the room occupied by the BMRA, Major H.G.F. Harlock, at HQ Southern Command. War Diary HQ 7 Div, G Branch, 20, 24 April 1940; April Appendix A; 17 August 1940, 1/5/14, AWM. War Diary HQ 7 Div, AQ Branch, 15, 29 April, 13, 31 May 1940, 1/5/15, AWM. Wilson diary, 17 August 1940. Long, *To Benghazi*, pp.39, 43n.

17. C.H. Wilson interview, Melbourne, 7 May 1981. Hasluck *The Government and the People 1939–1941*, p.167. War diary HQ 20 Bde, 7, 8, 15, 20 May 1940, 8/2/20, AWM. War Diary HQ 21 Bde, May 1940 (n.b. the 13th), 8/2/21, AWM. Long, *To Benghazi*, p.86.

18. Hasluck, *The Government and the People, 1939–41*, pp.67, 220–221. War Diary HQ 20 Bde, 31 May 1940, 8/2/20, AWM. Wilson diary, 7 June 1940. John W. O'Brien, *Guns and Gunners*, p.18.

19. See War Diary HQ 7 Div, G Branch, September 1940, Appendix 6, 1/5/14, AWM. The location of 20th Brigade units were: the 2/13th and 2/17th Battalions in New South Wales, with the 2/15th in Darwin. HQ 21st Brigade and the 2/14th Battalion were in Victoria, the 2/27th in South Australia, and the 2/16th in Western Australia. HQ 26th Brigade was in New South Wales close to the Victorian border with the 2/23rd Battalion, but the 2/24th and 2/48th Battalions, were in Victoria and South Australia respectively. For a discussion of the raising of the First AIF see Bean, *op cit*, Vo. 1, *The Story of Anzac*, pp.37–42.

20. 1 Aust Corps Circular G.43, War Diary HQ 7 Div, G Branch, September 1940, Appendix 2, 1/5/14, AWM. See Wigmore, *The Japanese Thrust*, p.29.

21. Letter, Lavarack to White, 11 July 1940, Lavarack papers 1. See War Diary HQ 7 Div G Branch, 2–13 September 1940, 1/5/14, AWM.

22. War Diary HQ 20 Bde, 7 June 1940, 8/2/20, AWM. Wilson diary, 24 May, 7 June, 2 July 1940. The experience of the 2/5th Field Regiment was probably typical of 7th Division units: 'As clothing arrived only in dribs and drabs, issue parades were all too frequent

interludes. The complicated peacetime routine still held sway, and months passed before the biggest and smallest of the men had received complete issues. It was not until field-service kits were complete that men began to feel like genuine soldiers.' As an example of the 'peacetime routine', 2,000 sets of underwear despatched to Puckapunyal to make good a shortage in two battalions there (the 2/14th and 2/2nd Pioneer) could not be issued immediately because the ordnance depot at nearby Seymour had closed for the King's birthday. See War Diary HQ 21 Bde, 17 June 1940, 8/2/21, AWM. O'Brien, *Guns and Gunners*, p.16. Wilson diary 1940. See War Cabinet Agendum 22/1940, Appendix B, CRS A2670, item 22/1940. E.F. Aitken, *The Story of the 2/2nd Australian Pioneer Battalion*, p.5.

23. War Diary HQ 7 Div, G Branch and AQ Branch, June 1940, 1/5/14 and 1/5/15, AWM. Aitken, *op cit*, p.10. W.B. Russell, *The Second Fourteenth Battalion*, p.11. Malcolm Uren, *A Thousand Men at War*, p.17. Stevens, unpublished manuscript, p.31. Wilson diary, 15 June 1940. Allan S. Walker, *Middle East and Far East, Medical Series*, vol.2, *Australia in the War of 1939–1945*, pp.28,31.

24. Long, *To Benghazi*, p.83n. Letter, Major-General R.N.L. Hopkins to author, 15 May 1981. Aitken, *op cit*, pp.9–10. War Diary HQ 7 Div, G Branch, May-June 1940, 1/5/14, AWM. Wilson diary, 2 July 1940.

25. Burns, *The Brown and Blue Diamond at War*, p.16. A.J. Hill to author, 16 July 1986. War Diary HQ 21 Brigade, 13 June 1940, 8/2/21, AWM. Henry, *The Story of the 2/4th Field Regiment*, p.11. O'Brien, *Guns and Gunners*, pp.20–1.

26. Although the allotment of transport to the AIF was increased early in August, this had little effect on training as most of the additional equipment was absorbed by the increasing needs of the 8th Division and the formation of the new brigade of the 7th Division, the 26th. Also, from 11 June Lavarack had the responsibility of training, in whole or in part, the corps troops in Australia. The 7th Division had the 2/3rd MG and 2/2nd Pioneer Battalions while the 8th Division had the 2/2nd MG and 2/1st and 2/3rd Pioneer Battalions. War Diary HQ 7 Div, G Branch, 1 May, 25 June, 1 July 1940, 1 August 1940, 1/5/14, AWM.

27. Long, *To Benghazi*, pp.88–89. Hasluck, *The Government and the People 1939–1941*, pp.229–230. The events of May and June 1940 brought home to the government one of the basic errors of Australian defence policy: the failure to recognise that the ability to defend Australia was in direct relation to the country's ability to manufacture the arms it would require in the event of war. See Long, *To Benghazi*, p.88.

28. Millar, *op cit*, pp.18–19. Memorandum, C.B. Laffan, Secretary to the Military Board, to Lavarack, 9 July 1940, Lavarack papers 1. General Staff Memorandum on Proposals for Raising and Training 250,000 Personnel, 6 July 1940, Lavarack papers 1.

29. Annotation on General Staff Memorandum on Proposals for Raising and Training 250,000 Personnel, 6 July 1940 and letter, Lavarack to White, 11 July 1940, Lavarack papers 1.

30. Annotation on General Staff Memorandum on Proposals for Raising and Training 250,000 Personnel, 6 July 1940, Lavarack papers 1.

31. War Cabinet Agendum 22/1940, Supplement No.4, CRS A2670, item 22/1940. Minutes War Cabinet Meeting, London, 15 May 1940, CAB 65/7, PRO. Long, *To Benghazi*, pp.86–87. War Diary HQ 7 Div, G Branch, 30 May 1940, general comments February 1941, 1/5/14, AWM. Maughan, *op cit*, p.10. Hasluck, *The Government and the People, 1939–41*, p.224n.

32. Hasluck, *The Government and the People 1939–1941*, p.222. War Cabinet Agendum

156/1940, Annex A, CRS A2671, item 156/1940.

33. Dominions Office Cablegram No.228, 28 June 1940, War Cabinet Agendum 156/1940, Annex A, CRS A2671, item 156/1940. War Cabinet Agendum 156/1940, Annex B, and Supplement No.1, Appendix B, CRS A2671, item 156/1940. War Cabinet Agendum 186/1940, CRS A2671, item 186/1940. War Cabinet Minute No.394, 3 July 1940, CRS A2673, item vol.3. War Cabinet Minutes Nos.398, 9 July 1940, and 459, 28 August 1940, CRS A2673, item vol.4. See also MP 729/7, item 42/421/166. Hasluck *The Government and the People 1939–1941*, pp.222–223.

34. War Cabinet Minute No.523, 23 September 1940, CRS A2673, item vol.4. See also MP 729/7, item 42/421/166. See Horner, *High Command*, pp.38–41 for a discussion of this episode. Hasluck, *The Government and the People 1939–1941 p.226*. Long, *The Six Years War*, pp.36–37.

35. War Cabinet Minute No.543, 1 October 1940, CRS A2673, item vol.4. Hasluck, *The Government and the People 1939–1941*, pp.225, 229.

36. Cable, Blamey to Menzies, 13 August 1940, and letter, Blamey to Menzies, 17 August 1940, Blamey papers 6A[3] and 2A[1], AWM. The Prime Minister replied on 21 August the government preferred Blamey to remain in the Middle East. Hetherington *Blamey: Controversial Soldier* p.106.

37. Wilson diary, 14 August 1940. War Cabinet Agendum 192/1940, CRS A2671, item 192/1940. War Cabinet Minute No.462, 2 September 1940, CRS A2673, item vol.3. War Diary HQ 7 Div, G Branch, 16 May1940 and 1 Aust Corps Circular G.43, September 1940, Appendix 2, 1/5/14, AWM.

8 - 'What sort of person does he think I am?'

1. Stevens, unpublished manuscript, pp. 36–37. War diary HQ 20 Bde, October 1940, 8/2/20, AWM. Letter, Sir Victor Windeyer to author, 24 March 1981. Long, *To Benghazi*, p.123. Personal notes, Lavarack Papers.

2. The four members of staff were Boase (AAQMG), Legge (DAQMG), Wells (GSO2) and Wilson (ADC). War Diary HQ 7 Div, G Branch, October and November 1940, 1/5/14, AWM. Stevens, unpublished manuscript, p.37. Norris, *No Memory for Pain*, p.110. Favourable reports of the conduct of the 7th Division in India were received in Australia. See cable Sturdee to Blamey, 3 December 1940, Blamey papers 5A, AWM.

3. Later, he would be made responsible for all units of the 1st Australian Corps and the 9th Division as well as his own 7th Division units in Palestine. Wilson diary, 10–23 November 1940. Commander-in-Chief's diary, 10, 14, 24 November 1940, Blamey papers, AWM. Letter, Blamey to Sturdee, 16 November 1940, Blamey papers 5A, AWM. Long, *To Benghazi*, pp.120–121. War Diary HQ 7 Div, G Branch, 23, 24, 26 November, 7 December 1940; see also 6,7 January 1941, 4 March 1941, 1/5/14, AWM. Wilson diary, 7–23 November 1940. War Diary HQ 20 Bde, 24–27 November 1940, 8/2/20 AWM. War Diary HQ 7 Div, AQ Branch, 7 December 1940, 1/5/15, AWM. Letter, Blamey to Spender, 29 November 1940, Blamey papers 8A[3], AWM. Norris, *op cit*, p.111.

4. Commander-in-Chief's Diary, 25 November 1940, Blamey papers, AWM. War Diary HQ 7 Div, AQ Branch, 28 November 1940, 1/5/15, AWM. J.D. Rogers, 'Say Not the Struggle', p.10, unpublished manuscript held by Mrs J.D. Rogers. Henry, *op cit*, p.37. Russell, *op cit*, p.21. Norris, *op cit*, p.112.

5. War Diary HQ 7 Div, AQ Branch, 17 December 1940, 1/5/15, AWM. 'Concentration of 7th Division', Blamey papers 2B[14], AWM. Almost as soon as the division had arrived a spirit of competition had sprung up between it and the 6th Division, as a letter from

Colonel G.A. Vasey (GSO1 of the 6th Division) to his wife in December showed: 'This 7 Div have a nasty smell under their collective nose and I intend to show them that from the efficiency point of view they have no excuse for it'. See letter, Vasey to wife, 15 December 1940, Vasey papers, Box 2, NLA MS3782.

6. O'Brien, *Guns and Gunners*, p.30. War Diary HQ 7 Div, AQ Branch, 11-12 December 1940, 1/5/15, AWM. War Diary HQ 7 Div, G Branch, 31 December 1940, 3 January 1941, 1/5/14, AWM. Long, *To Benghazi*, p.146. War Diary HQ 21 Bde, 1 December 1940, 8/2/21, AWM.

7. *Ibid*, p.34. Russell, *op cit*, p.26. Lavarack diary, 7 January, 5 March 1941. Henry, *op cit*, pp.39, 49. War Diary HQ 7 Div, G Branch, 14, 26–27 February, 1, 5, 23 March 1941, 1/5/14, AWM. Berryman diary, 10 March 1941, Berryman papers. War Diary HQ 21 Bde, 16 March 1941, 8/2/21, AWM. Fearnside (ed.), *Bayonets Abroad: A History of the 2/13th Battalion, A.I.F. in the Second World War*, p.32. Serle (ed.), *The Second Twenty-Fourth Australian Infantry Battalion of the 9th Australian Division*, p.27.

8. War Diary HQ 7 Div, AQ Branch, 5, 9 December 1940, 1/5/15, AWM. Letter, Vasey to wife, 17 November 1940, Vasey papers, Box 2. Long, *To Benghazi*, p.239.

9. There are frequent references in the divisional and brigade war diaries and Lavarack's and Wilson's personal diaries to visits made by Lavarack to formations and units. War Diary HQ 7 Div, G Branch, general comments January and February, 15 January 1941, 10, 13, 18 February, 3, 5, 28 March 1941, 1/5/14, AWM. Lavarack diary, 9 January, 10 February 1941. Burns, *op cit*, p.31.

10. Lavarack diary, 9 January, 10 February 1941. War Diary HQ 7 Div, G Branch, 10, 15 and Appendix 7 December 1940; 13, 17, 23, 24 January and 18 February, 10, 17 March 1941, 1/5/14, AWM. War Diary HQ 7 Div, AQ Branch, 10, 15 December 1940, 1/5/15, AWM. Long, *Greece, Crete and Syria*, p.533.

11. Maj-Gen R.N.L. Hopkins to author, 15 May 1981. War diary HQ 20 Bde, 23 September 1940, 8/2/20, AWM. Serle, *op cit*, pp.15, 23. 7 Aust Div Circulars G.2, 30 April 1940 and G.16, 24 June 1940, War Diary HQ 7 Div, G Branch, April-June 1940, Appendix 2A, 1/5/14, AWM. (See also 12 August 1940). War Diary, HQ 20 Bde, November 1940, 8/2/20, AWM. War Diary HQ 21 Bde, 4 December 1940, 8/2/21, AWM. Norris, *op cit*, p.113. Russell, *op cit*, p.22. Uren, *op cit*, p.30.

12. Lavarack diary, 7 January 1941. War Diary HQ 7 Div, G Branch, 14 January 1941, 1/5/14, AWM. War Diary HQ 21 Bde, 14 January 1941, 8/2/21, AWM. War Diary HQ 20 Bde, 14 January 1941, 8/2/20, AWM. Maughan, *op cit, p.*11. Long, *To Benghazi, p.83*. Long, *Greece, Crete and Syria, p.7*. Burns *op cit*, p.29. Russell, *op cit*, p.27.

13. Wilson diary, 4 February 1941. War Diary HQ 7 Div, G Branch, 4 February 1941; General Comments February and 20 March 1941, 1/5/14, AWM. 1/5/14, AWM). Cable, Menzies to Prime Minister's Department, 11 February 1941, CRS A5954, item Box 265 and letters Blamey to Spender, 1 February 1941, and Spender to Blamey, 7 February 1941, Blamey Papers, 6A [3] AWM). The previous month the Minister for the Army, Spender, and the CGS, Sturdee, had visited (see War Diary HQ 7 Div, G Branch, 2 January 1941, 1/5/14, AWM).

14. Maughan, *op cit*, pp.3, 6.

15. War Diary HQ 7 Div, G Branch, 24–25 February, 13–14, 27 March, general comments 1941, 1/5/14, AWM. Long, *Greece, Crete and Syria*, p.7. Maughan, *op cit*, p.7, 9. Lavarack diary, 25-27 February, 11 March 1941. Letter, Ochiltree to author, 31 August 1981.

16. Letter, Blamey to Minister for the Army, 11 March 1941, Blamey papers 2A[8] and 8A[3]. Letter and notes, Rowell to Lieutenant-Colonel E.E. Rich, 9 October 1945, CAB

106/710, PRO. See also undated notes by Rowell, Gavin Long Correspondence, S.F. Rowell, Part 2, AWM. Rowell also expressed this view to Blamey's biographer: 'Blamey simply didn't want Lavarack to go to Greece—not first anyway. He didn't tell me that, I suppose I assumed it. He liked Mackay, had great faith in him.' Hetherington papers, Box 2, AWM and Hetherington *Blamey: Controversial Soldier*, p.128, and Rowell, *Full Circle*, p.64. Letter, Blamey to Sturdee, 14 March 1941, Blamey papers 2A[7]. See also Cable, Menzies to Minister for the Army, 27 April 1941, Blamey papers 3A[1].

17. Rowell, *Full Circle*, p. 64. Carlyon, *I Remember Blamey*, pp.134–135. As early as 22 January Blamey had raised the possibility of grouping the 18th, 21st and 25th Brigades in the 7th Division because they were the three brigades most ready for war in the 7th and 9th Divisions. Horner, *High Command, p.*71.

18. Signals, Blamey to Lavarack, and Lavarack to Blamey, 27 February 1941, War Diary HQ 7 Div, G Branch, February 1941, 28 February 1941 and Appendix 27, 1/5/14, AWM. Lavarack diary, 28 February 1941. Wilson diary, 28 February 1941. Commander-in-Chief's Diary, 28 February 1941, Blamey papers.

19. Lavarack diary, 7 March 1941. Wilson diary, 7 March 1941.

20. Lavarack diary, 18 March 1941. Wilson diary, 18 March 1941. Letter, Blamey to Plant, 20 March 1941, Blamey papers 3A[2], and cable, Blamey to Minister for the Army, 31 March 1941, Blamey papers 2A[7]. Cable, Wavell to War Office, 3 March 1941, Great Britain, Cabinet Office *Principal War Telegrams and Memoranda, Middle East I*, no.(69). Long, *Greece, Crete and Syria*, pp.37, 39. Stevens, unpublished manuscript, p.35.

9 - 'A bloody insult'

1. War Diary HQ 7 Div G Branch, 3 April 1941, 1/5/14, AWM. Lavarack diary, 3 April 1941. Wilson diary, 3 April 1941. Playfair, *'The Germans Come to the Help of Their Ally' (1941)*, p.33. Long, *The Six Years War*, p.75. Cable, Wavell to VCIGS, 3 April 1941, Blamey papers, 2A[7], 3DRL 6643, AWM. See also cable, C-in-C Middle East to War Office, 3 April 1941, *Principal War Telegrams and Memoranda, 1940–1943, Middle East I.*, no. (36). Maughan, *op cit*, pp.64–65.

2. 'Narrative of Operations in Cyrenaica during period April 7–14, both inclusive, by Lt-Gen Sir John Lavarack' (hereinafter referred to as 'Narrative'), p.2, Lavarack papers 3 (see also AWM 51, item 123 and file 523/7/43). Lavarack diary, 4 April 1941. Wilson diary, 4 April 1941. See Maughan, *op cit*, p.113 where a similar account by Lavarack is recorded. Although the two differ in some minor details they are substantially the same. Lavarack, 'Narrative', p.2. Lavarack diary, 4 April 1941. War Diary HQ 7 Div G Branch, 4 April 1941, 1/5/14, AWM.

3. Cable, Wavell to Blamey, 4 April 1941, Blamey papers 2A[7], 3DRL 6643, AWM. On 4 April the CIGS contacted Blamey in Greece through Wilson (see Blamey papers 2A[7], 3DRL 6643, AWM). Lavarack told Blamey of these events on 5 April (cable in Blamey papers 2A[7]).

4. Collins, *Lord Wavell*, p.372. Cable, Blamey to Wavell, 5 April 1941. Cable, Wavell to Blamey, 5 April 1941, Blamey papers, 2A[7], 3DRL 6643, AWM (also included in *Principal War Telegrams and Memoranda, Middle East I, op cit*). Lavarack, 'Narrative', p.2. Lavarack diary, 5–6 April 1941. War Diary HQ 7 Div G Branch, 5–6 April 1941, 1/5/14, AWM. Maughan, *op cit*, p.85.

5. CIGS Diary of visit to Mediterranean, 1941, 6 April 1941, WO 106/2415. Maughan, *op cit*, p.115. Cable, Wavell to CIGS, 22 April 1941, *Principal War Telegrams and Memoranda, Middle East I*, no. (175). War Diary HQ 7 Div G Branch, 6 April 1941, 1/5/14,

AWM. Lavarack diary, 6 April 1941. Lavarack, 'Narrative', p.3.

6. 'Narrative', p.3. Lavarack diary, 7 April 1941. Wilson diary, 7 April 1941. War Diary HQ 7 Div G Branch, 7 April 1941, 1/5/14, AWM. Eden, *The Reckoning*, pp.278–279. Cable, C-in-C Middle East to War Office, 7 April 1941, *Principal War Telegrams and Memoranda, Middle East I*, no. (70). Cable, Mideast to Austforce, undated, Blamey papers, 4A, 3DRL 6643, AWM. See also Maughan, *op cit*, p.116.

7. Playfair, *op cit*, pp.29–30.

8. The *khamsin* is a fierce sand storm which is prevalent for about fifty days during spring (its name comes from the Arabic word 'khamsun', meaning 'fifty'). Liddell Hart, (ed.), *The Rommel Papers*, p.105.

9. Lavarack diary, 8 April 1941. Wilson diary, 8 April 1941. 'Narrative', p.3. War Diary HQ 7 Div G Branch, 8 April 1941, 1/5/14, AWM. Wilmot, *Tobruk*, pp.80–81. Collins, *op cit*, p.368. Maughan, *op cit*, p.109. Morshead had arrived in *Tobruk* the day before and had already discussed the defence of the fortress with Harding. See Hill, 'Lieutenant-General Sir Leslie Morshead: Commander, 9th Australian Division' in Horner (ed.), *The Commanders*, p.179.

10. Photographic copy of Wavell's instructions, Lavarack papers 3; also in Wilson papers. War Diary HQ 7 Div G Branch, April 1941, Appendix 5, 1/5/14, AWM. War Diary HQ Cyrcom, 8 April 1941, Appendix E, WO 169/1240, PRO. See also Maughan, *op cit*, p.117.

11. Lavarack diary, 8 April 1941. 'Narrative', p.4. Maughan, *op cit*, p.119. Wilmot, *op cit*, p.82.

12. Lavarack, 'Narrative', p.4. Maughan, *op cit*, p.119. Lavarack diary, 8 April 1941.

13. Maughan, *op cit*, pp.119–120. 'Narrative', p.4. Lavarack diary, 8 April 1941.

14. Lavarack, 'Narrative', p.4.

15. Lavarack, 'Narrative', pp.4–5. Wilmot, *op cit*, p.82.

16. Lavarack, 'Narrative', p.5.

17. Lavarack diary, 9 April 1941. Maughan, *op cit*, pp.121–122. Lavarack, 'Narrative', pp.4,6. See also War Diary HQ 7 Div G Branch, 8 April 1941 (refers to 9th), 1/5/14, AWM. Wilmot, *op cit*, pp.84–85.

18. Letter, Lieutenant-General Sir Thomas Daly to author, 4 July 1980. 'Narrative', p.6. Maughan, *op cit*, p.122. War Diary HQ 7 Div G Branch, 8 April 1941, 1/5/14, AWM.

19. 'Narrative', p.6. Lavarack diary, 9 April 1941. Maughan, *op cit*, p.122.

20. Liddell Hart, *The Rommel Papers*, p.121; also quoted in Maughan, *op cit*, p.123, with minor variations.

21. Cable, Lavarack to Wavell, 9 April 1941, Appendix A, War Diary HQ Cyrcom, Lavarack papers 3, 4. Maughan, *op cit*, p.124. Earlier that day Wavell had written to Blamey explaining the situation in Cyrenaica and enclosing a copy of his instructions to Lavarack. Letter, Wavell to Blamey, 9 April 1941, Blamey papers 33.1, 4A, 3DRL 6643, AWM.

22. Maughan, *op cit*, pp.122–125. Lavarack diary, 9–10 April 1941. Wilson diary, 10 April 1941. 'Narrative', pp.6–7.

23. Lavarack diary, 10 April 1941. See also Maughan, *op cit*, p.125. Cable, Wavell to VCIGS, 10 April 1941, *Principal War Telegrams and Memoranda, Middle East I*, no. (84).

24. 'Narrative', p.8. Lavarack diary, 10 April 1941. Maughan, *op cit*, p.129.

25. Lavarack diary, 10 April 1941. 'Narrative', p.8.

26. Maughan, *op cit*, pp.131–132.

27. Signal, Mideast to Cyrcom, 11 April 1941,War Diary HQ Cyrcom, 11 April 1941, Appendix A, WO 169/1240, PRO (a copy of this diary can also be found in Lavarack's papers). This telegram is misquoted in Maughan, *op cit*, p.138. Lavarack diary, 11 April 1941. Annotation by Lavarack on signal, Mideast to Cyrcom, 11 April 1941.

28. Signal, Mideast to Cyrcom, 11 April 1941, War Diary HQ Cyrcom, 11 April 1941, Appendix A, WO 169/1240, PRO. Signal, Lavarack to DCGS, 12 April 1941, War Diary HQ Cyrcom, 12 April 1941, Appendix D, WO 169/1240, PRO. See also Maughan, *op cit*, p.138.

29. Lavarack diary, 11 April 1941. 'Narrative', p.7.

30. Maughan, *op cit*, pp.132–134, 137.

31. War Diary HQ 9 Div G Branch, 11 April 1941, 1/5/20, AWM. Lavarack diary, 11–12 April 1941. Maughan, *op cit*, pp.138–139. Wilmot, *op cit*, p.95. Wilson diary, 12 April 1941.

32. Lavarack diary, 12 April 1941. Wilson diary, 12 April 1941. Maughan, *op cit*, pp.139–141.

33. C-in-C diary, 11 April 1941, 1930 hours, Blamey papers, 3DRL 6643, AWM. Maughan, *op cit*, pp.138–139, 143. Signal, Mideast to Cyrcom, 12 April 1941, War Dairy HQ Cyrcom, 12 April 1941, Appendix C, WO 169/1240, PRO. Wilson diary, 12 April 1941.

34. Horner, *Blamey,* Chapter 8.

35. Annotation by Lavarack on Signal, Mideast to Cyrcom, 12 April 1941, War Dairy HQ Cyrcom, 12 April 1941, Appendix C, WO 169/1240, PRO. Signal, Lavarack to DCGS, 12 April 1941, War Diary HQ Cyrcom, 12 April 1941, Appendix G, WO 169/1240, PRO. See also Maughan, *op cit*, p.143.

36. Maughan, *op cit*, pp.141–142. Wilson (diary, 12 April) gives the time as precisely 9 p.m. and the time of the previous message regarding the infantry tanks as 8 p.m. The order of these two messages is confirmed by Lavarack's diary and some indication of the time of arrival of the latter is given by Lavarack's comment that it came in 'late'. The 7th Division war diary also records that the message arrived at '2100'. Maughan, on the other hand, says that Wavell's cable regarding the reorganisation arrived in the morning and was followed by the message about the tanks (pp.141–143). It may be that he took the times from the transcripts of signals in the Cyrcom HQ war diary, which were probably the times of despatch written on the signals, and not the times of arrival. Lavarack did not receive the information in the signals until some 9–11 hours after the time given in the official history. Cable, DCGS to Lavarack, 12 April 1941, HQ Cyrcom War Diary 12 April 1941, Appendix B, WO 169/1240, PRO.

37. The message was ambiguous since it could have meant that HQ Western Desert Force was to assume command once HQ Cyrcom had arrived, or that Lavarack would assume command of Western Desert Force after he and HQ Cyrcom had arrived. The official history has opted for the argument that it was Lavarack who was to take over because command is exercised by commanders, not by headquarters, and also because the signal said 'in relief Gen Evetts'. Maughan, *op cit*, p.143. Signal, DCGS to Lavarack, 12 April 1941, HQ Cyrcom War Diary 12 April 1941, Appendix B, WO 169/1240, PRO.

38. Lavarack diary, 12 April 1941. Wilson diary, 12 April 1941.

10 - *'I am not conscious of failure at Tobruk...'*

1. Maughan, *op cit*, p.144.

2. Lavarack diary, 13 April 1941. Wilson diary, 13 April 1941. War Diary HQ 9 Div G

Branch, 13 April 1941, 1/5/20, AWM. Maughan, *op cit*, p.145. Original leaflet, Lavarack papers 4; Maughan quotes a leaflet on p.145, but it differs in minor detail.

3. Maughan, *op cit*, p.145.

4. Lavarack diary, 13 April 1941.

5. Maughan, *op cit*, pp.146, 148–150.

6. Lavarack diary, 14 April 1941. Wilson diary, 14 April 1941. Maughan, *op cit*, p.151.

7. Lavarack diary, 14 April 1941. Letter, Lavarack to Wilmot, 15 May 1943, Lavarack papers 12. Maughan, *op cit*, pp.151–153.

8. Wilmot, *op cit*, p.106. Maughan, *op cit*, pp.153–154.

9. Lavarack diary, 14 April 1941. Maughan, *op cit*, p.155. War Dairy HQ Cyrcom, 14 April 1941, Appendix B, WO 169/1240, PRO.

10. 7 Aust Div Circular G.16, 24 June 1940, War Diary HQ 7 Div G Branch, April-June 1940, Appendix 6, 1/5/14, AWM. Wilmot, *op cit*, pp.107–108. Maughan, *op cit*, p.156. Telegram, Wavell to War Office, 14 April 1941, *Principal War Telegrams and Memoranda, Middle East I, op cit*. See also Lewin, *Rommel as Military Commander*, p.39.

11. Lavarack, 'Narrative', p. 9. See also Maughan, *op cit*, p.158. Letter, Brigadier J.G. Ochiltree to author, 31 August 1981.

12. Signal, Wavell to Lavarack, 14 April 1941, War Diary HQ Cyrcom, 13, 14 April 1941, Appendix C, WO 169/1240, PRO. See also Maughan, *op cit*, p.157. Cable, Wavell to CIGS 13 April 1941, *Principal War Telegrams and Memoranda, Middle East I*, no. (94). War Diary HQ 7 Div G Branch, 13 April 1941, 1/5/14, AWM.

13. Letter, Plant to Blamey, 17 April 1941, Blamey papers 33.1 and 4A, 3DRL 6643, AWM. This has been confirmed by Field-Marshal Harding who was then BGS (letter, Harding to author, 31 August 1981).

14. Lavarack diary, 16 April 1941. Telegram, Wavell to CIGS, 13 April 1941, *Principal War Telegrams and Memoranda, Middle East I, op cit*. Beresford-Peirse was also a lieutenant-general.

15. Maughan, *op cit*, pp.157–158. Hetherington, *op cit*, p.162. Carlyon, *op cit*, p.52. See also p.31.

16. Lavarack diary, 14 April 1941. Lavarack thought Harding may have made the remark, but Harding has no recollection of the incident (letter, Harding to author, 4 October 1981). See also Horner, *High Command*, p.92. Playfair, *op cit*, pp.34,37. Quoted in Maughan, *op cit*, p.614.

17. Lavarack diary, 14, 16 April 1941.

18. Lavarack diary, 16, 30 April 1941. Signal, Wavell to Lavarack, 14 April 1941, War Diary HQ Cyrcom, 14 April 1941, Appendix C, WO 169/1240, PRO. Letter, Wavell to Lavarack, 13 May 1941, Lavarack papers 4, 5. See also War Diary HQ 7 Div, G Branch, May 1941, Appendix X, 1/5/14, AWM. Wavell had considered the possibility that he would have to use the remainder of the 7th Division in Cyrenaica (see cable, Wavell to Sturdee, 5 April 1941, Blamey papers 2A[7] 3 DRL 6643, AWM).

19. Letter, Lavarack to Wavell, 8 May 1941, Lavarack papers 4, 5. See also War Diary HQ 7 Div G Branch, 30 April 1941 and May 1941, Appendix X, 1/5/14, AWM. Lavarack diary, 30 April 1941. C-in-C diary, 30 April 1941, Blamey papers, 3DRL 6643, AWM.

20. Letter, Wavell to Lavarack, 13 May 1941, Lavarack papers 4, 5.

21. Telegram, Wavell to Dill, 22 April 1941, *Principal War Telegrams and Memoranda, Middle East I*, no. (175).

22. Telegrams, Wavell to VCIGS, 9 April 1941 and Wavell to Dill, 22 April 1941, *Principal War Telegrams and Memoranda, Middle East I, op cit.* Indeed, on 8 April he had told Sturdee that Lavarack probably would be appointed. Woollcombe, *The Campaigns of Wavell, 1939–1943*, p.105. Maughan writes that Wavell returned on the 12th (p.141). Annotation by Lavarack on a copy of Wavell's letter to him of 13 May, Lavarack papers 5. According to Lavarack, Wavell had shown Blamey Lavarack's letter and his reply.

23. Letter, Lavarack to Long, 26 September 1952, p.2. Gavin Long Correspondence, J.D. Lavarack, Part 1, AWM).

24. Robertson, *Australia at War 1939–1945*, p.15. Gavin Long, *The Six Years War*, p.65. Long *To Benghazi*, p.282. Horner, *High Command*, pp.92–94.

25. Lavarack diary, 8, 30 April 1941.

11 - 'He was almost in tears...'

1. Minutes, 'Conference 1415 hrs 22 Apr 41 Summoned by GOC', 525/1/2, AWM. '7 Aust Div Op Instn No 2. (Matruh Fortress)', War Diary HQ 7 Div G Branch, April 1941, 11 May 1941, Appendix 35, 1/5/14, AWM. Uren, *op cit*, p.38. Letter, Beresford-Peirse to Morshead, 8 May 1941, Blamey papers, 170.15, AWM.

2. Wilson diary, 8 May 1941.

3. Wilmoth interview, 5 May 1981. Carlyon, *op cit*, p.47. Hetherington, *op cit*, pp.157–158. Letter, Vasey to wife, 24 June 1941, Vasey papers, Box 2, NLA MS3782. Original emphasis.

4. Rowell to Hetherington, n.d., Hetherington papers, Box 2, 3DRL 6224, AWM. Carlyon interview, 6 May 1981. Horner, *Blamey*, Chapter 8.

5. Rowell to Long, 20 January 1947, quoted in Horner, *Blamey*, Chapter 8, Footnote 81

6. C-in-C's diary, 24 April 1941, Blamey papers, 3DRL 6643 AWM. Carlyon interview, 6 May 1981. Lavarack diary, 25 April 1941. Wilson diary, 25 April 1941.

7. Wilson diary (looseleaf), 25 April 1941.

8. Wilson interview, 12 May 1980. Lavarack diary, 29 April 1941. Wilson diary (looseleaf), 25, 29 April 1941.

9. Long, *Greece, Crete and Syria*, p.195. In March 1942 Savige denounced Herring. Letter, Hetherington to Herring, 25 November 1970, Hetherington papers, 3DRL 6224, AWM.

10. In 1980 Wilson remained certain that what he had written in his diary was correct. However, Elliott said in 1981 he had no recollection of attending a meeting at which Blamey's recall was discussed. Brigadier C.M.L. Elliott interview, 10 May 1981; Elliott to author 26 September 1982. Wilson interview, 12 May 1980.

11. F.J. Howard, 'Surviving the Hatchetmen', Melbourne *Herald*, 9 April 1974, p.34.

12. Howard interview, 7 May 1981; Rowell to Hetherington, 26 April 1974, Hetherington papers, file 419/89/9, 3DRL 6027. Blamey chastised Robertson in front of Menzies and Shedden, amongst others, for boasting of his exploits at Benghazi (see Hetherington, *op cit*, p.125).

13. Carlyon interview, 6 May 1981. Letter, Hetherington to Herring, 25 November 1970, Hetherington papers, 3DRL 6224, AWM.

14. Letter, Vasey to wife, 16 July 1941, Vasey papers, NLA MS3782, Box 2. See Horner, *Crisis of Command*, pp.183–185, 187, 211–212, 213.

15. Lavarack diary, 30 April 1941.

16. Wilson diary, 8 May 1941. Lavarack diary, 7–9 May 1941. War Diary HQ 7 Div G

Branch, 7 May 1941, & April 1941, Appendix 43, 1/5/14, AWM. Letter, Beresford-Peirse to Lavarack, 2 May 1941, Lavarack papers 3. Letter, Beresford-Peirse to Smith, c.12 May 1941, Blamey papers, 33.1, AWM.

17. Letter, Blamey to Smith, 14 May 1941, Blamey papers 33.1. Blamey to Prime Minister, 15 May 1941, Blamey papers, 6A[8], AWM.

18. Lavarack diary, 20–21 May 1941. Uren, *op cit*, p.38. Kisch to Beresford-Peirse, 24 May 1941, Beresford-Peirse to Lavarack, 25 May 1941, Lavarack papers 3. War Diary HQ 7 Div G Branch, May 1941, Appendix Z; April 1941, Appendix 35, 1/5/14, AWM.

12 - 'He did not want Lavarack as corps commander'

1. 'Extent of German Infiltration into Syria up to 7 June 1941, DDMI(I)/V1/2', Blamey papers 2B[8], AWM. Playfair, *op cit*, vol.2, pp.195, 197, 201–202. Warner, *Iraq and Syria 1941*, p.86. Lewin, *The Chief*, p.140. Telegrams, CIGS to Wavell, 27 April, 19 May 1941; C-in-C, Middle East to War Office, 4 May 1941; Prime Minister to Wavell, 9 May 1941; Wavell to CIGS, 17, 21 May 1941; War Office to the C-in-C, Middle East, 19, 20 May 1941; Wavell to Dill, 20 May 1941; Wavell to Prime Minister, 22 May 1941, *Principal War Telegrams and Memoranda, Middle East 1*, nos.(218), (25), (61), (125), (142), (139), (151), (154), (163) and (181). Long, *Greece, Crete and Syria*, pp.321–322, 326–327. Playfair, *op cit*, vol.2, p.203. Horner, *High Command*, p.7.

2. Playfair, *op cit*, vol.2, pp.210, 205. Long, *Greece, Crete and Syria*, p.33. Winterbotham, *The Ultra Secret*, p.9. Lewin, *Ultra Goes to War: The Secret Story*, *passim*. Hinsley, *British Intelligence in the Second World War*, vol.1, pp.422–423. 'Extent of German Infiltration into Syria up to 7 June 1941', p.1, and signal, Mice to Milpal, 15 June 1941, Blamey papers 2B[8], AWM. See Warner, *op cit*, pp.138–139.

3. War Diary HQ 7 Div G Branch, 22–23 May 1941, 1/5/14, AWM. '7 Aust Div Report on Ops in Syria', p.1, Blamey papers 51, AWM. Long, *Greece, Crete and Syria*, p.336. Lavarack diary, 23 May 1941. War Diary HQ 7 Div G Branch, 23 May 1941, 1/5/14, AWM.

4. Lewin, *The Chief*, pp.57, 87–88. See also Spears, *Fulfilment of a Mission*, pp.117–118, 123–127,132 for examples of Wilson's eccentricities. Letter, Blamey to Menzies, 7 June 1941, Shedden papers, CRS A5954, Box 265. Cable, CIGS to Wavell, 19/4/41, WO216/120, PRO. Later in the war, some Americans also were to form unfavourable impressions of Wilson. See Irving, *The War Between the Generals*, pp.259, 260, 261. 'H.Q. British Forces in Palestine and T.J. Operation Order No.7', 5 June 1941, WO 201/847, PRO. War Diary HQ 7 Div G Branch, June 1941, Appendix D, 1/5/14, AWM. Long, *Greece, Crete and Syria*, p.344.

5. 'H.Q. British Forces in Palestine and T.J. Operation Order No.7', 5 June 1941, WO 201/847, PRO. 'Plan "Exporter"', GHQ ME, 5 June 1941, Blamey papers 2B[8], AWM. Long, *Greece, Crete and Syria*, p.338. See also Playfair, *op cit*, vol.2, pp.206–207.

6. Hinsley, *op cit*, vol.I, p.425. In detail, there were 18 battalions of regular troops (including four Foreign Legion battalions), two tank regiments each equipped with 45 Renault R-35 light tanks armed with a 37mm gun, 150 locally-adapted armoured cars (some also with a 37mm gun), 30 batteries of artillery, and 11 battalions of Levantine troops of doubtful reliability. See Long, *Greece, Crete and Syria*, pp.334,358. Playfair, *op cit*, p.206.

7. 'Outline Plan for Operation "Exporter"', pp.10–11, WO 201/174, PRO. On 20 May the Chiefs of Staff signalled Wavell 'Defence Committee considered that [the] opportunity is too good to miss and the advance must be regarded as a political coup...rather than

as a military operation', signal War Office to the Commander-in-Chief, Middle East, 20 May 1941, *Principal War Telegrams and Memoranda, Middle East 1*, no. (151). Telegram, Prime Minister to Wavell, 21 May 1941, quoted in Churchill, *The Grand Alliance*, p.290. Long, *Greece, Crete and Syria*, pp.327–328, 337.'7 Aust Div Report on Ops in Syria', p.5, Blamey papers 51, AWM.

8. Letter, Lavarack to Long, 26 September 1952, 'Notes on Chapter 16', Gavin Long Correspondence, J.D. Lavarack, Part 1, AWM. Rowell, *op cit*, p.88. Lavarack diary, 5 June 1941. War Diary HQ 7 Div G Branch, 6 June 1941. Wilson, *op cit*, pp.111–112.

9. Blamey had already accepted that Lavarack would be a corps commander if the AIF Divisions and the New Zealand Division were formed into an Australian Corps and an Anzac Corps, thus constituting an Anzac Army, no doubt with Blamey as the commander. 'H.Q. British Forces in Palestine and T.J. Operation Order No.7', p.2, 5 June 1941, WO 201/847, PRO. War Diary HQ 7 Div G Branch, June 1941, Appendix D, 1/5/14, AWM. Rowell, *op cit*, p.84. Cable, Blamey to Menzies, 15 May 1941, Blamey papers, 6A[8], AWM. Long, *To Benghazi*, p.539, and *Greece, Crete and Syria*, pp. 340–341. Maughan, *op cit*, p.307.'H.Q. British Forces in Palestine and T.J. Operation Order No.7', p.2, 5 June 1941, WO 201/847, PRO. War Diary HQ 7 Div G Branch, June 1941, Appendix D, 1/5/14, AWM. Rowell, *op cit*, p.84. Cable, Blamey to Menzies, 15 May 1941, Blamey papers, 6A[8], AWM. Long, *To Benghazi*, p.539, and *Greece, Crete and Syria*, pp. 340–341. Maughan, *op cit*, p.307.

10. Rowell to Hetherington, notes, Hetherington papers, Box 2, AWM.

11. Rowell to Hetherington, notes, Hetherington papers, Box 2, AWM. Wilson diary, 23 May 1941. Lavarack diary, 30 May, 4 June 1941. War Diary HQ 7 Div G Branch, 4–5 June 1941, 1/5/14, AWM. Lavarack diary, 25 May 1941. Rowell, *op cit*, pp.85–86. Hetherington, *op cit*, p.170. See also Horner, *High Command*, pp.109–110. Signal, Mideast to Milpal, 2 June 1941, Blamey papers 2A[11], AWM. Long, *Greece, Crete and Syria*, p.341.

12. Rowell to Hetherington, notes and letter, Brigadier C.M.L. Elliott to Hetherington, 5 January 1971, Hetherington papers, Box 2, AWM. Long, *Greece, Crete and Syria*, p.340. Horner, *Blamey*, Chapter 9.

13. Lavarack diary, 22, 27, 31 May 1941. War Diary HQ 7 Div G Branch, 22, 28 May, 5 June (Appendix A) 1941, 1/5/14, AWM. Long, *Greece, Crete and Syria*, p.336–337. Berryman to Long, 16 June 1952, Gavin Long Correspondence, F.H. Berryman, Part 4, AWM '7 Aust Div Report on Ops in Syria', p.21, Blamey papers 51, AWM.

14. 'Report on the Operations - 1st Australian Corps - In the Campaign in Syria, June-July 1941', p.5, Blamey papers 51, AWM. 'H.Q. British Forces in Palestine and T.J. Operation Order No.7', Appendix A, 'Order of Battle', War Diary HQ 7 Div G Branch, 5 June 1941, 1/5/14, AWM. See also Long, *Greece, Crete and Syria*, p.338n. Playfair, *op cit*, vol.2, p.204. Wilson, *Eight Years Overseas*, p.111.

15. Naval Intelligence Division, *Syria*, Geographical Handbook Series, B.R. 513 (Restricted) (Reprinted 1944), pp.67–68. '7 Aust Div Report on Ops in Syria', p.6, Blamey papers 51, AWM.

16. War Diary HQ 7 Div G Branch, 31 May, 6–7 June 1941. '7 Aust Div Report on Ops in Syria', p.6–7, Blamey papers 51, AWM. Long, *Greece, Crete and Syria*, pp.337, 340. 'Notes on Chapter 16', 26 September 1952, p.1, Gavin Long Correspondence, J.D. Lavarack, Part 1, AWM. Lavarack diary, 31 May, 7 June 1941.

17. War Diary HQ 7 Div G Branch, 8 June 1941, 1/5/14, AWM. Wilson diary, 8 June 1941. Stevens, *op cit*, p.48. Long, *Greece, Crete and Syria*, pp.349–351.

18. Lavarack diary, 8 June 1941. War Diary HQ 7 Div G Branch, 8 June 1941, 1/5/14, AWM. '7 Aust Div Report on Ops in Syria', *op cit*, p.9. Long, *Greece, Crete and Syria*, pp.355–356. The official historian has commented: 'There was little time, however, to bring up the new battalion and organize an attack so soon' (p.368).

19. Long, *Greece, Crete and Syria*, pp.350–352, 356–357. Norris, *op cit*, p.120. Wilson, *op cit*, p.115. Interview, E.S. Eyers, 18 February 1981. The name of the first Australian casualty was Nicholas Koorey. He was seriously wounded and died less than two weeks later. Claire Hunter, 'I was lucky with my life', AWM online article, 5 October 2017, https://www.awm.gov.au/articles/blog/remembering-kelvin-koorey (accessed 3 June 2021).

20. Cable, Blamey to Minister for the Army, 8 June 1941, Blamey papers 2A[11], AWM and annotation on a copy of the cable in Lavarack papers 13. Long, *Greece, Crete and Syria*, pp.357–358, fn 4.

21. Lavarack diary, 9 June 1941. Wilson diary, 9 June 1941. Berryman diary, 9 June 1941. Long, *Greece, Crete and Syria*, p.368.

22. Lavarack diary, 9–10 June 1941. War Diary HQ 7 Div G Branch, 9 June 1941, 1/5/14, AWM. '7 Aust Div Report on Ops in Syria', *op cit*, p.9. Long, *Greece, Crete and Syria*, pp.369–370. Letter, Berryman to Long, 16 June 1952, Gavin Long Correspondence, F.H. Berryman, Part 4, AWM.

23. Stevens, *op cit*, p.51; Notes on Chapter 27, p.20, Gavin Long Correspondence, J.E.S.Stevens, AWM. AWM. War Diary HQ 7 Div G Branch, 11 June 1941, 1/5/14, AWM. 'Seventh Australian Division Report on the Operations in Syria 1941', p.18, Blamey papers 51, AWM.

24. 'Some Notes on the Landing of the SS Battalion on Morning of June 9', Blamey papers 2B[8], AWM. Cable, C-in-C Mediterranean to Admiralty, 9 June 1941, *Principal War Telegrams and Memoranda, Middle East 1*, no.(106). War Diary HQ 7 Div G Branch, 9–10 June 1941, 1/5/14, AWM. Lavarack and Wilson diaries 10 June 1941. '7 Aust Div Report on Ops in Syria', *op cit*, p.9. Long, *Greece, Crete and Syria*, pp.360–67, 375.

25. Notes by Colonel (later Lieutenant-General) V.C. Secombe, Lavarack papers 7.

26. Lavarack diary, 10–11 June 1941. War Diary HQ 7 Div G Branch, 10 June 1941, 1/5/14, AWM. Wilson diary, 10–12 June 1941. Long, *Greece, Crete and Syria*, pp.370–371, 386.

27. War Diary HQ 7 Div G Branch, 11 June 1941, 1/5/14, AWM. Long, *Greece, Crete and Syria*, pp.386–387. '7 Aust Div Report on Ops in Syria', *op cit*, p.9. Letter, Lavarack to Long, 14 February 1945, Gavin Long Correspondence, J.D.Lavarack, Part 2, AWM. Lavarack diary, 11 June 1941. Letter, Berryman to Long, n.d., Gavin Long Correspondence, F.H. Berryman, Part 3, p.7, AWM. 'Todforce' comprised the following: The Scots Greys; one squadron, 6th Australian Cavalry Regiment; one battery, 2nd Australian Anti-Tank Regiment; one section, 170th Light Anti-Aircraft Battery; one company, 2/3rd Machine Gun Battalion; one battery of 25pdr field guns; one section, Royal Australian Engineers.

28. War Diary HQ 7 Div G Branch, 11 June 1941, 1/5/14, AWM. Long, *Greece, Crete and Syria*, pp.375–378.

29. War Diary HQ 7 Div G Branch, 11–12 June, 1/5/14, AWM. Signal, Blamey to Sturdee, 12 June 1941, Blamey papers 2A[4], AWM. Wilson diary, 12 June 1941. Lavarack diary, 12 June 1941. See also letter, Lavarack to Long, 26 September 1952, 'Notes on Chapter 19', Gavin Long Correspondence, J.D.Lavarack, Part 1, AWM. Curtis Wilson wrote that Wavell 'Fubbed off recommendation by Lavarack for an immediate D.S.O. for Brig

Stevens with remark about waiting until the fight was won'—Wilson diary (looseleaf), 12 June 1941.

30. Lewin, *The Chief*, p.144, 146n. Playfair, *op cit*, vol.2, pp.244–246.

31. Telegram, the Commander-in-Chief, Palestine, to the War Office, 12 June 1941, *Principal War Telegrams and Memoranda, Middle East 1*, no.(168). Long, *Greece, Crete and Syria*, p.391–392. Letters, Lavarack to Long, 10 October 1952 and 26 September 1952 (notes Chapters 16 and 19), Gavin Long Correspondence, J.D. Lavarack, Part 1, AWM. For an exposition of Wavell's difficulties see Playfair, *op cit*, vol.2, pp.204–205.

32. Lavarack, Wilson and Berryman diaries, 12 June 1941. War Diary HQ 7 Div G Branch, 12 June 1941, 1/5/14, AWM. '7 Aust Div Report on Ops in Syria', *op cit*, p.9. Long, *Greece, Crete and Syria*, p.388.

33. '7 Aust Div Report on Ops in Syria', *op cit*, pp.9–10. Long, *Greece, Crete and Syria*, pp.378–379, 387–388. Lavarack diary, 12 June 1941. Letter, Lavarack to Long, 14 February 1945, Gavin Long Correspondence, J.D.Lavarack, Part 2, AWM.

34. Lavarack diary, 12 June 1941. War Diary HQ 7 Div G Branch, 13 June 1941, 1/5/14, AWM. Berryman diary, 13 June 1941. '7 Aust Div Report on Ops in Syria', *op cit*, p.9. Long, *Greece, Crete and Syria*, pp.387–388.

35. Long, *Greece, Crete and Syria*, pp.388–389. See also '7 Aust Div Report on Ops in Syria', *op cit*, p.10. War Diary HQ 7 Div G Branch, 13 June 1941, 1/5/14, AWM. Wilson diary, 13 June 1941.

36. Wilson diary, 14 June 1941. '7 Aust Div Report on Ops in Syria', *op cit*, p.9. The units under Monaghan's command included the 2/33rd Battalion, the 6th Australian Cavalry Regiment, the 10th Field Battery, and detachments of engineers and anti-tank guns (see Long, *Greece, Crete and Syria*, p.395). Lavarack appears to have altered the role of the Greys between the night of the 12th and the morning of the 14th from probing the routes leading out of the town to internal security (see Long, *Greece, Crete and Syria*, pp.387–388). Lavarack granted permission for a company attack on Poste Christofini, 'with the general intention of eventually seizing Hasbaya [to the west], which is still occupied by the French, and is rather a thorn in our sides'. War Diary HQ 7 Div G Branch, 14 June 1941, 1/5/14, AWM. Wilson diary, 14 June 1941.

37. Letter, Berryman to Long, 16 June 1952, Gavin Long Correspondence, F.H. Berryman, Part 4, AWM. Long, *Greece, Crete and Syria*, pp.380–381, 389–390. War Diary HQ 7 Div G Branch, 13–14 June 1941, 1/5/14, AWM. '7 Aust Div Report on Ops in Syria', *op cit*, p.10. Wilson diary, 13–14 June 1941.

38. The scratch reserve consisted of: the 2/3rd Machine Gun Battalion (less two companies) and the 2nd Anti-Tank Regiment (less three batteries) were in the Er Rama area; the 2/2nd Pioneer Battalion was at the Litani west of Merdjayoun; and the Scots Greys was in Merdjayoun itself. '7 Aust Div Report on Ops in Syria', *op cit*, p.10. Long, *Greece, Crete and Syria*, pp.382–384, 393. Wilson diary, 14 June 1941.

13 - 'We have Damascus in our pocket...'

1. '7 Aust Div Report on Ops in Syria', *op cit*, p.11. Telegram, Commander-in-Chief, Middle East to War Office, 15 June 1941, *Principal War Telegrams and Memoranda, Middle East 1*, no.(208). War Diary HQ 7 Div G Branch, 15 June 1941, 1/5/14, AWM. Wilson diary, 15 June 1941. Curtis Wilson noted that Sidon fell at 3 p.m. and that Lavarack became aware of the French counter-attack 'shortly afterwards', probably about 4.30 p.m. according to the divisional war diary. Long, *Greece, Crete and Syria*, pp.384–386, 394–395.

2. War Diary HQ 7 Div G Branch, 15 June 1941, 1/5/14, AWM. Long, *Greece, Crete and Syria*, pp.395–400. See Wilson, *op cit*, p.115. '7 Aust Div Report on Ops in Syria', *op cit*, p.10. Letter, Lavarack to Long, 1 October 1952, Gavin Long Correspondence, J.D.Lavarack, Part 1; and letter, Berryman to Long, 16 June 1952, Gavin Long Correspondence, F.H. Berryman, Part 4, AWM. Henri de Wailly, *Invasion Syria 1941*, p. 146.

3. Letter, Lavarack to Long, 1 October 1952, Gavin Long Correspondence, J.D. Lavarack, Part 1, AWM; cable, Blamey to Sturdee, 16 June 1941, Blamey papers 2A [4], AWM. Gavin Long Diaries and Notebooks, N66/26, 27, AWM. Berryman diary, 8 June 1941. Stevens, *op cit*, p.34. Lavarack left it to Allen to decide whether Monaghan remained in command of the 2/33rd Battalion. (Lavarack to Allen, 19 June 1941, Lavarack papers 7).

4. Allen to Long, Gavin Long Diaries and Notebooks, N66/26, AWM.Letter, Lavarack to Long, 14 February 1945, Gavin Long Correspondence, J.D.Lavarack, Part 2, AWM. See also Lavarack to Long, 26 September 1952, Gavin Long Correspondence, J.D.Lavarack, Part 1, AWM.

5. '7 Aust Div Report on Ops in Syria', *op cit*, p.38. Letter, Lavarack to Long, 14 February 1945, Gavin Long Correspondence, J.D.Lavarack, Part 2, AWM. De Wailly, *op cit*, pp. 45, 146.

6. War Diary HQ 7 Div G Branch, 15–16 June 1941, 1/5/14, AWM. '7 Aust Div Report on Ops in Syria', *op cit*, pp.10–11. Letter, Berryman to Long, 18 August 1952, Gavin Long Correspondence, F.H. Berryman, Part 4, AWM. Berryman to Long, n.d., Gavin Long Correspondence, F.H. Berryman, Part 3, AWM. Berryman diary, 15 June 1941. Long, *Greece, Crete and Syria*, pp.400–401, 405.

7. Hill, *op cit*, p.175. '7 Aust Div Report on Ops in Syria', *op cit*, pp.10–11. Long, *Greece, Crete and Syria*, pp.400–401. War Diary HQ 7 Div G Branch, 15 June 1941, 1/5/14, AWM. War Diary HQ 7 Div G Branch, 15 June 1941, 1/5/14, AWM.

8. War Diary HQ 7 Div G Branch, 16–17 June 1941, 1/5/14, AWM. Long, *Greece, Crete and Syria*, pp.400–404.

9. The units were: the Scots Greys; 6th Australian Cavalry Regiment (less two squadrons); 2/33rd and 2/25th Infantry Battalions; 2/2nd Pioneer Battalion (plus one company of the 2/5th Battalion); 2/5th Field Regiment (plus one troop 2/6th Field Regiment); one troop 57th Light Anti-Aircraft Battery; one section 2/5th Field Company; one company 2/3rd Machine Gun Battalion; and 8th Australian Anti-Tank Battery. The troops from the 2/3rd Machine Gun Battalion and 2/2nd Anti-Tank Regiment which had been sent north to guard Metulla the night before were not placed under Berryman's command immediately. Wilson diary, 16 June 1941. Berryman diary, 16 June 1941. Berryman to Long, n.d., Gavin Long Correspondence, F.H.Berryman, Part 3, AWM. '7 Aust Div Report on Ops in Syria', *op cit*, p.11. Long, *Greece, Crete and Syria*, pp.400, 401, 404–406. War Diary HQ 7 Div G Branch, 16–17 June 1941, 1/5/14, AWM.

10. Wilson and Berryman diaries, 17 June 1941. War Diary HQ 7 Div G Branch, 17 June 1941, 1/5/14, AWM. '7 Aust Div Report on Ops in Syria', *op cit*, p.12. Long, *Greece, Crete and Syria*, pp.408–409, 412–413.

11. De Wailly, *op cit*, pp.220-223.

12. Wilson and Berryman diaries, 17 June 1941. War Diary HQ 7 Div G Branch, 17 June 1941, 1/5/14, AWM. '7 Aust Div Report on Ops in Syria', *op cit*, p.12. Long, *Greece, Crete and Syria*, pp.408–409, 412–413.

13. Stevens, *op cit*, p.51. Letter, Lavarack to Long, 1 October 1952, Gavin Long Correspondence, J.D.Lavarack, Part 1, AWM. See War Diary HQ 7 Div G Branch, 18

June 1941, 1/5/14, AWM.

14. 'Report by General Sir H.M. Wilson on the Campaign in Syria', p.62, CAB 106/695, PRO. It should also be noted that in addition to the tactical problems, Lavarack had to deal as well with the civil administration of towns captured from the French, which included attempting to remedy problems such as food shortages. See 'Report No.1/41 from Political Officer attached to Australian Division Exporter', War Diary HQ 7 Div A&Q Branch, 12 June 1941, 1/5/15, AWM.

15. War Diary HQ 7 Div G Branch, 18 June 1941, 1/5/14, AWM. '7 Aust Div Report on Ops in Syria', *op cit*, pp.12–13.

16. Lavarack diary, 18 June 1941.

17. Rogers, 'Say Not The Struggle', p.54. See also Elliott to Hetherington, 5 January 1971, Hetherington papers, Box 2, AWM. Hetherington, *op cit*, p.171. The air of unreality surrounding Wilson's headquarters has been confirmed by Lieutenant-Colonel R.L. Holmes, an intelligence officer at one time attached to the headquarters (interview, 26 May 1983).Wilson diary, 16 June 1941.

18. Rowell to Hetherington, n.d., Hetherington papers, Box 2, 3DRL 6624, AWM. See documents held in CAB 106/122, PRO. Wilson diary, 16 June 1941. War Diary HQ 1 Aust Corps G Branch, 17 June 1941, 1/4/1, AWM. Letter, Blamey to Sturdee, 26 June 1941, Blamey papers 5A, AWM.

19. Lavarack diary, 18 June 1941. Wilson diary, 18 June 1941. Signal, Aust Corps to Ausforce, 18 June 1941, Blamey papers 2A[11], AWM. Long, *Greece, Crete and Syria*, pp.413–414, 440. Intelligence Summary No.22, HQ Aust Div Exporter, 17 June 1941, Lavarack papers 7. War Diary HQ 1 Aust Corps G Branch, 2–17 June 1941, 1/4/1, AWM. Rowell, *op cit*, pp.88–90.

20. War Diary HQ 1 Aust Corps G Branch, 18 June 1941, 1/4/1, AWM. 'Report on the Operations - 1st Australian Corps - In the Campaign in Syria, June-July 1941', Appendix A, 'Summary of Operations - Syrian Campaign 1941 up to 18 Jun 41', Blamey papers 51, AWM. Long, *Greece, Crete and Syria*, p.414. Signal, Blamey to Sturdee, 16 June 1941, MP729/7, item 35/421/48. Playfair, *op cit*, vol.2, p.215.

21. Narrative, Historical Section, Iraq and Syria, pp.53–54, CAB 44/127, PRO. Gavin Long Notebook 76, pp.26–28, AWM and also letter, Berryman to Long, 18 August 1952, Gavin Long Correspondence, F.H. Berryman, part 4, AWM. Lavarack diary, 18 June 1941. 'Seventh Australian Division Report on the Operations in Syria 1941', p.13, Blamey papers 51, AWM. Long, *Greece, Crete and Syria*, p.414.

22. 'Seventh Australian Division Report on the Operations in Syria 1941', p.13, Blamey papers 51, AWM. Long, *Greece, Crete and Syria*, pp.407, 411, 415–417. War Diary HQ 1 Aust Corps G Branch, 19 June 1941, 1/4/1, AWM. Signal, Wavell to War Office, 19 June 1941, *Principal War Telegrams and Memoranda, Middle East 1*. Cable, Blamey to Sturdee, 23 June 1941, MP729/7, item 35/421/48. Lavarack diary, 19 June 1941. 'Report on the Operations - 1st Australian Corps - In the Campaign in Syria, June-July 1941', pp.1–2, Blamey papers 51, AWM. '1 Aust Corps Op Instn No.21', War Diary HQ 1 Aust Corps G Branch, 19 June 1941, Appendix D, 1/4/1, AWM.

23. 'Report on the Operations - 1st Australian Corps - In the Campaign in Syria, June-July 1941', p.2, Blamey papers 51, AWM. Commander-in-Chief's diary, 19 June 1941, Blamey papers, AWM. Hetherington, *op cit*, p.172 (Hetherington wrote that Blamey telephoned Wilson before he left Lavarack's headquarters and then drove directly to Wilson's house. Blamey's official diary records that he telephoned on arrival in Jerusalem and fifteen minutes later arrived to see Wilson in person). Carlyon, *op cit*, p.59. Lavarack

diary, 19–20 June 1941. Berryman diary, 19 June 1941. 'Seventh Australian Division Report on the Operations in Syria 1941', p.13, Blamey papers 51, AWM. War Diary HQ 1 Aust Corps G Branch, 19 June 1941, 1/4/1, AWM. Long, *Greece, Crete and Syria,* pp.418, 443–446. War Diary HQ 7 Div G Branch, 19 June 1941, 1/5/14, AWM. Wilson diary, 19 June 1941.

24. Signal, Evetts to Lavarack, 20 June 1941, 225/1/11, AWM. War Diary HQ 7 Div G Branch, 20 June 1941, 1/5/14, AWM. 'Seventh Australian Division Report on the Operations in Syria 1941', p.14, Blamey papers 51, AWM. War Diary HQ 1 Aust Corps G Branch, 20 June 1941, Appendices F and G, 1/4/1, AWM. Lavarack diary, 20 June 1941. By the evening of the 20th Evetts' force comprised the 5th Indian and 16th British Brigades, and the 2/3rd, 2/5th and 2/3rd MG Battalions (Long, *Greece, Crete and Syria,* p.419). Letter, Lavarack to Long, 1 October 1952, Gavin Long Correspondence, J.D. Lavarack, Part 1, AWM.

25. Lavarack diary, 20 June 1941. 'Report on the Operations - 1st Australian Corps - In the Campaign in Syria, June-July 1941', p.2 and '6 Division Report on Syrian Operations June-July 1941', pp.1–2, Blamey papers 51, AWM. War Diary HQ 1 Aust Corps G Branch, 21 June 1941, 20 June 1941 Appendix G, and 1 Aust Corps Operation Instruction No.22, 20 June 1941 Appendix E, 1/4/1, AWM. See Long, *Greece, Crete and Syria,* pp.418–427; Bean, *Anzac to Amiens,* p.509.

26. Lavarack diary, 21 June 1941. Wilson diary, 21 June 1941. Letter, Lavarack to Long, 26 September 1952, 'Notes on Chapter 21', Gavin Long Correspondence, J.D. Lavarack, Part 1, AWM.

27. See Hetherington, *op cit,* p.172. Carlyon, *op cit,* p.59.

28. Carlyon interview, 6 May 1981 See Lavarack diary, 19 June 1941. War Diary HQ 1 Aust Corps G Branch, 21 June 1941, 1/4/1, AWM.

29. '1 Aust Corps Intelligence Summaries, Syria, Jun/Jul 1941', No.1, 20–21 June 1941, Lavarack papers 7. Long, *Greece, Crete and Syria,* pp.446–447. Berryman diary, 22 June 1941.

30. Lavarack diary, 22 June 1941. War Diary HQ 7 Div G Branch, 22 June 1941 and appendix, 1/5/14, AWM. 'Seventh Australian Division Report on the Operations in Syria 1941', p.15, Blamey papers 51, AWM. Letter, Allen to Long, 11 October 1952, Gavin Long Correspondence, A.S. Allen, AWM. Rowell, *op cit,* p.91. Letter, Lavarack to Long, 26 September 1952, 'Notes on Chapter 21', Gavin Long Correspondence, J.D. Lavarack, Part 1, AWM.

31. Letter, Lavarack to Long, 26 September 1952, 'General Note to Chapter 16' and 'Notes on Chapter 21', Gavin Long Correspondence, J.D. Lavarack, Part 1, AWM. See also Lavarack and Wilson diaries, 23 June 1941. Obviously Lavarack is referring to the country around Merdjayoun only, for Wavell had watched the fall of Damascus several days earlier (see Wilson, *op cit,* p.428).

32. Letter, Berryman to Long, n.d., Gavin Long Correspondence, F.H. Berryman, Part 3, AWM. Lavarack diary, 23 June 1941. Wilson diary, 23 June 1941. According to the official history, however, it was at about this time that Wavell was arriving at Lavarack's headquarters. Long wrote that Wavell spent the night of the 23rd there and that it was then, during discussions with Lavarack, that he offered the opinion that a battalion of infantry tanks would have been a better investment in Syria than in the Western Desert (Long, *Greece, Crete and Syria,* p.430n). It is clear, however, that this was not the case. Lavarack recorded in his diary that Wavell's remarks were made on the 22nd and that the commander-in-chief spent that night at 1 Aust Corps HQ (Lavarack diary, 22 June 1941). The timing of Wavell's visit is verified also by the

diaries of Lavarack's ADC and Berryman, and by the war diary of the 7th Division. (See Wilson diary, Berryman diary, and War Diary HQ 7 Div G Branch, 23 June 1941, 1/5/14, AWM. See also letter, Lavarack to Long, 26 September 1952, Gavin Long Correspondence, J.D. Lavarack, Part 1, AWM). Long, *Greece, Crete and Syria*, pp.447–448.

33. Lavarack diary, 21 June 1941. War Diary HQ 1 Aust Corps G Branch, 21 June 1941, 1/4/1, AWM. Long, *Greece, Crete and Syria*, p.430. 'Report on the Operations - 1st Australian Corps - In the Campaign in Syria, June-July 1941', pp.2–3, Blamey papers 51, AWM.

34. Intelligence notes, 23 June 1941, Lavarack papers 7. Signal, Blamey to Sturdee, 7 July 1941, Blamey papers 2A[4], AWM. '1 Aust Corps Intelligence Summaries, Syria, Jun/Jul 1941', No.4, 23–24 June 1941, Lavarack papers 7. Lavarack diary, 24 June 1941. 'Seventh Australian Division Report on the Operations in Syria 1941, p.15, and 'Report on the Operations - 1st Australian Corps - In the Campaign in Syria, June-July 1941', p.3, Blamey papers 51, AWM. Long, *Greece, Crete and Syria*, pp.431, 449.

35. Lavarack diary, 24–25 June 1941. War Diary HQ 7 Div G Branch, 24 June 1941, 1/5/14, AWM. War Diary HQ 1 Aust Corps G Branch, 24 June 1941, Appendix H, 1/4/1, AWM. 'Report on the Operations - 1st Australian Corps - In the Campaign in Syria, June-July 1941', p.3, Blamey papers 51, AWM.'1 Aust Corps Intelligence Summaries, Syria, Jun/Jul 1941', No.5, 24–25 June 1941, Lavarack papers 7. See also letter, Lavarack to Long, 26 September 1952, Gavin Long Correspondence, J.D. Lavarack, Part 1, AWM. Wilson diary, 25, 28 June 1941.

36. '6 Division Report on Syrian Operations June-July 1941', p.2, Blamey papers 51, AWM. GOC Intelligence Notes, 26 June 1941, Lavarack papers 7. Long, *Greece, Crete and Syria*, p.467. War Diary HQ 1 Aust Corps G Branch, 26 June 1941, 1/4/1, AWM. Letter, Lavarack to Long, 26 September 1952, Gavin Long Correspondence, J.D. Lavarack, Part 1, AWM.

14 - 'What he fears above all things is my success'

1. Lavarack and Wilson diaries, 26 June 1941. Letter, Lavarack to Long, 26 September 1952, p.7, 'Notes on Chapter 24', Gavin Long Correspondence, J.D. Lavarack, Part 1, AWM.

2. 'Report on the Operations - 1st Australian Corps - In the Campaign in Syria, June-July 1941', p.4, Blamey papers 51, AWM. Lavarack diary, 26 June 1941. Long, *Greece, Crete and Syria*, p.467. The 17th Brigade comprised the 2/3rd and 2/5th Infantry Battalions, and the 2/2nd Pioneer Battalion.

3. 'Report on the Operations - 1st Australian Corps - In the Campaign in Syria, June-July 1941', p.4 and 'Seventh Australian Division Report on the Operations in Syria 1941', p.16, Blamey papers 51, AWM. Long, *Greece, Crete and Syria*, p.467n.

4. '1 Aust Corps Intelligence Summaries, Syria, Jun/Jul 1941', No.9, 28–29 June 1941, Lavarack papers 7. GOC Intelligence Notes, 29 June 1941, Lavarack papers 7.

5. Quoted in Long, *Greece, Crete and Syria*, p.511. Curtis Wilson's diary (29 June) suggests that Lavarack received permission the day before to send the message, not on the 30th as Long has recorded. Unfortunately, Lavarack made no entry in his diary for the 29th. De Wailly, *op cit*, pp.129, 261-3, 266 (de Wailly gives the wrong date for Lavarack's message to Dentz). Smith, *England's Last War Against France*, p.262.

6. Lavarack diary, 2 July 1941. Long, *Greece, Crete and Syria*, p.474. War Diary HQ 7 Div G Branch, 1–2 July 1941, 1/5/14, AWM. '1 Aust Corps Intelligence Summaries, Syria,

Jun/Jul 1941', No.12 (1/2 July 1941), (No.13, 2/3 July 1941), Lavarack papers 7. War Diary HQ 1 Aust Corps G Branch, 4 July 1941, 1/4/1, AWM. 'Seventh Australian Division Report on the Operations in Syria 1941', p.16; '6 Division Report on Syrian Operations June-July 1941', p.2; 'Report on the Operations - 1st Australian Corps - In the Campaign in Syria, June-July 1941', p.4, Blamey papers 51, AWM.

7. Lavarack diary, memorandum at the end of June 1941, 4 July 1941. Wilson diary, 4 July 1941. GOC Intelligence Notes, 3–5 July 1941, Lavarack papers 7. Long, *Greece, Crete and Syria*, pp.474, 477. War Diary HQ 7 Div G Branch, 3 July 1941, 1/5/14, AWM. See also '1 Aust Corps Op Order No.4', War Diary HQ 1 Aust Corps G Branch, 4 July 1941, Appendix R, 1/4/1, AWM.

8. '1 Aust Corps Op Instn No.27', War Diary HQ 1 Aust Corps G Branch, 2 July 1941, Appendix M, 1/4/1, AWM. 'Report on the Operations - 1st Australian Corps - In the Campaign in Syria, June-July 1941', p.2, Blamey papers 51, AWM. Long, *Greece, Crete and Syria*, pp.469, 525.

9. Lavarack diary, memorandum at the end of June 1941, 4 July 1941. Wilson diary, 4 July 1941. See also '1 Aust Corps Op Order No.4', War Diary HQ 1 Aust Corps G Branch, 4 July 1941, Appendix R, 1/4/1, AWM.

10. Lavarack and Wilson diaries, 6 July 1941. '1 Aust Corps Intelligence Summaries, Syria, Jun/Jul 1941', No.16, 5/6 July 1941, Lavarack papers 7. War Diary HQ 7 Div G Branch, 6 July 1941, 1/5/14, AWM.

11. War Diary HQ 7 Div G Branch, 6–7 July 1941, 1/5/14, AWM. '1 Aust Corps Intelligence Summaries, Syria, Jun/Jul 1941', Nos 16 (5–6 July), 17 (6–7 July 1941), No.18 (7–8 July 1941), Lavarack papers 7. Lavarack diary, 6–7 July 1941. Wilson diary, 6 July 1941. See also Long, *Greece, Crete and Syria*, p.505.

12. Lavarack diary, 7 July 1941.

13. '1 Aust Corps Intelligence Summaries, Syria, Jun/Jul 1941', No.17, 6–7 July 1941, Lavarack papers 7. Lavarack diary, memorandum at the end of June 1941.

14. '1 Aust Corps Intelligence Summaries, Syria, Jun/Jul 1941', No.18, 7–8 July 1941, No.19, 8/9 July 1941, Lavarack papers 7. '1 Aust Corps Op Instn No.29', War Diary HQ 1 Aust Corps G Branch, 8 July 1941, Appendix T, 1/4/1, AWM. War Diary HQ 7 Div G Branch, 8 July 1941, 1/5/14, AWM. Lavarack diary, 8 July 1941. Wilson diary, 8 July 1941. Allen to Long, Gavin Long Notebooks and Diaries, N66/24, AWM.

15. '1 Aust Corps Intelligence Summaries, Syria, Jun/Jul 1941', No.19, 8/9 July 1941, Lavarack papers 7. War Diary HQ 1 Aust Corps G Branch, 9 July 1941, 1/4/1, AWM. War Diary HQ 7 Div G Branch, 9 July 1941, 1/5/14, AWM. Long, *Greece, Crete and Syria*, p.502. Lavarack diary, 9 July 1941. 'Report on the Operations - 1st Australian Corps - In the Campaign in Syria, June-July 1941', p.5, Blamey papers 51, AWM.

16. Lavarack diary, 9 July 1941. See also War Diary HQ 1 Aust Corps G Branch, 9 July 1941, 1/4/1, AWM. War Diary HQ 7 Div G Branch, 9 July 1941, 1/5/14, AWM.

17. War Diary HQ 1 Aust Corps G Branch, 9 July 1941, 1/4/1, AWM. War Diary HQ 7 Div G Branch, 9 July 1941, 1/5/14, AWM. 'Report on the Operations - 1st Australian Corps - In the Campaign in Syria, June-July 1941', p.5, Blamey papers 51, AWM. Long, *Greece, Crete and Syria*, pp.502–503. Lavarack diary, 10 July 1941. '1 Aust Corps Intelligence Summaries, Syria, Jun/Jul 1941', No.20, 9–10 July 1941, Lavarack papers 7. GOC Intelligence Notes, 10 July 1941, Lavarack papers 7.

18. '6 Division Report on Syrian Operations June-July 1941', p.3, Blamey papers 51, AWM. Long, *Greece, Crete and Syria*, p.509. Lavarack diary, 9–10 July 1941. War Diary HQ 1 Aust Corps G Branch, 10 July 1941, 1/4/1, AWM. '1 Aust Corps Intelligence Summaries,

Syria, Jun/Jul 1941', No.20, 9–10 July 1941, Lavarack papers 7. 'Report on the Operations - 1st Australian Corps - In the Campaign in Syria, June-July 1941', p.5, Blamey papers 51, AWM. De Wailly, *op cit*, pp.234-5.

19. There was some confusion about whether Lavarack had approved all Evett's attacks. Questions about the role of his division in and around Damascus were ignored by Evetts in correspondence with the author, although answers to others were provided (letters, author to Evetts, 12 April 1981; Evetts to author, 24 April 1981). See letter, Lavarack to Long, 26 September 1952, and Draft of Chapter 25 'The Battle of Damour', page 63, note 1. 'Notes on Chapter 25', Gavin Long Correspondence, J.D. Lavarack, Part 1, AWM. Lavarack diary, 9 July 1941. GOC Intelligence Notes, 10 July 1941, Lavarack papers 7.

20. Letter, Berryman to Long, 18 August 1952, Gavin Long Correspondence, F.H. Berryman, Part 4, AWM. Letter, Lavarack to Long, 10 October 1952, Gavin Long Correspondence, J.D. Lavarack, Part 1, AWM. Evetts took the Australian 2/3rd Battalion from line of communications duties despite orders that he was not to do so unless he could replace it with another battalion. Interview with Evetts, 11 December 1946, Historical Section Files (Archivist and Librarian Services) 1939 to 1967, Comments Iraq and Syria, CAB 106/896, PRO. Wilson diary, 9 July 1941, 19 September 1941, 8 November 1941.

21. '6 Division Report on Syrian Operations June-July 1941', pp.3–4, Blamey papers 51, AWM. 'Report on the Operations - 1st Australian Corps - In the Campaign in Syria, June-July 1941', p.5, Blamey papers 51, AWM. War Diary HQ 1 Aust Corps G Branch, 11 July 1941, 1/4/1, AWM. See also Long, *Greece, Crete and Syria*, pp.504–505, 509–511. Lavarack diary, 11 July 1941. '1 Aust Corps Intelligence Summaries, Syria, Jun/Jul 1941', No.21, 10–11 July 1941, Lavarack papers 7. Wilson diary, 11 July 1941.

22. Lavarack diary, 11 July 1941. Long, *Greece, Crete and Syria*, pp.511–513.

23. Long, *Greece, Crete and Syria*, p.513 (see also p.511). War Diary HQ 7 Div G Branch, 11 July 1941, 1/5/14, AWM. War Diary HQ 1 Aust Corps G Branch, 11 July 1941, 1/4/1, AWM. '1 Aust Corps Intelligence Summaries, Syria, Jun/Jul 1941', No.22, 11–12 July 1941, Lavarack papers 7.

24. Letter, Lavarack to Blamey, 11 July 1941, Blamey papers 8A[3], AWM. See also Long, *Greece, Crete and Syria*, p.512; Mockler, *Our Enemies the French*, pp.186–187. Lavarack's letter was forwarded by Blamey to the minister for the army, Spender. Blamey added: 'I know nothing of the circumstances, but I do know we have a considerable amount of trouble with the B.B.C. and I thought perhaps I should forward this privately to you' (letter, 19 July 1941, Blamey to Spender, Blamey papers 8A[3], AWM). Spender replied that he would place the matter before the prime minister (letter, Spender to Blamey, 7 August 1941, Blamey papers 8A[3], AWM).

25. '1 Aust Corps Intelligence Summaries, Syria, Jun/Jul 1941', No.22, 11–12 July 1941, Lavarack papers 7. See also Long, *Greece, Crete and Syria*, p.511; '7 Aust Div Report on Ops in Syria', *op cit*, p.19; '17 Australian Infantry Brigade Report on Operations in Syria - July 1941', p.14, Blamey papers 50, AWM.

26. Hetherington, *op cit*, pp.325–326. Hetherington's source for this story is Wills himself, who told him: 'In Syria the ceasefire was to be at midnight. Tubby Allen, very tight, rang up and said the French hadn't ceased firing on his front and he was going to open fire again. I told him he mustn't —if he had it might have led to a general resumption of the fighting and added to the casualties on each side—but he was difficult. I went and woke Lavarack and told him the trouble. I said, "Will you speak to General Allen, sir [?]" "No I won't", he snapped and turned over in bed dismissing me. I managed to get

hold of John Chapman and told him Lavarack had issued instructions that in no circumstances were the Australians to reopen fire.' Wills to Hetherington, n.d., Hetherington papers, Box 2, 3DRL 6224, AWM.

27. It will be recalled that Lavarack's order issued at 9.10 p.m. on the 11th had stated that full military precautions were to be taken. Notes by Lavarack, 12 July 1941, Lavarack papers 7. War Diary HQ 7 Div G Branch, 12 July 1941, 1/5/14, AWM.

28. Notes by Lavarack, 12 July 1941, Lavarack papers 7.

29. Notes by Lavarack, 12 July 1941, Lavarack papers 7. War Diary HQ 7 Div G Branch, 12 July 1941, 1/5/14, AWM. Lavarack diary, 12 July 1941.

30. Lavarack diary, 12 July 1941.

31. Notes by Lavarack, 12 July 1941, Lavarack papers 7. '1 Aust Corps Intelligence Summaries, Syria, Jun/Jul 1941', No.22, 11–12 July 1941, Lavarack papers 7. War Diary HQ 7 Div G Branch, 12 July 1941, 1/5/14, AWM.

32. It is worth reiterating that this incident appears in Hetherington's second Blamey biography published after Lavarack's death, when there was no risk of facing a libel suit. See Bridge, Carl, review of David Horner, *Blamey: the Commander-in-Chief*, in *Journal of the Australian War Memorial*, Issue 34.

33. '1 Aust Corps Intelligence Summaries, Syria, Jun/Jul 1941', No.22, 11–12 July 1941, Lavarack papers 7. War Diary HQ 7 Div G Branch, 12 July 1941, 1/5/14, AWM. Long, *Greece, Crete and Syria*, pp.511–3. Wilson diary, 12 July 1941. Wilson, *op cit*, p.119. Rowell, *op cit*, p.93.

34. Quoted in Long, *Greece, Crete and Syria*, p.514. Letter, Lavarack to Long, 26 September 1952, 'Notes on Chapter 25', Gavin Long Correspondence, J.D. Lavarack, Part 1, AWM. See Wilson diary (including looseleaf), 12 July 1941.

35. Lavarack diary, 12 July 1941. Wilson diary (looseleaf), 12 July 1941. Slessor later complained that he had been obstructed by British officers in his attempt to report the signing of the armistice (see MP729/7, item 55/421/38). Lavarack disagreed, however, stating that Slessor was treated no differently to other correspondents. Blamey told Spender that 'Slessor was excitable and tactless' (see cable, Blamey to Spender, 4 August 1941, MP729/7, item 55/421/38).

36. Lavarack diary, 12 July 1941. Wilson diary, 12 July 1941. There have been published several accounts of the initialling of the armistice and it is interesting to note that generally they differ, sometimes remarkably, in the incidents they describe and the sequence in which events unfolded. While taking note of these accounts, and using them where they are unambiguous, most reliance has been placed upon primary sources, such as Lavarack's and Curtis Wilson's diaries, notes made by Wilson, and war diaries and intelligence summaries. See also Norris, *op cit*, p.124; Spears, *op cit*, pp.123–126.

37. Allen to Long, Gavin Long Notebooks and Diaries, N66/23–4, AWM. *Sydney Morning Herald*, 18 July 1941, p.6.

38. *Hasluck, The Government and the People 1939–1941, pp.341, 344–345, 348. See Long, Greece, Crete and Syria, p.526.*

39. Letter, Lavarack to Long, 26 September 1952, 'Notes on Chapter 25', Gavin Long Correspondence, J.D. Lavarack, Part 1, AWM. Lavarack diary, 16 July 1941. 'Seventh Australian Division Report on the Operations in Syria 1941', p.19, Blamey papers, 51, AWM. Stevens, *op cit*, p.56, Stevens papers. *Sydney Morning Herald*, 18 July 1941, p.6. De Wailly, *op cit*, p.294.

40. Lavarack diary, 15 July 1941. Commander-in-Chief diary, 15 July 1941, Blamey papers,

AWM. Carlyon interview, 6 may 1981. Wilson diary, 15 July 1941, original emphasis.

41. Letter, Lavarack to Bracegirdle, 13 December 1941, Lavarack papers 13.

42. Recommendation for the award of KBE, 29 September 1941, Lavarack papers 13 and CAB 106/379, p.22, PRO. Letter, Lavarack to Long, 26 September 1952, p.7, 'Notes on Chapter 24', Gavin Long Correspondence, J.D. Lavarack, Part 1, AWM. Letter, Blamey to Forde, 11 October 1941, Blamey papers 8A[3], AWM.

43. Letter, Lavarack to Long, 30 June 1952, Lavarack papers 7. Blamey saw it differently. At the time he wrote to Spender, 'To help along I organized a temporary brigade under Savige consisting of the two battalions that were in best condition, 2/3 and 2/5[,] and the 2/1 Pnr Bn' (letter, Blamey to Spender, 8 September 1941, Blamey papers 2A[10]; letters, Blamey to Minister for the Army, 11 May 1941 and Blamey to Sturdee, 22 May 1941, Blamey papers 2A[8], AWM.

44. Letter, Blamey to Spender, 8 September 1941, Blamey papers 33.1, AWM. Blamey also despatched a similar signal to Spender during the fighting, see Blamey to Minister for the Army, 21 June 1941, MP729/7, item 35/421/48. See also Blamey to Sturdee, 26 June 1941, Blamey papers 5A, AWM.

45. Long, *Greece, Crete and Syria*, p.529. Notes by Colonel (later Lieutenant-General) V.C. Secombe, Lavarack papers 7.

15 - 'It may be necessary to take risks'

1. Rowell, *op cit*, p.94. Letter, Blamey to Spender, 18 August 1941, Blamey Papers 33.1, AWM. Letter, Lavarack to Blamey, 3 August 1941, War Diary HQ 1 Aust Corps, 1/4/1, AWM. Lavarack to Long, 26 September 1952, 'Notes on Chapter 26', Gavin Long Correspondence, J.D. Lavarack Part 1, AWM. Long, *Greece, Crete and Syria*, pp.516–517, 519–521, 534–535. Cables, Blamey to Menzies, 2 and 11 August 1941, Blamey papers 2A[4], AWM. Letter, Allen to Long, 11 October 1952, Gavin Long Correspondence, A.S. Allen, AWM.

2. C.E.M. Lloyd, 2nd Preliminary Interview, Canberra, 19 July 1948, Gavin Long Correspondence, C.E.M. Lloyd, AWM. Telegram, Minister of State to Prime Minister, 22 December 1941, PREM 3/63/3, PRO. Letter, Lavarack to Long, 26 September, 1952, 'Notes on Chapter 29', Gavin Long Correspondence, J.D. Lavarack, Part I, AWM. See Long, *Greece, Crete and Syria*, p.555, note 5. Maughan, *op cit*, passim. Horner, *High Command*, pp.114–124. Letter, Blamey to Spender, 8 September 1941, Blamey papers 2A[10], AWM

3. Draft cable, Churchill to Curtin, 7 January 1942 and minute, J.M. Martin to Ismay, 19 January 1942, PREM 3/63/3, PRO.

4. Annotation by Churchill on a minute from Atlee, 28 February 1942, PREM 3/63/3, PRO. Letter, Lavarack to Long, 26 September, 1952, 'Notes on Chapter 29', Gavin Long Correspondence, J.D. Lavarack, Part I, AWM.

5. Cables, Australian High Commissioner, London to Australian Prime Minister, 25 December 1941; and CGS to Minister for the Army, 5 January 1942, MP729/7, item 38/422/415A. Wigmore, *op cit*, pp.163–164, 190. Hasluck, *The Government and the People, 1942–45*, p.32. Long, *The Six Years War*, p.138.

6. Lavarack diary, 8–19 January 1942. Berryman diary, 10 January 1942. Cable, Wavell to Chiefs of Staff, 12 January 1942, *Principal War Telegrams and Memoranda, 1940–1943, Far East*, no.(174), p.81. Long, *The Six Years War*, p.138.

7. Long, *Greece, Crete and Syria*, pp.549–550.

8. Cables Blamey to Curtin, 8 and 19 January 1942, MP729/7, item 38/422/415A and Blamey papers, 6A[4], AWM. '1 Aust Corps. Precis of inward and outward telegrams dealing with powers of GOC AIF', 'Report of Comd 1 Aust Corps for period 26 Jan 42 - 21 Feb 42 in the N.E.I.', Appendix A, Lavarack papers 9.

9. Lavarack was accompanied by Brigadier F.H. Berryman (BGS), Brigadier W. Bridgeford (DA&QMG), Brigadier C.S. Steele (CE), Lieutenant-Colonel K.A. Wills (GSO2 Intelligence), Lieutenant-Colonel D. Cleland (AQMG), Major E. Mander-Jones (GSO3 Intelligence), Captain C.H. Wilson (ADC), Lieutenant T.A.M. Boulter (Cipher Officer), Warrant Officer, Class 1 D. Linklater (Chief Clerk). Lavarack diary, 21–27 January 1942. Berryman diary, 27 January 1942. War Diary HQ 1 Aust Corps Air Party, 21–27 January 1942, Lavarack papers 9 and 1/4/4, AWM. Signals, Army Melbourne to Abdacom, 22 January 1942, and Ausforce to Austcorps, 14 January 1942, Blamey papers 2B[9], AWM. Wigmore, *op cit*, pp.442–443. Wavell, *Despatch by the Supreme Commander of the ABDA Area to the Combined Chiefs of Staff on the Operations in the South-West Pacific, 15 January 1942 to 25 February 1942*, (hereinafter referred to as Despatch), p.8. Wigmore, *op cit*, pp.442–443.

10. Lavarack and Berryman diaries, 27 January 1942. Wigmore, *op cit*, p.443. Letter, Lavarack to Sturdee, 6 February 1942, Lavarack papers 13.

11. Lavarack diary, 27–28 January 1942. Berryman diary, 27 January 1942. Cable, Wavell to Sturdee, 28 January 1942, *Principal War Telegrams and Memoranda, 1940–1943, Far East*, no.(377), pp.164–165. Horner, *High Command*, p.176. Wigmore, *op cit*, p.443.

12. Hasluck, *The Government and the People 1942–1945*, pp.3–4, 36. Signal, Lavarack to Sturdee, 31 January 1942, Lavarack papers 13. 'Report of Comd 1 Aust Corps for period 26 Jan 42–21 Feb 42 in the N.E.I.', Appendix B, Lavarack papers 9 (copies are also held in K.A. Wills papers 8, DRL6201, AWM and CAB 106/153, PRO). Lavarack diary, 31 January 1942.

13. Lavarack diary, 1–3 February 1942. 'Defence of South Sumatra. Notes of Appreciation by BGS as result of recce with GOC on 1–3 Feb 42'; 'Action on Appreciation on Defence of South Sumatra', 4 Feb 42, Appendix B; and 'Notes on Situation in South West Pacific - 2 February 42', Appendix C, War Diary HQ 1 Aust Corps Air Party, Lavarack papers 9. Original emphasis. See Also Wigmore, *op cit*, pp.443–444.

14. Wigmore, *op cit*, p.443n. Letter, Lavarack to Sturdee, 6 February 1942, Lavarack papers 13.

15. Letter, Lavarack to HQ SWPC, 5 February 1942 (mis-dated 5 January), MP 729/7, item 2/421/26. Letter, Lavarack to Sturdee, 6 February, 1942, CRS A5954, Box 573.

16. Cables, Curtin to Blamey, 7 February 1942 and Blamey to Curtin, 8 February 1942, Blamey papers 6A[4], AWM. Minutes, Secretary, Department of the Army to Secretary, Military Board, 22 January 1942; CGS to Secretary, Department of the Army, 28 January 1942, MP729/6, item 2/401/221.

17. Lavarack and Berryman diaries, 8–9 February 1942. Wilson diary, 8 February 1942. War Diary HQ 1 Aust. Corps Air Party, 8 February 1942, Lavarack papers 9. Signal, Curtin to Lavarack, 8 February 1942, Lavarack papers 13. Wigmore, *op cit*, p.443. Lodge, *The Fall of General Gordon Bennett*, p.141.

18. Signal, Lavarack to Curtin, 9 February 1942, Lavarack papers 9. See also 'Report of Comd. 1 Aust. Corps for period 26 Jan 42 - 21 Feb. 42 in the N.E.I.', Appendix B, Lavarack papers 9 and CAB 106/153, PRO.

19. Lavarack diary, 11 February 1942. Berryman diary, 11,12 February 1942.

20. Lavarack diary, 10, 12 February 1942, Wigmore, *op cit*, p.454. See Berryman diary, 9,

11, 12 February, 1942; Wilson diary, 10 February, 1942. 1 Aust Corps Op Instn no. 1', 11 February, 1942, War Diary HQ 1 Aust Corps Air Party, 13 February 1942 and Appendix B, Lavarack papers 9. Wigmore, *op cit*, p.454. Cable, Lavarack to Sturdee, 12 February 1942, Lavarack papers 9. '1 Aust Corps. Precis of inward and outward telegrams dealing with powers of GOC AIF', 'Report of Comd 1 Aust Corps for period 26 Jan 42 - 21 Feb 42 in the N.E.I.', Appendix A, Lavarack papers 9.

21. Cable, Curtin to Wavell, 13 February 1942, Lavarack papers 13 and MP 729/7, item 38/422/461A. Cable, Sturdee to Lavarack, 13 February 1942, Lavarack papers 13. Annotation by Sturdee (dated 15 February) on letters to him from Lavarack, 6 February 1942, CRS A5954, Box. 573.

22. Cable, Lavarack to Sturdee (for Prime Minister), 13 February 1942, Lavarack papers 9. Berryman diary, 13 February, 1942.

23. Cable, Lavarack to Sturdee (for Prime Minister) dated 13 February 1942 (sent 14 February 1942), CRS A 5954 Box 573. Wigmore, *op cit*, pp.444, 506.

24. Lavarack diary, 13 February 1942, Wilson diary 13 February 1942. Cable, ABDA Comm to Britman Washington (for combined Chiefs of Staff), 13 February 1942. A copy is contained in *Principal War Telegrams and Memoranda, 1940–1943, Far East*, no. 141, pp.48–49. See also 'Report of Comd 1 Aust Corps for period 26 Jan 42 - 21 Feb 42 in the N.E.I.' Appx B, Lavarack papers 9, and CAB 106/153, PRO. Wigmore, *op cit*, p.444.

25. Lavarack and Berryman diaries, 14 February, 1942. War Diary HQ 1 Aust Corps Air Party, 14 February, 1942, Lavarack papers 9. Wigmore, *op cit*, p.453.

26. Lavarack and Berryman diaries, 14 February, 1942. War Diary HQ 1 Aust Corps Air Party, 14 February, 1942, Lavarack papers 9. Lavarack diary, 15 February 1942. Bond (ed.), *Chief of Staff. The Diaries of Lieutenant.-General Sir Henry Pownall*, vol. 2, p.87.

27. Wigmore, *op cit*, pp.454–455. Letter, Lavarack to Long, 7 October 1953, Gavin Long Correspondence J.D. Lavarack, Part 1, AWM. Lavarack diary, 15 February 1942. Wavell, Despatch, p.14. Long, *The Six Years War*, p.161. Lavarack's Chief Engineer, Brigadier C.S. Steele, was in Palembang when Blackburn's force was landed. In a report submitted a few days later he was critical of the part played by Lavarack's HQ in the brief episode, especially on the question of orders for Blackburn. However, Steele was not aware of all the factors affecting the situation. See 'Report on operations in South Sumatra 14–17 Feb 42', 19 February 1942, Lavarack papers 9.

28. Cable, Sturdee to Lavarack, despatched 14 February, 1942. War Diary HQ 1 Aust Corps Air Party, 15 February, 1942, Appendix B, Lavarack papers 9. See also '1 Aust Corps. Precis of inward and outward telegrams dealing with powers of GOC AIF', 'Report of Comd 1 Aust Corps for period 26 Jan 42 - 21 Feb 42 in the N.E.I.', Appendix A, Lavarack papers 9. See cable Blamey to Sturdee, 15 February 1942, Blamey papers 6A[4], AWM.

29. Long, *To Benghazi*, pp.100–101. Wigmore, *op cit*, p.65. Minute, Sturdee to Forde, 3 February 1942, MP 729/7, Item 2/421/44. Instructions, Forde to Lavarack, 31 January 1942, MP729/6, item 2/401/221 (also Lavarack papers 13).

30. 'Papers by the Chief of the General Staff on Future Employment of A.I.F.', 15 February 1942, and covering letters, Sturdee to Curtin, CRS A5954, item box 573. Wigmore, *op cit*, pp.675–677 (see also pp.444–445). Cable, Wavell to Curtin and Sturdee, 14 February 1942, CRS A5954, Box 573. Letter, Sturdee to Long, 9 November 1953, Gavin Long Correspondence, V.A.H. Sturdee, AWM.

31. Wigmore, *op cit*, pp.445–46.

32. Cable, Curtin to Churchill, 15 February 1942, CRS A5954, Box 573. See also Wigmore,

op cit, p.446. Sturdee's paper was endorsed by the Australian Chiefs of Staff on 16 February (see 'Future Employment of A.I.F. Report by Chiefs of Staff', 16 February 1942, CRS A5954, Box 573). Sturdee threatened to resign as CGS if the government did not press for the return of the AIF to Australia (see Horner, *Crisis of Command*, p.43.) Cable, Wavell to Churchill, 15 February 1942, WO 106/3302, PRO.

33. Cable, Lavarack to Curtin, 15 February, 1942, Lavarack papers 9 and 13. Original emphasis. Lavarack diary, 15 February, 1942. Cable, Curtin to Lavarack, 14 (?) February 1942, Lavarack papers 13. See also 'Report of Comd 1 Aust Corps for period 26 Jan 42-21 Feb 42 in the N.E.I.', Appx B, Lavarack papers 9.

16 - 'Emphatically a bad business'

1. Cable, Wavell to Dill and Churchill, 16 February 1942, WO 106/3302, PRO. Wavell, *Despatch*, pp.14–15. Wigmore, *op cit*, p.446.

2. Lavarack diary, 16 February 1942. Cable, Lavarack to Sturdee and Curtin, 16 February, 1942, and 'Report of Comd 1 Aust Corps for period 26 Jan 42 - 21 Feb 42 in the N.E.I.', Appendix B, Lavarack papers 9. Long, *The Six Years War*, p.161. Wigmore, *op cit*, pp.446–7. Wigmore writes that Lavarack cabled Curtin on the 17th, which was probably the date of receipt in Australia.

3. Lavarack diary, 17 February, 1942. Berryman diary, 17 February, 1942. Gavin Long Notes and Diaries, N1/22–23, AWM. See also War Diary HQ 1 Aust Corps Air Party, 16 February, 1942, Lavarack papers 9.

4. Lavarack, Berryman and Wilson diaries, 17 February, 1942. War Diary HQ 1 Aust Corps Air Party, 17 February 1942 and Appendix B, Lavarack papers 9. Wigmore, *op cit*, p.455.

5. The units ordered to disembark were the 2/3rd Machine Gun Battalion, 2/2nd Pioneer Battalion, 2/6 Field Company, 105th General Transport Company, the 2/2nd Casualty Clearing Station, and company headquarters and one platoon of the Guard Battalion, plus some stragglers and details. Cable C-in-C South-West Pacific to War Office, 18 February 1942 *Principle War Telegrams and Memoranda, 1940–1943, Far East*, no.(188). Lavarack diary, 18 February 1942. Signal, ABDAcom to HQ 1 Aust Corps, 18 February, 1942, Lavarack papers 13. Wigmore, *op cit*, pp.446-7, 457. Cables, Lavarack to Sturdee and Curtin, 16 and 18 February, 1942, Lavarack papers 9. See also 'Report of Comd 1 Aust Corps for period 26 Jan 42 - 21 Feb 42 in the N.E.I.', Appendix B, Lavarack papers 9. Cable, Curtin to Wavell, 18 February, 1942, CRS A5954, Box 573.

6. Lavarack diary, 18 February 1942. Cable, Wavell to Curtin, 18 February, 1942, CRS A5954, Box 573, 'Report of Comd 1 Aust Corps for period 26 Jan 42 - 21 Feb 42 in the N.E.I.', Appendix B, Lavarack papers 9 and CAB 106/153, PRO. See cable C-in-C, South-West Pacific to the British Joint Staff Mission, Washington, and the War Office, 18 February 1942, *Principle War Telegrams and Memoranda, 1940–1943, Far East*, no.(188). See also Wavell, *Despatch*, p.15.

7. Cable, Lavarack to Sturdee and Curtin, 18 February, 1942 and annotation these on Lavarack papers 9. Wigmore (p.450) incorrectly states that this cable was sent on the 19th. See also 'Report of Comd 1 Aust Corps for period 26 Jan 42- 21 Feb 42 in the N.E.I.', Appendix B, Lavarack papers 9. Berryman and Wilson diaries, 18 February, 1942.

8. Wigmore, *op cit*, pp.447–450, 459. See cable, Curtin to Page, 19 February, 1942, Blamey papers 6A[4], AWM and CRS A5954, Box 573.

9. Letter, Lavarack to Sturdee, 19 February 1942, Lavarack papers 13.

10. Lavarack diary, 19–20 February 1942. Letter, Lavarack to Sturdee, 19 February 1942, Lavarack papers 13. Wigmore, *op cit*, p.456. Cable, Curtin to Lavarack, 20 February 1942, Lavarack papers 13. 'Report of Comd 1 Aust Corps for period 26 Jan 42 - 21 Feb 42 in the N.E.I.', Appendix B, Lavarack papers 9.

11. Lavarack diary, 20 February 1942. Wigmore, *op cit*, pp.456–457. Cable, Combined Chiefs of Staff, Washington to Wavell, 20 February 1942, WO 106/3302, PRO. Wavell, *Despatch*, p.16.

12. Lavarack diary, 20 February 1942. Cable, Lavarack to Curtin, 21 February 1942; 'Report of Comd 1 Aust Corps for period 26 Jan 42–21 Feb 42 in the N.E.I.'; and '1 Aust Corps Op Instn no. 4', War Diary HQ 1 Aust Corps Air Party, 21 February, 1942, Appendix B, Lavarack papers 9. Wigmore, *op cit*, p.457.

13. Blackburn was promoted to brigadier on 22 February. Wigmore, *op cit*, p.457. Letter, Lavarack to Blackburn, 21 February, 1942, and '1 Aust Corps Op Instn no. 3', War Diary HQ 1 Aust Corps Air Party, 21 February, 1942, Appendix B, Lavarack papers 9 and 1/4/4, AWM. 'Report by Brigadier A.S. Blackburn, GOC AIF Java on Operations of the AIF in Java, Feb Mar 42' p.1, CAB 106/139 PRO. Lavarack, Wilson and Berryman diaries, 21 February 1942. See also note to Minister for External Affairs, probably by Shedden, c. 22 February, 1942, CRS A 5954 Box 573. Wigmore, *op cit*, p.456–458.

14. Lavarack diary, 22–23 February 1942. Wilson diary 22 February, 1942. See also Wigmore, *op cit*, p.459. Lodge, *The Fall of General Gordon Bennett*, pp.199–200. The allegation was repeated in Joynt, *Breaking the Road for the Rest*, p.187.

15. Cable, Curtin to Page, repeated Casey, Lavarack, Wavell, 19 February, 1942, copies in Lavarack papers 8, CRS A5954, Box 573 and Blamey papers 6A[4], AWM. Wigmore, *op cit*, p.450 (see pp.450–452 for a detailed discussion of the diversion of the AIF convoys). Horner, *High Command*, p.159. Wigmore, *op cit*, p.457. Cable, Curtin to Page, 19 February 1942, Blamey papers 6A[4], AWM.

16. Lavarack diary 24 February, 1942 (see also 28th). Advisory War Council Minutes Nos 785 and 786, 24 February 1942, copies held in CRS A5954, Box 573. See Wigmore, *op cit*, pp. 464–465 (for details of the cables which passed between Curtin and Churchill see pp.450–452). Letter, Lavarack to Long, 7 October 1953, Gavin Long Correspondence, J.D. Lavarack Part 1, AWM.

17. Cables, Curtin to Page and Curtin to Wavell, 24 February 1942, CRS A5954, Box 573. Wigmore, *op cit*, p.459.

18. Lavarack diary, 27 February, 1942. Wigmore, *op cit*, p.459. Horner, *High Command*, p.166. Letter, Wavell to Lavarack, 22 December 1943, Lavarack papers 8. Letter, Lavarack to Long, 7 October 1953, Gavin Long Correspondence, J.D. Lavarack, Part 1, AWM.

19. See Letter, Lavarack to Sturdee, 19 February 1942, Lavarack papers 13. Letter, Lavarack to Long, 7 October 1953, Gavin Long Correspondence, J.D. Lavarack, Part 1, AWM. See also letter, Lavarack to Long, 10 October 1952.

20. See 'Observations by C.G.S', on cable, Lavarack to Sturdee and Curtin, 27 February 1941, and in War Cabinet Agendum no.106/1942, copy in CRS A5954, Box 573.

21. Maughan, *op cit*, pp.343–351. A.J. Sweeting, review of Norris, *op cit*, in *Army Journal*, no.262, March 1971, p.53. Letter by Berryman in *Army Journal*, no.265, June 1971, pp.52–53.

22. Gavin Lang Notebook and Diaries, C.E.M. Lloyd, N1/27, AWM. See cable, Lavarack to Sturdee and Curtin, 18 February 1942, CRS A5954, Box 573. Letter, Lavarack to Curtin, 5 September 1943, CRS A5954, Box 266.

23. Curtis Wilson, 'Java Adventure', unpublished manuscript, p.5, Wilson papers. This paper formed the basis of 'Java Interlude' prepared by the Military History Section a copy of which is in file 556/2/1, AWM. Lavarack diary 13, 15 February 1942. Letter, Lavarack to Sturdee, 19 February 1942, Lavarack papers 13.

24. Letter, Lavarack to Sturdee, 6 February 1942, Lavarack papers 13. Undated notes by Wilson, Wilson papers. Wilson interview, 12 May 1980. Letter, Lloyd to Wigmore, 14 July 1948, Personal Records - World War II, Major-General C.E.M. Lloyd, AWM 67. Bond, *op cit*, p.91.

25. Lavarack diary, 14 April 1942.

17 - 'There is no generosity in Blamey'

1. Lavarack diary, 24–28 February 1942. Extract from Commonwealth Gazette, 16 April 1942, CRS A5954, Box 1506. War Cabinet Minute No. 1989, 11 March, 1942, CRS A2673, vol. XI. War Cabinet Minute No. 1906, in CRS A5954, Box 573, and signal, Curtin to Blamey, 20 February, 1942, Blamey papers 6A[4], AWM.

2. Gavin Long Diaries and Notebooks, D3/27, AWM.

3. Interview, C.H. Wilson, 12 May 1980. Horner, *High Command*, p.183.

4. Vasey was a regular, Herring and Steele citizen officers. In November 1941 Vasey wrote to his wife that 'Ned [Herring] thinks Joe is just too impossible. He says he will have a real row with him one day. I'm all for it'. In the same letter Vasey wrote of his fears that Bennett, then visiting the Middle East, would be appointed GOC AIF. Letter, Vasey to wife, 29 November 1941, Vasey papers, Box 2, folder 4, NLA. Chapman, *op cit*, p.262. Letter, Herring to Hetherington, n.d.; Herring to Hetherington, 2 December 1970, Hetherington papers, Box 2, AWM. Hetherington, *op cit*, p.213. Horner, *Crisis of Command*, pp.57–58.

5. Lavarack diary, 21, 23 March 1942. Rowell, *op cit*, p.105. Berryman diary, 20 March 1942. Apparently Berryman did not mention Herring or Luxton to Lavarack. Letter, Lavarack to Forde, 23 March 1942, 33/1/4 AWM.

6. After discussing the new command organization with Sturdee, Lavarack had recommended to the Minister that he should command the First Army and Mackay the Second Army. Headquarters First Army opened on 15 April. Horner, *High Command*, p.183. Lavarack diary, 12–13 March, 26–27 March, 1, 11,13 15 April 1942. Commander-in-Chief's diary, 26 March, 13 April 1942, Blamey papers, AWM.

7. Horner, *Crisis of Command*, pp.92–95, 276. Memorandum, Sturdee to Supreme Headquarters, South West Pacific, 4 April 1942, Blamey papers 23–72 AWM. McCarthy, *South-West Pacific Area—First Year*, p.26. 'Summary of Operational Efficiency, Formations—First Aust Army', 15 May 1942, Lavarack papers 10.

8. When formed, First Australian Army comprised seven divisions. In July 1942 the 1st US Corps (32nd and 41st Divisions) was established in the First Army area. By April 1943 First Army was composed of 2nd Corps (6th, 7th and 9th Divisions, with a total of eight brigades), 4th Division (6th, 11th, 12th and 14th Brigades), 3rd Armoured Division (2nd Armoured and 1st Motorised Brigades) and Torres Strait Force. In August 1943 the major formations under Lavarack's headquarters were 2nd Corps (6th Division and 2/7th Cavalry (Commando) Regiment), 4th Division (3rd Brigade), 3rd Armoured Division (2nd Armoured Brigade), 11th Brigade and Torres Strait Force. Lavarack diary, 14 July, 7, 20 August 1942. McCarthy, *South-West Pacific Area—First Year*, p.120. Luvaas (ed.), *Dear Miss Emm—General Eichelberger's War in the Pacific 1942–1945*, p.31. Dexter, *The New Guinea Offensives*, pp.16, 280n.

9. Lavarack diary, 20 August, 18 September 1942 (original emphasis).

10. Berryman diary, 16 and 18 September 1942. The entry for the 18th was obviously added some time later. Letter, Hopkins to author, 14 January 1983.

11. Hetherington, *op cit*, pp.248, 323. (see Bean, *op cit*, Vol. 2, *The Story of Anzac*, *op cit*, pp.781–783). Interview, J.A. Wilmoth (ex-ADC to Blamey), 5 May 1981. Interview, F.J. Howard, 7 May 1981). See Berryman diary, 18 September 1942 and letter, Hopkins to author, 14 January 1983, both of which refer to Murdoch's opposition to Blamey. Lavarack diary, 13, 16 March and 6 July 1942. Letters, Hopkins to author, 14 and 30 January, 1983.

12. Lavarack diary, 24 September, 22 October 1942. Hetherington *op cit*, pp.239–258; McCarthy, *South-West Pacific Area—First Year*, pp.235–240. Rowell, *op cit*, pp.127–131. See Horner, *High Command*, pp.251–253; *Crisis of Command*, pp.169–173, 176–177.

13. Lavarack diary, 28, 29 October 1942.

14. Lavarack diary, 28, 29, 30 (original emphasis), 31 October 1942; 4, 25 November 1942. See also Hetherington *op cit*, pp.261–262 Lavarack's ADC recalled that Lavarack was rebuked on several occasions for being absent from his headquarters. Wilson interview, 12 May, 1980.

15. Lavarack diary, 5 November 1942. (See 28 December 1942, where Lavarack criticizes 'Blamey's craze for disorganisation of existing arrangements and preferences for "ad hoc" set-ups', and 31 December 1942).

16. Lavarack diary, 5 November 1942. Later Lavarack was also critical of MacArthur's presence in New Guinea, which he saw as a publicity-hunting (Lavarack diary, 16 November 1942). Letters, Forde to Curtin, 11 February 1944, CRS A816, item 58/ 301/112; Blamey to Forde, 11 November 1943, CRS A5954, Box 1506. Horner, *Crisis of Command*, pp.275–276.

17. Lavarack diary, 1 April, 28 October, 5 November 1942. Letter, Lavarack to Blamey, 5 November 1942, Blamey papers 170.8, AWM. Lavarack had met MacArthur about a week before, when he thought the American to be 'very nervous'. Lavarack could not decide if MacArthur was a 'genuine good soldier or not' (see Lavarack diary, 23 March, 1942). See also Commander-in-Chief's diary, 1 April 1942, Blamey papers, AWM.

18. Lavarack diary, 22 November 1942. Letter, Brigadier Sir Frederick Chilton to author, 6 September 1983. Letter, Brigadier Sir Charles Spry to author, 27 July 1981.

19. Lavarack diary, 7 September, 5, 9 October and 7, 12 November 1942. Berryman diary, 3 August, 1942. Lavarack was just as angry with Major-General C.H. Simpson, SO-in-C at Land Headquarters: 'Simpson should know better...[He] has failed to foresee and provide and is not fit for his job' (see also entry for 17 November 1942).

20. Letter, Blamey to Forde, 17 November 1943, CRS A5954, Box 1506. First Australian Army Operation Instruction, August 1943, Blamey papers 30.2, AWM. Lavarack diary, 1 January 1943.

21. Lavarack diary, 7 October 1942,4, 17 January, 6 April 1943. Berryman diary, 3 August 1942.

22. Lavarack diary, 9 January 1943, Lavarack papers 11. Letter, Lavarack to Blamey, 21 May 1942, Blamey papers 43–51, AWM). Lavarack noted at this time that Mackay also was unhappy about the position of Second Army (Lavarack diary, 12 January 1943). Minutes of PM's War Conference, Canberra, 14 January 1943, CRS A5954, Box 1.

23. Letter, Dunstan to Rowell, 29 September 1942, Rowell papers 9, AWM. Gavin Long Diaries and Notebooks, D9/34, 5 October 1943, AWM. Garrett to Hetherington, n.d., Hetherington papers Box 2, AWM. Garrett finished the war as BGS of the 2nd Corps

and was CGS 1958–1960. Letter, A.J. Sweeting to Hetherington, 11 February 1972, Hetherington papers, Box 2, AWM. Letter, Lumsden to General Sir Alan Brooke, 22 November 1943, WO216/96, PRO.

24. Letters, Hopkins to author, 14 January, 3 September 1983.

25. Lavarack diary, 10 February 1943, Lavarack papers 11. See Horner, *High Command*, p.213 and *Crisis of Command*, p.60 for a different point of view.

26. Lavarack diary, 20 February 1943, Lavarack papers 11. Letter, Blamey to Forde, 17 November 1943, CRS A5954, Box 1506. McCarthy, *South-West Pacific Area —First Year*, pp.7, 25. Gavin Long Diaries and Notebooks, 5 September 1943, D9/19, AWM.

27. Letter, Lavarack to Blamey, 21 September 1943, Blamey papers 98, AWM. The signal referred to by Lavarack, dated 20 August, 1943, and Blamey's reply (in which he said Lavarack's suggestion that advanced HQ First Army go to New Guinea was 'unworkable'), dated 2 September 1943, is in Blamey papers 170.8, AWM.

28. Letter, Blamey to Lavarack, 25 October 1943, Blamey papers 170.8, AWM.

29. Hetherington, *op cit*, p.325.

30. Carlyon, *op cit*, p.128.

31. Senior Military officers. Prime Minister's War Conference Minute, Canberra, 27 September, 1943, CRS A5954, Box 4. Dexter, *op cit*, p.507. Gavin Long Diaries and Notebooks, D3/27, AWM. See also letters, Blamey to Forde, 16 November 1943, Blamey papers 92 and Curtin to Forde, 20 December 1943, Blamey papers 6/1, AWM. The necessity of having a high-ranking officer in Washington is explained in Horner, *Crisis of Command*, p.332, n.42.

32. *Melbourne Herald*, 3 August 1943 (see also 30 June and 11 & 18 August 1943).

33. 'Lieutenant-General Lavarack - Advice regarding relation of stowing of 6th and 7 Divisions to question of diversion to Burma','Prime Minister's Statement to Press, Perth, 15 August 1943', CRS A5954, Box 266.

34. Cable, Lavarack to Northcott, 17 August 1943; and letter, Shedden (?) to Northcott, 18 August 1943, CRS A5954, Box 266. The minutes of the meeting of the Advisory War Council on 24 February record that 'Lieut.-General Lavarack stated that the ships conveying the first and second flights of the A.I.F. from the Middle East had not been tactically loaded, and if the first flight had been diverted to Burma, the troops could not have been landed as an effective fighting force, as it was probable many of the units would have had incomplete fighting equipment. It would have taken approximately 21 days after their arrival to re-sort the equipment available and have the troops ready for the field'. Advisory War Council Minute no. (756), 24 February 1942, copy held in CRS A5954, Box 573. See also Advisory War Council Minute no. (785), 24 February 1942. Wigmore, *op cit*, p.464. Letter, Lavarack to Curtin, September 1943, CRS A5954, Box 266.

35. Letter, Curtin to Lavarack, 21 September 1943, CRS A5954, Box 266. See 'Note on General Lavarack's letter of 5th September to Prime Minister', 9 September 1943, CRS A5954, Box 573. Letter, Lavarack to Curtin, 30 September 1943, CRS A5954, Box 266.

36. Letter, Wavell to Lavarack, 22 December 1943, Lavarack papers 8.

37. In February 1946 Sturdee proposed that C.E.M. Lloyd, with whom he had clashed during the war, take Lavarack's place. Melbourne *Herald*, 19 November 1945. Berryman diary, notes for January 1944; and letter, Berryman to wife, 20 February 1944, Berryman papers. Minute, Sturdee to Forde, 4 February 1946, CRS A5954, Box 16\506. Gillison, *Royal Australian Air Force 1939—1942*, p.475. Hetherington, *op cit.*, p.379. Gavin Long, *The Final Campaigns*, p.23.

18 - 'He has not had a good war'

1. Letter, Lavarack to Long, 14 February 1945, Gavin Long Correspondence, J.D. Lavarack, Part 2, AWM. Letter, Curtin to Forde, 2 March 1945, CRS A816, item 11/301/544. Hasluck, *The Government and the People 1942–1945*, pp.434–435; 469–470; P.M. Reid interview, 16 February 1981. Lavarack explained some of the difficulties at the conference to Northcott (see Letter, Lavarack to Northcott, 27 May 1945, Blamey papers, 6.1, AWM). See also cables between Lavarack and Australia, December 1945-January 1946, in CRS A816, item 52/301/223. Hasluck, *Diplomatic Witness*, pp.203–204; see also p.191.

2. Letters, Blamey to Lavarack, 4 August 1944; Lavarack to Blamey, 1 September 1944 and 18 October 1944, Blamey papers, 6.1, AWM. See also Horner, *High Command*, pp.373, 423, 428. Long, *The Final Campaigns*, pp.393–394. Letter, Wilson to Brooke, 12 June 1945, CAB 127/47, PRO. Wilson, *op cit*, pp.252, 254.

3. Cable, Lavarack to Forde, 19 June 1945 and Forde to Lavarack, 20 June 1945, CRS A816, item 31/301/349. Cable, Blamey to Lavarack, 18 April 1945 (see also Lavarack to Blamey, 16 April 1945), Blamey papers, 6.1, AWM.

4. Letter, Lady Lavarack to Mrs. J. Vasey, 28 April 1945, Vasey papers, Box 1, Bundle 4, NL MS3782, NLA. P.M. Reid interview, 16 February 1981. *Washington Post*, 1 April 1945. *Commonwealth Parliamentary Debates*, Senate, 28 February 1945, vol.181, p.130. Letter, Blamey to Menzies, 1 March 1945, Blamey papers 136.21, AWM. Long, *The Final Campaigns*, pp.57-58; Hasluck, *The Government and the People 1942–1945*, pp.572–573. 'The Appointment of a Chief of the General Staff and the Relation of his views to Operational Strategy in the Southwest Pacific Area', 7 December 1945, CRS A5954, Box 1506.

5. Quoted in Horner, *Blamey*, Chapter 14.

6. Letters, Lavarack to Forde, 26 May 1945 and Forde to Lavarack, 11 July 1945, Blamey papers 146, AWM.

7. Lavarack to Forde, 28 May 1945, CRS A5954, Box 1506.

8. Letter, Blamey to Lieutenant-General Sir Bernard Freyberg, 1 April 1948, Blamey papers, item 3, PR 85/355, AWM.

9. Commander-in-Chief's diary, 31 July 1945, Blamey papers, 144, AWM. Letter, Blamey to Forde, 23 July 1945, CRS A5954, Box 1506. Minutes, Forde to Chifley, 1 April 1946; and Fitzgerald to Sturdee, 4 March 1946, CRS A5954, Box 1506. Hetherington, *op cit*, pp.377–378. Long, *The Final Campaigns*, p.579.

10. Telegram, Evatt to Chifley, 19 November 1945, CRS A5954, Box 1506. Lavarack diary, 22 August 1942.

11. *Herald* and *Age*, 19 November 1945; *Herald*, 20 November 1945.

12. *Herald*, 20 November 1945.

13. *Age*, 19 November 1945. 'Machinery for Higher Direction of the Army', Notes on War Cabinet Agendum No. 542/1945, 17 December 1945; 'The Machinery for the Higher Direction of the Services', pp.6–7, 26 May 1945; and minute, F.R. Sinclair, Secretary, Department of the Army to Shedden, 7 February 1946, CRS A5954, Box 1506. Minute, Sinclair to Secretary, Superannuation Board, 26 November 1946, MP 742/1, item L/1/2261.

14. Letters, Forde to Lavarack, 30 October 1946, MP 742/1, item L/1/2261.

19 - A Rearguard Action

1. Lavarack Papers, 7571, SLQ. Lavarack to Sir Frederic Eggleston, 31 October 1946, Eggleston papers, MS 423/1/351.

2. Letter, Lavarack to Long, 26 September, 1952, 'Notes on Chapter 29', Gavin Long Correspondence, J.D. Lavarack, Part 1, AWM.

3. *Ibid.* See Letter, Lavarack to Long, 26 September 1952, Gavin Long Correspondence, J.D. Lavarack, Part 1, AWM. Handwritten note by C.H. Wilson, n.d., Wilson papers. Lavarack diary, 8 July 1942. *Active Service with Australia in the Middle East*, pp.34, 60–65. Letter, Lavarack to Morshead 16 August 1943, Lavarack papers 6.

4. Draft article, p.31, 'Siege of Tobruk', Blamey papers 2B[11], AWM. Lavarack diary, 14 July 1942.

5. Lavarack diary, 17 July, 12 August and 14 December 1942. See also diary entries for 9 January and 16 March 1943. See 'Tobruk Rat' (C.E.M. Lloyd), 'Tobfort', *Salt*, 10 May 1943. Unpublished interview with Lavarack, p.1, Lavarack papers 6. Letter, Blamey to Lavarack, 6 August 1943, Lavarack papers 6.

6. Unpublished interview with Lavarack, p.1, Lavarack papers 6; annotation on letter, Blamey to Lavarack, 6 August 1943; Lavarack to Morshead, 29 May 1943; Morshead to Lavarack, 11 August 1943; Lavarack to Morshead, 16 August 1943; and Blamey to Lavarack, 6 August 1943, Lavarack papers 6. Letters, Lavarack to Wilmot, 15 May, 28 May, 5 June 1943, Lavarack papers 12.

7. Letter, Lavarack to Long, 26 September 1952, 'Notes on Chapter 29', Gavin Long Correspondence, J.D. Lavarack, Part 1, AWM. Letter, R. Evans to author, 28 May 1980. Carlyon, *op cit*, pp. x, 136, 139. Hetherington, *op cit*, pp.64–70. Long, *The Final Campaigns*, p.64.

8. Semmler, *The War Diaries of Kenneth Slessor*, pp.483, 561). See Hetherington, *op cit*, pp.401–403.

9. 'Extract from Personal Letter from Lt. Gen Sir John Lavarack', CAB 106/384, PRO. Smart passed Lavarack's comments on to the War Cabinet Historical Section (see letter, Smart to Colonel H.B. Latham, 15 May 1944, CAB 106/384). Letter, Wilson to Latham, 7 December 1950, Gavin Long Correspondence, Field-Marshal Lord Wilson, AWM. Letter, Lavarack to Ismay, 22 February 1949, Ismay papers II/3/140/1, Liddell Hart Centre for Military Archives.

10. Letter, Lavarack to Long, 26 September 1952, 'Notes on Chapter 27', Gavin Long Correspondence, J.D. Lavarack, Part 1, AWM (see also annotation thereon). Long, *Greece, Crete and Syria*, p.526. Lodge, *The Fall of General Gordon Bennett*, pp.296–306.

11. Horner, *Blamey*, Ch.4, fn.125.

12. Carlyon, *op cit*, p.61. Interview, C.H. Wilson, 12 May 1980. Menzies to Hetherington, n.d., Hetherington papers, Box 2, AWM. Letter, Long to Rowell, 14 October 1948, Rowell papers 11, AWM.

13. See Department of Defence files relating the promotion of Blamey to field-marshal: CRSA5954, 1508/8 and MP742/1, B/5/4043, National Archives of Australia. The files relating to Blamey's promotion were exempt from public disclosure until 1996. See also Deasey, David J., 'Some myths relating to the promotion to field marshal of Sir Thomas Blamey in 1950', *United Service*, June 2019.

14. McKernan, Michael, *The Strength of a Nation*, p.405.

15. In a letter to the Acting Minister for the Army, James Fraser, in 1945 an army chaplain stated that the Australian soldiers at the front had no confidence in Blamey and that he

had deprived the troops of more competent commanders:

As a chaplain I have walked, talked, marched and slept with officers and men, and can state without the slightest fear of contradiction that this confidence is completely lacking as far as the majority of the members of the Army are concerned. They trust neither his abilities or [sic] his motives. Many are convinced that his personal ambitions have over-rided [sic] any sense of justice and fair play that he may possess. In the pursuit of personal ambition he has removed men far more capable than himself from their positions.

The chaplain quoted one army officer serving in New Guinea who had said bluntly that 'Blamey threw away lives in New Guinea'. Subsequently Fraser's own enquiries confirmed the chaplain's allegations. (Quoted in Horner, *Blamey*, ch.22.) Although Monash was included in the 1988 bicentenary list of 200 great Australians compiled by 'Heritage 200', Blamey was not. The co-chair of the committee was a former junior army officer, Alan Coates, who called Blamey a 'prick' and announced: 'I buried three men because of his arrogance...I'll never forgive him.' He threatened to resign and go public if Blamey were chosen. (Quoted in McKernan, *The Strength of a Nation*, p.406.)

16. Horner quotes a 1976 review of Hetherington's biography of Blamey in which Robert O'Neill makes a similar observation. Horner, *Blamey*, Ch.23, fn.101.

17. Obituary quoted in Horner, David, 'Lavarack, Sir John Dudley (1885–1957)' *Australian Dictionary of Biography*, vol.15 (MUP, 2000). Slim quoted in *The Canberra Times*, 5 December 1957. The newspaper also reported: 'The Leader of the Opposition, Dr. Evatt, said yesterday Sir John Lavarack had rendered outstanding service to Australia on the battlefield and as one of principal military advisers during the last war. He had rendered service of equal value in his long and distinguished term as Governor of Queensland.'

18. Maughan, *op cit*, p.157.

Conclusion

1. Lavarack diary, 24 February 1942 (the entry was made at a later date). Long to Rowell, 14 October 1948, Rowell papers 11.

2. Sir Frank Berryman, quoted in Dean, *op. cit.*

3. Long, *Greece, Crete and Syria*, p.555.

4. Horner, *High Command*, pp.252-253.

5. Lavarack to Secretary, Military Board, 'Army Headquarters Internal War Book', 11 October 1935, Military Board Ag.92/1935, CRS A2653, vol.1 1935. Horner, *High Command*, p.210.

6 Interviews, N.D. Carlyon and J.A. Wilmoth, 5 and 6 May 1981 respectively. Carlyon, *op cit*, pp.61, 128.

7 Interview, P.M. Reid (Lavarack's ADC), 16 February 1981. Letter, Hopkins to author, 3 September 1983. See Hetherington, *op cit*, pp.62, 121-22.

8. Letters, Hopkins to author, 15, 31 May 1981 and 3 September, 1983. Rowell, op cit, p.132. Letter, Vasey to wife, 29 August 1941, Vasey papers, Box 2, MS 3782, NLA. Horner, Blamey, chs.12, 19 and 23. Horner, *High Command*, p.215 (see also p.374).

9. Letters, Hopkins to author, 15, 31 May 1981 and 3 September, 1983. Hopkins wrote that there was a 'definite pro-militia influence surrounding Blamey'. Lavarack diary, 27 November 1942. Horner, *High Command*, pp.215, 374. Horner, *Blamey*, ch.19. Dexter, *op cit*, p.780.

10. Interviews, N.D. Carlyon and J.A. Wilmoth, 5 and 6 May 1981 respectively. Carlyon, *op cit*, pp.61, 128. Lavarack told Gavin Long in 1952 that 'I do not consider that I myself was in any way inferior to Blamey as a commander' in the Middle East. Lavarack to Long, 26 September 1952, Gavin Long Correspondence, J.D. Lavarack, Part 1. Menzies to Long, Gavin Long Notebooks and Diaries, D11/22.

11. Some troops reportedly jeered openly when Blamey addressed them on film, booing, hooting and yelling 'Get back to your brothels, Blamey!' Blamey's shortcomings were neatly encapsulated in a review of the most recent biography of Blamey, which noted not only drunkenness, but 'his political vindictiveness and favouritism; his grasping materialism and overweening ambition; his tawdry sex life; his propensity to thumb his nose at public opinion; and his harsh, authoritarian politics...'. Allegations that Blamey took a cut of army contracts and his fraudulent claims to collect overseas allowances, as well as the possibility that he somehow contrived to be paid a dual salary to cover his distinct command and administrative roles, tarnished the image of the Commander-in-Chief. Robertson, *Australia at War*, p.44. Horner, *Blamey*, chs.15, 22. Carl Bridge, review of Horner, *Blamey: the Commander-in-Chief*, *op cit*.

12. Gavin Long Notebooks and Diaries, D5/49 (see also N37/45). Lumsden to General Sir Alan Brooke, 22 November 1943, WO216/96, PRO. 'Replies to Questionnaire and Conversation between C.S.4 and A.C.N.B.' c.mid-1942, WO 216/120.

13. Gavin Long Notebooks and Diaries, D11/22-23.] 15. Ellis, *op cit*, p.36.

14. Lavarack to Forde, 17 June 1945, CRS A816, item 31/301/349 in which Lavarack expressed his disappointment.

Bibliography

I The Lavarack papers

The Lavarack papers consist of three bound diaries and thirteen folders, as well as photographs. They are not extensive and almost exclusively relate to Lavarack's Second World War career, though there is some personal material. Moreover, some items are duplicated, especially in folders 3, 4, and 5. Lavarack's diaries for 1941 and 1942 and his account of his time in *Tobruk* (Folder 3) were especially useful.

Diaries:

1940—small appointment diary with minimal detail
1941–42—full diaries with useful personal detail

Folders:

'Letters on defence policy. Copies 1. To Richmond 2. To Dill'
'The Squires Letter and Correspondence with Gavin Long'
'J.D.L.'s Narrative of Operations in Cyrenaica during period 7–14 April. Tobruk. At end of file: Prelude to Syrian Campaign'
'Papers recovered from 2nd Echelon by Lieutenant-General Sir J.D. Lavarack...'
'Copies of Tobruk Papers. April 8–14, 1941'
'Tobruk'
'Syria'
'Java, Part I'
'Java, Part II'
'General'
'Personal Diary, 1 Jan - 8 Apr 43'
'Personal, Part I'
'Personal, Part II'

The collection was held by Dr J.O. Lavarack at the time of first publication. Copies of a number of documents in the collection were also held in public institutions at that time. Some of the Lavarack papers are now held in the John Oxley Library, State Library of Queensland, Australia.

II Official Records, Australia

(a) Australian Archives

CA 3, Cabinet Secretariat (1901–1968)

CRS A2694 Menzies and Fadden Ministries, (Folders and Bundles of) Minutes and Submissions (not complete), 1932–1939

CRS A2697 Menzies and Fadden Ministries, Minutes and Submissions (not complete), 1939–1941

CRS A2700 Curtin, Forde and Chifley Ministries—Folders of Cabinet Agenda, 1941–1949

CRS A2703 Curtin, Forde and Chifley Ministries—Folders of Cabinet Minutes (with indices) 1941–1949

CRS A3258 Lyons and Page Ministries—Folders of Cabinet Submissions

CA 6, Department of Defence (I) (1905–1921) and CA 19, Department of Defence (II) (1921–1936)

CRS A289 Correspondence Files, Multiple Number Series, 1906–1917

CRS B197 Secret and Confidential Correspondence Files, Multiple Number Series

CA 12, Prime Minister's Department, Central Office, Melbourne and Canberra (1911–1971)

CRS A1606 Correspondence Files, Secret and Confidential Series, Third System, 1926–1939

CRS A1608 Correspondence Files, Secret and Confidential Series, 1939–1945

CRS A461 Correspondence Files, Multiple Number Series, Third System, 1934–1950

CP 4/2 Correspondence

CP 30/3 Correspondence of the Rt. Hon. J.A. Lyons, 1931–1937

CA 19, Department of Defence (II) (1936–1939) and CA 36, Department of the Army (1939–1945)

MP 133/2 Secret and Confidential Correspondence Files, Multiple Number Series

MP 508/1 Correspondence Files, Multiple Number Series, 1939–1942

MP 729/2 Secret and Confidential Correspondence Files, Multiple Number Series with A, B, C, D or E prefix

MP 729/6 Secret Correspondence Files, Multiple Number Series, 1939–1945

MP 729/7 Classified Correspondence Files, Multiple Number Series, 1940–1942

MP 729/8 Classified Correspondence Files, Multiple Number Series, 1945–1957

MP 742/1 General Correspondence Files, Multiple Number Series, 1943–1951

MP 826 Defence Schemes, c.1906–1938

CA 37, Department of Defence Co-ordination (1939–1942) and CA 46, Department of Defence (III) (1942-)

CRS A663 General Correspondence (Unclassified) Series, 'O' Multiple Number System, 1940–1957

CRS A664 Correspondence Files, Multiple Number System (Class 401), 1924–1940

CRS A816 Correspondence Files, Multiple Number System (Class 301), (Classified),

BIBLIOGRAPHY

1935–1957

CRS A5954 Defence Records Collected by Sir Frederick Shedden

CRS A6828 Chief of the General Staff's (Australia) periodical letters to the Chief of the Imperial General Staff, 1934–1940

AA 1971/216 Council of Defence Records

CA 88, Naval Board of Administration

CRS A2585 Naval Board Minutes, 1905-

CA 89, Military Board of Administration

CRS A2653 Proceedings of the Military Board

CA 289, Defence Committee

CRS A2031 Defence Committee Minutes

CA 495, Advisory War Council (1940–1945)

CRS A2679 Advisory War Council Agenda, 1940–1945

CRS A2680 Advisory War Council Agenda Files, 1940–1945

CRS A2682 Advisory War Council Minutes [Books], 1940–1945

CRS A2684 Advisory War Council Minutes Files, 1940–1945

CA 1468, War Cabinet Secretariat (1939–1946)

CRS A2670 War Cabinet Agenda, 1939–1946

CRS A2671 War Cabinet Agenda Files, 1939–1946

CRS A2673 War Cabinet Minutes [Books] [Decisions], 1939–1946

CRS A2676 War Cabinet Minutes Without Agenda Files, 1939–1946

CP 81, Papers of F.M. Forde

(b) Australian War Memorial

AWM 4 War Diaries, 1914–1918 War

War Diary HQ Royal Artillery 5th Division, 13/14

AWM 51 Ex-Confidential Documents. Item 123: 'Narrative of Operations in Cyrenaica during period April 7–14, both inclusive, by Lt-Gen Sir John Lavarack'

AWM 52 War Diaries, 1939–1945 War

War Diary HQ 1 Aust Corps G Branch, 1/4/1

War Diary HQ 1 Aust Corps Air Party, 1/4/4

War Diary HQ 7 Div, G Branch, 1/5/14

War Diary HQ 7 Div, AQ Branch, 1/5/15

War Diary HQ 9 Div G Branch, 1/5/20

War Diary HQ 20 Bde, 8/2/20

War Diary HQ 21 Bde, 8/2/21

AWM 54 Written Records, War of 1939–1945. The file numbers have been cited with the suffix 'AWM'

AWM 67 Gavin Long Papers. Documents used in the preparation of the official history, including diaries, notebooks and correspondence

AWM 183 Australian War Records Section Biographical Forms. Alphabetical index to biographical details of service in the First World War.

Blamey papers. There are two collections held by the Memorial. The first, designated as 3DRL 6643, consists of much official and semi-official material and was donated soon after Blamey's death. The other, smaller collection, containing more personal material, was donated in 1985 and is catalogued as PR 85/355

III Official Records, United Kingdom. Papers held in the Public Record Office, London

Cabinet Office

CAB 2 Committee of Imperial Defence Minutes, 1902–1939

CAB 4 Committee of Imperial Defence, Miscellaneous Memoranda, 1903–1939

CAB 9 Committee of Imperial Defence, Colonial/Overseas Defence Committee Memoranda, 1887–1939

CAB 16 Committee of Imperial Defence, Ad-Hoc Sub-Committees, 1905–1939

CAB 21 Cabinet Registered Files, 1916–1959

CAB 27 Committees, General Series to 1939

CAB 32 Imperial Conferences, 1917–1937

CAB 44 Cabinet Office Historical Section, Official War Historians: Narratives (Military)

CAB 53 Committee of Imperial Defence, Chiefs of Staff Committee, 1923–1929

CAB 63 Hankey papers, 1908–1944

CAB 65 War Cabinet Minutes (WM Series)

CAB 66 War Cabinet Memoranda (WP and CP Series)

CAB 79 War Cabinet, Chiefs of Staff Committee, Minutes of Meetings, 1939–1946

CAB 103 Historical Section Registered Files, 1915–1959

CAB 106 Historical Section Files (Archivist and Librarian Series), 1939–1967

CAB 127 Private Collections: Ministers and Officials, 1922–1961

Prime Minister's Office

PREM 1 Prime Minister's Office, Correspondence and Papers, 1916–1940

PREM 3 Prime Minister's Office, Operations Papers, 1938–1946

PREM 4 Prime Minister's Office, Confidential Papers, 1939–1946

War Office

WO 79 Various Private collections, 1709–1939

WO 95 War of 1914–1918 War Diaries, 1914–1922

WO 106 Directorate of Military Operations and Intelligence

WO 169 War of 1939–1945 War Diaries, Middle East Forces, 1939–1946

WO 201 Military Headquarters Papers, Middle East Forces, 1939–1946

WO 216 Chief of the Imperial General Staff, Papers, 1935–1954

WO 217 War of 1939–1945, Private War Diaries

Admiralty

ADM 205 First Sea Lord Papers

IV Unpublished official reports

'Report of Comd 1 Aust Corps for period 26 Jan 42 - 21 Feb 42 in the N.E.I.', Lavarack papers 9

'Report on the Operations - 1st Australian Corps - In the Campaign in Syria, June-July 1941', Blamey papers 51, AWM

'Seventh Australian Division Report on the Operations in Syria 1941', Blamey papers

51, AWM

'6 [British] Division Report on Syrian Operations June-July 1941', Blamey papers 51, AWM

'17 Australian Infantry Brigade Report on Operations in Syria - July 1941', Blamey papers 50, AWM

V Unpublished private papers

(a) Australia

Bennett, Lieutenant-General H.G., ML MSS 807, Mitchell Library, Sydney

Berryman, Lieutenant-General Sir F.H., private collection

Blamey papers. (See Australian War Memorial)

Eggleston, Sir Frederic, MS 423/1/351, NLA

Hetherington, John, 3DRL 6224 and 6027, AWM

Hughes, W.M, MS 3924, National Library of Australia

Mackay, Lieutenant-General Sir Iven. DRL 6850, Australian War Memorial

Milne, Colonel E. MS 1456, National Library of Australia

Page, Sir Earle. DRL 3682, Australian War Memorial and MS 1633, National Library of Australia

Piesse, E.L. ('Albatross'), MS 882, National Library of Australia

Rogers, Brigadier J.D., 'Say Not the Struggle', unpublished manuscript held by Mrs J.D. Rogers

Rowell, Lieutenant-General Sir S.F., 3DRL 6763, AWM

Savige, Lieutenant-General Sir Stanley, 3DRL 2529, AWM

Stevens, Major-General Sir J.E.S., 'A personal story of the service, as a citizen soldier', unpublished manuscript, 3DRL 3561, AWM

Vasey, Major-General G.A., MS 3782, NLA

Wills, Brigadier Sir K.A., DRL 6201, AWM

Wilmot, Chester. MS 1692, National Library of Australia

Wilson, C.H., private collection loaned to author

———, 'Java Adventure', unpublished manuscript, Wilson papers and file no.556/2/1, AWM

(b) United Kingdom

Baldwin, Stanley, Cambridge University Library, Cambridge

Birdwood, Field-Marshal Lord, Imperial War Museum

Hankey, Maurice, Lord, Churchill College, Cambridge

Ismay, Lieutenant-General Lord, Liddell Hart Centre for Military Archives, King's College, London

Kisch, Brigadier F.H., WO 217, Public Record Office, London

Lyttelton, Oliver (1st Viscount Chandos), Churchill College, Cambridge

Montgomery-Massingberd, Field-Marshal Sir Archibald, Liddell Hart Centre for Military Archives, King's College, London

Richmond, Admiral Sir H.W., National Maritime Museum, London

Roskill, Captain S.W., Churchill College, Cambridge

Squires, Lieutenant-General E.K., private collection loaned to author

VI Correspondence

Brigadier H.J. Bates, 28 May 1980
Brigadier A.T.J. Bell, 22 September 1980
Brigadier S.J. Bleechmore, 19 August 1980
Colonel J.P. Buckley, 22 September 1982
Sir Samuel Burston, 24 September 1982
Brigadier S.H. Buckler, 17 September 1980
Lieutenant-General Sir Mervyn Brogan, 26 May, 29 June 1980
Brigadier Sir Frederick Chilton, 6 September 1983
Colonel E.L. Cook, 1 June 1980
Lieutenant-General Sir Thomas Daly, 4 July 1980
Mr Keith Dunstan, 28 September 1982
Brigadier C.M.L. Elliott, 26 October 1982
Brigadier F.R. Evans, 28 May 1980
Lieutenant-General Sir J.F. Evetts, 15 March and 24 April 1981
Major-General C.H. Finlay, 20 June 1980
Field-Marshal Lord Harding, 31 August and 4 October 1981
Rt Hon Sir Paul Hasluck, 9 April 1981
Major-General R.N.L. Hopkins, 15, 31 May, 9 June 1981; 14 January, 30 January and 3 September 1983
Brigadier D.R. Jackson , 12 June 1980
Dr J.O. Lavarack, 3 June 1980; 21 February, 7 June, 18 October 1981; 15 November 1982
Mr Peter Lavarack, 18 September 1981
Brigadier E. Logan, 27 May 1980
Major H.B. McKenzie, 26 May 1980
Colonel M.C. Morgan, 3 June 1980
Brigadier J.G. Ochiltree, 31 August 1981
Brigadier M.P. O'Hare, 10 June 1980
Major Warren Perry, 23 April 1981
Major-General B.W. Pulver, 25 February 1981
Brigadier F.P. Serong, 6 June 1980
Brigadier Sir Charles Spry, 25 May, 27 July 1981
Brigadier W.W. Wearne, 28 May 1980
Mr C.H. Wilson, 9 April 1980, 1 March 1981
Sir Victor Windeyer, 24 March 1981
Mr A.E. Woodward, 23 March 1981

VII Interviews

Colonel J.D. Andrew, Canberra, 27 April 1981
Major-General T.F. Cape, Canberra, 17 June 1980
Mr N.D. Carlyon, Melbourne, 6 May 1981
Mr L.G. Darling (Rowell's ADC), Melbourne, 5 May 1981
Brigadier C.M.L. Elliott, Canberra-Perth via telephone, 10 May 1981
Mr E.S. Eyers (Lavarack's wartime ADC), Sydney, 18 February 1981
Major-General C.H. Finlay, Canberra, 6 April 1982

Mr A.J. Hill, Canberra, 9 May 1984.

Lieutenant-Colonel R.L. Holmes (wartime intelligence officer attached to Wilson's headquarters), Canberra, 26 May 1983

Major-General R.N.L. Hopkins, Canberra-Adelaide via telephone, 29 August 1984

Mr F.J. Howard, Melbourne, 7 May 1981

Dr. J.O. Lavarack, Melbourne, 3 May 1981

Mr P.M. Reid (Lavarack's ADC), Sydney, 18 February 1981

Brigadier F.W. Speed, Brisbane, 6 August 1980

Dr S.W. Williams (DADMS, 7th Division), Canberra, 8 May 1981

Mr J.A. Wilmoth (Blamey's ADC), Melbourne, 5 May 1981

Mr C.H. Wilson (Lavarack's wartime ADC), Melbourne, 12 May 1980

General Sir John Wilton, Canberra, 24 June 1980

Lady Helen Wilton, Canberra, 10 August 1983

VIII Official Histories

(a) Australia

Bean, C.E.W., T*he Official History of Australia in the War of 1914–1918*:
— Volume I, *The Story of Anzac: From the Outbreak of War to the End of the First Phase of the Gallipoli Campaign, May 4, 1915* (Angus & Robertson, Sydney, thirteenth edition 1942)
— Volume II, *The Story of Anzac: From 4 May, 1915, to the Evacuation of the Gallipoli Peninsula* (Angus & Robertson, Sydney, 1924)
— Volume III, *The Australian Imperial Force in France 1916* (Angus & Robertson, Sydney, thirteenth edition 1942)
— Volume IV, *The Australian Imperial Force in France 1917* (Angus & Robertson, Sydney, thirteenth edition 1943)
— Volume V, *The Australian Imperial Force in France During the Main German Offensive, 1918 (Angus & Robertson, Sydney, tenth edition 1943)*
———, *Anzac to Amiens* (Australian War Memorial, Canberra, 1946)

Dexter, David, *The New Guinea Offensives* (Australian War Memorial, Canberra, 1961)

Gillison, Douglas, *Royal Australian Air Force 1939–1942* (Australian War Memorial, Canberra, 1962)

Hasluck, Paul, *The Government and the People, 1939–41* (Australian War Memorial, Canberra, 1952)
———, *The Government and the People, 1942–45* (Australian War Memorial, Canberra, 1970)

Long, Gavin, *To Benghazi* (Australian War Memorial, Canberra, 1952)
———, *Greece, Crete and Syria* (Australian War Memorial, Canberra, 1953)
———, *The Final Campaigns* (Australian War Memorial, Canberra, 1963)
———, *The Six Years War: A Concise History of Australia in the 1939–45 War (Australian War Memorial, Canberra, 1973)*

McCarthy, Dudley, *South-West Pacific Area—First Year*, (Australian War Memorial, Canberra, 1959)

Maughan, Barton, *Tobruk and El Alamein* (Australian War Memorial, Canberra, 1966)

Walker, Allan S., *Middle East and Far East, Medical Series*, vol.2 (Australian War Memorial, Canberra, 1953)

Wigmore, Lionel, *The Japanese Thrust* (Australian War Memorial, Canberra, 1957)

(b) United Kingdom

Gibbs, N.H., *Grand Strategy*, Volume I, *Rearmament Policy* (HMSO, London, 1976)

Hinsley, F.H., *British Intelligence in the Second World War*, vol. I, (HMSO, London, 1979)

Playfair, I.S.O., *History of the Second World War, The Mediterranean and Middle East*, vol. II, *'The Germans Come to the Help of Their Ally' (1941)* (HMSO, London, 1956)

IX Commonwealth Parliamentary Papers

'Report for the Inspector-General of the Australian Military Forces by Lieut.-General Sir H.G. Chauvel', Part 1, 31 May 1929, p.8, *Commonwealth Parliamentary Papers, General*, 1929–30–31, vol.2

X Official publications

Active Service with Australia in the Middle East (AWM, Canberra, 1941)

The Army List of the Australian Military Forces, Parts 1 & 2, 1 June 1940.

Gradation List of officers of the Australian Military Forces, Active List, vol.1, 18 January 1945

Department of Defence, *Historical Listings*, May 1976

Naval Intelligence Division, *Syria*, Geographical Handbook Series, B.R. 513 (Restricted) (Reprinted 1944)

General Sir Archibald Wavell, *Despatch by the Supreme Commander of the ABDA Area to the Combined Chiefs of Staff on the Operations in the South-West Pacific, 15 January 1942 to 25 February 1942* (HMSO, London, 1948)

XI Books, chapters and articles

(a) Books

Aitken, E.F., *The Story of the 2/2nd Australian Pioneer Battalion* (2/2nd Pioneer Battalion Association, Melbourne, 1953)

Andrews, E.M., *The Writing on the Wall: The British Commonwealth and Aggression in the Far East, 1931–1935* (Allen & Unwin, Sydney, 1987)

Bean, C.E.W., *Two Men I Knew* (Angus & Robertson, Sydney, 1957)

Bond, Brian, (ed.), *Chief of Staff: The Diaries of Lieutenant-General Sir Henry Pownall, vol. 2* (Leo Cooper, London, 1974)

Burns, John, *The Brown and Blue Diamond at War* (2/27th Battalion Ex-Serviceman's Association, Adelaide, 1960)

Carlyon, Norman D., *I Remember Blamey* (Macmillan, Melbourne, 1980)

Chapman, Ivan D., *Iven G. Mackay: Citizen and Soldier*, (Melway, Melbourne, 1975)

Churchill, Winston S., *The Second World War, vol. 3, The Grand Alliance* (Cassell, London, 1950)

Collins, Major-General R.J., *Lord Wavell* (Hodder & Stoughton, London, 1948)

Dennis, Peter, et al , *The Oxford Companion to Australian Military History* (OUP, Melbourne, 1995)

de Wailly, Henri, *Invasion Syria 1941* (I.B. Taurus, London, 2016)

Eden, Anthony, *The Reckoning* (Houghton Mifflin, Boston, 1965)

Fearnside , G.H., (ed.), *Bayonets Abroad: A History of the 2/13th Battalion, A.I.F. in the*

Second World War (Printed by Waite & Bull, Sydney, 1953)

Gray, T.I.G., *The Imperial Defence College and the Royal College of Defence Studies 1927–1977 (HMSO, Edinburgh, 1977)*

Great Britain, Cabinet Office, *Principal War Telegrams and Memoranda, Middle East I* (KTO Press, Nendeln, 1976)

———, *Principal War Telegrams and Memoranda, 1940–1943, Far East (KTO Press, Nendeln, 1976)*

Hamill, Ian, *The Strategic Illusion: The Singapore Strategy and the Defence of Australia and New Zealand, 1919–1942* (Singapore University Press, Singapore, 1981)

Hasluck, Paul, *Diplomatic Witness: Australian Foreign Affairs, 1941–1947* (MUP, Melbourne, 1980)

Henry, R.L., *The Story of the 2/4th Field Regiment* (Merrion Press, Melbourne, 1950)

Hetherington, John, *Blamey: Controversial Soldier* (AWM, Canberra, 1973)

Hill, A.J., *Chauvel of the Light Horse* (Melbourne University Press, Melbourne, 1978)

Horner, David, *Blamey: The Commander-in-Chief* (Allen & Unwin, Sydney, 1998; electronic version 2020)

Horner, D.M., *Crisis of Command* (ANU Press, Canberra, 1978)

———, *High Command*, (AWM, Canberra and George Allen & Unwin, Sydney, 1982)

———, (ed.), *The Commanders* (George Allen & Unwin, Sydney, 1984)

Howard, Michael, *The Continental Commitment* (Maurice Temple Smith, London, 1972)

Hughes, W.M., *Australia and War Today: The Price of Peace* (Angus & Robertson, Sydney, 1935)

Irving, David, *The War Between the Generals* (Allen Lane, London, 1981)

Joynt, W.D., *Breaking the Road for the Rest* (Hyland House, Melbourne, 1979)

Keegan, John, *The Face of Battle* (Jonathan Cape, London, 1976)

Keogh, E.G., *Middle East 1939–43* (Wilke, Melbourne, 1959)

Lewin, Ronald, *Rommel as Military Commander* (B.T. Batsford, London, 1968)

———, *Ultra Goes to War: The Secret Story* (Hutchinson, London, 1978)

———, *The Chief* (Farrar-Straus-Giroux, New York, 1980)

Liddell Hart, B.H., *History of the First World War* (Book Club Associates, London, 1973)

———, (ed.), *The Rommel Papers* (Harcourt, Brace and Company, New York, 1953)

———, *The Memoirs of Captain Liddell Hart*, vol.2 (Cassell, London, 1965)

Lodge, A.B., *The Fall of General Gordon Bennett* (Allen & Unwin, Sydney, 1986)

Luvaas , Jay, (ed.), *Dear Miss Emm—General Eichelberger's War in the Pacific 1942–1945* (Greenwood Press, Westport, Conn., 1972)

Marder, Arthur J., *Old Friends, New Enemies: The Royal Navy and the Imperial Japanese Navy. Strategic Illusions, 1936–1941* (Clarendon, Oxford, 1981)

McCarthy, John, *Australia and Imperial Defence 1918–1939: A Study in Sea and Air Power* (University of Queensland Press, St Lucia, 1976)

McIntyre, W. David, *The Rise and Fall of the Singapore Naval Base, 1919–1942* (Macmillan, London, 1979)

Millar, T.B., *Australia's Defence* (Melbourne University Press, Melbourne, 1969)

Mockler, Anthony, *Our Enemies the French* (Leo Cooper, London, 1976)

Murfett, Malcolm H., *Fool-proof Relations: The Search for Anglo-American Naval Cooperation During the Chamberlain Years, 1937–1940* (Singapore University Press, Singapore, 1984)

Neidpath, James, *The Singapore Naval Base and the Defence of Britain's Eastern Empire, 1919–1941* (Clarendon, Oxford, 1981)

Norris, F. Kingsley, *No Memory for Pain* (Heinemann, Melbourne, 1970)

O'Brien, John W., *Guns and Gunners*, (Angus & Robertson, Sydney, 1950)

Piesse, E.L. (under the pseudonym 'Albatross'), *Japan and the Defence of Australia* (Robertson & Mullens, Melbourne, 1935)

Richmond, Admiral Sir Herbert, *Statesmen and Sea Power* (Clarendon, Oxford, 1946)

Robertson, John, *Australia at War 1939–1945* (William Heinemann, Melbourne, 1981)

Robertson , John, and McCarthy, John, *Australian War Strategy 1939—1945: A Documentary History* (University of Queensland Press, St Lucia, 1985)

Roskill, Stephen, *Hankey. Man of Secrets, vol.3, 1931–1963* (Collins, London, 1974)

———, *Naval Policy Between the Wars, vol.2, 1930–1939 (Collins, London, 1976)*

Ross, A.T., *Armed and Ready: The Industrial Development & Defence of Australia, 1900–1945 (Turton & Armstrong, Sydney, 1995)*

Rowell, S.F., *Full Circle* (Melbourne University Press, Melbourne, 1974)

Russell, W.B., *The Second Fourteenth Battalion* (Angus & Robertson, Sydney, 1948)

Sayers, Stuart, *Ned Herring: A Life of Sir Edmund Herring* (Hyland House, Melbourne in association with Australian War Memorial, Canberra, 1980)

Semmler , Clement, (ed.), *The War Diaries of Kenneth Slessor* (University of Queensland Press, St Lucia, 1985)

Serle , R.P., (ed.), *The Second Twenty-Fourth Australian Infantry Battalion of the 9th Australian Division* (Jacaranda, Brisbane, 1963)

Smith, Colin, *England's Last War Against France,* (Phoenix, London, 2010).

Spears, Major-General Sir Edward, *Fulfilment of a Mission* (Leo Cooper, London, 1977)

Uren, Malcolm, *A Thousand Men at War* (Heinemann, Melbourne, 1959)

Wavell, General Sir Archibald, *Generals and Generalship* (Times Publishing, London, 1941)

Warner, Geoffrey, *Iraq and Syria 1941* (Davis-Poynter, London, 1974)

Williams, Sir Richard, *These Are Facts* (AWM/AGPS, Canberra, 1977)

Wilmot, Chester, *Tobruk* (Angus & Robertson, Sydney, 1944)

Wilson, Field-Marshal Lord, *Eight Years Overseas* (Hutchinson, London, 1950)

Winterbotham, F.W., *The Ultra Secret* (Futura, London, 1975)

Woollcombe, Robert, *The Campaigns of Wavell, 1939–1943* (Cassell, London, 1959)

(b) Chapters and articles

Andrews, E.M., 'The Broken Promise—Britain's Failure to Consult its Commonwealth on Defence in 1934, and the Implications for Australian Foreign and Defence Policy', *Australian Journal of Defence Studies*, vol.2, no.2, November 1978

B.B.J., 'Defence-or What?', *Bulletin*, 22 July 1936

Bridge, Carl, review of David Horner, *Blamey: the Commander-in-Chief* (Allen & Unwin, Sydney, 1998), in *Journal of the Australian War Memorial*, Issue 34.

Gow, Neil, 'Australian Army Strategic Planning 1919–1939', *Australian Journal of Politics and History*, Vol.XXIII, No.2, August 1977

Deasey, David J., 'Some myths relating to the promotion to field marshal of Sir Thomas Blamey in 1950', *United Service*, June 2019.

Ellis, M.H. ['Ek Dum'], 'Lavarack', *Bulletin*, 18 December 1957

Gilchrist, Hugh, 'The Australians in Macedonia', *Sabretache* , vol.23, July/September

1982

Hill, A.J., 'Lieutenant-General Sir Leslie Morshead: Commander, 9th Australian Division' in D.M. Horner (ed.), *The Commanders* (George Allen & Unwin, Sydney, 1984)

Horner, D.M., 'Staff Corps versus Militia: the Australian Experience in World War II', *Defence Force Journal*, No.26, January-February 1981

Horner, David, 'Lavarack, Sir John Dudley (1885–1957)' *Australian Dictionary of Biography*, vol.15 (MUP, 2000)

———, 'Sir Frederick Shedden: The Forerunner' in Furphy, Samuel (ed.)*The Seven Dwarfs and the Age of the Mandarins: Australian Government Administration in the Post-War Reconstruction Era (ANU Press, 2015)*

Howard, F.J., 'Surviving the Hatchetmen', *Melbourne Herald*, 9 April 1974

Hunter, Claire, 'I was lucky with my life', Australian War Memorial Online Article, 5 October 2017, https://www.awm.gov.au/articles/blog/remembering-kelvin-koorey

Lavarack, J.D., 'The Defence of the British Empire, with Special Reference to the Far East and Australia', *Army Quarterly*, vol. XXV, No.2, January 1933.

Lavarack, Dr Peter, 'My Grandfathers Were Both Heroes to Me', *Sunshine Coast Daily*, 22 April 2018

Lloyd, C.E.M. ['Tobruk Rat'], 'Tobfort', *Salt*, 10 May 1943

Lodge, A.B., 'A Share of Honour: Lavarack and Tobruk, April 1941', *Journal of the Royal United Services Institute of Australia*, vol.5, no.1, April 1982

———, 'Lieutenant-General Sir John Lavarack: From Chief of the General Staff to Corps Commander', in D.M. Horner (ed.), *The Commanders* (George Allen & Unwin, Sydney, 1984)

Perry, Warren, 'Sir Frederick Shedden', *Victorian Historical Magazine*, vol.42, no.3

———, 'Lieutenant-General Henry Douglas Wynter', *Victorian Historical Magazine*, vol.43, no.2

———, 'Wynter, Henry Douglas (1886–1945)', *Australian Dictionary of Biography* (Melbourne University Press, 2002) Volume 16.

———, 'Lieutenant-General Sir John Dudley Lavarack. Australia's 14th Chief of the General Staff', *Victorian Historical Journal*, vol.46, no.2

Primrose, B. N., 'Equipment and Naval Policy 1919–1942', *Australian Journal of Politics and History*, vol.23, no.2, August 1977 Check

Richmond, Admiral Sir Herbert, 'An Outline of Imperial Defence', *Army Quarterly*, July 1932

———, 'Imperial Defence', *Army Quarterly*, October 1933

Simington, Margot, 'The Southwest Pacific Islands in Australian Interwar Defence Planning', *Australian Journal of Politics and History*, vol.XXIII, No.2, August 1977

Sweeting, A.J., review of F. Kingsley Norris, *No Memory for Pain* (Heinemann, Melbourne, 1970) in Army Journal, no.262, March 1971

Thorby, H.V.C., 'I Saved Our Little Ships', *Sydney Morning Herald*, 22 December 1957

Trotter, Ann, 'The Dominions and Imperial Defence: Hankey's Tour in 1934', *Journal of Imperial and Commonwealth History*, May 1974

XII Theses

Dean, Peter J., 'The Making of a General: Lost Years, Forgotten Battles. Lieutenant General Frank Berryman 1894-1941', Ph. D. Thesis, UNSW, 2007

Dowse, Simon, 'The Growth in Influence of the Defence Secretariat between 1929 and 1936', B.A. (Hons) Thesis, UNSW, 1981

McNarn, M.R., 'Sir Robert Archdale Parkhill and Defence Policy 1934–1937', B.A. (Hons) Thesis, UNSW, 1979

Neumann, Claude, 'Australia's Citizen Soldiers, 1919–1939: A Study of Organisation, Command, Recruiting, Training and Equipment', M.A. Thesis, UNSW, 1978

Primrose, B.N.,'Australian Naval Policy, 1919–1942: A Case Study in Empire Relations', Ph.D. Thesis, ANU, 1974

Ross, A.T. , 'The Arming of Australia: The Politics and Administration of Australia's Self Containment Strategy for Munitions Supply 1901–1945', Ph.D. Thesis, UNSW, 1986

Acknowledgements

(to the first edition, 1998)

MANY PEOPLE HAVE kindly helped me with the research and the writing of this book by consenting to be interviewed, corresponding, recommending sources, and by reading and commenting on the text. Others have provided welcome encouragement and support over the years. In the latter category, my parents, of course, have endured for longest and worried the most (though perhaps not in equal measure). Now is as appropriate a time as any to say to them that you brought it all upon yourself and I for one am grateful that you did.

It seems as if it were only yesterday that I received my first history lecture from Alec Hill at Duntroon. Since that time I have continued to benefit from Alec's profound knowledge of military history and ability as a writer. Both he and Patsy have been a constant source encouragement and I am privileged to enjoy their friendship.

I am especially grateful that I embarked on this book because it sent me in search of General Ernest Squires' papers and thereby introduced me to his daughter Margaret Lodge. Thanks to her generosity (and that of her sister Mrs Lorna Essame and brother Vice-Admiral Robin Squires) the papers were sent from England to be used in the writing of this book. It was to be the beginning of a long and happy association of which I have been the prime beneficiary.

I am indebted to Dr and Mrs J.O. Lavarack for the time they gave and for the unconditional loan of the Lavarack papers. Mr Curtis Wilson, Lavarack's wartime ADC, also gave generously of his time and loaned me his personal papers. I express my gratitude to the many correspondents who considered my queries and patiently replied, and to the staffs of the various libraries and archives mentioned in the pages which follow for assistance over many years. In particular, I thank the Council and staff of the Australian War Memorial, not least for the award of the first AWM Postgraduate Scholarship which allowed me to start work on Lavarack's career in 1980.

I am pleased that the work begun then is to culminate in a book which will be part of a series produced with the encouragement of the Australian army. I have had a connection with the army for as long as I can remember and, in particular, I have always been grateful for the education the army gave me at Duntroon in the 1970s. I hope that, in some way, it has received a return on its investment with the completion of this study of Lavarack, which in many respects is a companion volume to my earlier book, *The Fall of General Gordon Bennett.*

David Horner, the editor of the series, suggested in 1979 that I write about Lavarack when I was searching for a thesis topic. He also encouraged me to write this book and provided welcome advice during its preparation. In addition, he and his colleague Nikki Baker have kindly arranged many details in Australia which would normally have fallen to me had I been in the country. They have made my task much easier and I remain grateful to them.

There have been others who have shared the load at various times. Although they are too numerous to mention by name, they too have my thanks. During the last year of revising the book Anne McMillan has kept me pointed in the general direction of sane endeavour as I tried, sometimes successfully, to juggle conflicting commitments. I am, as ever, grateful that she has far more tolerance than I have a right to expect. However, she has drawn the line at taking responsibility for any errors there may be in this book. If no-one else steps forward to shoulder that particular burden, then I accept the possibility that they just might be mine.

Brett Lodge,
London, July 1997

Index